W9-BLH-140

ARCHITECTURAL EXCELLENCE

500 Iconic Buildings

ARCHITECTURAL EXCELLENCE

500 Iconic Buildings

General Editor

Paul Cattermole

FIREFLY BOOKS

A FIREFLY BOOK

Published by Firefly Books Ltd. 2008

First printing

Library and Archives Canada Cataloguing in Publication
Cattermole, Paul
    Architectural excellence : 500 iconic buildings / Paul Cattermole.
Includes bibliographical references and index.
ISBN-13: 978-1-55407-358-0
ISBN-10: 1-55407-358-8
    1. Architecture — History. I. Title.
NA200.C37 2008   720.9   C2008-903286-1

Publisher Cataloging-in-Publication Data (U.S.)
Cattermole, Paul.
    Architectural excellence : 500 iconic buildings / Paul Cattermole.
[512] p. : col. photos. ;   cm.
Includes bibliographies and index.
Summary: A collection of architectural icons, organized chronologically, from prehistoric cave dwellings in Turkey, to buildings commissioned for the 2008 Olympics in China.
ISBN-13: 978-1-55407-358-0
ISBN-10: 1-55407-358-8
1. Architecture — Pictorial works. 2. Visionary architecture.
3. Fantastic architecture. I. Architectural excellence : five hundred iconic buildings. II. Title.
720 dc22   NA209.5.C38847   2008

Published in Canada by Firefly Books Ltd., 66 Leek Crescent, Richmond Hill, Ontario L4B 1H1

Published in the United States by Firefly Books (U.S.) Inc., P.O. Box 1338, Ellicott Station, Buffalo, New York 14205

Printed in China

Designed by John Shuttleworth, Compendium Design

Cover designed by Erin R. Holmes

General Editor: Paul Cattermole
Contributors: Paul Cattermole (**PC**), Sandra Forty (**SF**), Clare Haworth-Maden (**CHM**), Judith Millidge (**JM**), Ian Westwell (**IW**), Emily Wood (**EW**)

Photograph Credits:
(Abbreviations: t=top; b=below; l=left; r=right; m=middle)

Alamy Philip Scalia 182

Arcaid 8, 42-43, 138, 334, 344 both, 357, 493; Inigo Bujedo Aguirre 353 452, 469, 498t; Archenova 4-5; Architekturphoto 443; artur/Oliver Heissner 167; Alex Bartel 94, 229b, 280, 331, 332, 367, 378-79, 396b; Bisou foto/Fabpic 500t; Achim Bednorz 58-59; Achim Bednorz/Bildarchiv-Monheim 77t, 140l; Bildarchiv Monheim 406t, 432b; Patrick Brice 395; Stefan Buzas 387; Lynne Bryant 286; Richard Bryant 12 both, 87, 112, 114b, 125, 145b, 170-71, 173, 177 both, 178, 181, 192, 198, 206b, 209, 212b, 231, 232-33, 236, 240, 241, 243t, 251t, 253, 262b, 263, 264-65, 268-69, 275, 277t, 281, 287, 318b, 326-27, 335, 347, 360b, 382b, 384b, 385, 393, 396t, 397, 402, 403, 406b, 410b, 412, 417, 418b, 419, 421, 424, 427t, 448, 454b, 457, 459, 461, 462b, 464-65, 467b, 468, 480, 496-97, 498b; Chuck Choi 500b; David Churchill 15, 133, 184-85, 290-91, 442; David Clapp 19bl, 78-79, 115, 164t, 203; Niall Clutton 217b, 258-59; Jeremy Cockayne 356, 423; Joe Cornish 67, 70t, 104, 118t, 139, 153, 300b 413; Nick Dawe 304, 306-07, 313b; Uwe Dettmar 80t; Colin Dixon 16b, 18m, 34, 76, 249t, 407; Sarah J Duncan 200-01; Peter Durant 169t; Richard Einzig 333t, 363, 370b, 386; Mondadori Electa 51, 95, 102b; Gisela Erlacher 235t, 243b; Mark Fiennes 179, 206t, 242, 250, 349, 351, 414t; Werner Forman 3, 24, 30, 72, 88, 90, 120-21, 137t; Scott Frances/ESTO 308t; Roman von Gatz 239; Marc Gerritsen 492, 504b; John Gollings 380-81; Farrell Grehan 31t, 324-25; Lisa Hammel/Annet van der Voort 434r;

Michael Harding 364-65, 446-47; Thomas A. Heinz 249b, 311; Jochen Helle 124b, 223, 254, 270, 434l; Gavin Jackson 216, 298, 299, 345, 400l; Ben Johnson 155, 408; Nick Kane 303, 304t, 354, 449, 454t, 460, 490-91; Rainer Kiedrowski 18t, 25, 55, 65, 70b, 74, 191; Martine Hamilton Knight 225, 248, 301, 458t; Ian Lambot 409; Lucinda Lambton 158t, 193, 199, 211, 222; John Edward Linden 19m, 109, 207, 228, 230r, 247, 289, 318t, 342-43, 392, 420, 428-29, 430, 435, 440-41, 445, 472, 475b, 483, 487b, 499; Joe Low 482t; Benedict Luxmoore 473, 478; Paul M.R. Maeyaert 28t, 141, 276; Marcel Malherbe 18b, 122t, 398-99, 431, 475t; Bill Maris/ESTO 323; Tim Mitchell 183, 297; Florian Monheim 75, 152, 154, 160, 166b, 169b, 190, 252, 278-79; Florian Monheim/Roman von Gatz 214-15, 255t, 411; Kadu Niemeyer 372-73, 438-39, 467t; Robert O'Dea 319; Clay Perry 100-101; Richard Powers 355; Will Pryce/Thames & Hudson 28b, 40-41, 44t, 96, 99, 102t, 123, 132t, 134-35, 137b, 142, 186, 218, 221, 229t, 257, 262t, 288, 317, 360t, 374, 432t; Ralph Richter/architekturphoto 487t; Schutze & Rodemann/Bildarchiv-Monheim 84, 97t, 117, 118b, 196-97, 219t, 377, 400r; Natalie Tepper 47, 71, 122b, 188-89, 266-67, 309, 316, 389, 418t, 426, 433; Bill Tingey 234, 358, 376, 422, 436-37, 466, 488; Richard Turpin 126, 148-49, 444t; Richard Waite 162, 187, 208, 320, 474; Alan Weintraub 321b, 328-29, 330t, 341, 350, 370t, 414b; Alan Williams 394t; Charlotte Wood 210, 330b

Corbis 158b, 313t, 458b, 494-95; Peter Adams 404-05; Albig/dpa 315t; Paul Almasy 213; Craig Aurness 416; Gaetano Barone/zefa 89; Morton Beebe 321t; Kristi J. Black 86; Jonathan Blair 143; Christophe Boisvieux 38-39; Ashley Cooper 479b; Christopher Cormack 166t; Peter Durant/Arcaid 484-85; Edifice 486; Michele Falzone/JAI 113; Robert Francis 371; Free Agents Ltd 226-27; George Hammerstein/Solus-Veer 285; Robert Harding World Imagery 56b, 110-11, 294-95; Jason Hawkes 489; Thomas A. Heinz 300t; Chris Hellier 340; 338; Jon Hicks 401; Andrew Holbrooke 382t; Angelo Hornak 13, 106, 346, 352; Harald A. Jahn 255b; Bob Krist 62t; Jacques Langevin 450-51; Charles & Josette Lenars 315b; Jean-Pierre Lescourret 85; James Leynse 260, 453; Ludovic Maisant 256; Stefan Matzke 501; Phil O'Connor/Loop Images 277b; Bryan Pickering; Eye Ubiquitous 204-05; Paul Prince/Loop Images 314; Louie Psihoyos 444b; Carl & Ann Purcell/ 114t; Jose Fuste Raga 502-03; Enzo & Paolo Ragazzini 145t; Paul A. Souders 176; Hubert Stadler 116; George Steinmetz 50; Keren Su 108; Murat Taner/zefa 273; Paul Thompson 388; Vanni Archive 29; Sandro Vannini 481t; Ivan Vdovin 77b; Roger Wood 54t; Adam Woolfitt 11, 336-37; Michael S. Yamashita 58t

fotoLibra Tim Anderson 305b; Aditya Bajaj 35, 62b 130-31; Robert Banham 172; David Beasley 220; Martin Bennett 339, 359; Jenny Brice 410t, 455; Einar Borchsenius 32-33, 46b; Arnold De Bruin 292-93; Sean W. Burges 348; David Carter 368-69; Robert Cochran 132b ; Kim Comber 19br, 284; Kathy Cox 165; John Davies 150l; Gareth Dewar 19tr, 506; Robert Down 194; Edwin Edwards 97b; Keith Erskine 390, 425; Steven Everitt 146-47, 384t; Malcolm Forrow 308b; Philip Gordon 244; Harry Van Gorkum 282-83, 361; David Harding 274; Neil Harris 31b, 98 both, 129; Gwyn Headley 80b; Martin Hendry 168, 202; Peter Herbert 119, 174, 175; Barry Hitchcox 151; Nick Jenkins 19l, 136; Ceri Jones 82-83; Frances Kay 159; Norman Kelly 128, 212t; Karolina Krolikowska 261; Raymond Lofthouse 48; Sergey Lutskiy 312; Leo Marriott 219b; Stephen McAdam 27; Philip McElhinney 127; Ellen McKnight 462t; Ben McMillan 92-93, 505; Scott Murray 245; Deborah Nicklen-Daggon 37; Gordon Nicol 124t; Bernard O'Kane 16t, 52-53, 56t, 58b, 59, 66, 73, 81, 310; Eli Pascall-Willis 366; Lesley Pegrum 68, 150r; Ricardo Pimentel 156-57; Alex Ramsay 44b, 161, 163, 375; Lee Robinson 64; Al Sermeno 195; Rodger Shagam 383; Bryan Smith 482b; Mark Staples 107; Uwe Stiens 49; James Symington 69; David Stuckey 22-23; Glyn Thomas 45; Patrick Tweddle 91, 164b, 456; Peter Vallance 26; Adrian Wain 144; Jim Walker 271; Anthony Wallbank 238, 296, 333b; Hugh Walton 46t, 391; Alan Ward 103; Tony Watkins 251b; Simon Weir 54b; David Whittam 18 bl, 36, 63; Rob Wyatt 217t; David Young 272

Getty Images 9, 230l, 476-77, 507; AFP 105, 427b, 470-71, 504t; Daryl Benson 20-21; Ken Gillham 469; Robert Harding World Images 394b; Nicholas Pitt 140r

Japan Guide 479t

Library of Congress Prints and Photographs Division 224, 235b

David Lyons 57

Raj Rewal Associates 481b

RIBA Library Photographs Division 246; Bernard Cox 302; Luis Renau 322

Jo St Mart 362, 415

Shutterstock 463

Structurae 180

Wikipedia 237

Contents

Foreword

Deciding on the world's 500 most excellent buildings is not only a privilege, it's an enjoyable challenge. Every year someone lovingly prepares a list of the 100 Greatest Singles of All Time. Nothing over 60 years old ever appears on the list. In this book Cattermole has bucked the trend, stuck his neck out and dared to dart back into prehistory to choose these superb examples of architecture.

The reader will wonder what the criteria were for this selection. What epitomizes architectural excellence? Is it practicality? Economy? Beauty? Originality?

Three simple keys have allowed a building entry to this volume, and they are style, function, and context. Throughout the book these three watchwords underscore the choice of each project. As the author writes, this is "a careful selection of seminal buildings by key practitioners of architecture." He draws out the comparison between the indigenous and the international, and each building is featured as a project, with the architect, completion date, location, style and period listed.

No two architectural historians worth their mortarboards would agree upon the world's five most influential buildings, let alone 500, but Cattermole will be more praised than excoriated for his selections. When compiling such a work editors are inevitably swayed by personal passions, the subjective nature of the task leading to pleasingly unique results. Cattermole's interest in both "architecture as process" and the "architecture of defense" shines through in his intriguing selection of obscure, but fascinating forts and factories that seldom make it into print. A different editor could have easily told a different story, for the history of architecture offers riches in all directions. As President of the Folly Fellowship, my own passions would have made the omission of the Athenian Tower of the Winds unthinkable; it has become one of

The octagonal Tower of the Winds in Athens has a frieze around the top that depicts the Greek wind gods. The date of its construction is uncertain, but was certainly before 50 BCE.

the most imitated structures in history, with countless facsimiles gracing landscaped parks across the world. But then, such decisions are the editor's joyous privilege and a welcome subject for debate.

The curious evolution of architectural fashion is clearly traced here. There had to be a better way of building than simply piling stones on top of each other. It took millennia before the invention of the arch, but that breathtaking concept marks our transition from shelter to civilization.

Every architect is influenced by his predecessors, every designer strives to add something unique, but the broad river of architectural style dredges its own channel. How dated the copies of Gehry's Guggenheim Museum in Bilbao will look in 30 or 40 years time! Will we see echoes of its groundbreaking design in the buildings of 2050, in the same way that today's commercial and domestic architecture is indebted to Gropius, Le Corbusier, and Mies van der Rohe?

The history of architecture is peppered with brave yet unsuccessful attempts to divert the stylistic mainstream. Jože Plečnik in Austro-Hungary wrought wonders with the traditional colonnaded portico in the first half of the 20th century, creating a new capital and daring to use three instead of the traditional four or more columns. But his work, still exciting and thrilling to see today, has no followers. In 1828 Sir John Soane built a lodge to Pell Wall Hall in Shropshire, England, a design so revolutionary that it could have altered the course of architecture in England forever — but the river of style flowed inexorably past.

When President Kennedy welcomed 49 Nobel Prize laureates to the White House in 1962, he announced the event as,

> the most extraordinary collection of talent and of human knowledge that has ever been gathered together at the White House — with the possible exception of when Thomas Jefferson dined alone.

Kennedy was rightly impressed by the brilliant individuals around him, but in architectural terms the most amazing gathering of modern talent had already occurred in Peter Behrens' design practice in Berlin during the early years of the 20th century. His assistants were Walter Gropius, Le Corbusier, and Mies van der Rohe — indisputably the most influential architects of the past century.

A successful building needs to perform efficiently, even if its purpose is purely decorative. In 1786 Golghar, a huge-domed grain store, was built in Patna, India, following a famine in 1770. For seven years of plenty men toiled up and down the beautiful twin spiral staircases around the dome to empty their sacks. Then came the years of famine, and it was discovered that the doors at the bottom opened inwards.

Any pedestrian that has battled the fierce wind between skyscrapers, will regret that architects of skyscrapers never reread

Vitruvius. Writing in the 1st century BCE, the father of architectural writing opened his thesis with the effect of winds on town planning:

> For if the streets run full in the face of the winds,
> their constant blasts rushing in from the open
> country, and then confined by narrow alleys, will
> sweep through them with great violence. The lines of
> houses must therefore be directed away from the
> quarters from which the winds blow, so that as they
> come in they may strike against the angles of the
> blocks and their force thus be broken and dispersed.

"Form follows function," the saying popularized by Louis H. Sullivan, has been a byword in architecture for over a century. Only in the last 15 or 20 years have we begun to see that old argument for austerity and economy turned on its head. But when you look at a domestic house built in the first decade of the 21st century, it is not substantively different from one built 200 years earlier. Town houses barely move on in a century. Human beings retain the same needs and desires and require the same functionality. Our natures can no more change than the beaks of eagles.

Some architects have designed buildings without visiting the site. These buildings are oblivious of their surroundings; the *sharawaggi* is absent. "Sharawaggi" does not appear in every dictionary or, sadly, every architect's vocabulary. This strange and wondrous word made its appearance in English in 1685, when Sir William Temple wrote about the comfortable context of a building in the landscape: "The Chinese have a particular Word to express it; and where they find it hit their Eye at first sight, they say the Sharawadgi is fine or is admirable." In modern terms we would interpret it as the feng shui of architecture — the considered placement of a building in its proper environment. Temple's knowledge of other languages may not have been encyclopedic — he described German as, "a language I should never learn unless it were to fright children when they cry" — and it seems that *sharawaggi* originated from a Japanese Kyushu dialect word which became obsolete over 400 years ago. To use an 18th-century term of approbation, building without being aware of the genius of the place is not architecture, it is a dictatorship. Google Earth can only take you so far — consider the story of the winds.

A list of 500 of the most famous buildings in the world would differ greatly from this book. Some structures achieve such global recognition that they become tropes for their country — the Leaning Tower of Pisa, the Eiffel Tower, the Statue of Liberty, the Taj Mahal.

The rise of the celebrity architect is nothing new. To rephrase Lord Acton, celebrity distorts; total celebrity distorts totally. Architects were famous before Christ; they see no reason to stop being famous now. In any one decade there are usually five to ten big beasts, such as the Fosters, Rogers, Pianos, Jahns, Peis, Nouvels and Hadids of this century.

To them fall the choicest cuts, the pick of the world's commissions. Airports are particularly sought after as they yield big budgets and high profiles. When Thailand needed a new airport at Bangkok they sent for German Helmut Jahn, who delivered a monumental structure of undeniable magnificence — just what the customer ordered. Norman Foster went one better and built the world's largest building as Terminal 3 of Beijing International Airport. They take the fame and the glory, but have a remarkable ability to fade into the background when problems arise — the architect of London Heathrow's Terminal 5 was modest to the point of invisibility.

Sometimes the architect's arrogance oversteps the mark: when the principal of the Southern Baptist College in Lake Wales, Florida complained to Frank Lloyd Wright that the roof of his newly built office leaked right on to the desk, a three-word cable came back: "Move your desk."

Sadly for the profession there is no Nobel Prize for Architecture. There are plenty of awards, and a plethora of ceremonies, but given that architecture has a rather longer pedigree than Hollywood, it is surprising that there is nothing like the Oscars for buildings. The difficulty of course is the vagaries of taste; the *dernier cri* of 30 years ago is the premier call for today's wrecking ball.

Reclining on the Olympian slopes of the 21st century, it is easy to glance condescendingly down to the 18th century and grant recognition to their low-tech shacks; through a mist of 300 years, great beacons of architecture shine through as brightly as the light of common day. Now we can look back on the masterpieces of the past and award them the recognition their makers craved. Harder by far is to look back 30 years and decide what will be remembered in the years to come.

The profession would love the fame. There are more drama queens in architecture than in Tinseltown. But none of the architectural awards have captured the public's imagination. The Stirling Prize excites young British architects, but it merits scarcely more than a passing mention in North America. So until an international jury institutes the "Architectural Oscars," this book will serve as a primer and a guide.

No art form galvanizes public opinion like architecture. A painting has to be visited to be viewed, a novel must be read, but every passer-by sees a building, and every one will have a viewpoint. The articulate amateur is conventionally conservative: "eyesore," "monstrous erection," "carbuncle" are common epithets for any proposed new building. The Swiss Re Building in the City of London, better known as the Gherkin, was the exception that proves the rule, and was immediately welcomed into the affections of Londoners.

In this book you will discover some of the most outstanding buildings ever constructed. These towers, domes, theaters and temples have exerted a powerful influence on the imagination of patrons, the public and the architectural profession.

Style, function and context are the defining attributes of the architectural assemblage you hold in your hands, but they all share one further quality that cannot be quantified, cannot be priced and could never be predicted.

Splendor.

Gwyn Headley

Introduction

Architecture and Identity

This journey through 500 buildings begins with one bomb. On the night of May 10, 1941, at the height of the London Blitz, a tumbling incendiary from a German plane struck the British Houses of Parliament. Of the 14 attacks the building sustained during World War II, this was the most devastating. The ensuing fire consumed the debating chamber of the House of Commons leaving behind a blackened shell at the heart of government.

The Palace of Westminster, (to give it its more regal title), was no stranger to such sudden destruction. The structure that bore the Luftwaffe's aggression owed its very existence to a blaze of 1834 which had swept away the majority of Westminster's Tudor and medieval buildings dating back as far as the 11th century. This fiery demolition prompted an architectural competition, won in 1836 by Charles Barry and the flamboyantly named Augustus Welby Northmore Pugin. A neoclassicist by inclination, the talented Barry had been obliged to tap Pugin's mastery of Gothic revival as the judging panel had deemed this to be the most appropriate style with which to clothe a British institution. To most of the contemporary Establishment, the Gothic style was inherently patriotic, backed up by centuries of noble national precedents from parish churches to great cathedrals. By contrast, the once fashionable neoclassical style was increasingly regarded as a foreign import, tainted by its dangerous associations with tumultuous revolutions in France and America. As a consequence of its creators' opposing

Left & below: Discretely hidden behind Pugin's forest of neogothic spires, Britain's House of Commons remained a bombed-out ruin for the duration of World War II.

dispositions, the winning design was a hybrid, Barry's highly symmetrical classical plan almost dripping with Pugin's ornate Gothic detailing. This compromise clearly rankled with purist Pugin, who indignantly declared the result to be "All Grecian, sir; Tudor details on a classic body." It was into this tense marriage of classical and Gothic that the German bombs dramatically intervened.

The vital matter of rebuilding the Commons Chamber was addressed before the war was even over. In 1944 the prestigious commission was awarded to the prominent architect, Sir Giles Gilbert Scott. Designer of both the ubiquitous red telephone box and the iconic Battersea Power Station (see page 314), Scott was an Establishment figure and former president of the RIBA (Royal Institute of British Architects). In his inaugural speech as president in 1935 he had made an impassioned appeal to those at the ideological (and stylistic) extremes of his profession. He urged both diehard traditionalists and hardline modernists to look for common ground and pursue an architectural "middle line." For Scott, this meant transforming power station chimney flues into striped classical columns and placing 19th century "Soane domes" atop his inherently modern telephone boxes. His calls fell largely on deaf ears and, despite some notable commissions, Scott soon found himself out of sync with the progressive times.

His 1942 proposal for rebuilding Coventry Cathedral (another recipient of the Luftwaffe's attentions) was flatly rejected by the Royal Fine Arts Commission on the grounds that it was neither sufficiently avant-garde or traditional, but an unsatisfactory amalgam of the two. Eight years later, a competition panel would choose the uncompromisingly modern design of Basil Spence for Coventry's spiritual home (see page 353); a clear indicator of the new direction to be found in British postwar architecture.

Though Scott did not suffer the same ignominy with his Westminster proposal he did find himself deviating inexorably away from his own "middle line." Sensing everywhere the heavy hand of history he concluded that only a piece in the same Gothic perpendicular style would be appropriate within the context. Despite the shortcomings of the original chamber, such as poor acoustics and insufficient seating, Scott rejected the idea of creating even a moderately modern intervention, arguing that it would jar disastrously with the work of Barry and Pugin. His proposal that the interior be rebuilt in its original form ironically placed him amongst the staunch traditionalists he had earlier sought to convert. Thoroughly approving of this line of action, Sir Winston Churchill (himself a national institution) is alleged to have made the telling observation; "We shape buildings, thereafter they shape us." The Commons agreed. Following a debate on January 25, 1945, a free vote was held, with the motion to rebuild in Barry's mold being carried by 121 votes to 21. Scott duly oversaw the building of a five-story block within the walls of the original, the double-height debating chamber accounting for the top two floors. First used on October 26, 1950, its Gothic finery continues to present an illusion of unbroken occupancy stretching back far further than its true vintage.

Stories in Architecture

This tale of a national icon restored serves as a helpful introduction to the three recurring themes found within these pages: style, function, and context. In a state of constant flux, this trio of concepts is constantly tugging architects in different directions, often leading practitioners to reach radically different conclusions to their contemporaries. Architecture does not happen in isolation, for it is largely a mirror to society, its built forms reflecting the traditions, fashions, customs, beliefs, and aspirations of the people who commission it. Styles come and go as these factors change, leaving behind a document of that moment in time. A single building may offer an interesting historical snapshot, but without the support of its forebears and successors its meaning is substantially diluted. In much the same way that a single mosaic tile can offer only a single color, individual buildings need to be placed together within a timeline before the patterns of the wider picture can be described. A quick overview of these three strands of narrative will bring alive the hidden stories that lie waiting in this survey of the built environment.

The Strictures of Style

Westminster's marriage of convenience, between the Gothic and the classical, was symptomatic of 19th century architecture's overriding obsession with style. Whether they were derived from the ruined monuments of ancient Rome, Greece, and Egypt, or based upon Europe's own medieval cathedrals, the whole of Western architecture seemed locked into a recurring cycle of historical revivals that all claimed to hold the authenticity of antiquity. The so-called "Battle of the Styles" was not limited to Europe, being waged across the British Empire wherever public buildings were required. Under the baking sun of the Indian subcontinent, Bombay became a forest of Gothic spires while its rival, Calcutta, was home to a neoclassical colony. Little concession was made to the climate or to India's own architectural heritage — itself the product of successive invasions, and the co-existence of Hindu and Muslim. For their part, the various cultures of the Middle and Far East kept largely to themselves, honing and refining their own indigenous patterns of building that had continued without interruption for centuries. Conquest or contact through trade periodically exposed the West to the shapes of Arabia and the Orient, leading to architectural oddities such as the Prince Regent's indulgent Royal Pavilion (see page 185) with its Mogul domes.

Across the Atlantic, America was also borrowing freely from the past. Like France, the young republic saw the classicism of

Athens as being synonymous with the ideals and origins of democracy. From the "Age of Enlightenment" onward, the use of neoclassical forms signaled the break from the oppressive old regimes of church and monarch, the principal patrons of the Gothic. The fact that the Greeks had originally painted their buildings in bright colors was known, but largely ignored, the wealthy patrons' preference being for tasteful white marble facades, as seen on their Grand Tours of Europe. The result was a host of fluted Corinthian and Ionic columns, rising like ghostly shadows of their ancient ancestors. From the White House to The Capitol (see pages 190 and 212), this Christian nation was quite happy to appropriate the classical orders of pagan antiquity for its own purposes.

What finally upset this obsessive gazing into the past was the arrival of new forms and new materials. With the rumbling approach of the Industrial Revolution came new building types for which there were no historic precedents. The railway station in particular became the subject of some unfortunate stylistic confrontations, clearly seen in London's St. Pancras (see page 216). Here the red brick Gothic splendor of the Midland Grand Hotel by Sir George Gilbert Scott (Giles' grandfather) makes no attempt to couple up with William Henry Barlow's even more impressive iron and glass train shed, then the largest single-span structure in the world. For the emerging younger generation of architects the structural possibilities of these new industrial materials offered a way out of the stylistic cul-de-sac. Gradually, cast iron, plate glass, reinforced concrete, and finally, steel broke the stranglehold of brick and stone and helped forge a new architecture informed by its materiality, not its symbolic meaning. This new mood at the turn of the century was hammered home by the Austrian architect Adolf Loos, whose vitriolic essay "Ornament and Crime" (1908) branded the use of any stylist devices as "degenerate." His approach advocated stripping buildings back to their purist form, thereby avoiding the inherent obsolescence brought about by changes in taste and fashion.

The attacks of Loos and his contemporaries heralded the birth of modernism, and the beginning of the most eclectic century of architecture the world had ever seen. The story of architecture's eventful stylistic journey is retold here through a careful selection of seminal buildings by key practitioners, covering almost five millennia between them. Tracing the timeline, the reader can follow the continuous narrative of construction from ancient originals through Victorian revivals to the high-tech structures of today. Ultimately, even the belligerent modernist has to acknowledge his debt to the past.

Form and Function

Scott's decision to reinstate, rather than reengineer, the stately House of Commons stands directly at odds with modernist ideology, as articulated in the well worn maxim, "Form follows function." Consequently, the epicenter of one of the most technologically advanced democracies in the world once again donned the faux-medieval robes originally prescribed for it by dusty Victorian romantics. Instead of addressing the specific needs of a modern debating chamber, Scott continued with Pugin's and Barry's ode to the medieval great halls, whose open spaces were intended to accommodate multiple functions, from state banquets to legal trials. The result is decorative and reassuringly solid, but with significant practical failings already alluded to. Those wishing to speculate as to how a progressive modernist might have tackled the task can make a direct comparison with Norman Foster's 1999 intervention at the Reichstag in Berlin, Germany (see page 459). Here, a modern circular debating chamber was crowned with a glass dome and mirrored light cone, all successfully inserted into another bombed-out Victorian shell, (this time in the opposing neoclassical style). In contrast to Westminster's closed stone keep, the transparent Reichstag has tourists queuing around the block to gain access to its dome's panoramic spiral ramps. The recent process of devolution in the U.K. has afforded architects fresh opportunities to reassess the practicality and symbolism of democratic forms, resulting in the Scottish Parliament and the National Assembly for Wales (see pages 491 and 498), whose characters differ sharply with the formality of Westminster. Admittedly, they both had the benefit of a blank canvas on which to draw, but neither Miralles nor Rogers made any recourse to historical pastiche in their efforts to break down the barriers between the governors and the governed.

The actual mantra that "form follows function" was first popularized by the American architect Louis Sullivan, widely credited as the father of the Chicago skyscraper. His original utterance, "That form ever follows function," was made in an article of 1896, published in *Lippincott's Magazine* and entitled "The Tall Office Building Artistically Considered." Sullivan was concerned with the aesthetics of the emerging generation of steel-framed high-rise buildings which would come to dominate the modern cityscape. But, far from advocating a minimal, utilitarian structure devoid of any decoration, Sullivan was simply suggesting that the tower's exterior treatment be appropriate to the form. Instead of flicking through the stale pattern books of history, he proposed that new styles be evolved

Above left: The glittering glass dome that now crowns the scarred stone shell of Berlin's Reichstag hints at the extent of the modern interventions that lie within.

Left: Beneath the dome, the Reichstag's debating chamber is flooded with natural light, diffused in all directions by its mirrored metal stalactite.

in their place. Adorning his multistory Carson Pirie Scott Department Store of 1899 (see page 235), the flowing Art Nouveau patterns of his flamboyant cast iron traceries are evidence of a love of ornament that might have delighted even Pugin. It fell to the purist Adolf Loos and the modernists who followed, (such as Walter Gropius and Le Corbusier), to design buildings deliberately stripped of ornament to reflect the phrase in its more dogmatic, contracted form. Le Corbusier, too, had a knack for soundbites, his 1923 book *Vers une architecture* ("Towards a new architecture") referring to the house as a "machine for living in." As famous as the phrase that preceded it, the clinical white precision of his 1931 Villa Savoye (see page 295) is held up as an icon of logical modernist functionality. Ironically, Corbusier would later abandon the harsh rectilinear lines of his early work and create large scale architectural forms that were as free-flowing and organic as Sullivan's applied decoration, (see Notre Dame du Haut, page 336).

Not content with simply documenting the rise of modernism, this survey sets out to challenge the popular notion of "form follows function" being a purely 20th century concept. Widening the search beyond the narrow modernist definition, it opens the way to re-evaluate historic structures that also have an inherent functionality. The Shaker's Round Barn (see page 212), begun in 1826, is a notable 19th century example of architecture as process, with the internal circulation of the wagon tracks and harnessing of gravity bearing witness to the Brethrens' quest for greater efficiency. However, the use of logical layouts and unembellished, utilitarian forms goes back much further than this agricultural example. The inclusion of a significant number of military structures is quite deliberate, for if Le Corbusier's villas were "machines for living," then Vauban's citadels (see page 142) were undoubtedly "machines for killing." The cold calculation with which military engineers arranged their interlocking fields of fire and built embrasures and parapets to defeat specific projectiles, puts their fortresses in a brutally functional category all of their own. Even the medieval castles of Krak de Chevaliers and Malbork (see pages 76 and 99), with their concentric rings of defenses, staggered turrets, and deadly arrow slits have a cold mechanical precision. The final irony is that their pointed towers and crenulated walls were later adopted as purely decorative forms by Victorian architects, wishing to recreate a vision of noble chivalry that ignored the bloody realities of medieval warfare.

A Sense of Place

Scott's judgment that only a Gothic carbon copy could sit with the remaining fabric of Westminster might appear to lack daring, but it demonstrates his sensitivity to both the commission's physical and psychological context. Effectively a symbolic act of restoration, he was faithfully rebuilding the inner shrine of a democracy that had resisted the tide of Fascism to emerge scarred, but victorious. That comforting

sense of continuity restored, of war wounds healed, would seem to support Churchill's assertion that buildings "shape us." Communities are loathe to alter their familiar monuments, which have the power to inspire and unify in a very public manner.

Most architects do not have the handrail of such an historic building to lean upon. They must find other means of injecting their buildings with a "sense of place" to achieve that satisfying air of permanence. In the absence of applied decoration, this is most commonly explored through form and materials, the latter being particularly pertinent in an eco-conscious age. The Industrial Revolution may have helped free architects from the

straightjacket of style, but the liberation of the new railway network also began to erode centurys' old traditions of vernacular architecture. The importing of affordable "foreign" materials (Welsh slate, Italian pan-tiles, London stock brick) to once-isolated backwaters meant that local materials, and the skills to use them, went into terminal decline. In the age of profit-driven property developers, this gradual process of

Above: The swirling lines of Sullivan's sensuous cast iron traceries wrap their way around the first floor of the Carson Pirie Scott Building, Chicago, Illinois.

Right: Elevated on slender ranks of white piloti, the hard machined forms of Le Corbusier's Villa Savoye lightly hover above the soft green lawn.

national homogenization is almost complete. The result is a soulless sea of clones. It is difficult to form an attachment to a mass-produced mock-Tudor house knowing that its glued-on timber frames, that thin veneer of regionality, disguise an anonymous breeze-block carcass. The unique may have largely given way to the ubiquitous, but architects frequently fight against the economic tide to imbue their buildings with material meaning. Richard Rogers' National Assembly for Wales (see page 498) makes a patriotic virtue of its Welsh slate podium, even though blocks of near identical Chinese slate could have been imported at a fraction of the price. Conversely, the seemingly indigenous green oak laths that form the ground-breaking Downland Gridshell (see page 473) were sourced from carefully managed forests in France, not England. In this instance the desire to act in a sustainable fashion took precedence over national pride, as shipping material the short distance from Normandy produced far fewer carbon emissions than trucking timber down from suppliers in northern England. The desire to respond to a building's context must sometimes be tempered with a sustainable pragmatism.

Form can also be a powerful tool, for past glories can be invoked in far more imaginative ways than pure revival or pastiche. The Bibliotheca Alexandrina (see page 480) is an outstanding example, subtly infused with memories of Ancient Egyptian mythology. Its forest of concrete columns, with their simple flared capitals, produces echoes of Luxor's hypostyle halls, transplanting the lines of pagan temples into an awe-inspiring 21st-century library for the whole of the Middle East. Jean Nouvel's Arab Institute (see page 409) follows a similar vein, its screening façade of photosensitive apertures cleverly tapping into the clients' architectural heritage by recalling the pattern (and function) of the traditional Islamic mashrabiya. Far more subtle than outright duplication, these deft architectural moves provide context-driven precedents for architects across the world.

Accelerated Iconography

This story both begins and ends with a bang, for the last 100 years have seen an explosion of divergent ideas that are helping shape a world of unconventional icons. The fact that almost three-fifths of the 500 buildings that follow were completed after 1900 demonstrates how architecturally rich the past century has been. The great social upheavals of the two world wars proved a major catalyst for change. The first replaced large reactionary regimes and empires with numerous youthful states, keen to express their identity. The second drove a wave of avant-garde modernists to flee Europe and disseminate their ideas in

Britain and America where they took root and flourished. It remains one of history's great ironies that Hitler and Stalin did more to spread the modernist ideology they loathed than any other motive force.

If the advent of air travel made the modern world a smaller place, then the internet and computer-aided design have compressed it still further. In an increasingly mobile society, the superstars of international architecture flit back and forth across the globe to accept their high profile commissions. They are outpaced only by their own designs, which whiz through high-speed internet links to deliver precise digital instructions to distant site managers or computerized cutters. The speed with which ideas can now be tried, tested and built with structural certainty has reduced the labor of experimentation to accelerate the rate of change by encouraging ever more daring forms. The question remains as to whether these rapidly prototyped icons have the same power to "shape us" as did their distant forebears. Whatever a building's age, it should still tell us something meaningful about the moment of its completion. With the guiding strands of style, form, and context in hand, we are now ready to begin our search for architectural excellence.

Paul Cattermole

Above left: Beneath the dramatically sloping disc of the Bibliotheca Alexandria in Egypt lies a latter-day hypostyle hall where centuries of wisdom are now shared.

Left: Like a kinetic Islamic textile, the dilating ocular of the Arab Institute in Paris regulates the strong French sun with sliding metal shutters.

Timeline

Like every strand of human history, the story of architecture declines to be constrained by the strict boundaries of the centuries. Subject to forces in the wider world its evolution has come in fits and starts, frequently hindered by war and famine only to be fanned by religious fervor or the discovery of exotic climes. The last century may have been defined by radical new technologies, but as architects experiment with ever more advanced materials, they still find themselves revisiting forms that have been with us since the dawn of time.

The reader will soon discern the recurring cycle of rediscovery and reinvention within these pages, as each generation reveals its debt to those that have gone before. The broad swathes of time employed to divide this book serve as a useful navigation tool when searching through nearly five millennia of man's endeavors. Listed by completion date, these 500 buildings form a compelling narrative that touches upon every aspect of human history for, ultimately, architecture is but a mirror to the cultures that call it home.

The monuments erected by the builders of the ancient world are all the more remarkable for the limited technologies they could bring to bear. Seemingly intended to last for all eternity, their scale and sheer longevity remain a constant source of inspiration, offering up a plethora of pure forms, ripe for reinterpretation.

Emerging from the doldrums of the Dark Ages, Europe's skyline was dominated by the twin forms of castle and cathedral, upholding faith and the feudal system. Often centuries in the making, the soaring spires and slender arches of the organic Gothic become the touchstone for Victorian architects, dreaming of a truly European style.

Ancient World   **Dark Ages**   **Medieval Period**   **16th Century**

With the fall of the Roman Empire the era of classical refinement faltered. But even as these Mediterranean monuments crumbled, sophisticated new cultures were producing original and exciting forms. From the Mayan jungles to Moorish Spain, the world's architectural vocabulary was being constantly enlarged to express new beliefs, amongst them the growing might of Islam.

The Renaissance saw ancient Rome reborn, with the pagan models rescued from antiquity to be pressed into service as the palaces of Christian pontiffs and princes. Slowly spreading out across Europe, the advancing ranks of columns, urns, and porticos mingled with medieval forms to produce the elegant chateaus that line the Loire, and the stately residences of England's Tudor elite.

The refined Renaissance gave way to the exuberant baroque and Europe was engulfed by a wave of energetic icons. While palaces and churches embraced all things theatrical, the military engineers focused purely on the practical, their fortresses designed with deadly geometric precision. All the while the Mogul masters of India were commissioning that continent's finest landmarks.

Bankrolled by colonial expansion, the cities of Europe became filled with lavish buildings decked out in past styles. Yet the Victorian obsession with historicism was increasingly at odds with the needs of the modern age. It was arguably the great engineers who tapped the zeitgeist best, with their colossal cast iron railway stations and glittering exhibition halls.

The elite of 21st century architecture continue to exploit the possibilities of digital design, proposing ever more elaborate buildings that would have been inconceivable a decade ago. Freed by technology to model, test, and modify without constraint, the only question is whether the world can sustain such a relentless building boom. What form must future buildings take to safeguard all our tomorrows?

17th Century	18th Century	19th Century	20th Century	21st Century

In the Age of Enlightenment the ruins of antiquity captivated the wealthy young aristocracy on their grand tours. They returned to their estates to build the great columned houses of Europe, standing amid rolling artificial hills and lakes, dotted with follies. Yet the illusion of this contrived serenity was soon undermined by violent revolution and the costly Napoleonic wars.

Within a single century of conflict, both literal and ideological, the world of architecture evolved beyond all recognition. From the swirling lines of art nouveau, through the abstraction of art deco, to the strict rationality of pure modernism; the first half of the century saw a shift toward reduction, only for post-modernism to bring it back full circle with its eclectic mix of many styles.

The Citadel of Üçhisar

Architect: Unknown

Completed: Unknown—somewhere between
3500–2000 BCE (Early Bronze Age)

Location: Cappadocia, Anatolia, Turkey

Style/Period: Prehistoric/Early Bronze Age

No one can say for certain when people first hollowed out their homes from the rocks of Cappadocia. Archaeologists can distinguish between those caverns hewn with metal tools and those made with stone, but from there the trail goes cold. The region lies under a blanket of soft tuff stone formed from layers of consolidated volcanic ash, now eroded by centuries of wind and flood into the most surreal of landscapes. Its human history is as tumultuous as its topography, and civilizations from the ancient to the medieval constantly wrestled for control. It was in the folds of these lunar dunes that the early Christians took refuge from a persecuting Roman war machine, and where a stand was made against the tides of Arab invaders encroaching upon Byzantine territory.

Given Cappadocia's history as a troubled frontier, it was inevitable that the rocky outcrop of Üçhisar became inhabited. The highest peak in the region, the citadel is a natural defensive position, offering panoramic views for wary lookouts scanning the horizon. Easy to carve but hardening to a crust once hewn, the great stone stump is riddled with tunnels, tombs and chambers to create a literal "living rock." With the constant comings and goings of its troglodyte community, the citadel would have resembled a busy termite mound, its occupants burrowing ever deeper as the population expanded. Even in its now abandoned state, this prehistoric tower block has a raw, primitive power that speaks of centuries of human interaction with the landscape. **PC**

Stonehenge

Architect: Unknown

Completed: 2600–2100 BCE (main phase)

Location: Salisbury Plain, Wiltshire, England

Style/Period: Neolithic

Stonehenge is one of the most instantly recognizable prehistoric monuments in the world and has been a UNESCO World Heritage Site since the mid-1980s, yet little is known about those who built it, how they built it or its precise purpose. What is known is that the site was not built quickly — archaeologists believe it took some 3,000 years in all and that the work was done in a number of stages using various materials. First there was a circular earth bank and ditch enclosure that was dug around 3100 BCE. The second phase involved the construction of wooden structures, including a timber building within the earthworks.

Although there were later periods of work on the site, phase three, which is divided into various subphases and lasted from around 2600 BCE to 2100 BCE, saw the arrival of the large blocks of stone that can be seen today. These include the extremely large sarsen stones, originally 30 in all, which were linked by lintels to form a circular enclosure. Various theories have been put forward to explain the purpose of Stonehenge, including some that can only be described as bizarre, but it is generally thought to have been a pagan religious site. **IW**

Great Sphinx

Architect: Unknown

Completed: Mid-3rd millennium BCE

Location: Giza, near Cairo, Egypt

Style/Period: Ancient Egyptian

The half-human–half-lion Great Sphinx is one of the most famous sculptures on the planet, yet it remains an elusive monument, one that has provoked fierce debate between archaeologists and others over the date of its construction, its builder and its role. It is agreed that the sphinx was carved out of the limestone of the Giza plateau and was part of a religious and burial complex on the bank of the River Nile, and that it is the largest monolithic statue in the world — being 241 feet (73 m) long, 20 feet (6 m) wide and 65 feet (20 m) tall — and most certainly the oldest.

Most Egyptologists credit the east-facing Great Sphinx to Khafra, a pharaoh who is thought to have ruled between 2520 BCE and 2494 BCE, and who built the second largest of the nearby Great Pyramids, although some have suggested that other rulers from around the same time were responsible for its construction. More radically, some have suggested that the monument is much older, dating back between 8,000 to 10,000 years, largely on the basis that the sphinx shows clear signs of erosion by rainwater that could only have taken place in the latter, wetter period. **IW**

Great Pyramid of Khufu

Architect: Hemon

Completed: c. 2560 BCE

Location: Giza, near Cairo, Egypt

Style/Period: Ancient Egyptian

Hemon (n.d.) was the cousin of Khufu, a pharaoh who reigned from 2589 BCE to 2566 BCE and ordered the building of a pyramid — which remains the world's largest — to house his remains. The four-sided structure is the only one of the Seven Wonders of the World still standing, and its sheer monumentality ensured that it would be included in that select list. When completed, it was 482 feet (147 m) high. It was built with huge granite blocks covered in a sheathing of polished limestone blocks. The precision with which they were cut and positioned was equally remarkable, and consequently the pyramid has a stunning mathematical and geometric precision. Each base side, for example, originally measured 755 feet (230 m).

The pyramid interior consists of two main burial chambers and one that was never completed, as well as the Grand Passage and various other galleries. There are two narrow shafts that rise to the outer surface that probably had some religious significance relating to astronomy. The Great Pyramid, which would have shone in the sun and may have had a dazzling gilded pinnacle, would have inspired reverence and awe among the ancient Egyptians. Although it has suffered centuries of wear, it is still the ancient world's most iconic architectural statement. **IW**

Temple of Karnak

Architect: Unknown

Completed: 1640 BCE

Location: Luxor, Nile Valley, Egypt

Style/Period: Ancient Egyptian

The Temple of Karnak is the ancient world's largest religious site and covers an area of some 247 acres (100 ha) on the east bank of the River Nile, close to what was once known as Thebes and is now called Luxor. The temple complex was built during the reigns of a number of pharaohs, including Ramesses I, Seti I and Ramesses II, and the greater part of the work was completed between 2040 BCE and 1640 BCE. It consists of several temples of various sizes, and the largest of them are dedicated to Amun, the king of the gods, Mut, the queen of the gods, and Montu, the solar and warrior god.

There are also several great entrance pylons, the Sacred Lake and various perimeter walls. The site's greatest architectural feature is the extensive Hypostyle Hall, which would have had a height of 82 feet (25 m) when completed. It has a central section that consists of 12 sandstone columns in two rows of six. These columns are each flanked by seven rows of nine columns that rise to a height of 42 feet (13 m) to create a vast hall. Somewhat unusually, significant sections of the columns' rich decoration have survived the ravages of time. **IW**

Palace of Knossos

Architect: Unknown

Completed: c. 1400 BCE

Location: Knossos, Crete, Greece

Style/Period: Minoan

The Palace of Knossos was built gradually over a period of around 300 years beginning in c. 1700 BCE, and it became the political and ceremonial heart of the powerful Bronze-Age Minoan civilization. The impressive remains today, many of which were rebuilt by the wealthy, self-taught English archaeologist Arthur Evans in the early 20th century, probably largely date from the Late Minoan Period. The palace was built on an epic scale — it covers some 6 acres (2.43 ha) and contains 1,300 rooms of various sizes and functions.

The palace has the expected throne rooms and ceremonial spaces, but it also contains a theater and practical storage rooms that housed large clay jars for preserving foodstuffs, as well as mills and presses to process grains and olives. The complex displays advanced architectural techniques and has, among other things, a sophisticated water management system. Clean water was brought in by aqueduct over a distance of some 6 miles (10 km) and distributed by pipes; there was a method of removing excessive runoff from storms, and waste water was also displaced by a sewage system that included the earliest known flushing toilets. **IW**

Lion Gate

Architect: Unknown

Completed: c. 1250 BCE

Location: Mycenae, Peloponnese, Greece

Style/Period: Early Ancient Greek

The hilltop city of Mycenae was the heart of a great civilization that dominated much of southern Greece and the Eastern Mediterranean during the Bronze Age and undoubtedly had contact with ancient Egypt. The imposing Lion Gate is the most important and impressive entrance into the citadel and is cut through walls that are commonly referred to as "cyclopean," as it was once believed that the massive carved stone blocks could only have been moved by the race of one-eyed giants known as cyclops.

The gate consists of two upright stone blocks and a massive lintel above which there is a carved triangular stone that helps direct the force of the stone blocks to the side, down into the two uprights. It is carved with two rampant lionesses — reinforcing the belief that the Myceneans had contacts with Africa — which are separated by a column that is believed to be a reference to a goddess and is in a style that suggests a connection with the Minoan civilization on Crete. The Lion Gate impacted on the later Greeks of the Classical world, who took the Mycenaean architectural inheritance and refined it to create their own great buildings. **IW**

Choga Zambil

Architect: Unknown

Completed: c. 1250 BCE

Location: Dur Untash, Khuzestan, Iran

Style/Period: Mesopotamian

Choga Zambil ("large basket-shaped hill") in the southwest of Iran is the world's biggest ziggurat. It lies at the center of the Elamite city of Dur Untash, which was built on a plateau overlooking the River Daz and is part of a large religious complex that contains irregular double walls and various other temples. The complex's outer walls measure some 3,900 feet (1,200 m) by 2,600 feet (800 m). The ziggurat itself was built by King Utash-Gal in what is usually known as the

Middle Elamite Period (c. 1500–1000 BCE) and was dedicated to Inshushinak, the bull-god of Susa.

The ziggurat has four sides that measure 344 feet (105 m) each. Today it rises to a height of 80 feet (24 m), but in its original form it would probably have been twice that height and topped by a temple from where the bull-god ascended to heaven each night. The ziggurat, which was built in brick and cement, was once richly decorated. The exterior blazed with glazed blue and green terra-cotta, while the interior was decorated in glass and ivory. The temple complex was never actually completed, and the city was sacked by the Assyrian King Ashurbanipol around 640 BCE and thereafter abandoned. **IW**

Treasury of Atreus

Architect: Unknown

Completed: c. 1200 BCE

Location: Mycenae, Peloponnese, Greece

Style/Period: Early Ancient Greek

The Treasury of Atreus was excavated but misnamed by German archaeologist Heinrich Schliemann in the late 19th century. It is actually a *tholos*, or beehive tomb, and is sometimes referred to as the Tomb of Agamemnon. Thanks to its scale and the quality of the craftsmanship, it is one of the most impressive monuments to the skills of the Bronze Age Myceneans. The *tholos* is a semi-subterranean circular room made by very carefully placing carved stone blocks that are angled on their interior face so that, as they rise, they form a self-supporting dome. The *tholos* has a diameter of 48 feet (15 m) and a height of 44 feet (14 m) — dimensions that made it the tallest and widest dome in the world for more than 1,000 years.

The *tholos* is reached by way of a 118-foot (36 m) *dronos* ("open passageway") that is made from beautifully carved stone blocks, and entrance to the tomb is by way of a pyramidal-covered gateway that has two huge stone lintels. There is a void triangle above the doorway, which is typical of Mycenaean architecture. It deflects the thrust of the upper part of the building onto the supports of the doorway. **IW**

Ishtar Gate

Architect: Unknown
Completed: c. 575 BCE
Location: Babylon, Iraq
Style/Period: Babylonian

The imposingly large Ishtar Gate, which is named after the Babylonian goddess of fertility, love and war, was the most important of the eight entrances that led to the inner city of Babylon. Situated along the northern length of a great defensive wall, it was ordered by King Nebuchadnezzar II, who reigned from 605 to c. 562 BCE, and who was responsible for developing and revitalizing his capital. The Processional Way, a route with ritual significance, went through the gate.

The gate is covered in blue glazed bricks that alternate with low reliefs made from glazed polychromatic bricks that depict both real and imaginary animals. The animal reliefs are of two types: aurochs, an extinct species of cattle, and sirrush, which are scaly dragons with catlike forelegs, hind legs with eagle's talons, a snakelike tongue and a crest. The gate's roof was constructed in cedar, as was the large pair of double doors. The remains of the gate were uncovered during the early 20th century by the German archaeologist Robert Koldewey, and a full-size copy of it was constructed in Berlin's Pergamon Museum. The gate was actually one of the original Seven Wonders of the World but was replaced by the Pharos of Alexandria in the 6th century CE. **IW**

Temple of Poseidon

Architect: Unknown
Completed: c. 550 BCE
Location: Paestum, Calabria, Italy
Style/Period: Ancient Greek/Doric

Paestum was the Roman name for a Greek city in southern Italy that they captured around 273 BCE, but the name given to it by its founders, colonists from the city-state of Sybaris who arrived at the end of the 7th century BCE, was Poseidonia. The city was laid out on a plateau of travertine stone, which became the chief building material. Within the walls, which are some 3 miles (5 km) long, are a number of large buildings, including three temples. The most impressive of these temples has been known by a number

of names, including the Basilica, because it was once assumed to be a civic rather than religious building, and the Temple of Poseidon, because 18th century archaeologists mistakenly assumed it was named after the Greek god of the sea like the city.

In reality, the Greeks dedicated the temple to Hera, the goddess of fertility and the wife of Zeus, and inscriptions and other evidence unearthed by archaeologists confirmed its true name. The building is in the Doric style, with simple large columns that are fluted, but less so than later Greek architectural orders, and it is the best-preserved example of the earliest form of Greek classical architecture. **IW**

Gate of the Nations

Architect: Unknown

Completed: Reign of Xerxes I (486–465 BCE)

Location: Persepolis, Iran

Style/Period: Persian

Work on the construction of Persepolis, the capital of the Persian Archaemenid Empire, began during the reign of Darius I, and the construction continued under his son and successor, Xerxes, at whose command the Gate of Nations was built. It was the imposing entrance to the city's inner sanctum, including its great throne room, and the title refers to the subject nations ruled by the empire. The gate, actually a reception room with three double-leafed doorways, was built in mud brick and had a roof supported by four columns. It was not especially large, each side being around 16 feet (5 m) wide.

Two gates, those to the east and west, led to the outside world, while the southern gate opened into the yard, beyond which lay the large throne reception room, where visitors would honor and pay tribute to the emperor. The western door is flanked by symbolic bulls with the head of a bearded man, while the eastern doorway is adorned with winged bulls. The gate also carries script in three languages that informed any visitor that Xerxes had ordered it to be built. The interior contained a stone bench that ran parallel to the walls. The anticipation of moving from a windowless enclosed space through a large courtyard into the throne room must have been immense. **IW**

Parthenon

Architects: Iktinos, Kallikrates, Pheidias

Completed: c. 432 BCE

Location: Acropolis, Athens, Greece

Style/Period: Hellenistic

The largely Doric-style Parthenon is the most dominant and significant building on the hilltop Acropolis, not least because it was dedicated to Athena, the goddess who gave her name to the most important of classical Greece's city-states, the home of democracy. Although the temple was not the largest of the ancient world, it is widely considered the most beautiful because of its seemingly perfect geometry. It was also the most highly and skillfully decorated building of its type, and many beautiful friezes were sculpted to record the history, religion, myths and legends of the Athenian state.

The building actually housed a large, long-gone statue of Athena, but its precise function is a matter of debate. No evidence of an altar has ever been found, and many rituals normally took place in the open air anyway. Some have suggested that the Parthenon was actually used as a treasury, a view that has gained ground in recent years. Whatever the case, the Parthenon is the most important building of the classical Greek age, despite the enormous amount of damage done to it down the centuries, and it is wholly symbolic of the golden era of Athens. **IW**

Erechtheion

Architect: Mnesicles (attributed)

Completed: c. 405 BCE

Location: Acropolis, Athens, Greece

Style/Period: Hellenistic

This Ionic temple, within which various rites were conducted, stands on sloping ground to the north of the Pantheon and is one of the Acropolis's great architectural treasures. It was probably erected to replace an earlier temple that was destroyed by the Persians around 480 BCE. Built in white marble, it is unusual in that it is asymmetrical with two porches projecting outward from the north and south. It is also remarkable because it is built on a slope so that its west and north sides are some 9 feet (3 m) taller than the south and east sides.

The central block of the temple is a simple rectangle divided into four compartments, the largest of which lies to the east. It has a wall with engaged (partly embedded) columns at the western end and a fine portico at the eastern end. To the north there is a porch with a high Ionic colonnade, while to the south is the shorter porch of the Caryatids. This, the most well known part of the Erechtheion, consists of a flat roof supported by six finely and individually sculpted female figures. The temple was once decorated with a frieze that ran all along its walls. **IW**

Great Stupa

Architect: Unknown

Completed: c. mid-3rd century BCE

Location: Sanchi, Madhya Pradesh, India

Style/Period: Buddhist

Positioned on a hill adjacent to the village of Sanchi, the Great Stupa is part of the greatest and oldest collection of Buddhist structures in India. Sanchi includes temples, monasteries and stupas, the hemispherical mounds that formed memorial shrines. The first stupas were built in the 3rd century BCE by Emperor Ashoka, a convert to Buddhism. The largest of the shrines is known as the Great Shrine or, more prosaically, Stupa 1. It was originally built in large burnt bricks and mud, but it subsequently underwent a major expansion. It was also subject to various renovations and additions over the following centuries.

In its final form the Great Stupa, which is 120 feet (37 m) across, consists of a sandstone hemisphere with a flattened top from which rises a three-tiered symbolic parasol set inside a square railing. A third of the way up the structure is a round terrace enclosed by a fence that was used in ritual circumambulations. At ground level there is a stone processional walkway enclosed by a stone balustrade pierced by four intricately carved gateways positioned at the cardinal points. The Great Stupa is one of the best-preserved Buddhist shrines anywhere, and its evolution charts the rise, flowering and fall of Buddhism in India. **IW**

Temple of Horus

Architect: Unknown

Completed: 57 BCE

Location: Edfu, Egypt

Style/Period: Ancient Egyptian

This temple complex dedicated to Horus, the falcon god, is the second largest in Egypt and is the best preserved, largely because it spent many centuries mostly buried under a deep layer of desert sand. The temple dates back to Ptolemaic Egypt, an era when Greeks ruled the land. Its many inscriptions, despite suffering attacks by Christians, have helped to shed light on the language, myths, and religious practices of Ptolemaic Egyptians.

Work began on the site in 237 BCE, and the temple was built over an existing structure that was orientated east-west and looked out over the River Nile. The new temple was, unusually, orientated from north to south, with the massive, imposing entrance pylon facing south. Construction was undertaken in a number of stages. After the original work was completed, a great hypostyle hall of 18 columns was built, and this hall was followed by the courtyard and pylon gateway some 25 years later, which is 118 feet (36 m) high and decorated with carvings of Ptolemy XII defeating his enemies. Work ended when a double-leaved cedar door was hung in the gateway. The complex also includes various other rooms, including the Great Hall. The temple fell into disuse from the 3rd century CE, when the Romans imposed Christianity on the Egyptians. **IW**

Maison Carrée

Architect: Unknown

Completed: c. 19–16 BCE

Location: Nimes, Provence, France

Style/Period: Ancient Roman

Marcus Agrippa, a leading Roman politician and son-in-law of the Emperor Augustus, ordered the construction of the temple now known as the Maison Carrée ("Square House"), and it was later dedicated to his two sons. The unknown architect produced a beautifully proportioned building that is austere yet elegant. The temple was built using local limestone and is almost perfectly symmetrical — the ratio being virtually two (lengths) to one (width). This quintessential classical Roman building sits on a 9-foot (3 m) high podium, and entrance is by way of 15 steps that lead to the six Corinthian columns that support the pediment.

The portico is three columns deep, roughly one-third of the building's entire length, while the temple itself is an enclosed, windowless room that is supported by eight columns that are half embedded in the outside walls. The temple has had many uses — it became a Christian church in the 4th century and has subsequently been used as a house, stable, archive store and currently hosts various exhibitions. It is, most importantly, the purest and most tangible expression of the ideals of austerity, dignity and order that were so prized within the Roman Empire. **IW**

Pont du Gard

Architect: Unknown

Completed: 60 CE (begun sometime after 40 CE)

Location: Vers-Pont-du-Gard, near Remoulins, France

Style/Period: Roman

The largest aqueduct in the Roman world, the imposingly proportioned Pont du Gard, forms the most visible element of an even greater feat of ancient engineering. Stretching out across 31 miles (50 km) of French countryside winds a masonry channel that once kept the civilizing spas of Roman Nîmes supplied with water from the spring of Eure. Long since plundered for its stone, some 90 percent of the channel was built underground with a barrel-vaulted roof and mortar-lined walls that prevented both contamination and evaporation. With only a 39-foot (12 m) height difference from end to end, Nîmes' vast umbilical cord was obliged to hug the contours of the landscape, maintaining a gentle angle of descent that kept the waters flowing on a 24- to 30-hour journey to their destination.

When confronted by the deep gorge of the River Gardon, the Roman engineers' response was to project the pipeline out into the void, carrying it upon a bridge that soars some 160 feet (49 m) above the river's surface. The number of mortarless yellow limestone arches multiplies through its three tiers, from 6 to 11, then 47, with the largest spanning 80 feet (24.5 meters). The Roman architect has gone unrecorded, since the only mark on its stone piles is the Latin inscription *men totum corium* — "this structure has been measured in its entirety." The Pont du Gard's listing as a UNESCO World Heritage Site provides a fitting measure of its significance today. **PC**

Colosseum

Architect: Unknown

Completed: 80 CE

Location: Piazza del Colosseo, Rome, Italy

Style/Period: Roman

The 70,000-seat Colosseum, originally known as the Flavian Amphitheater, is the largest Roman amphitheater ever built. It is elliptical in shape, and its longest axis measures 617 feet (188 m) and its shortest 512 feet (156 m). It is built in brick and concrete with a cladding of travertine and has four levels that, from the exterior, can be identified by the succession of columns of different classical styles rising up to a height of 157 feet (48 m). The first three arcades have, from the ground up, Doric, Ionic and Corinthian columns, while the fourth has Composite pilasters. The lower level has 76 arcades, through which the crowds entered and left the venue.

The Colosseum was much more than an awe-inspiring building, as it played a key role in Rome's everyday life and politics. It was both symbolically and actually at the heart of both the city and the empire. Emperors sponsored gladiatorial and other games to celebrate key dates in the empire's history, to display their own power and wealth, and used such events to keep the capital's population in order. After the fall of the empire, the amphitheater was used as a fortress and eventually as a quarry, and much of its stone was used in later buildings in the capital. **IW**

Roman Baths

Architect: Unknown
Completed: c. 2nd century CE
Location: Bath, Somerset, England
Style/Period: Ancient Roman

Bath is the site of Britain's only geothermal spring and, as such, it was a place of worship from the earliest times. The Celts worshipped their goddess Sulis at the site and, when the Romans arrived, they named the town Aquae Sulis and built their own temple dedicated to the goddess of arts and crafts, Minerva. Work on the temple began between 60–70 CE, and the complex grew over the following centuries until the comparatively small city had a shrine and baths that were out of proportion to its own population's needs. This suggests that the temple and baths were a place of pilgrimage for the Romans of Britain and, most probably, from elsewhere in the empire.

The complex consists of three main elements — the sacred spring, the temple (one of only two stone ones in the country) and the bathhouse. The bathhouse incorporates a large and, unusually, hot bath (*caldarium*), a warm bath (*tepidarium*) and a cold bath (*frigidarium*). The caldarium is rare because the expense of heating water on such a scale would have made such an extravagance financially ruinous, whereas in Bath the hot water was freely available. The baths, which are the best-preserved Roman religious spa complex, are a UNESCO World Heritage Site. **IW**

Trajan's Markets/ Forum of Trajan

Architect: Unknown, probably Apollodorus

Completed: 117 CE (begun 98 CE)

Location: Rome, Italy

Style: Roman

The ruins of the Forum of Trajan seen in Rome today are a perpetual reminder of what was once a magnificent tribute to the military prowess of Marcus Ulpius Traianus, Roman emperor from 98 to 117 CE. Trajan returned to Rome cloaked in military glory after his resounding victory over the Dacians, annexing the land that is today Romania into the Roman Empire. He ordered the forum be built to reinforce the power of the empire and his own part in its glory. It was described by the historian Ammianus Marcellinus (330–395 CE) as "beggaring description and never again to be imitated by mortal men."

Set 16 feet (5 m) below the modern street level and probably built under the direction of the architect Apollodorus, the forum was entered through a triumphal arch that opened onto a massive plaza laid with marble. In the center stood a towering bronze statue of Trajan on horseback, likely to have stood some 39 feet (12 m) high. Surrounding it to the east and west was a Corinthian colonnade; to the north was a huge basilica, behind which were two libraries on either side of the Trajan's Column. Trajan's Markets, built at the same time and lying to the east, contained a vaulted hall and multilevel market. **EW**

Hadrian's Villa (Villa Adriana)

Architect: Unknown

Completed: 124 CE

Location: Tivoli, Lazio, Italy

Style: Roman

Built originally as a retreat for Emperor Hadrian, the villa's structure reflects architectural styles in keeping with Hadrian's wide experiences from a lifetime's traveling. Set on a hillside just outside modern-day Tivoli, away from the politics of Rome, the villa quickly became Hadrian's preferred residence. Made up of over 30 buildings, it

covered a huge area of some 250–300 acres (80–120 ha), much of which remains unexcavated.

Alongside the traditional villa, the complex included a Greek and Latin library, a grand court (Piazza d'Oro), guest accommodation (*hospitalia*), baths, temples, a Greek theater, barracks and gardens. One of the most important surviving buildings is the Maritime Theater, which was effectively an island set in the middle of a pool and linked to a round portico, probably by a draw or swing bridge. The house on the island, complete with an audience hall, dining room (*triclinium*), a library and baths, is believed to have been Hadrian's retreat within a retreat. Underground is a network of tunnels used by servants to reach the various parts of the site; aboveground was reserved for the more illustrious residents. In 1999 Hadrian's Villa was named a UNESCO World Heritage Site and was described as "a masterpiece that uniquely brings together the highest expressions of the material cultures of the ancient Mediterranean world." **EW**

Pantheon

Architect: Unknown
Completed: 125 CE
Location: Piazza della Rotunda, Rome, Italy
Style/Period: Roman

The original driving force behind the construction of this structure was the statesman Marcus Agrippa, who wanted to create a temple to celebrate the 12 most important Roman gods. The original building was damaged by a fire in 80 CE, and it was extensively restored by two later emperors, Domitian and Trajan. The current temple was the work of Emperor Hadrian, and the Pantheon was rebuilt under his patronage between 118 and 125. This produced the original and quintessential classical Roman structure, one of great composition and order.

The Pantheon was groundbreaking in that it was not the typical rectangular structure, as previous such temples were, but rather a square from which a high-vaulted concrete dome rises. The latter, a revolutionary feat of engineering, was accomplished by inserting hidden niches in the walls and brick arches as supports. By gradually reducing the thickness of the walls, the dome's downward thrust was reduced, and the stress redirected to the foundations. The dome is beautifully proportioned — its diameter is equal to its height from the floor. The Pantheon, which is now a Christian church, is by far the best-preserved example of the classical form, and its great qualities proved an inspiration to innumerable architects. **IW**

The Library of Celsus

Architect: Unknown

Completed: c. 125 CE

Location: Ephesus, Turkey

Style: Ancient Roman

Julius Celsus Polemeanus, governor of Asia in 115 CE, successfully ensured he would be remembered eternally by leaving 25,000 denarii toward a library when he died at the age of 70. His son, Gaius Julius Aquila, fulfilled his father's ambition, building a library capable of holding 12,000 scrolls alongside Celsus's marble tomb.

In a style influenced by Greek architecture, nine full-length steps lead to three main entrances, each with a window above that would have allowed the sunlight to flood in. Sets of Corinthian columns marked the three entrances, with the center one set slightly higher than the other two. Directly above, another set of columns frames the windows, and there is some indication that the library was originally three stories high. Also flanking the entrances are four statues, which represent wisdom (Sophia), knowledge (Episteme), intelligence (Ennoia) and virtue (Arete). Inside was a single high-ceilinged reading room, surrounded on three sides by storage spaces for the scrolls of manuscripts, which were kept in cupboards in niches. Behind were double walls, probably designed to protect the manuscripts from humidity. On the fourth side was a semicircular recess, under which lay Celsus's remains. **EW**

Odeon of Herodes Atticus

Architect: Unknown

Completed: c. 161 CE

Location: Acropolis, Athens, Greece

Style/Period: Ancient Greek

This *odeon* (theater) was cut into the southern slope of the Acropolis ("high city") in Athens at a time when it was no longer a great political and creative city-state, but rather a vassal of the Roman Empire. Atticus was a scholar and philosopher who had spent time in Rome teaching members of the nobility, including Emperor Marcus Aurelius.

He was also extremely wealthy and financed a number of public buildings across Greece, including his eponymous theater, which was in part built to commemorate his recently deceased wife, Aspasia Regilla.

The steep southern slope of the Acropolis, the religious and political heart of the city-state, was an ideal site for the 5,000-seat semicircular theater, where plays and concerts were performed and speeches were made, often in an attempt to recapture the city's golden age. The theater's orchestra is a semicircular flat area, where dancing and singing by the chorus took place, and has a raised platform behind for the actors and a substantial pierced and colonnaded facade through which they entered and exited the stage. The Odeon of Herodes Atticus is the best-preserved late classical Greek theater and is still in use. **IW**

The Theater of Aspendos

Architect: Zeno
Completed: 180 CE (begun 161 CE)
Location: Antalya, Turkey
Style: Ancient Greco-Roman

Built during the reign of Emperor Marcus Aurelius (161–180 CE), the spectacular Theater of Aspendos is still used today. Under the stewardship of the Greek architect Zeno, whose statue stands in the south *parados*, a spectacular theater arose, which remains one of the best examples not only of Roman theater building, but also of the influence of Hellenistic architecture on Roman design. Examples of this influence include what once was a 7-foot (2 m) high stage, compared with the more usual "western"-style height of about 4 feet (1.2 m). The theater was probably built on the site of an earlier stage.

Inscriptions on either side of the *skene* (backdrop building) attribute its construction to wealthy brothers Curtius Crespinus and Curtius Asupicatus and dedicate it to "the Gods of the Country and the Imperial House." The *cavea* (seating area), built of high-quality limestone, is set over two levels with 41 rows of seats, the top row of which is surrounded by a colonnaded gallery with regular vaulted arches. Towers on either side of the stage connect the *skene* to the *cavea*. A parapet between the audience and the *cavea* was added in the 3rd century, and the Suljuk leader Alaeddin Kaykabat I made further changes, including tile decorations and the towered entrance, in the 13th century. **EW**

Al Khazneh

Architect: Unknown

Completed: c. 100 BCE–200 CE

Location: Petra, Wadi Mousa, Jordan

Style/Period: Ancient Roman

Petra remained lost to the world until Johann Burckhardt, a Swiss explorer, stumbled upon it in 1812. Although this city carved in sandstone appears off the beaten track, it actually stands on what once would have been important north-south and east-west trade routes. Its citizens must have grown wealthy on the trade, as the city covers some 4 square miles (10 sq. km) and has a sizeable amphitheater that can hold an audience of up to 3,000. Yet little is known of the people who lived in the city, the Nabataeans, traces of whom have been found nowhere else.

Al Khazneh ("the Treasury"), which may have been originally built as a tomb, is Petra's most well-known structure, and it clearly shows that the Nabataeans were influenced by, but also reinterpreted, classical Greek and Roman architectural styles. The top half of its facade is divided by Corinthian columns and has a small *tholos* (rotunda), while the lower portion is a pedimented portico with six columns and is decorated with two sculptures thought to be Castor and Pollux. The Treasury was probably one of the last buildings to be carved in Petra, as no other structures show such a mix of styles, and it is therefore effectively unique. **IW**

Arch of Septimus Severus

Architect: Unknown

Completed: c. 203 CE

Location: Forum, Rome, Italy

Style/Period: Roman/Parthian

Severus was a notable Roman general who went on to rule the empire between 193 and 211, and this prototype triumphal arch was erected to celebrate a war he and his two sons, Caracalla and Geta, won against the Parthians in 197. Built in brick and stone with highly decorative white marble cladding, it is in the northeast of the Forum and was originally approached by a flight of steps. It consists of one large central archway flanked by two smaller arches. The main arch has a highly coffered semicircular vault and lateral openings that connect with the subsidiary arches, features that were copied in later such monuments.

The three archways rest on piers, in front of which stand detached Composite columns that sit on pedestals. Other decorations include carvings of winged victory and inscriptions concerning the royal family's role in the Parthian War. The south pier contains a staircase that leads to the roof, where a four-horse chariot with statues of the emperor and his two sons once stood. Unlike many Roman monuments, the arch is still largely intact; it later formed part of a church, so its stone was not plundered for other uses. **IW**

Arg-é Bam

Architect: Unknown

Completed: c. 224–250 CE

Location: Kerman Province, Iran

Style/Period: Persian Adobe

Made from the earth itself, the humble adobe brick has been the mainstay of Middle Eastern architecture for over three millennia. A thoroughly sustainable material, its constant maintenance needs make it difficult to date, as each successive layer of render is indistinguishable from the first. Hiding their precise age behind centuries of accretions stand the imposing ruins of the Arg-é Bam (Citadel of Bam), whose delicately crenulated walls were likely raised during Persia's early Sassanian period. Clinging to the contours of an artificial hill, the citadel dominates the northwest quadrant of the abandoned city of Bam, once an important trading center along the legendary Silk Road.

Enclosing an area of approximately 2 million square feet (180,000 sq. m) within its walls, the fortress qualifies as the world's largest adobe building. Its inherent sandy uniformity makes it appear to be morphing out of the landscape, as though sheered up by some tectonic force. Tragically it was just such an event that spelt the end for Bam's fine ramparts, when on the night of December 26, 2003, it was struck by a massive earthquake measuring 6.6 on the Richter scale. In a matter of seconds, a monument that had stood for centuries was reduced to dust. A UNESCO World Heritage Site, the citadel's destruction provoked an international response, and Iran was inundated with offers of assistance. There are grand plans for its reconstruction but, for the time being at least, the great adobe citadel remains returned to its natural state. **PC**

Arch of Constantine

Architect: Unknown

Completed: 315 CE

Location: Via Triumphalis, Rome, Italy

Style/Period: Roman (Corinthian)

This honorary arch, the largest still standing in Rome, was erected on the orders of Emperor Constantine I to celebrate his decisive victory over Maxentius at the Battle of the Milvian Bridge in 312. It was built over the route taken by triumphant generals and armies when they returned to the city. The beautifully proportioned arch is some 65 feet (20 m) high, 82 feet (25 m) wide and 23 feet (7 m) deep, and it is pierced by three archways, the central being the highest at 39 feet (12 m). The lower part is built out of marble blocks, while the attic consisted of marble riveted to brick. The whole is beautifully decorated with Corinthian columns, sculptures and bas-relief. Some elements, those known as *spolia* (spoils), were taken from existing buildings, sometimes partly resculpted, and attached to the new arch.

The work probably began in late 312 and was completed some three years later. Classicists have argued why it was thought necessary to use *spolia* at all — was it because of the short build time? Or was it because the sculptors then available were less skilled than their predecessors? Whatever the reason, the arch became something of a blueprint and an archetype for other monuments, not least the far larger Arc de Triomphe in Paris. **IW**

Dark Ages 500–1200 CE

Hagia Sophia

Architects: Anthemius of Tralles, Isidore of Miletus
Completed: 537 CE
Location: Sultanahmet Square, Istanbul, Turkey
Style/Period: Christian Classicism

Hagia Sophia, once a mosque and today a museum, was originally a Christian place of worship, known as the Church of the Holy Wisdom until 1453. It was commissioned by Emperor Constantine as the crowning glory of Constantinople, the new city he had founded. Work commenced in 326, but the Emperor Justinian rebuilt the basilica between 532 and 537. Anthemius and Isodore, both better known as scientists, drew up the ambitious plan. The latter was a renowned teacher of stereometry — the measurement of volumes — and physics; the former was an expert in projective geometry.

They produced a building that was the epitome of Byzantine architecture and the largest cathedral in the world for over 1,000 years. It ran counter to the prevailing architectural norms: the building's huge central dome has a span of 107 feet (33 m) and rises more than 164 feet (50 m) above the nave. Various interlocking domes, part domes and apses compress the main walls so that they can support the central dome's great weight. The church was the first to use what is termed the pendentive, a method that solves the problem of how to make the curve of a dome meet with the right angle of its supporting wall. The use of the pendentive gives the church its complex geometry. **IW**

Taq-i-Kisra

Architect: Unknown

Completed: 532–579 CE

Location: Iraq

Style: Sassanid

Dominating the landscape by its sheer size and majesty, Taq-i-Kisra is the world's largest single-span arch. This impressive example of Sassanid architecture protected the ceremonial throne room of the original imperial palace of Ctesiphon, one of the great cities of ancient Mesopotamia, and set in what is now the Mada'in region of Iraq, some 20 miles (35 km) southeast of modern Baghdad.

The entry *iwan* is a vaulted three-sided structure that was a trademark of Sassanid architecture. It was built without a centering device and the sidewalls taper from 23 to 13 feet (7–4 m). It originally led to a central hall flanked by two large rooms, and their size indicates that it was used purely for ceremony and audience, rather than as a residence. The six-level facade was made up of columns, entablatures and arches. Built mainly of brick, excavation also suggests the existence of glass mosaics and marble. The Arab historian Qazwini also mentioned a mural of the Sasanian King Anushirvan Khusraw (531–579 CE) in the throne room. Much of the ruins were destroyed by floods in the late 19th century. Only parts of the *iwan* and the front of the palace, both facing east, survive. **EW**

Dome of the Rock

Architects: Yazid ibn Salam and Raja ibn Haywah

Completed: 691 CE

Location: Temple Mount, Jerusalem, Israel

Style/Period: Early Islamic

The Dome of the Rock shelters the rock from where the prophet Mohammed ascended to heaven on a horselike creature, a Buraq, in the company of the angel Gabriel. It is therefore one of Islam's holiest sites. Jerusalem was captured by Muslim forces in 637, and the driving force behind the Dome of the Rock's construction was an Umayyad caliph, Abd al-Malik ibn Marwan.

The two men given the task of creating the building were primarily engineers, and it appears they took their inspiration from the Christian Church of the Holy Sepulchre in Jerusalem's Old City. Work began in 685.

The Dome of the Rock is considered to be the earliest surviving mosque and, indeed, the oldest Muslim building in the world. It stands centrally on a manmade platform and consists of an octagonal building with a golden dome topped by a symbolic full moon orientated toward Mecca. The 115-foot (35 m) dome was made entirely of gold, but it is now aluminum covered in gold leaf. The stunning polychromatic tiles (now modern copies) were originally given by Suleiman the Magnificent in the 16th century. The Dome of the Rock embodies many of the stylistic elements that would come to typify Islamic religious architecture. **IW**

Temple 1 (Mayan Step Pyramid)

Architect: Unknown

Completed: c. 695 CE

Location: Tikal, Guatemala

Style/Period: Mayan

Tikal Temple 1, also known as the Temple of the Great Jaguar, is one of several pyramids found in the spectacular ancient Mayan city of Tikal, an archaeological site in the Petén Basin region of north Guatemala. Temple 1 and its counterpart, Temple 2, dominate what is known as the Great Plaza at the heart of Tikal. They were built under the instructions of Ha Sawa Chaan-K'awil, who ruled from 682–734. His was a successful reign, which saw Tikal restored to wealth and power after a period known as the hiatus,

and the temples were a visual embodiment of that success.

Temple 1 is a tall, fairly narrow structure of nine levels, measuring some 148 feet (45 m) high on a base of 98 x 111 feet (30 x 34 m). Temple 2, which faces toward the rising sun, was completed during K'awil's reign, but Temple 1, which faces the setting sun, was intended to house his tomb and was therefore not completed until after his death. In 1979 the Tikal National Park, of which Temple 1 is an integral part, was declared a UNESCO World Heritage Site and described as "one of the major sites of Mayan civilization," lying in the heart of the jungle. **EW**

Umayyad Mosque

Architect: Unknown
Completed: 715 CE
Location: Old City, Damascus, Syria
Style/Period: Islamic/Byzantine

When Muslim forces took Damascus in the 630s, they converted an existing Byzantine church in the Old City into a mosque, but one where both Muslims and Christians were free to worship. However, an Umayyad caliph, Al-Walid I, decided that something grander was needed, so he bought the church from its Christian owners, knocked it down and built the Umayyad, or Grand, Mosque that stands in the Syrian capital today. The new mosque was based on the Prophet Mohammed's home in Medina, and much of the skilled work was undertaken by Byzantine craftsmen.

Construction work on the mosque began in 706, and when it was completed its sheer scale made it not only the most impressive mosque in the Muslim world, but also the largest building anywhere in the world. The lavish interior was undoubtedly inspired by the Dome of the Rock in Jerusalem, but the Grand Mosque's layout of courtyards, praying areas and arcades, and features such as its three minarets, also made it a much-copied blueprint for all larger mosques. It ranks high as a place of worship, and only Mecca and Medina surpass it as a pilgrimage destination. **IW**

Palace of Ukhaidir

Architect: Unknown
Completed: 778 CE
Location: Iraq
Style/Period: Abbasid

The palace fortress of Ukhaidir, one of the best-preserved palaces of the early Abbasid period, rises majestically in a valley on the edge of the plain desert 75 miles (120 km) southwest of Baghdad. Built toward the end of the 8th century by Abbasid caliph Isa ibn Musa, it is essentially a fortified complex of halls, courtyards, living quarters and a mosque. The total enclosure measures 574 feet x 554 feet (175 m x 169 m), and, with its

vaulted rooms, some sections are up to 69 feet (21 m) high.

Constructed using stone and plaster, the palace has strong defenses with very thick walls, arrow slits and a portcullis at each gateway in the center of the four sides. Round towers at each corner and semicircular towers along the sides gave additional protection from attack. The skill of the architects can be seen in the use of vaults and arches throughout the complex; for the first time flattened arches were used to support a brick vault. This style was copied in Andalusia, eventually influencing European Gothic architecture. Decorative pointed arches, which are now a characteristic part of Muslim architecture, were first used at Ukhaidir, and so it is not surprising that the palace is considered one of the great monuments of early Islam. **EW**

Gallus/Gallarus Oratory

Architect: Unknown

Completed: c. 800 CE

Location: County Kerry, Ireland

Style/Period: Early Christian

The best preserved early Christian church in Ireland, Gallus, or Gallarus Oratory, on the Dingle Peninsula in County Kerry is thought to have been built in the 7th or 8th centuries, although monastic settlements were built in remote areas of Ireland as early as the 6th century. It looks out over the harbor of Ard na Caithne, but, in the tradition of the time, the building was used for prayer and contemplation and is dimly lit.

In his poem "In Gallarus Oratory," Seamus Heaney evokes the mystical atmosphere of this ancient site:

"You can still feel the community pack This place: it's like going into a turfstack,/ A core of old dark walled up with stone/ A yard thick."

According to legend, anyone who climbs out through the window will be spiritually cleansed, but the feat is almost impossible as the "window" in question is just 7 inches (18 cm) long and 5 inches (12 cm) wide. Built of stone without mortar, it is a good example of the corbel vaulting technique developed by Neolithic tomb makers. The stones are laid at an angle, lower on the outside than on the inside, allowing rainwater to run off, preserving this monument for hundreds of years. **EW**

Ziggurat of the Great Mosque of Samarra

Architect: Unknown

Completed: 852 CE

Location: Samarra, Iraq

Style: Sassanid

Standing over 171 feet (52 m) high, the 9th century Ziggurat of Samarra, or Minaret al-Malwiya is testament to the love of building of the last great Abbasid caliph, Al-Mutawakkil (reigned 847–861). The distinctive spiral minaret is part of the Great Mosque of Samarra, which was for a long time the largest mosque in the world, and was built by Al-Mutawakkil to mark his succession as caliph.

The minaret stands 89 feet (27 m) away from the mosque but is connected to it by a ramp. The base is 108 square feet (33 sq. m) and almost 9 feet (3 m) high. The minaret rises out of the base, and a ramp spirals the minaret counterclockwise five times. Holes on the outer edge of the ramp indicate that it might once have had some form of handrail. At its top, it reaches the doorway to a round platform decorated with eight point-arch recesses. There are traces of a wooden pavilion used to protect the muezzin. Apart from the minaret, much of the majestic mosque lies in ruins, although the walls remain largely intact. In 2005 the top of the minaret was slightly damaged by an insurgent explosion, targeted because American troops had apparently been using it as a lookout tower. **EW**

Cathedral Church of the Holy Cross

Architect: Manuel (architect monk)

Completed: 921 CE (begun 915 CE)

Location: Eastern Anatolia, Turkey

Style: Armenian

Built of pink sandstone under the guidance of the architect monk Manuel, the Cathedral Church of the Holy Cross has been surrounded by controversy for many years. It was built on the instructions of King Gagik I, who founded a settlement on Akdamar Island in Lake Van. Legend has it that the island takes its name from the plaintive cry of a young man dying in the lake as he tried to reach his lover, Tamar, whose father had extinguished her guiding light. It is the only surviving medieval Armenian church with most of its wall paintings intact, although they are in a poor state of repair.

The inside of the cathedral, which until 1915 was part of a monastic settlement, measures just under 49 feet x 38 feet (15 m x 11.5 m). It is all that remains both of King Gagik's buildings on the island and of the monastic settlement, having survived the massacres and looting of the 1915 Armenian Genocide. The cross at the top, however, did not survive. Following traditional Armenian architectural style, the cathedral's most interesting feature is the carvings around its exterior walls. While mostly of biblical scenes, these carvings have been variously interpreted to meet ethnic requirements. Following a restoration program, the cathedral reopened in March 2007 but, controversially, as a secular museum. **EW**

Saminid Mausoleum

Architect: Unknown

Completed: 943 CE

Location: Samani Park, Bukara, Uzbekistan

Style/Period: Early Islamic

This 10th century mausoleum is commonly referred to as the Tomb of Ismail Samani, the founder of the Tajik Samanid Empire. The Samanids were a people of Persian origin, and their dynasty was founded by Saman Khuda. Samanid Islamic influence in Central Asia began to spread from the mid-8th century. Bukara, a key staging post on the Silk Road between Europe, the Middle East and China, became the Samanid capital in 850. The tomb marked a new era in Central Asian architecture, as it incorporated local traditions of working in baked brick, and it was finished to a higher and more complex standard than had been seen before. Construction started in 892.

The tomb incorporated architectural elements plucked from older traditions and structures, chiefly those relating to earlier civilizations such as the Sassanids, but the geometry was largely Islamic in concept. It consists of a slightly tapered cube topped by an inset dome, and each of its four facades is identical. The highly decorative brickwork is especially intricate, giving the tomb the look of a woven basket. Overall the tomb is not a particularly large building — it measures 35 square feet (11 sq. m) — but its style was to have a profound influence on the region's future architecture. **EW**

La Mezquita

Architect: Unknown

Completed: 987 CE

Location: Old Town, Cordoba, Spain

Style/Period: Moorish

The Moors landed in Spain from North Africa during 711 and overthrew the reigning Visigoth Empire the following year. The invaders eventually established Cordoba as the capital of their new caliphate in 756, and the first caliph, Abd Ar Rahman I, celebrated the new caliphate's emergence by constructing La Mezquita, or Grand Mosque (*mezquita* is Spanish for mosque), to rival the great mosques found elsewhere in the Muslim world. Work began in 785, but the mosque was subsequently extended by later rulers and did not reach its current form and extent until the late 10th century.

The builders relied on column-mounted horseshoe arches — inspired by those found on Roman aqueducts, which are unique to Cordoba in the Muslim world — to give imposing height to the mosque's ceiling. The arches themselves are made from red and white brick, and they stand on a total of 865 columns made of granite, jasper, marble and onyx. The complex is unique in one other way: the main *mihrab* (prayer niche) does not face Mecca. Cordoba fell to the forces of catholic Spain in 1236, and La Mezquita was converted to a Christian cathedral from 1523 onward. The city is now a UNESCO World Heritage Site. **IW**

Longhua Pagoda

Architect: Unknown

Completed: Late 10th century

Location: Shanghai, China

Style: Chinese

Part of the Longhua Temple, the oldest and largest temple in Shanghai, the Longhua Pagoda is itself the tallest structure in the complex, standing over 131 feet (40 m) high. First erected in 242 CE, during the Three Kingdoms period, the Longhua Temple has since been destroyed and rebuilt many times, and it is noted for its Buddhist scripture, gold seals and Buddhist statues of the Tang, Ming and Qing dynasties. According to legend, the pagoda and 12 others were built on the orders of Sun Quan to house the cremated remains of the Buddha.

Destroyed by war, the Longhua Pagoda was rebuilt in 977 CE, and its style reflects that of the Song dynasty (960–1279), with seven octagonal stories, each smaller than the one below, based on a brick structure. Each story is decorated with balconies and banisters. At the end of each upturned eave hangs a brass bell, designed to catch the wind. Inside, a wooden staircase leads to the upper floors. The foundations, unearthed during repairs in the 1950s, are formed from 20 layers of brick. Renovations in the 1980s saw the center pillar restored and a new pagoda top, weighing over four tons, (3.6 metric tonnes) installed. **EW**

Kandariya Mahadev Temple

Architect: Unknown

Completed: 1029 (begun 1017)

Location: Madhya Pradesh, India

Style: Indo-Khmerism

Built in the 11th century (during the Chandella dynasty) in Madhya Pradesh and dedicated to Lord Shiva, the Kandariya Mahadev Temple is one of the largest and most magnificent Hindu temples. Its design of a central spire rising 101 feet (31 m) surrounded by 84 smaller pillars is intended to represent Meru, the holy mountain of Shiva. This sandstone structure is as long as it is tall.

The temple takes its name from *Kandariya* ("cave") and *Mahadev* (one of several names for Shiva). Inside are the porch (*ardhamandapa*), a pillared outer hall (*mandapa*), a great hall (*mahamandapa*), the innermost sanctum (*garbagriha*) where the marble *linga* (symbol) of Shiva is kept and the walkway (*pradakshina*) around it. Ornate carvings and statues abound inside and out, depicting gods and goddesses and other, sometimes erotic, images. Some 226 statues have been counted inside the temple and a further 646 outside, most nearly 3 feet (1 m) high. The ceilings are particularly impressive, and the pillars supporting them are intricately carved. In 1986 the Khajuraho Group of Monuments, of which the Kandariya Temple is one, was declared a UNESCO World Heritage Site; the citation described the sculptures as "among the greatest masterpieces of Indian art." **EW**

The White Tower

Architect: Unknown
Completed: 1097 (begun 1078)
Location: Tower of London, London, England
Style/Period: Norman

Following his defeat of King Harold at the Battle of Hastings in 1066, William "the Conqueror," Duke of Normandy, lost little time in firstly having himself crowned King William I of England and, secondly, establishing a firm grip on his kingdom. One symbol of the military might of this new dynasty of Norman kings, as well as a formidable fortress occupying a commanding position on the northern bank of the River Thames on the east side of England's capital, London, was the White Tower, which was began in 1078 and completed in around 1097,

ten years after William's death in 1087.

Constructed by Norman masons under the supervision of Bishop Gundulf of Rochester, this classic Norman hall, or *donjon*, soared to a height of 90 feet (28 m), and its rectangular footprint measured 118 x 106 feet (36 x 33 m). A stronghold first and foremost, the White Tower's massive, ashlar-dressed ragstone-rubble walls — 15 feet (5 m) thick at the base with crenellated battlements running along the top — were pierced by arrow loops, while four corner turrets acted as watchtowers. With a bailey stretching down to the Thames, the keep was further defended by existing walls to the south and east, ditches to the north and west and an earthwork surmounted by a wooden palisade. **CH-M**

Great Ball Court and Temple of the Jaguars

Architect: Unknown

Completed: 900–1100

Location: Chichén Itzá, Yucatán Peninsula, Mexico

Style: Maya Toltec

Little is known about life in Chichén Itzá, the largest ruined Mayan city on the Yucatán Peninsula and home to the Great Ball Court and the Temple of the Jaguars. Yet the carvings on both give some idea. There are additional ball courts in Chichén Itzá and other Mayan cities, but the Great Ball Court, as its name suggests, is the largest at 544 feet (166 m) long and 223 feet (68 m) wide. Walls 39 feet (12 m) high, each with a central ring set near the top, are angled inward at the base. Set within are carved panels depicting the "games" once held here.

Images of heavily protective clothing and, in one case, a player holding the decapitated head of another, indicate that this was no trivial pastime. Whether it was the leader of the losing side who was executed or the winning captain given the dubious "honor"

of sacrifice, we will never know.

There are temples at both ends of the court, one now in ruins. On the southeastern side is the Temple of the Jaguars. Columns on either side of the entrance are carved with serpents, and the upper chamber overlooks the ball court. Nearby is the Tzompantli, a stone platform carved with skulls, where some believe the heads of the sacrificed were displayed. **EW**

Temples and Stupas of Bagan (Pagan)

Architect: Unknown

Completed: 11th–13th centuries

Location: Bagan, Myanmar (Burma)

Style: Buddhist

With more than 2,500 monuments dating primarily from the 11th to 14th centuries and ranging in size, style, and decoration, Bagan (also called Pagan) is a major historical landmark and an unrivaled example of Buddhist architecture. The structures juggle for space in this spectacular

ancient city, once the majestic capital of northern Burma. Set 8 miles (13 km) along the Ayeyarwady River and 2 miles (3 km) inland, the collection is characterized by three distinct structures: stupas, originally mounds built to contain sacred Buddhist relics; temples, which held sacred images; and monasteries, which range from single rooms to complexes of several buildings. There are also other buildings, such as libraries.

Testament to huge royal wealth and power, the structures reflect the Mon traditions of the royal family and its craftsmen. Many of the structures were damaged by an earthquake in 1975. Probably the best-preserved building is the Ananda Temple, built by King Kyanzitthar (1064–1113), whose life-sized statue can be found in the western sanctum. The temple's base is 174 feet (53 m) square, and it rises in terraces to a height of nearly 167 feet (51 m). Inside are four images of Buddha standing 31 feet (9.5 m) high and decorated with gold leaf, each facing a different direction. **EW**

Kalyan Minaret

Architect: Unknown

Completed: 1127

Location: Bukhara, Uzbekistan

Style: Mongul/Islamic

Towering over the ancient city of Bukhara and considered the symbol of the city, the Kalyan Minaret is the only building to survive the ravages of Genghis Khan, who captured and destroyed the rest of the city in 1220. Built in 1127 of baked brick, the minaret soars 151 feet (46 m) into the sky, tapering in diameter from 29 feet (9 m) at the bottom to around 20 feet (6 m) at the top. According to legend, the first minaret built here quickly collapsed, and the foundation of the rebuild — mortar and plaster mixed with camels' milk — was left for two years to ensure it had hardened so the disaster was not repeated. Decorating the minaret are 14 parallel bands, none of which is repeated. Inside, a narrow brick spiral staircase leads to the crown where 16 arch windows face every direction. It is from here that the muezzin called the faithful to prayer.

The minaret had other uses too. Its height and panoramic views made it an ideal watchtower (although this was not enough to stop Genghis Khan), and anecdotal stories tell of it also being used as a point of execution: wrongdoers were thrown from the top to die on the stones below. **EW**

Mont-Saint-Michel

Architect: Various

Completed: 1135 (first phase)

Location: Estuary of the River Couesnon, Normandy, France

Style/Period: Romanesque/Gothic

Mont-Saint-Michel evolved as a heavily defended religious center and an important medieval place of pilgrimage, largely because of its location in Normandy, which was a dangerous place to be during the Hundred Years' War between England and France. The English besieged the complex during 1423 and 1424. The granite island lies a little offshore and is cut off from the mainland for part of the day, when the tide is high. This natural defense was improved by various man-made features, a process that culminated with the construction of towers, ramparts and courtyards during the reign of Charles VI.

The abbey has been remodeled several times through the centuries, partly because of collapses. The first building on Mont-Saint-Michel was built in the Romanesque style by William de Volpiano (962–1031) in the 11th century, but subsequent alterations were made in the Gothic style, most noticeably to the main facade, and rebuilding work continued until around 1521. The abbey also survived the French Revolution, when its religious status was revoked and it became a prison. However the prison closed in 1863, and it became an iconic French historical monument. Its significance was confirmed in 1979, when it was given the status of a UNESCO World Heritage Site. **IW**

The Round Tower

Architect: Unknown

Completed: 1179 (begun 1173)

Location: Windsor Castle, Windsor, Berkshire, England

Style/Period: Norman

Like the White Tower in London, the Round Tower was intended both to represent the imposing expression, in unyielding stone, of Norman might and to act as a defensive stronghold. William the Conqueror ordered its construction above the River Thames to the west of London in 1075.

Conforming to the favored Norman motte-and-bailey style of castle construction, the first keep (or donjon) rose above a motte (a mound, in this case, of natural chalk) and was enclosed by one bailey to the east and another to the west. All of these elements are identifiable today, although significant modifications were made over the centuries. Between 1173 and 1179, for instance, when Henry II was England's king, the royal apartments and outer walls of the Upper Ward (and part of the Lower Ward's too) were remodeled. It was also at this time that the original keep (which was probably of wood rather than stone) was replaced with a new stone shell keep, the Round Tower being raised inside the walls of the first keep to a height of around 34 feet (11 m). Wooden buildings were constructed within this shell keep, which were used to conduct the day-to-day business of Windsor Castle. **CH-M**

Borgund Stave Church

Architect: Unknown

Completed: c. 1180

Location: Borgund, Norway

Style: Medieval

Stave churches are Norway's most important contribution to world architecture. Surviving stave churches — named after the huge wooden posts (staffs) placed in the corners and other important connecting points of the building — are almost exclusive to Norway, although there is one in Sweden and another in Poland. Of the 28 still standing in Norway, Borgund is the best example.

Built probably around 1180, based on dating of the timber, and dedicated to St. Andrew, the Borgund Stave Church is extremely well preserved, its timber protected from the damp ground by stone foundations. There is some evidence that it was built on the site of an earlier construction, possibly another church. Perhaps the most surprising of its features are the carved dragons' heads that adorn the roof. Equally impressive are the elaborately carved west door and the belfry. Inside, men and boys would stand on the south of the aisle and women and girls on the north. Only the elderly or disabled were afforded seats. The pulpit dates from the late 16th century and the altarpiece from the early 17th century. A faithful replica of the church was erected in Rapid City, South Dakota, in 1969, an area that had originally been settled by Scandinavian immigrants to the United States. **EW**

Durham Cathedral

Architect: Unknown

Completed: 1189

Location: Durham, Northumberland, England

Style/Period: Romanesque

Durham Cathedral — also called the Cathedral Church of Christ, St. Mary the Virgin and St. Cuthbert of Durham — stands on imposing high ground overlooking a loop in the River Wear. It was, however, highly vulnerable to attack from Scotland, across the nearby border, so its founder, William de Saint Carileph, the Bishop of Durham, was given leave to build a castle as well, a unique decision in English history. Construction work on the cathedral began in 1093 on the site of an Anglo-Saxon church that had been built over the grave of St. Cuthbert. The main vault was completed in 1133, but the building program continued for another 60 years or so.

The cathedral's exterior is purely Gothic in style, especially the central tower, but the interior is rather different and follows the Romanesque style, with the great pillars carved with various geometric patterns, including chevrons and diamonds. However the most significant architectural feature is the nave's rib-vaulted roof with concealed flying buttresses. Durham is believed to be the earliest example of such features, and they became the norm for cathedrals across medieval Europe. Durham remains the most complete example of a Norman cathedral in the whole of England. **IW**

Angkor Wat

Architect: Unknown

Completed: First half of the 12th century

Location: Siem Reap City, Siem Reap, Cambodia

Style/Period: Indo-Khmerism

Angkor Wat temple complex stands at the heart of a vast city and was commissioned in the 12th century by Suryavarman II, king of the Khmer Empire from 1113–c. 1150, who ordered a royal mausoleum and a temple dedicated to the Hindu deity Vishnu be built in the state's capital. The complex mixes two key elements from the religious architecture

of the time — a temple mountain and towers of varying heights — which are surrounded by various other temples built with galleries. The temple mountain symbolizes the home of the Hindu gods, Mount Meru, while the five towers are arranged as a quincunx, a geometric pattern like the five spots on a dice or domino, to represent the five peaks of the holy mountain.

The whole rectilinear site is surrounded by a wall some 2 miles (4 km) long and a wide moat, which respectively represent the mountains and oceans that surround Meru. The whole of Angkor Wat was highly decorated with carvings and bas-reliefs, and it marked a defining moment in Khmer architecture. It was much copied across the empire but never bettered and certainly never matched in sheer scale. The complex has effortlessly progressed from its origins as a Hindu temple to a place of Buddhist worship in the 14th and 15th centuries to one of the world's great attractions. **IW**

Church of St. George

Architect: Unknown

Completed: 1200

Location: Lalibela, North Wollo, Ethiopia

Style/Period: Afro-Christian

The town of Lalibela in northern Ethiopia is home to 11 unique monolithic churches hewn out of solid volcanic rock with roofs at ground level, of which St. George is the finest example. After Muslims captured the city in 1187, the project was initiated by King Gebre Mesqel Lalibela, who wanted to create a version of Jerusalem in this dusty backwater in the middle of nowhere. He largely succeeded — the churches have been in use for more than 800 years, and they remain a center for pilgrimage.

Unlike the other 10 churches, St. George, the last to be completed, is not connected to the rest by either passages or bridges. It takes the form of a Greek cross on a stepped plinth. The roof is carved with concentric Greek crosses, while the walls are largely unadorned except for simple carved bands. The walls are punctured by a few windows at higher levels that end in pointed arches decorated with flowers. The overall design, especially the cruciform shape, suggests that, although the town appears isolated, it must have had strong links with the wider Christian world. **IW**

Citadel of Aleppo

Architect: Unknown

Completed: 1209

Location: Aleppo, Syria

Style/Period: Medieval Islamic

Subject of a major restoration program by the Aga Khan Trust for Culture, the majestic Citadel of Aleppo is one of the oldest and largest castles in the world. Its elliptical (oval) base is 492 yards (450 m) long and 388 yards (355 m) wide. Rising to height of 164 feet (50 m), the top measures 935 x 542 feet (285 x 160 m).

Although originally built in the 10th century by Sayf al-Dawla, this imposing structure owes much of its "modern" form to Sultan al-Zahir al-Ghazi, Saladin's son, who ruled Aleppo between 1193 and 1215. His efforts transformed the fortress into a thriving city, complete with palatial homes, mosques, defenses and basic utilities. It was at this time that the Great Mosque, complete with 69-foot (21 m) minaret, was built, as was the ingenious entrance block. This entrance was almost impenetrable to intruders, whose only way in involved several changes of direction while being subjected to onslaughts of boiling liquid from above. The defenses, however, were not sufficient to prevent attack by the Mongols in 1400–1401, but restoration work by Sayf al-Din Jakam, Mamluk governor of Aleppo in 1415, saw the building of two new advance towers and the Mamluk palace. In 1986 the Ancient City of Aleppo was declared a UNESCO World Heritage Site. **EW**

Temple of Htilominlo

Architect: Unknown

Completed: 1211

Location: Myanmar (Burma)

Style/Period: Buddhist

Rising over 150 feet (46 m), the Htilominlo is a fine example of late Bagan temples. Built in the early 13th century, Htilominlo commemorated the spot where King Nantaungmya was chosen from among five brothers to become successor to the throne. In style, it is similar to the Sulamani Temple, built by his father some 20 years earlier.

The three-story temple is built of red brick, with some stones, on a low platform. The shrine's main entrance hall is extended on the eastern side. Some of the original stucco carvings can still be seen, along with small green and yellow glazed sandstone plaques. Inside, on the ground floor, a large image of Buddha set at the back of a small shrine is one of the few intact, albeit restored, brick-and-stucco images, many having long since been destroyed by those seeking relics. There are four Buddhas in total, each facing a different direction. The remains of murals can also still be seen, as can several horoscopes, originally painted to protect the building from harm. The temple was damaged by an earthquake in 1975 but has since been restored to its former glory. **EW**

Cathedral of Notre Dame, Chartres

Architect: Unknown

Completed: 1220

Location: Chartres, Eure-et-Loir, France

Style/Period: Gothic

The Cathedral of Notre Dame in Chartres southwest of Paris, is considered one of the finest, most awe-inspiring examples of High Gothic architecture, and it set standards that were copied in many other ecclesiastical buildings constructed in the 13th century. Work began in 1145, using the foundations of the previous Romanesque church that had burned down in 1134, and the greater part of the main building was erected remarkably speedily between 1194 and 1220. The cathedral, also known as Chartres Cathedral, is built in limestone and has an unusual, now vivid green, copper roof. Its other distinguishing features are the two towers dating from the 1140s, one rising to 345 feet (105 m), and the other reaching 370 feet (182 m), which were completed in 1513.

The cathedral is cruciform and incorporates a large nave with particularly high vaulting that required the construction of numerous innovative high buttresses. The cathedral height also meant that the builders had to pioneer new methods of working at such elevations. It set new precedents in various other decorative art forms, not least in sculpture, and the volume of stained glass, used on an epic scale to complete a total of 150 individual windows. **IW**

Notre Dame de Paris

Architect: Maurice de Sully

Completed: 1235

Location: Place du Parvis de Notre Dame, Paris, France

Style/Period: Gothic

Notre Dame (Our Lady) cathedral sits on an island in the middle of the River Seine in Paris on a site occupied first by a Roman temple, then by the city's first Christian church and then the first church to be known as Notre Dame, which was built during the reign of Frankish King Childebert I. Construction work on the current Notre Dame cathedral was initiated by Sully, the bishop of Paris, in 1163, with Pope Alexander III laying the foundation stone.

Work continued for the next 100 years or so, and then Notre Dame remained largely untouched until the spire was erected in the 19th century during a bout of restoration directed by Eugène Viollet-le-Duc.

Notre Dame is the first archetypical cathedral of the Early Gothic period and, as such, initiates the movement away from the Romanesque style. It was particularly innovative in two areas. First, its more naturalistic decorations, as can be seen in the Gallery of Kings on the western facade above the three great entrances. And second, it employed new building techniques: the external flying buttresses, which take the load exerted by the cathedral's high vault, make it possible for the internal columns to be much more slender than traditional supports. **IW**

Sainte-Chapelle

Architect: Unknown

Completed: 1248

Location: Boulevard du Palais, Paris, France

Style/Period: Gothic

This outstanding ecclesiastical building was created both to house holy relics acquired from Constantinople (Istanbul) by King Louis IX and to act as a royal chapel. It is sited next to today's Palace of Justice, which was, until the second half off the 14th century, a royal palace. The chapel's main entrance was originally on the grander, higher first floor, where it connected directly to the palace's apartments, and it was here that the various relics were displayed.

The exterior of the chapel is simple and

mostly unadorned — the buttresses are wholly undecorated, for example, and are purely there to carry the weight of the roof and interior vaulting. The interior is a different matter. It is a symphony of colored decoration, sculpture and beautiful stained-glass windows that depict scenes from the Old and New Testaments. The chapel is an outstanding example of the Rayonnant style of Gothic architecture, in which the traditional bulky masonry is reduced to a skeletal system to support large areas of stained glass. The term is derived from the radiating stone spokes found in rose windows. **IW**

Krak de Chevaliers

Architect: Unknown

Completed: 1250

Location: Homs Gap, Homs, Syria

Style/Period: Medieval

Despite being ravaged by earthquakes on several occasions, the immensely strong Krak de Chevaliers (Knights' Fortress) is the best-preserved Crusader castle anywhere — it even houses rare Crusader frescoes — and was the largest ever built in the Holy Land. It stands atop a high hill that guards what was the only viable route from Antioch to Beirut and the Mediterranean Sea, and it is close to the border with Syria, the center of Muslim resistance during the Crusades. An existing castle on the site was given to the the Hospitallers, a religious order of knights, in 1142, who set about strengthening its defenses as they intended to make the fortress their headquarters.

Their work marked a revolution in castle design. They constructed a second massive wall around the castle, with masonry some 10 feet (3 m) thick, studded with seven even thicker towers. The outer wall was on a lower level so that, if the castle fell, the attackers could still be fired upon by the surviving garrison from the second, higher interior wall. The Krak de Chevaliers, the first so-called concentric castle, was such a revolutionary design that it was much copied in Europe, not least by England's King Edward I, who had visited it in person. **IW**

Salisbury Cathedral

Architect: Unknown

Completed: c. 1270

Location: Salisbury, Wiltshire, England

Style/Period: English Gothic

Salisbury, or rather the Cathedral of St. Mary, was the spearhead of a plan to build a new city, originally called New Sarum, to replace a much earlier nearby settlement, Old Sarum. This Early English Gothic cathedral is remarkable in many ways, not least for the speed of its construction. It was largely, and uniquely among English medieval cathedrals, completed within a century, with the greater part of the work taking place over just 38 years, starting in 1220. It is therefore unique architecturally, as it is constructed in just one style. The central tower and spire, the tallest in England at 404 feet (123 m), were added 50 years later, made possible by the development of flying buttresses that could carry their 6,397-ton (5,803 metric tonnes) weight.

The cathedral, which is a mixture of Portland stone and marble, is in the shape of a double cross. Its main entrance is at the west end, while inside a high rib-vaulted ceiling is supported on Gothic arches. Its cloisters are also the largest in England. The fabric of the building has suffered, largely because the great weight of the tower and spire have caused some bowing of the walls, but it still stands — even though it rests on foundations no more than 4 feet (1.2 m) deep and dug into marshy ground. **IW**

Cathedral of St. Étienne

Architect: Unknown
Completed: 1275 (begun 1195)
Location: Place Étienne-Doulet, Bourges, France
Style/Period: Early and High Gothic

The Cathedral of St. Étienne — today a UNESCO World Heritage Site — is one of the most highly prized buildings in Bourges. Not only is this sacred edifice an important example of the Gothic style of architecture, but the stained-glass windows that softly illuminate the interior are notable for their great age and artistry. This cathedral in central France also features five portals set into the western facade (when three were the norm), two horseshoe-shaped aisles, a triforium alongside the outer aisle, an elevated inner aisle, giving it a height of 70 feet (21 m) to the outer aisle's 30 feet (9 m). The structure's five-level elevation also sets it apart, as does its lack of a transept. The nave measures 49 feet (15 m) in width, 400 feet (122 m) in length and 121 feet (37 m) in height.

Building work started in 1195 and was completed in 1275, a comparatively short period in cathedral building, hence the harmonious merging of elements of the Early Gothic (such as sexpartite rib vaults) and High Gothic (flying buttresses, for example) styles. Dedicated to St. Étienne (St. Stephen), it is an imposing expression of the profound Christian piety that permeated medieval French society. **CH-M**

Cloth Hall, Ypres

Architect: Unknown
Completed: 1304 (begun 1202)
Location: Ypres, West Flanders, Belgium
Style/Period: Flemish Gothic

Although, strictly speaking, the Cloth Hall, or *Lakenhalle*, admired by modern visitors to Ypres is a reconstruction — the first having been flattened during World War I — it is such a faithful replica of the original that this fact merely makes an interesting footnote to the building's history.

Seven hundred years before Ypres became a battleground, this Flemish town in

southwestern Belgium had been a prosperous center of the European wool and cloth trade. The Cloth Hall, built in the heart of the market square between 1202 and 1304, was therefore both an important place of business and an expensive manifestation of the town's significance and wealth. (Today it houses the In Flanders Fields Museum, which commemorates Ypres's more tragic claim to fame.)

The surface decoration is detailed, and the pointed arches that pierce the hall's frontage are numerous, but much of the building's impact lies in the simplicity of its Gothic design. Most notable are its unbroken horizontal facade, which measures 440 feet (134 m) long, its steep roof that rises above that and the central belfry tower, whose spire soars above four corner turrets to a height of 230 feet (70 m). **CH-M**

Tomb of Rukn-i-Alam

Architect: Unknown

Completed: 1324 (begun 1320)

Location: Multan, Punjab, Pakistan

Style/Period: Indo-Mogul (Persian influences)

The imposing tomb of Shah Rukn-i-Alam in Multan, Pakistan, is a stunning example of Mogul architecture. Built between 1320 and 1324 by the Tughluq ruler of Delhi, Ghiyas-ud-Din Tughluq, supposedly for his own remains, it was instead donated by his son to the family of the saint Rukn-i-Alam. Originally buried in his grandfather's tomb, the body of Rukn-i-Alam was transferred here and today is surrounded by 72 of his descendents.

Built in red brick with a visible timber frame and intricately decorated with glazed tiles, the octagon-shaped tomb rises over three stories to 115 feet (35 m). The walls of the first story, which give an interior diameter of 49 feet (15 m), are 13 feet (4 m) thick. Towers taper to the top at each point of the octagon. The second story is a smaller 26-foot (8 m) octagon, and crowning the whole is a magnificent dome, supposedly the second largest in the world, at a diameter of 49 feet (15 m). The exterior is decorated with carved brick and blue and white mosaic tiles. Inside, the wooden *mehrab* (indicating the direction to face for prayer) is considered one of the earliest examples of its kind. The tomb was renovated during the 1970s and remains an important pilgrimage site for thousands every year. **EW**

Caernarfon Castle

Architect: Master James of St. George

Completed: c. 1324

Location: Caernarfon, Gwynedd, Wales

Style/Period: Medieval

England's King Edward I spent years trying to subdue and pacify the Welsh. He began his campaign in 1277, but as his opponents proved elusive, he embarked on a huge castle-building project to isolate his enemies and dominate the locals physically and psychologically. Edward proved himself to be a great innovator and used the most modern castle-building techniques. Caernarfon Castle, which was started in 1283, was a simple design, but it was immensely strong and took approximately 50 years to build.

It is, however, somewhat different from the other five great castles built by Edward I and was probably the costliest. It obviously functioned as a fortress, but it was also designed as a propaganda weapon. Edward I knew that there was a legend that the Byzantine emperor Constantine the Great had been born in Caernarfon, and the king had visited the latter's capital, Constantinople (now Istanbul), while on a Crusade to the Holy Land. Edward I thus ordered that the castle's walls, originally rendered and whitewashed, be built in the banded masonry style he had seen in the Byzantine capital. Caernarfon's hexagonal towers were also copied and not repeated elsewhere by the king. **IW**

La Torre di Pisa

Architect: Unknown

Completed: 1350

Location: Piazza del Duomo, Pisa, Italy

Style/Period: Romanesque

Better known as the Leaning Tower of Pisa, this cylindrical campanile, or bell tower, is part of a trio of ecclesiastical structures built as a group, the others being the cathedral itself and a circular baptistery. Construction work on the tower, the last of the trio to be built, began in 1173 probably, but not definitively, guided by Pisano. Only three stages had been completed before the tower began to list as a result of shallow foundations and unstable subsoil. Work resumed again in 1275, when the first attempt to correct the subsidence was made. Seven stages had been completed by 1301, and the final stage — the bell tower housing itself — was finished in the middle of the century.

The tower, which was built in stone, marble and limestone, is an outstanding example of the Romanesque style of architecture. And its various stages are covered in many fine marbles and carvings, especially over the main doorway, where various grotesque animals can be seen. Despite its lean (currently stabilized), the tower is also something of an innovative feat of engineering, in that the outer rings of columns support the core. **IW**

Siena Cathedral

Architect: Unknown

Completed: 1380 (begun early 13th century)

Location: Piazza del Duomo, Siena, Italy

Style/Period: Italian Gothic

The black and white striped *campanile* (bell tower) of Siena's *duomo* (cathedral) has dominated the skyline of this Tuscan city since medieval times. The nave is also notable, both for its length and for the hexagonal crossing beneath the central dome. Once inside, the cathedral reveals itself to be a treasure house of art, be it in the form of the marble mosaic flooring, the pulpit, the statuary, the frescoes or the font, while the black and white internal walls and columns echo the campanile, displaying the symbolic colors of Siena.

Work on the Cathedral of Santa Maria Della Assunta commenced during the first half of the 13th century and finished in 1380. Visitors approaching the trio of portals are confronted by an elaborately decorated facade in the Tuscan Gothic style. The lower half of the facade was designed by the master mason Giovanni Pisano around 1284, and the upper half was added in 1376, under the supervision of Giovanni de Cecco. There had been plans to enlarge the cathedral even more significantly in 1339, but the decimation of Siena's population (and, consequently, of the funds and labor required for the construction) by the Black Death, which hit the city in 1348, stymied this plan. **CH-M**

Bodiam Castle

Architect: Unknown
Completed: 1385
Location: Bodiam, East Sussex, England
Style/Period: Medieval

The Hundred Years' War between France and England was largely fought in France, but the French did make occasional raids along England's southern coast. A royal license was given to Sir Edward Dallyngrigge to crenellate (fortify) his manor house to protect the local area, but he chose instead to build a wholly new castle not far away.

Bodiam ticks all of the right boxes for a late medieval castle, or at least it seems to. It has a square ground plan with round towers at each of the four corners, square towers in the middle of each wall and a moat. However, doubt exists whether it was built for defense or as the home of a nouveau riche knight who had done well out of the war with France and wanted to show off his new status. Castles were becoming obsolete in the late 14th century, largely because the well-to-do wanted more comfortable living quarters and advances in military technology, chiefly the development of the cannon, were making castles far too vulnerable to attack. It is telling that Bodiam's walls are a mere 2 feet (60 cm) thick. **IW**

Palazzo Davanzati

Architect: Unknown
Completed: Late 14th century
Location: Via di Porta Rossa, Florence, Italy
Style/Period: Italian Renaissance

Although Italian *palazzi*, like the Palazzo Davanzati (Davanzati Palace), had a practical purpose — to provide accommodation for their owner, his family and their servants — the title of "palace" gives a clear indication of their owners' wealth and pretensions to grandeur.

The Palazzo Davanzati was built for the Davizzi family, although the *palazzo* is now named after the Davanzatis, to whom ownership later passed and whose coats of arms still decorate the building's exterior. In the late 14th century Florence was an independent republic, awash with wealth (the Davizzis were prosperous wool merchants) and flowering as a center of Italian Renaissance thought and culture. Its Renaissance pedigree is evident in the Palazzo Davanzati, which demonstrates an unmistakable adherence to the principles of the architecture of ancient Rome later popularized by the influential Italian architect Leon Battista Alberti. Thus the five-story sandstone facade incorporates street- and roof-level *loggias* (an open gallery that overlooks an open court), while its windows display Roman arches. More arches are featured in the courtyard to the rear, well away from the dust and noise of the street. The Palazzo Davanzati was extensively restored during the 20th century, and it is now a museum displaying the traditional Florentine home. **CH-M**

Palace of the Alhambra

Architect: Unknown
Completed: 1390
Location: Granada, Spain
Style/Period: Moorish

The Alhambra (*Al Hambra* is Arabic for "the red") began life as a multifunctional Moorish complex, one that acted as a fortress, mosque and palace for the local Muslim rulers. However the design — the building is made of sun-dried brick (originally whitewashed) — owes much to traditional Christian strongholds of the period. Work began in 1238 during the Nasrid dynasty.

Granada was reconquered by the Christian King Charles V in 1492, and, rather than have this powerful symbol of Moorish rule pulled down, he set about giving some of the buildings new roles. Parts of the complex were demolished though, so that architect Pedro Machuca (1490–1550) could build a new Renaissance-style palace. The Moorish style can still be seen among the preexisting buildings and the beautiful water gardens.

The Alhambra has been rather fortunate to survive at all, as in the past some parts were deliberately vandalized, other elements were wantonly blown up, and it underwent a somewhat unsympathetic restoration. Nevertheless, it remains the finest example of Moorish art in its final flourish in Europe, at a time when Granada's isolation from the rest of the Arab world forced its artists and architects to develop their own particular style, free from Byzantine influences. **IW**

Trulli

Architect: Unknown
Completed: 14th–15th centuries
Location: Alberobello, Puglia, Italy
Style/Period: Vernacular

The *trulli* – whitewashed round houses with conical roofs – of Alberobello in southern Italy are admired by tourists for their rustic charm. In a country not short of outstanding architecture, they are remarkable buildings. Constructed in the 14th and 15th centuries using ancient drystone techniques from roughly worked limestone quarried from neighboring fields, they were originally designed to be as easy to dismantle as they were to erect. This meant that recalcitrant householders could be dispossessed easily by the local count, who could also avoid paying a tax on new settlements. At the merest hint of a tax inspector, the *trulli* could be transformed into tax-free rubble.

Most of the *trulli* were built without mortar on naturally occurring rock bases to form one-room circular buildings. The stones were simply laid on top of one another to form two parallel walls that provided excellent insulation against the unforgiving Mediterranean heat and the winter cold. The conical roofs were formed from layers of smaller slabs, each layer projecting slightly inward. Some were decorated with symbols and talismans to protect the inhabitants. Inside, wooden floors and door frames provide additional stability. In 1996 UNESCO designated the town a World Heritage Site, with the citation, "The *trulli* of Alberobello represent the remarkable survival of what is essentially a prehistoric building technique, that of drystone walling, for domestic use in a western European country." **JM**

Westminster Abbey

Architect: Unknown

Completed: c. 1400 (begun 1040s)

Location: London, England

Style/Period: English Gothic

As well as playing a uniquely symbolic role in English, and later British, history as the sacred place where its monarchs are traditionally crowned and where many are also entombed, Westminster Abbey is an outstanding example of English Gothic architecture in the center of London, England's capital city.

Its history can be traced back to the 1040s, when King Edward the Confessor ordered the erection of an abbey dedicated to St. Peter the Apostle on the site of a Benedictine monastery. During the mid-13th century, work on rebuilding the abbey began at the behest of King Henry III, this time in the French-influenced Gothic style. And by the end of the reign of King Richard II (1377–1400), masons working under the direction of Henry Yevele

had fulfilled the task.

This structure has continued to be the essence of Westminster Abbey, although significant modifications were subsequently made, such as the addition of King Henry VII's Lady Chapel and the completion of the western towers atop the western front. The abbey's Gothic pedigree and character are instantly recognizable in its flying buttresses, pointed-arch portals and windows, and in its high, vaulted nave (which, in 1375, was constructed in accordance with the Perpendicular style). **CH-M**

Changdokkung Palace

Architect: Unknown

Completed: 1405

Location: Korea

Style/Period: Medieval Korean

Built in 1405 by King Taejong, the original palace, apart from the wooden main entrance – the Tonhwamun Gate – was

destroyed during the Japanese invasion of 1592 and rebuilt in 1611 during the reign of the Chosun King Kwanghoegun. Changdokkung Palace is the finest example among the five surviving Chosun palaces and was used as the official royal residence by 13 successive kings, until 1910.

Laid out over 77 acres (31 ha), it is also the largest of the palaces, and its buildings and gardens are well preserved. Entrance to the palace is over the Kumchungyo Bridge, the oldest stone bridge in Seoul, which is carved with mythical beasts to ward off evil. The main throne hall (*injongjon*) burned down in 1803, and the building there today, with its double roof and red and blue ceiling decorations, reflects the style of the later Chosun dynasty. It is now a museum, housing the magnificent royal ceremonial costumes, the royal coach, sedan chairs and early cars used by the royal family. An equally important part of the palace complex is the secret garden (*piwon*), landscaped in 1623 and complete with sloping paths, ancient pavilions and an unusual square lotus pond. **EW**

The Forbidden City

Architect: Unknown

Completed: 1420 (begun 1406)

Location: Beijing, China

Style/Period: Chinese Ming Dynasty

A compound rather than a single building or, indeed, a city, the Forbidden City (so called because access to it was forbidden to ordinary Chinese people) was built between 1406 and 1420 to act as the Ming emperors' imperial palace (*Gu Gong*) after it was decided to establish the capital in Beijing. Enclosed by a wall 30 feet (9 m) high and a moat 150 feet (46 m) wide, the Forbidden City was constructed on a 250-acre (around 1 million sq. m) site with a footprint measuring 3,152 x 2,470 feet (961 x 753 m). Those permitted to enter did so through the double-roofed Meridian Gate (*Wumen*), whereupon they would arrive at the Golden River, spanned by five marble bridges. Today visitors who venture farther into the complex — which is divided into the outer (south) and inner (north) courts — can view nearly 1,000 buildings that are typically long and low slung and have curved roofs. Three impressive ceremonial halls standing on a marble platform in the outer court — the Hall of Supreme Harmony (*Taihedian*), the Hall of Middle Harmony (*Zhongedian*) and the Hall of Protective Harmony (*Baohedian*) — date from the 17th century, when much reconstruction work took place. The Forbidden City is now a museum and a UNESCO World Heritage Site. **CH-M**

Ca' d'Oro Palazzo

Architects: Giovanni Bon and Bartolomeo Bon

Completed: c. 1436

Location: Grand Canal, Venice, Italy

Style/Period: Gothic/Venetian

This exercise in Venetian Gothic was created as a waterside mansion for the city-state's public prosecutor, Marino Contarini. The Palazzo Santa Sofia was more commonly known as *Ca' d'Oro*, or "Golden House," because of the once spectacular, but now entirely faded, gilt and polychromatic decorations that graced its elegant facade. The building was created by a father-and-son team of architects, Giovanni and Bartolomeo Bon, who were also responsible for the Doge's Palace in nearby St. Mark's Square. Work on the palace began in 1428.

The palace, which was built in stone and marble, has a distinctively "split" yet harmonious facade — to the right is a largely solid wall with nine recessed windows, while to the left is a more open space. On the left a recessed colonnaded portico leads from the boat moorings directly into the palace's main entrance hall and sits beneath two rows of balconies and arches topped by an intricately carved parapet. The overall style reflects Venice's extensive trading links with Christian Orthodox Constantinople (now Istanbul), Moorish Spain and the Islamic Far East. The arched balconies on the left-hand side of the palace are undoubtedly inspired by Moorish architecture. **IW**

Florence Cathedral

Architects: Filippo Brunelleschi, Arnolfo di Cambio, Giotto di Bodone, Francesco Talenti

Completed: 1436 (begun 1296)

Location: Florence, Italy

Style/Period: Italian Gothic/Italian Renaissance

Three Italian architects are mainly credited with the creation of Florence's cathedral church, Santa Maria del Fiore, but of the three, it is Filippo Brunelleschi's name that has become associated with the *duomo* (cathedral). Arnolfo di Cambio's Gothic design was initially followed when work began in 1296. Construction was largely prompted by wealthy Florence's desire to outshine the new cathedrals that had recently boosted the prestige of rival Tuscan cities. Impetus flagged during the first half of the 14th century, with only Giotto's free-standing campanile (bell tower) completed. However, the appointment of Francesco Talenti (and others) prompted a revival, and enlargement, of the building program, and the nave was completed by 1380. Only the dome remained to be constructed.

Brunelleschi won a competition to solve the problem of bridging a 138-foot (42 m) wide crossing and construct the basilica's crowning glory. He began work in 1420. His Classically inspired octagonal cupola is inventively constructed in herringbone brickwork without a supporting framework — it's on a drum with a double shell and ribbing and tapers inward and upward toward the apex. This cupola has become an iconic structure that symbolizes the Italian Renaissance, and it remains the largest masonry dome in the world. It was finished in 1436, with a lantern being added in 1461 and in 1466, a ball and cross. **CH-M**

Herstmonceaux Castle

Architect: Unknown

Completed: 1441

Location: Herstmonceaux, East Sussex, England

Style/Period: Medieval

Although it has the outward appearance of a strongly built medieval castle, Herstmonceaux is no such thing — it was built for comfort as a large country house, not a defendable place. It has the square shape and octagonal and semioctagonal towers of a traditional castle, but in reality the walls would have been too thin to stand up to gunfire, and it is also overlooked to three sides. The castle was commissioned by the Treasurer of Henry VI's household, Sir Roger Fiennes, a veteran of the Hundred Years' War. His new position gave him considerable status, and he needed a country house to reflect his importance and wealth.

Built in the mid-15th century, Herstmonceaux was revolutionary as it was one of the first brick buildings erected anywhere in England, and today it is the oldest brick building in the country. As there was no local expertise in such materials, Fiennes brought in Flemish craftsmen to undertake the construction work in Flanders brick. The castle's architecture is significant, marking a transition from traditional medieval stone buildings to the brick that typifies the Renaissance architecture of the Tudor age. **IW**

Doge's Palace

Architects: Various

Completed: c. 1442

Location: St. Mark's Square, Venice, Italy

Style/Period: Italian Gothic

The doges were the elected ruler of the medieval Venetian city state, which had grown rich on maritime trade; evidence of its wealth and prestige can be evinced from the palace at the heart of the city. It was, in fact, a multifunctional building, as it not only contained the ruler's living quarters but also meeting chambers, courts, offices, and prison cells. The complex was built into two stages, although it underwent various modifications after they had been completed. The first

stage, which began in around 1340 saw the completion of the south-facing façade that overlooks the Venetian Lagoon, while the second saw the completion of the more ornate façade overlooking St. Mark's Square.

The palace is largely Gothic in style, but it has various unique features that largely reflect the site's geographical and geological realities and gave rise to the term Venetian Gothic. The towering, heavy style associated with soaring Gothic architecture was simply not possible on land prone to subsidence, so the Venetians built squatter buildings to reduce the weight, but incorporated somewhat exaggerated Gothic features. The Doge's Palace is characterized by ornate arcading faced with rose and white marble, another weight-reducing feature. **IW**

Warwick Castle

Architect: Unknown
Completed: 1450
Location: Warwick, Warwickshire, England
Style/Period: Medieval

There has been some form of defensive structure on this site on the banks of the River Avon since the early 10th century, when it was protected by an Anglo-Saxon earth rampart, but the castle seen today began to evolve in 1068, when King William I the Conqueror built a traditional dry-moated motte (mound) and bailey (courtyard) out of earth and wood. This was followed in 1260 by a more substantial motte-and-bailey castle, which was built on the same site from stone.

Over the following centuries the castle gradually grew larger and larger as new walls and towers were constructed to the most modern design concepts of the day. Caesar's Tower was built in 1350 and the similar Guy's Tower was finished some 45 years later. The last major defensive feature was the massive gate-house and barbican, which were completed in 1450. Thereafter the castle became less of a stronghold and more of a family home. New additions tended to be purely domestic — the state rooms were extended in 1540, Capability Brown landscaped the garden in 1750 and a state dining room was completed in 1763. Warwick therefore encapsulates the rise and demise of the castle. **IW**

Wat Chedi Luang

Architect: Unknown

Completed: Mid-15th century (begun late 14th century)

Location: Chiang Mai, Thailand

Style/Period: Buddhist

Once home to the famous Emerald Buddha, the temple of Wat Chedi Luang remains an important Thai attraction without it. Building started at the end of the 14th century, and the temple was intended to hold the remains of the father of King Saen Muang Ma. The king never lived to see the results, and it was left to his widow and, later, King Tilokaraj to complete the work. By this time the *chedi* (or stupa) stood some 295 feet (90 m) high and 177 feet (54 m) wide at its base, dominating the surrounding landscape. Modeled on Mount Meru, which sits in the center of Chiang Mai, it remains an excellent example of 14th-century Lanna-style architecture. In a shrine near the entrance to the *chedi* is a brass and mortar Buddha image that dates to the late 14th century. A *viharn* (hall) also houses a reclining Buddda.

In 1468 Wat Chedi Luang housed the revered Emerald Buddha statue (a misnomer as the figurine is actually made of jade). The statue remained in the temple for 80 years, but it was moved after the *chedi* was partially destroyed by an earthquake in 1545. The end of the 20th century saw the *chedi* undergo further restoration, although some view the work more in keeping with Central Thai than with Lanna style. **EW**

Darb-I Imam

Architect: Unknown

Completed: 1453

Location: Iran

Style/Period: Persian

Built on the site of an ancient cemetery in Isfahan, the one-time capital of Persia, the venerable Darb-I Imam (literally "the shrine of the Imams") reflects several architectural and aesthetic styles within its complex of courtyards, shrines and cemetery. The original sections, of which a decorated entrance porch, a square hall and a mausoleum survive, were built in the mid-15th century by Jalal al-Din Safarshah. The rest of the monument is of Safavid origin (1502–1722). Unusually, the shrine has two enameled tile domes, both Safavid and built by Hasaini Shahristani — the larger dome in 1601–02 and the smaller in 1670–71 — reflecting the importance of the burial ground. The shrine is particularly important because it holds the tombs of two Imamzadeh, Ibrahim Tabataba'i and Zayn al-'Abidayn 'Ali, who are descendents of Ali, son-in-law of the prophet Muhammad.

Particularly notable is the exquisite decorative mosaic work within the shrine, with glazed and unglazed tiles making intricate abstract, geometric and floral patterns. In recent years the *girih* tiles (sets of five tiles commonly used in Islamic architecture) of the shrine have been closely studied because they are laid in a pattern that can extend forever without repeating. **EW**

Malbork Castle

Architect: Unknown

Completed: 1457

Location: Malbork, Zulawy, Poland

Style/Period: Gothic

This large brick castle was founded by the Order of the Teutonic Knights, a German religious order that had plans to establish a Christian state in what was then heathen East Prussia. In 1309 their leader, Grand Master Sigfried von Feuchtwangen, decided to establish a new Ordensburg (headquarters town) and named it Marienburg (Mary's Town) after the order's patron, the Virgin Mary. The work on the headquarters castle by the River Nogat continued into the mid-15th century and when it was completed the Teutonic Knight's had the largest Gothic castle ever built in Europe and one of the largest brick structures in the world.

Malbork actually consists of three distinctive sections, which are known as the High, Middle and Low Castles, and each performed certain specific functions The Low Castle consists of St. Lawrence's Church, along with various practical buildings such as an armory, stables, and various workshops. The Middle Castle is a living area with the grand master's palace, an infirmary, a large refectory and accommodation for the garrison. The High Castle is the main defensive position and consists of several moats and curtain walls with towers. Partially destroyed during World War II, the castle has been extensively restored and is now a UNESCO World Heritage Site. **IW**

Little Morton Hall

Architect: Unknown

Completed: 1480

Location: Congleton, Cheshire, England

Style/Period: Tudor

Little Moreton Hall in the north of England was the family home of the Moreton family. They became immensely rich landowners, partly because they were tax collectors, and partly because they had heads for business. The effects of the Black Death in the mid-14th century, for example, enabled them to purchase land cheaply. Successive generations added to and refined a picturesque hall, a family home that was begun in the mid-15th century. Its charm lies in the fact that it has few right angles and seems almost on the point of collapse.

At first sight the hall appears wholly medieval, as it is a timber-framed building with a wattle-and-daub infill set on a stone plinth. Yet on closer inspection much of the detailing, and some of the rooms, have a distinctively Elizabethan feel and owe more to the Renaissance style. This is most evident on the exterior, where the decorative motifs — chevrons, lozenges and quatrefoils — are all distinctly Elizabethan, as are the interior fireplaces and bay windows. The long gallery, which was added in the second half of the 16th century, was used for promenading during inclement weather, and it is a type of domestic room unknown in the medieval period. **IW**

Albi Cathedral

Architect: Unknown

Completed: 1480 (begun 1282)

Location: Albi, France

Style/Period: Southern Gothic

The town of Albi in southern France lent its name to the Albigenses, members of a Christian sect that flourished in the region between the 11th and 13th centuries, and whom the Roman Catholic Church regarded as heretics. A crusade was accordingly waged against them between 1208 and 1229, and the Albigensian heresy was eventually stamped out in 1244. The history of religious conflict in the town, and the established Church's victory, offer crucial explanations for the building of a cathedral in Albi in 1282 and the fortresslike form it assumed, on its elevated site overlooking the River Tarn.

On its completion in 1480, the rosy-colored Gothic-style Cathedral of St. Cecile had the distinction of being the largest brick structure in the world, and at 256 feet (78 m) high, its bell tower — finished in 1492 — dominates Albi's skyline. Its unadorned external appearance, such as ramparts, parapets and narrow windows, has military overtones, and its proximity to Spain is reflected in its huge Catalan-influenced, hall-like nave and internal buttresses. Entry is through a portal created by Dominique de Florence; once inside, the eye is overwhelmed by the richly colored and imaginatively rendered religious artwork. **CH-M**

Milan Cathedral

Architect: Various

Completed: 1486 (main work)

Location: Milan, Italy

Style/Period: Gothic

Milan's great Gothic cathedral lies at the heart of the northern Italian city, both literally and metaphorically, but it was a building project that took some 500 years to reach fruition. Antonio da Saluzzo, a Roman Catholic archbishop, had the original idea for a cathedral with a cruciform nave and transept in 1386, and he intended to build on some old Roman ruins. Construction stopped and started over the next several centuries, largely due to shortages of funds and arguments over architectural styles. Nevertheless the cathedral played an important role in introducing the High Gothic style, which was pioneered in northern Europe, into Italy.

Given its long gestation period, the cathedral displays an array of styles — the eastern apse is French Gothic, the cupola is Renaissance, while the facade is Neoclassical — yet it is more than the sum of its parts. The building was constructed on a truly monumental scale and is one of the largest in the world. It can house 40,000 visitors at a time and is decorated both inside and out with more statues, 3,159 in total, than any other building in existence. Yet for all its monumentality it has great delicacy, partly because of its astonishingly decorated roof. **IW**

Machu Picchu

Architect: Unknown
Completed: c. 1500 (begun 15th century)
Location: Near Cuzco, Peru
Style/Period: Incan/Pre-Columbian/Peruvian

What remains of the once-inhabited city of Machu Picchu stands swathed in clouds, 7,972 feet (2,430 m) above sea level, on a plateau on a ridge between two mountains. Typical of Andes-challenged Incan architecture, the site is defined by its steep man-made terraces (which aid agriculture); its huge enclosing walls; its ramps, steps and fortifications; and the breathtakingly high quality of its stonework. The ruined mortar-free and polished-masonry buildings — numbering between 100 and 200 — that make up this ghost town are believed to have been used as palaces, houses, storehouses and temples, and it is thought that, essential agricultural elements apart, Machu Picchu served primarily as a sacred sanctuary. Such significant structures as the Intihuatana (Temple of the Sun) were constructed so they would align with the sun at certain times of the year, indicating the sun's paramount importance in both the Incas' sacred belief system and their social order. The site's functioning aqueducts, drains and fountains further testify to the Incas' expertise in building and engineering.

Unknown to nonindigenous Peruvians until its discovery by U.S. explorer Hiram Bingham in 1911, this UNESCO World Heritage Site has since been visited by so many tourists that it is now rapidly deteriorating and is in danger of suffering irreparable damage. **CH-M**

Orvieto Cathedral

Architects: Arnolfo di Cambio and Lorenzo Maitani

Completed: 1500 (begun 1290)

Location: Orvieto, Italy

Style/Period: Italian Gothic

Orvieto's *duomo* (cathedral) has more profound links with the papacy than many other Roman Catholic centers of worship: it was erected on the instructions of Pope Urban IV (to house the Corporal of Bolsena), its foundation stone was laid by Pope Nicholas IV in 1290, and the adjoining Palazzo dei Papi (Papal Palace) was once inhabited by a number of popes.

The design of this Umbrian *duomo* was based on a basilica-style plan by the Florentine stonemason Arnolfo di Cambio, but it was later modified and amended by the Sienese architect and sculptor Lorenzo Maitani, who took charge from around 1310. It was Maitani who was responsible for the eye-catching gold-highlighted and mosaic-inlaid facade; he is credited with sculpting many of its stone figures and bas-reliefs

himself. Stripes — white marble and bluish basalt — are a notable feature of the exterior walls and interior columns.

A number of pieces of sacred art grace the inside of the *duomo*, with the Chapel of the Madonna di San Brizio being famous for its frescoes painted by Luca Signorelli around 1500. Another chapel, the Chapel of the Corporal, contains a golden reliquary in which is kept the miraculously bloodstained corporal that prompted the cathedral to be established. **CH-M**

Novodevichy Convent

Architect: Unknown

Completed: c. 1500

Location: Russia

Style/Period: Byzantine/Kievan

Steeped in Russian military, literary and artistic history and resembling a mini-Kremlin, the Novodevichy ("New Maidens") Convent is a superb example of medieval Russian architecture. It was built in the early

16th century by Crown Prince Vassily III, who had vowed in 1514 to build a convent dedicated to the Virgin of Smolensk if he was victorious in recapturing the city from Lithuania. Its location, on the left bank of the Moscow River, gave it an important defensive role. The five-domed Smolensk Cathedral possibly dates from the original build in 1524–1525, although its style is more akin to that of Vassily's son, Ivan the Terrible, leading many to believe that it was rebuilt in the mid-16th century.

Within the cathedral are a stunning 16th-century wall fresco and an irreplaceable iconostasis with icons from the 16th and 17th centuries. The convent also contains churches, a refectory and living quarters, all in the Moscow baroque style of red brick and white detail. Equally arresting is the six-tier bell tower soaring to a height of 236 feet (72 m). In 2004 the "Ensemble of the Novodevichy Convent" was declared a UNESCO World Heritage Site as representing the most outstanding example of Moscow baroque. **EW**

The Tempietto

Architect: Donato Bramante

Completed: c. 1502 (begun around 1502)

Location: San Pietro in Montorio, Rome, Italy

Style/Period: Italian High Renaissance

Despite its diminutive size — it measures 26 feet (8 m) in diameter and 43 feet (13 m) in height — the Tempietto is regarded as one of the most important examples of High Renaissance architecture. This masterpiece was designed by Donato Bramante to commemorate the spot where St. Peter is said to have been crucified, making it a martyrium. Limited space within the cloister of the Church of San Pietro in Montorio may have dictated a structure that was equally restricted, but its pleasing classical proportions (it is said to have been inspired by the ancient Roman Temple of Vesta) and conformity to the Platonic ideals that were then fashionable caused the "Little Temple" to become both a symbol of the divine and an enormously influential building.

Three steps lead up to a peristyle comprising granite Doric columns that enclose a central circular cella (the building's main body). The columns support an entablature, whose decorative frieze is soberly adorned with triglyphs and metopes; niches punctuate the section above, and a hemispherical dome surmounts the entire structure. The total effect is an unmistakable architectural link between 16th-century Rome and ancient Rome, as well as perfect simplicity and harmony. **CH-M**

King's College Chapel

Architects: Reginald Ely and John Wastell

Completed: 1515

Location: Cambridge, Cambridgeshire, England

Style/Period: Gothic

This beautiful essay in the Late Gothic (or Early Perpendicular) style was commissioned by King Henry VI in 1441. The work began around 1446 but soon ran into problems.

England became embroiled in the War of the Roses, a prolonged dynastic conflict, and Henry suffered a major setback when he lost the Battle of Towton, after which he went into exile in Scotland. Work eventually resumed in 1506, during the reign of Henry VII, and was completed by his son, Henry VIII. Yet the chapel has a strong sense of unity, despite its various patrons and having taken some 70 years to complete.

The design's cohesiveness was largely due to Reginald Ely, Henry VI's master stonemason, who designed the building, and John Wastell, who was responsible for the stunning Tudor fan vault, which is the world's largest. The chapel, which is a long narrow rectangle, is flooded with light that pours in through stained glass windows, which were mostly produced by Dutch craftsmen hired by Henry VIII. The whole thrust of the opulent, beautifully crafted interior — windows, columns and pilaster — is directed upward, to lead the eye heavenward and toward the delicate vaulting. **IW**

Liuhe Pagoda

Architect: Unknown

Completed: 1524 (twice destroyed)

Location: Hangzhou, Zhejiang, China

Style: Chinese

The 196-foot (60 m) high Liuhe Pagoda stands at the foot of the Yuelun Hill on the Qiantang River in Zhejiang Province. It is the oldest standing pagoda in Hangzhou. Literally meaning "Six Harmonies," its name comes from the six Buddhist ordinances, meaning "harmonies of the heaven, earth, north, south, east and west." Originally built during the Northern Song dynasty (960–1127), the pagoda was destroyed by war in 121 and rebuilt during the Southern Song dynasty (1127–1279). From the beginning, it has acted as a lighthouse for sailors, although its other role was to control the Dragon King and thereby calm the river's tidal bore, during which a wall of water up to 30 feet (9 m) high rushes upstream. Additional eaves were added during the Ming dynasty (1368–1644) and Qing dynasty (1644–1911).

Built of wood and brick, the octagonal structure has a deceptive exterior that appears to have 13 floors, even though on the inside there are only seven. The stories are reached via a spiral stone staircase, and the walls and ceilings are decorated with carved and painted images of landscapes and real and mythological creatures. It is considered a leading example of traditional Chinese architecture. **EW**

St. George's Chapel, Windsor Castle

Architect: Unknown

Completed: 1528 (begun 1475)

Location: Windsor, Berkshire, England

Style/Period: Late Perpendicular Gothic

King Edward IV initiated building work on St. George's Chapel (formerly the Chapel of St. Edward the Confessor) in the Windsor Castle complex in 1475, and the work was initially directed by master mason Henry Janyns. But it was not until 1528, during the reign of King Henry VIII, that work was completed, with the crucial addition of elegant interior fan vaulting. Ever since, St. George's Chapel, situated in the castle's Lower Ward, has been an acclaimed example of the Late Perpendicular style of Gothic architecture. As its name suggests, the Perpendicular style's essential elements are straight verticals, and other characteristic features include large, broad windows, vertically divided skeletal support structures and general simplicity of ornamentation, all of which are evident in the chapel.

Parts of the interior are certainly colorful, however. Dedicated to the patron saint of the Order of the Garter (which was founded in 1348), St. George's Chapel has been this chivalric order's chapel for centuries. Inside, each of the order's eminent living members has been allocated his or her own stall in the choir, and the interior is decorated with their heraldic devices and brass stall plates naming their predecessors. The chapel is also the burial place of ten monarchs (including, appropriately, Edward IV and Henry VIII). **CH-M**

Tudor Wing, Hampton Court Palace

Architect: Unknown

Completed: 1530 (begun 1515)

Location: Hampton, Surrey, England

Style/Period: Tudor

The aggrandizement of Hampton Court, near Richmond, Surrey, was an exercise in the expression of wealth, stature and power on the part of Thomas Wolsey. He ordered work to begin on his newly leased property in 1515, the same year in which he became a Roman Catholic cardinal and lord chancellor of England. Already a grand country house in the 14th-century style, Hampton Court was transformed by Wolsey into a palace fit for a cardinal, complete with suites for his royal patron, King Henry VIII. Elements borrowed from Italian Renaissance style were clearly meant to impress and included such details as the repeated use of symmetry, Giovanni da Maiano's busts of Roman emperors and a piano nobile ("noble floor," the main floor in a Renaissance building); modish English contributions included extensive brickwork and ostentatious chimneys.

Unfortunately for Wolsey, his political, financial and personal fortune depended on the goodwill of his monarch and master, and when he lost this, he lost Hampton Court, which became a royal palace in 1528 and has remained so ever since. Although Hampton Court Palace was later partially enlarged by Christopher Wren, and many of the Tudor apartments were reconstructed during the 18th century, the spirit of its early 16th-century flowering is still evident, notably in Base Court (an outer courtyard surrounded by guest accommodation). **CH-M**

Casa de Pilates

Architects: Don Fadrique de Ribera and Don Per Afán

Completed: 1531 (begun 1480)

Location: Seville, Spain

Style/period: Mudéjar/Gothic/Renaissance

Popularly believed to be a copy of the house of Pontius Pilate in Jerusalem — hence the name — the 16th century Casa de Pilates (Pilate's House) was built by Moorish and Christian architects. It's an unusual combination of Mudéjar, Gothic and Renaissance styles. The house owes its place in architectural history primarily to Don Fadrique, the first Marquis of Tarifa, who departed on a European grand tour and pilgrimage to the Holy Land in 1519. When he returned home, enthused by the splendors of Renaissance Italy, he was inspired to recreate a Way of the Cross that would incorporate the house and the Cruz del Campo shrine on the edge of Seville. The first station of the cross is marked at the house by a marble cross.

The house's majestic Renaissance marble gateway arch was made by the Genoan craftsman Antonio María of Aprile in 1529. The intricate plasterwork and decorative tiling of the magnificent main courtyard is typically Mudéjar, while its surrounding arches are topped with Gothic banisters. The collection of statues, — which include Roman depictions of Minerva and Ceres and a 5th-century Greek representation of Athena — were collected by Don Per Afán, a later owner of the house. The Mudéjar influence can also be seen inside the house, particularly the grand staircase with its intricate tiling and dome. **EW**

Mir-i Arab Madrasa

Architect: Unknown

Completed: c. 1536

Location: Kalon Square, Bukhara, Uzbekistan

Style/Period: Islamic/Shaybanid

Mir-i Arab Madrasa (Islamic religious school) is named after a Yemeni sheikh who exerted a powerful influence on the 16th century ruler of the Uzbek state, Ubaydallah Khan. Bukhara grew rich thanks to the trade moving along the Silk Road and the school was constructed just as the city was entering its most glorious period. Mir-i Arab provided the funds to finance the large building project and it has been suggested that he may well have been the architect as well. When completed it was one of the best examples of a madrasa.

The most notable features are two large vivid blue domes either side of a large gateway that is richly decorated with mosaics, plaster relief work, and paintings. The luminosity of the domes is enhanced by the fact that most of the surrounding buildings are a dusty brown color. The gateway leads to a large central courtyard. Roughly square in shape, it has an iwan (summer classroom) in the center of each of the four sides and a double height arcade along each one. More than 100 quite spacious cells act as accommodation for the students, who study Islamic literature, law, and Arabic during their time at the school. The complex also contains a mosque and various tombs, including that of its benefactor. **IW**

Château de Fontainebleau

Architect: Gilles le Breton
Completed: 1547 (begun 1528)
Location: Fontainebleau, Île-de-France, France
Style/Period: Mannerist

The spectacular transformation that King François I of France presided over at the royal hunting lodge in Fontainebleau — in Île-de-France, southeast of Paris — was the envy of his fellow monarchs. The Italian mannerist artists François I hired to create his "new Rome" in France, such as Rosso Fiorentino and Francesco Primaticcio, had such an inspirational influence that Fontainebleau gave its name to a French school of mannerist painting and sculpture. The School of Fontainebleau featured high-relief stucco, plaster strapwork and decorative paintings.

The Italianate château's design is based on a series of courts, and features introduced from Italy include the mannerist interior decoration that embellishes the Gallery of François I. The design, however, also retains traditional French elements, such as the vertically arranged windows in the Porte Dorée, and Gilles le Breton, the architect and master mason primarily in charge of the château's transformation, was French. He was responsible for the Porte Dorée (the Golden Gate), parts of the Cour de l'Ovale (the Oval Court), parts of the Cour du Cheval Blanc (the Court of the White Horse) and the Gallery of François I. That the château and its park are today a UNESCO World Heritage Site further demonstrates the importance of the work done here. **CH-M**

Villa Barbaro

Architect: Andrea Palladio
Completed: 1554 (begun c. 1549)
Location: Maser, near Treviso, Italy
Style/Period: Mannerist

Many of the distinctive hallmarks of mannerism, the Italian architect Andrea Palladio's famous style, are evident in the Villa Barbaro, which was commissioned by the patrician, powerful and well-to-do brothers Daniele and Marc'antonio Barbaro. It was constructed in the village of Maser, near Treviso, in the Venetian Republic (now Veneto, a northeastern region of Italy), during the mid-16th century.

The villa's overall appearance is strikingly symmetrical, with a facade consisting of five parts: a pavilion at either end with an arcaded wing leading from each to a projecting central structure. The centerpiece is classical in style, and it is no accident that it resembles a Roman temple, as it features four Ionic columns inspired by the Temple of Fortuna Virilis in Rome. This central building was a grand reception area, and the two-story living quarters were situated behind the arcades of the flanking wings. The pavilions also have two-stories, and the upper sections, whose pediments frame sundials, acted as dovecotes, while the lower sections were used for domestic or farm purposes.

Inside the central block of the Villa Barbaro are frescoes painted by Paolo Veronese and stuccowork by Alessandro Vittoria. The grounds boast a *tempietto* ("little temple"), also designed by Palladio, and a *nymphaeum* (a statue-adorned grotto). **CH-M**

Cathedral of St. Basil the Blessed

Architect: Postnik Yakovlev
Completed: 1561
Location: Red Square, Moscow, Russia
Style/Period: Russian Orthodox

Formerly known as the Cathedral of the Virgin of the Intercession on the Moat, St. Basil's was built as much as a political statement as a place of worship. Ivan IV (the Russian monarch commonly referred to as "Ivan the Terrible") commissioned Postnik Yakovlev to commemorate a great victory over the Mongols' previously all-conquering Golden Horde, the capture of the Khanate Kazan on the Virgin's feast day in 1554. It was a victory that saved Russia. The site for the new cathedral — in the very heart of Moscow — was to leave the local people in no doubt about the strength of Ivan's rule.

Yakovlev (n.d.) constructed a cathedral that comprises a symmetrical group of eight

(later 10) chapels set around a central pillar. St. Basil's is an extraordinarily geometrically complex building, resembling an eight-point star and inspired by the Byzantine architectural tradition. The interior walls of the small chapels are decorated with a mix of pilasters, arches and cornices. The

embroiderylike and brightly painted exterior seen today is not original but was added in around 1670. St. Basil's has come to represent the first flowering and most beautiful example of the ecclesiastical architectural style termed Russian Orthodox. **IW**

Olavinlinna Castle

Architect: Unknown

Completed: 1562 (begun 1475)

Location: Lake Saimaa, Savonlinna, Finland

Style/Period: Medieval

Olavinlinna Castle, or the Castle of St. Olaf (*Olofsborg* or *Sankt Olofsborg* in Swedish) — St. Olaf being a patron saint of knights — dates back to 1475, when a fortified building was first raised on this rocky island in Lake Saimaa. Its founder Erik Axelsson Tott (a Danish knight), intented to defend the Savonia region of Finland against Russian incursions from the east. Although Finland is now an independent nation, it was part of Sweden during this period and was coveted by nearby Russia (which annexed it in 1809), and consequently many battles were fought between these two mighty northern powers on Finnish soil. Russian forces occupied the castle itself in 1743.

The fortress, which was constructed of stone, is encircled by crenellated walls. Entry is from the west, through a vaulted gateway that leads into an inner courtyard. There were once five round towers, but only three of these still stand, including the Church Tower and the Bell Tower. The tower's massive walls are punctuated only by arrow loops, and the viewing platforms at the top that served as watchtowers are equally well protected against attack. The castle compound also contains a bailey, living quarters and various halls. **CH-M**

Villa Foscari

Architect: Andrea Palladio

Completed: 1563 (begun 1549)

Location: Near Mestre, Italy

Style/Period: Mannerist

Built during the mid-16th century for Nicolo and Luigi Foscari (scions of an aristocratic Venetian family) on a bank of the Brenta River near Mestre, the Villa Foscari also goes by the names Villa Malcontenta and La Malcontenta (*malcontenta* meaning "discontented woman" in Italian and referring to a Foscari wife who later lived there).

In common with many of the villas (typically part country retreats and part working farms) that the Italian architect Andrea Palladio designed in the north-eastern Veneto region of Italy, when approached head on, Villa Foscari has the outward appearance of an august Roman temple, thanks to the volute-topped Ionic columns that support its impressive pediment. This pediment, the building's central section, projects forward from the main body of the villa, and it is reached by two elegant flights of stone steps on either side — Palladio's symmetrical blueprint is evident everywhere at the Villa Foscari. The view of the villa from the rear is equally balanced and harmonious. Although it lacks a portico and columns, a smaller pediment echoes the larger, triangular classical feature at the front. The villa itself is rectangular, with two central attic gables protruding upward at the front and back of the hipped roof. **CH-M**

Villa Farnese

Architect: Giacomo Barozzi di Vignola

Completed: 1569

Location: Caprarola, Viterbo, Italy

Style/Period: Italian Renaissance

This retreat was built for the immensely wealthy Cardinal Alessandro Farnese, the grandson of Pope Paul III, one of many people of status who liked to escape Rome's stifling summer heat by heading for cooler climes in the so-called *villeggiatura* (the countryside). Farnese intended to impress other members of high society with an imposing, fortresslike structure that entirely overpowers the lesser buildings around it. He commissioned Vignola, a noted exponent of the largely Italian mannerist style of the Renaissance period, to design his mansion.

The stone mansion, which was sited on a slight hill to give it even more impact, is massively imposing, but it was integrated into its gardens with great skill, reflecting the rediscovery of classical style in the Renaissance period. The building has an unusual pentagonal plan, possibly because it was built on the foundations of a fortress of that shape. It also strayed from a purely Classical design by having a circular, rather than angular, courtyard. Villa Farnese is considered Vignola's greatest work and one of the finest mannerist buildings ever built. **IW**

Villa Capra

Architect: Andrea Palladio

Completed: 1569 (begun 1565)

Location: Near Vicenza, Italy

Style/Period: Mannerist

The Villa Capra's alternative names — La Rotonda and Villa Rotonda — reveal something about the villa that Andrea Palladio erected on a hilltop near Vicenza (a town in the northeastern Veneto region of Italy), "rotunda" being architectural shorthand for a building with a circular plan, usually with a dome. In fact, although a dome is indeed present above a circular hall at the heart of Villa Capra, the main building's ground plan is essentially square, and overall it is cruciform. The four arms of the cross terminate in flights of stairs, each of which leads up to a hexastyle (six-columned) portico, or loggia, that resembles a classical Roman temple and is typical of Palladio's style. The choice of circle, square and cross shapes as fundamental elements of the building's design enabled Palladio to achieve a perfectly symmetrical building (symmetry being another of this influential Italian architect's hallmarks). The dome, however, was lower than Palladio had originally intended, being added by Vicenzo Scamozzi, whose inspiration was the Pantheon in Rome.

The Villa Capra was commissioned during the 1560s by Paolo Almerico, a cleric and native of Vicenza, who, following a career that had culminated at the papal court, envisaged himself retiring to a residence whose splendor reflected his exquisite taste, wealth and stature. **CH-M**

Lal Qila

Architect: Unknown

Completed: 1573

Location: Agra, Uttar Pradesh, India

Style/Period: Mogul

Lal Qila, better known as the Red Fort, is much more than a fortress. This vast site was more of a walled palatial city and the administrative heart of the Mogul Empire. Emperor Akbar the Great began construction of the great red sandstone walls, which are more than 65 feet (20 m) high and run for some 1½ miles (2.5 km), in 1565. Successive Mogul rulers made further additions and improvements, which culminated during the reign of Shah Jahan in the 17th century.

The semicircular fort was eventually filled with all the buildings needed to run an empire, and thus it constituted the most extensive collection of Mogul architecture anywhere in the empire. Unfortunately many of the fort's residential, religious and administrative buildings were destroyed during various conflicts, ending with the 1857 Indian Mutiny. British forces swept away many structures when they retook the fort. Nevertheless some fine Mogul buildings remain, including the stunning white marble

Moti Masjid (Pearl Mosque), the Diwan-i-am and Diwan i-Khas (the Halls of Public Audiences and Private Audiences), the Musamman Burj (Octagonal Tower) and Jehangir's Palace. The fort is a UNESCO World Heritage Site. **IW**

Great Wall of China

Architect: Unknown

Completed: 1575 (begun 214 BCE)

Location: China

Style/period: Chinese

Built as a series of many walls to ward off invasion from the north, the Great Wall of China winds majestically some 4,000 miles (6,400 km) from east to west in northern China. Known to the Chinese as the "Long Wall of Ten Thousand Li" (a Chinese unit of distance), the Great Wall's origins have been traced back as far as the 7th century BCE, although much of the brick and stone structure seen today dates from the Ming dynasty (1368–1644).

The Great Wall of China starts at the Jiayuguan Pass of Gansu Province in the west and ends at the Shanhaiguan Pass of Hebei Province in the east, where the symbolic monument of the "first door under heaven" can still be seen. The wall is up to 26 feet (8 m) high and was fortified by 25,000 towers and 15,000 outposts. Passageways lined with battlements run along the top. Sections of the wall are subject to conservation projects, but others have been damaged or destroyed by man and nature. In 1987 the Great Wall of China was declared a UNESCO World Heritage Site because "its historic and strategic importance is matched only by its architectural significance." **EW**

Château de Chenonceau

Architects: Philbert de l'Orme and Jean Bullent
Completed: 1576
Location: Chenonceau, Indre-et-Loire, France
Style/Period: French Renaissance

This beautiful French Renaissance château, which was built over the River Cher in the Loire Valley (and is stunning reflected by the river), owes its current form to a succession of owners. Thomas Bohier tore down much of the original structure and created the Marques Tower, a basic rectangular keep with four towers, between 1515 and 1521. Thereafter, the castle was largely developed and maintained by a succession of women, and it is sometimes referred to as the Château des Femmes. (Castle of Women)

King Henry II gave the château to his mistress, Diane de Poitiers, who commissioned Philibert de l'Orme to built the five-arched bridge linking the keep with the Cher's left bank. Work began in 1556 and was completed three years later. Henry II's wife, Catherine de Medici, took over the château after his death in 1559, and she had Jean Bullant add the three-story gallery to the bridge in 1576. The castle was allegedly saved from destruction during the French Revolution by the intervention of Louise

Dupin, wife of the owner, who subtly changed its name from Chenonceaux, which was well known as a royal palace, to the present Chenonceau. IW

Xian Bell Tower

Architect: Unknown

Completed: 1582 (first built 1384)

Location: Xian, Shaanxi Province, China

Style/period: Chinese

The largest and best-preserved wooden tower in China, the Xian Bell Tower stands on a 116-square foot (35 sq. m) and 28-foot (8 m) high brick base, and it rises 118 feet (36 m) over the busy city streets. Built in 1384 by the first Ming emperor, Zhu Yuanzhang, in what was the city center, the subsequent expansion of Xian meant that it was moved 1,000 yards (1 km) to the east in 1582. According to legend, the emperor, who was from a lowly background, built the tower to ward off the "dragon power" of any blue-blooded opposition that might aim to take his throne.

The three layers of eaves, complete with green glazed tiles, and the 20-foot (6 m) gold-plated roof crown are excellent examples of Ming dynasty architecture. Inside are two stories, reached by a spiral staircase. A plaque on the second story records the tower's 16th-century relocation. Arches 20 feet (6 m) high in the base allow access under the tower. The original bell in the tower was the Tang-dynasty copper Jingyun Bell (now in Xian's Forest of Stone Steles Museum). The current, much smaller, bell dates from the Ming dynasty. It was used to ring in dawn, while the drums of the Drum Tower a short distance away marked dusk. EW

Church of Santa Maria di Loreto

Architects: Antonio Sangallo (Sangallo the Younger) and Jacopo del Duca

Completed: c. 1582 (begun 1507)

Location: Rome, Italy

Style/Period: Italian High Renaissance

The Church of Santa Maria di Loreto's dome appears to vie with the nearby Trajan's

Column to reach the farthest into the sky. It is a testimony to the classically inspired vision of architect Antonio Sangallo (Sangallo the Younger) that a 16th-century place of Christian worship does not look out of place alongside an ancient monument to an emperor's battlefield triumphs. And yet when he began work on the church in 1507, which was commissioned by the Confraternita dei Fornari (the Guild of Bakers) to replace a smaller, earlier structure, the Florentine-born Sangallo was just starting to make a name for himself in Rome, mainly as an architectural draftsman.

By the time Sangallo finished his contri-

bution to the church's construction in 1534, the lower part had been completed. Built of brick and travertine marble, this lower section was based on a square ground plan above which rose an octagonal story, the overall effect being simple, elegant, well proportioned and reminiscent of ancient Rome. The final flourishes — the tall dome and the elaborate cagelike lantern at its apex — were added by Jacopo del Duca between around 1573 and 1582. The interior of the church contains semicircular chapels and is notable for its statues of angels and saints. CH-M

Stirling Castle

Architect: Unknown

Completed: c. 1583 (main complex)

Location: Castle Hill, Stirling, Scotland

Style/Period: Medieval/Tudor

Imposing Stirling Castle, which was built from the 1370s onward on a high crag of volcanic rock, was sited to defend two vital points — the main north-south route between Highland and Lowland Scotland, where a ford crossed the River Forth, and the main route running between the country's east and west coasts. It was Scotland's most important stronghold until the mid-18th century. However, although it was placed under siege on several occasions and major battles were fought in its vicinity, Stirling was more than a fortress. Above all it was the heart, the capital and the administrative headquarters of the Stuart dynasty that ruled the kingdom of Scotland during the 15th and 16th centuries.

While the castle's strong defenses are impressive, it is the domestic and administrative buildings dating from the late 15th century that are the most architecturally interesting. These include a trio of partly Late Gothic buildings — the Great Hall with its fine hammer-beam ceiling erected by James IV in 1503, the Royal Palace (1540–1542), which is one of the earliest buildings in Britain to have Renaissance-style decoration, and the Royal Chapel of 1594. Stirling Castle is thus considered to be one of the most important collections of buildings, both historically and architecturally, not only in Britain, but also in Western Europe. **IW**

Palazzo Farnese

Architects: Antonio da Sangallo and Michelangelo

Completed: 1589 (begun c. 1519)

Location: Rome, Italy

Style/Period: Italian High Renaissance

The long, horizontal and rectangular facade of the Palazzo Farnese (Farnese Palace) is an imposing sight, as it was intended to be when the Florentine architect Antonio da Sangallo (Sangallo the Younger) drew up plans for a grand palazzo that would project the dignity of the noble Farnese family. (And the Farnese clan was about to become preeminent. Cardinal Alessandro Farnese — whose palazzo it was and who commissioned Sangallo —became Pope Paul III in 1534, while Pierluigi Farnese received the dukedom of Parma in 1545.) Following Sangallo's death in 1546, the work was completed by Michelangelo, with modifications, particularly to the top floor, which received a projecting cornice.

Noteworthy especially on account of its monumental appearance, the Palazzo Farnese comprises three floors divided by string courses. The walls of plain cut stone are bounded by quoins, punctuated by rows of windows (numbering between 12 and 13 on the facade) and measure 184 feet (56 m) wide. The central rusticated portal on the ground floor is surmounted by a window designed by Michelangelo, above whose architrave can be seen Pope Paul III's coat of arms. The flanking windows on the piano nobile (noble floor) have alternating curved and triangular pediments. To the rear, enclosed by the building's four sides, is a square courtyard, or *cortile*. **CH-M**

Hardwick Hall

Architect: Robert Smythson
Completed: 1597
Location: Doe Lea, Derbyshire, England
Style/Period: Tudor

Hardwick Hall was commissioned by the much-married Elizabeth, Countess of Shrewsbury — better known as Bess of Hardwick — after the death of her fourth husband, the Earl of Shrewsbury, left her even more impressively wealthy than she was before. The countess, who was of comparatively lowly origins and wanted to reflect her new status, commissioned Robert Smythson to build a country house to better any other. He came up with a design that melded the Renaissance style found in Europe with cutting-edge British technology. These, together with Bess's money, allowed the use of expensive glass on a scale never witnessed before.

The house, which is symmetrical on every side, has several interesting features. At the time such buildings were usually built in an E-shape in honor of Queen Elizabeth I, but Hardwick Hall is cross-shaped, possibly reflecting the owner's Catholic leanings. Smythson also introduced some novel features, such as placing the staterooms on the second rather than first floor. Hardwick remains the finest, most perfectly realized Elizabethan house in Britain, and no one can be in any doubt about its origin, as the exterior balustrades were carved with the initials "ES" for its owner, Elizabeth, Countess of Shrewsbury. **IW**

17th Century

The Globe Theatre

Architect: Unknown

Completed: 1614 and 1997 (begun 1614 and 1987)

Location: Southwark, London, England

Style/Period: Elizabethan

The Globe Theatre that comes into view on crossing London's Millennium Bridge toward Bankside is the third of this name, and although it looks authentically Elizabethan, it dates from 1997. The first Globe Theatre was erected by Cuthbert Burbage in 1599. William Shakespeare's plays were staged here by the Lord Chamberlain's Men (Shakespeare's acting company) until 1613, when the firing of a cannon during *Henry VIII* set the thatched roof ablaze, burning the timber building to the ground. The second Globe Theatre rose from the ashes in 1614. It welcomed audiences until 1642, when the Puritans shut it down, and it stood until 1644, when it was demolished.

Construction of this third Globe Theatre — the pet project of the U.S. movie director Sam Wanamaker, who wanted to create as exact a replica of the second Globe Theatre as possible as close to its original site as possible — got under way in 1987. The New Globe Theatre, or Shakespeare's Globe Theatre, was completed in 1997. The timber-framed, plasterwork and thatched Globe is a round building three stories high, whose center is open to the sky, like an amphitheater. "Groundlings" (members of the audience) stand in the pit at the foot of the raised apron stage, exposed to the elements; covered seating is available on the three levels surrounding the pit. **CH-M**

Sultan Ahmet Mosque

Architect: Sedefhar Mehmet Aga

Completed: 1616

Location: Sultanahmet Square, Istanbul, Turkey

Style/Period: Islamic

This building, which is better known as the Blue Mosque, was commissioned by Sultan Ahmet I, who ordered his chief royal architect, Mehmet Aga to erect an imposing mosque opposite the former Byzantine church Hagia Sophia (see page 52) in what was then Constantinople. The architect's design was perfectly symmetrical and consisted of a square building topped by a great dome that was in turn flanked on each side by a number of semi-domes. These were surrounded by a further grouping of turrets, domes, and semi-domes. The complex was given six minarets in two rows of three, a comparatively rare style in Ottoman mosques.

Although the interior's domes and upper parts are painted rather crudely in blue, the lower walls of the interior are covered in blue and green tiles that are decorated with all manner of plant motifs, including carnations, lilies, roses, and tulips. Mehmet Aga was one of the ablest pupils of Koca Mimar Sinan Aga, the greatest of all Ottoman designers who produced more than 300 buildings. The Blue Mosque was the former's masterpiece but it is clearly influenced by Sinan Aga and marks the high point of the classical era of Ottoman architecture. **IW**

Himeji-jo

Architect: Ikeda Terumasa
Completed: 1618 (rebuilding began 1580)
Location: Himeji, Hyogo Prefecture, Japan
Style/period: Medieval Japanese

The original castle at Himeji, built by the *daimyo* Toyotomi Hideyoshi in the late 16th century, was destroyed by Ikeda Terumasa. The fortress he built in its place is the Himeji-jo (Himeji Castle) visible today. Unlike many castles built in the Shogun period, the wooden Himeji-jo's towers, ramparts and earthen walls have survived war and the ravages of nature almost intact. Made up of 83 buildings, it can be seen from any part of the city of Himeji, and its white plastered walls brought it the local nickname *Shirasagi-jo* ("Castle of the White Heron").

Built at the top of Himeyama hill, the structure is divided into inner and outer walled zones. The main keep, with its five projecting roofs, and three smaller keeps are placed in the center of the inner zone. The famous main tower stands over 150 feet (46 m) high. Particularly unusual is the castle's highly complicated defense system, whereby a labyrinth of paths and walls lead eventually to the keep, but only via a series of defensive positions that were intended to prevent any invaders from reaching their target. In 1993 Himeji-jo was declared a UNESCO World Heritage Site and described as "the finest surviving example of early 17th-century Japanese castle architecture." **EW**

Sheikh Luft Allah Mosque

Architect: Mohammed Reza ibn Ustad Hosein Banna Isfahani
Completed: 1619
Location: Imam Square, Isfahan, Iran
Style/Period: Persian/Islamic

This outstandingly beautiful mosque in Isfahan — the holy city that became the capital of the Safavid Empire in 1592 — was built on the orders of Abbas the Great — the fifth Safavid shah of what was then Persia — to honor his father-in-law, who was also a renowned cleric. The mosque takes its name from Sheikh Luft Allah Maisi Al-Amili, who was invited to Isfahan by Abbas and lived at the location. The mosque, arguably the most beautiful in the world, sits in a square but stands at 45 degrees to it so that it is orientated toward Mecca.

The highly decorated brick mosque is somewhat unusual because its tiled dome is a sandy color, not the brilliant blue that is common to all other Safavid mosques. It has an elegant simplicity, the interior consisting of the dome and eight supporting arches. What is startling is the effect of the thousands of tiles that cover the walls. These tiles, completed in outstanding detail, are a heady mix of flowers and calligraphy, and include arches defined by blue cable tiles. The dome is equally beautifully decorated, with a central sunburst surrounded by teardrop-shaped medallions that shrink in size as they rise up the dome. The mosque's interior is akin to a dazzling jewel box. **IW**

Jag Mandir

Architect: Unknown

Completed: 1620

Location: Rajasthan, India

Style/period: Mogul

Used originally as a hideaway by the Mogul Prince Khurram (later Emperor Shah Jahan) in 1623–1624, the stunning three-story white marble Jag Mandir palace stands on an island on the southern edge of Lake Pichola. It is one of the few examples of Mogul-style architecture in Udaipur.

The lavish Islamic-style domed main pavilion (Gul Mahal) used by Prince Khurram and his family is topped with the Muslim crescent, and the interiors are richly decorated. There was originally a throne made from a single block of serpentine, but it is now lost. The palace's intricate *pietra dura* (decorative stonework) provided some of the inspiration for the Taj Mahal, built by Shah Jahan in later years in memory of his favorite wife, Mumtaz Mahal, who stayed with him at Jag Mandir. The palace complex includes further pavilions — one made from 12 marble slabs and another that was used for women's chambers — and a mosque. There is a stunning courtyard of black and white tiles, as well as beautiful gardens with pathways lined with marble balustrades and columns. Guarding the entrance are eight life-sized marble elephants. The palace's reputation as a safe haven was reinforced during the 1857 Indian Mutiny, when it was used to shelter European families hiding from the mutineers. **EW**

Frederiksborg Slot

Architects: Hans van Steenwinckel and Lorents van Steenwinckel
Completed: 1622 (begun 1602)
Location: Hillerød, Sjaelland, Denmark
Style/Period: Dutch/Danish Renaissance

When King Christian IV of Denmark and Norway decided to rebuild a castle constructed in the 16th century in honor of his father, King Frederick II (after whom Frederiksborg is named), his intention was to create a Renaissance palace whose splendor would dazzle his contemporaries. Frederiksborg Slot (Frederiksborg Castle) sits on three islets in the center of Slotsø (Palace Lake) in the city of Hillerød, northeastern Sjaelland (Zealand). In order to achieve his vision for Frederiksborg, Christian IV hired the Dutch architects Hans and Lorents van Steenwinckel. This explains why certain aspects of this erstwhile royal Danish residence are reminiscent of Dutch Renaissance buildings, including the sandstone decorative features adorning the long, rectangular facade, the extravagantly large gables and the deep roofs and spiky spires that were covered in copper (or verdigris). That Christian's palace unquestionably outshone his father's upon its completion in 1622 is evident by comparing two adjoining, and relatively diminutive, round towers that survive from Frederick II's time.

While Frederiksborg's exterior is massive and magnificent yet simple, harmonious and compact, the largely Italianate-style interior is breathtakingly lavish and elaborate. Although a fire devastated much of Frederiksborg in 1859, it was faithfully reconstructed and today houses Denmark's Museum of National History. **CH-M**

Saint Peter's Basilica

Architects: Donato Bramante, Raphael, Michelangelo, Giacomo della Porta, Carlo Maderno and others
Completed: 1626 (begun 1506)
Location: Rome, Italy (now Vatican City)
Style/Period: Italian High Renaissance/Mannerist/Baroque

Some of the most stellar names in Renaissance art and architecture worked on Saint Peter's Basilica, Roman Catholicism's preeminent church, in the Vatican. Donato Bramante was first commissioned by Pope Julius II in 1506 to reconstruct the basilica that traditionally marked Saint Peter's tomb. He devised a Greek-cross plan (with the altar in the center), which was surmounted by a huge dome and surrounded by four smaller domes and towers at each corner. On Bramante's death in 1514, work continued under Raphael and Fra Giocondo and then under Antonio da Sangallo, a subsequent chief architect, who all amended Bramante's design.

The baton was passed to Michelangelo between 1547 and 1564, and it was he, more than any other architect, who implemented Bramante's vision, albeit making a few radical amendments, such as shifting a square 45 degrees to Bramante's original ground plan and adding a huge drum to support the piers of the dome. Giacomo della Porta contributed various domes between 1578 and 1590, and it was Carlo Maderno who extended the nave to form a Latin cross and created the baroque western facade, which he did between 1602 and 1626. The resulting travertine-marble church is an imposing 435 feet (133 m) high with a surface area of 163,182 square feet (15,160 sq. m). **CH-M**

The Queen's House

Architect: Inigo Jones
Completed: 1635 (begun 1616)
Location: Greenwich, London, England
Style/Period: Palladian

The Queen's House has the distinction of being the first building in the Palladian style to be constructed in England. Its architect, Inigo Jones, studied in Italy, where he came into contact with Andrea Palladio's work. Appointed surveyor of the king's works in 1615, Jones was occupied with the royal palaces until the outbreak of the English Civil War in 1642.

Work on the Queen's House, in Greenwich, southeast London, was divided into two phases: the laying of the foundations between 1616 and 1618, and the raising of the grand, classically inspired house between 1629 and 1635. Its resemblance to an Italian villa is unmistakable, not least in the three-part facades, with their projecting central portions — although Jones included some original touches. The ground plan was based on two parallel, rectangular and symmetrical masonry buildings joined by a bridge, under which ran a public road. At the center of the northern block was a cubic hall, and angled flights of steps led from the building's two sides to the terrace. Both blocks had two floors, with a loggia on the upper floor, below a balustrade, and rustication on the lower floor. The Queen's House was the residence of James I's queen, Anne of Denmark, and later of Queen Henrietta Maria, Charles I's wife. **CH-M**

Pol Khaju

Architect: Unknown

Completed: 1650

Location: Isfahan, Iran

Style/Period: Persian/Islamic

Pol Khaju is both functional and beautiful: a bridge of 24 graceful arches that also acts as a weir regulating the flow of the great Zayendah River from the Zagros Mountains east through to Isfahan, the one-time capital of Persia (modern-day Iran).

Built by Shah Abbas II in 1650, during the golden age of Safavid rule in Isfahan, Pol Khaju (pol is Farsi for bridge) is a two-story bridge. The upper level has a central aisle for horses and carts, and there are covered paths on either side for pedestrians, as well as vaulted niches where people still meet and chat. At 433 feet (132 m) long and some 45 feet (14 m) wide, the bridge had sluices used to control the river flow and, in the 17th century, to flood an ornamental lake.

Like the slightly older Sei-Si Pol upriver, Pol Khaju has an octagonal pavilion in its center, which provided space for tearooms and allowed travelers to admire the view of the city, known proudly by its inhabitants as "half the world." And if they tired of the view they could admire the intricate tile decorations characteristic of Safavid Isfahan, which adorned the interior and the area around the exterior arches on the lower level. The finest tiling and faience was reserved for the two royal pavilions set either side of the central span, and it has recently been restored. **JM**

The mausoleum itself was constructed on a sandstone plinth at the end of a garden of flowerbeds and watercourses. Every part of the main structure is decorated with calligraphy in bas-relief, abstract patterns or floral devices inlaid with precious and semiprecious gemstones.

The Taj Mahal, which displays elements of Indian, Islamic, Persian and Turkish styles, is actually the centerpiece of a well-balanced complex of buildings, whose minarets are smaller than those of the mausoleum, which accentuate its size. These minarets were also cleverly built, at a slight angle, so that if they collapsed they would fall away from the Taj Mahal. The mausoleum's purpose, its ornate decoration and its beautiful symmetry have ensured it is India's national symbol and one of the world's most instantly recognizable pieces of architecture. **IW**

Katsura Imperial Villa

Architect: Unknown

Completed: 1663 (begun 1615)

Location: Kyoto, Japan

Style/period: Japanese

Considered one of the finest examples of Japanese architecture and garden design, the Katsura Imperial Villa was built in the Edo period by Prince Toshihito (1579–1629), with later additions by his son Prince Toshitada (1619–1662). Younger brother of Emperor Go-Yozei, Toshihito was the founder of the Hachijo-no-miya line.

The villa comprises the Old Shoin (*shoin* is Japanese for "building"), built around 1615, the Middle Shoin and the New Palace, all of which were built using natural materials. The complex includes an imperial hall, a moon-viewing platform, teahouses and the villa itself. Although smaller than the villa we see today — the New Palace was added by Toshitada in honor of a visit by Emperor Gomino-o in 1658 — Toshihito's villa was noted for its simplicity and elegance but was still large enough to hold moon-viewing parties. After he died, when his son was just ten years old, the villa went into decline for several years, until the boy was old enough to enjoy it. Toshitada's additions are slightly more in line with the later, more

Taj Mahal

Architect: Ustad Ahmad Lahauri

Completed: 1653

Location: Agra, Uttar Pradesh, India

Style/Period: Mogul

When Mumtaz Mahal, the beloved second wife of Mogul ruler Shah Jahan, died in childbirth in 1631, the emperor was left heartbroken — his hair is said to have turned gray overnight. He immediately ordered the building of an unparalleled white mausoleum, made from Makrana marble and dedicated to her memory. He gathered together some 20,000 workers, many highly skilled craftsmen from India and Persia (Iran), to build the Taj Mahal.

decorative, Sukiya style. Restoration work in 1983 sympathetically addressed problems with sagging floors and rotten wood. The elaborate strolling garden is considered a masterpiece of design and is believed to be based on the ancient Tale of Genji, a traditional story of courtly love and intrigue. **EW**

Bacon's Castle

Architect: Unknown

Completed: 1665 (begun 1655)

Location: Surry County, Virginia, United States

Style/Period: Jacobean/English Colonial

When Bacon's Castle was erected in Surry County in 1665, Virginia was still an English colony, and colonists looked to the other side of the Atlantic Ocean for a lead when it came to fashionable styles and trends to follow (although given the distance involved, the information was often a little dated). This tendency explains why the grand house commissioned by Arthur Allen, a wealthy planter, is Jacobean in appearance.

Constructed of brick and with timber used extensively inside, Bacon's Castle (originally known as the Arthur Allen House or Allen's Brick House) is a two-story house with a deep roof flanked on each side by large, curved Flemish gables and a row of three tall chimneys. It would have been rectangular in form had not two bays projecting from the center of the front and back facades created a cruciform ground plan.

The name change, to Bacon's Castle, happened after 1676, when Nathanial Bacon's men evicted Arthur Allen's son and heir from his home and then occupied and fortified it. The house has been subjected to many modifications over the centuries, including the addition of a Greek-revival-style wing. Recently restored, it is now open to the public. **CH-M**

San Carlo alle Quattro Fontane

Architect: Francesco Borromini

Completed: 1667

Location: Quirinal Hill, Rome, Italy

Style/Period: Baroque

This masterpiece of baroque style was commissioned by Cardinal Francesco Barberini, a nephew of Pope Urban VIII, from Francesco Borromini. The site was located at an intersection with a fountain in each corner, hence its name, Quattro Fontane ("four fountains"), and provided a limited space in which to construct a church. It was also the architect's first commission, but he overcame his lack of experience to produce a seemingly large church in a small space. As he could not design a normal Greek cross, one with four equal arms, he came up with an oval design and combined it with suggestions of a Greek cross, which was somewhat outside the style's architectural norms. He also used concave and convex bays on the exterior to give the church a feeling of movement and size. The main body of the church was completed in 1641, and the undulating facade in 1667.

Borromini also used trompe l'oeils in the interior to give the illusion of greater height to the church's dome. These effects consist of geometric coffers (recessed panels) one on top of the other that gradually decrease in size. The coffering is undoubtedly unusual, as it consists of a mix of circles with octagonal molding, unequal hexagons and Greek crosses. **IW**

Sheldonian Theatre

Architect: Sir Christopher Wren

Completed: 1668

Location: Oxford, England

Style/Period: English Baroque

Gilbert Sheldon, the archbishop of Canterbury and future chancellor of Oxford University, gave Christopher Wren his second architectural commission in 1663. Sheldon wished to provide a secular space in which the university's business could be discussed and settled, rather than use the nearby Church of Saint Mary the Virgin. Polymath Wren was actually a professor of astronomy and an internationally renowned mathematician at the time, but he had recently visited Rome, where he had been inspired by the Theatre of Marcellus and had read the works of Marcus Vitruvius Pollio, the 1st-century architect whose *De Architectura* remains the only surviving such work from the era of classical Rome.

Work began in 1664. Wren built a D-shaped structure in the baroque style using locally sourced limestone and wood. The largest column-free building of its day, it can accommodate up to 1,000 people in tiered seating. The finished building comprised a two-story facade topped with a broken pediment. The interior ceiling is flat and painted with blue skies to give the illusion of an outdoor classical theater. The building's most radical piece of design — a complex roof support structure — is actually hidden from view. **IW**

Sant'Andrea al Quirinale

Architect: Gian Lorenzo Bernini

Completed: 1670

Location: Via del Quirinale, Rome, Italy

Style/Period: Baroque

Bernini was the leading baroque sculptor and architect in 17th-century Rome. In 1658 he was commissioned by Pope Alexander VII to build this masterpiece — sometimes referred to as the "baroque pearl" — of the most flamboyant of architectural styles on Rome's Quirinal Hill. Camillo Pamphili, a Jesuit cardinal, acted as patron, and his crest appears over the main entrance. The exterior of the church of Sant'Andrea (Saint Andrew the Apostle) is comparatively plain

and breaks no architectural molds, but the interior shows Bernini at the height of his powers as both sculptor, arguably his forte, and architect.

The church is elliptical in plan because of the constraints of the site, and thus the shorter axis leads from the entrance to the altar. There is a circular central area with a stunning dome that has a golden oculus at its center. This leads to eight separate chapels, four of which are square and four are oval. The interior is lavishly decorated with sculptures, paintings and ornamental Carrara marble. Bernini considered the church his finest work and is alleged to have spent many hours admiring his own accomplishment.
IW

Riddarhuset

Architects: Simon de la Vallée, Jean de la Vallée and Justus Vingboons

Completed: 1674 (begun c. 1641)

Location: Stockholm, Sweden

Style/Period: Classical and Baroque

The Riddarhuset (literally "House of Knights" or "House of Nobles" in Swedish) was, until 1866, Sweden's political equivalent of the British House of Lords. Its aristocratic representatives met in the building, which has stood in Stockholm, Sweden's capital city, since the nobles commissioned it during the 17th century.

If the Riddarhuset resembles Salomon de Brosse's Palais du Luxembourg in Paris, France, it is not that surprising, since the initial designs were drawn up by a Frenchman, Simon de la Vallée. He settled in Sweden in 1637, was appointed royal architect in 1639 and died in 1642. His well-traveled son, Jean de la Vallée, picked up where his father left off and worked with the Dutch architect Justus Vingboons (who designed the facades) to complete the Riddarhuset around 25 years later.

The monumental-looking Riddarhuset — within which modish French and Dutch elements are combined with traditional Swedish features — has a rectangular footprint with two wings projecting from the southern side, toward Lake Mälar. Vingboons's Dutch Palladian-style facades follow a symmetrical, classically inspired, giant-order design, with the central four columns supporting a pediment. The verdigris-covered roof is of the traditional Swedish "Säteri" type and is surmounted by gilded statues. **CH-M**

Château de Versailles

Architects: Louis Le Vau and François d'Orbay
Completed: 1678 (begun 1661)
Location: Versailles, France
Style/Period: Classical and Baroque

The grand palace at Versailles, on the outskirts of Paris, France, was once a hunting lodge, constructed in 1623 for King Louis XIII. Versailles became a favorite retreat of the French royal family, and his son Louis XIV resolved to build a splendid palace here that would reflect and project the glory of the "Sun King."

Work on aggrandizing the relatively modest original chateau began in 1661, under the direction of Louis Le Vau, but it was soon decided that it was too small. From 1668, Le Vau encased the chateau in a rectangular "envelope" of stone. The result was a dazzling and symmetrical balustrade-topped building, comprising three stories lined with windows. A central arched terrace was part of the garden facade, and there were numerous embellishments in the form of stone figures. The royal apartments were on the first floor (the piano nobile), and the elaborate interior decoration was masterminded by Charles Le Brun.

Landscaping, designed by André Le Nôtre, transformed the surrounding parkland into breathtakingly impressive formal gardens, the integrated effect conveying beauty, grandeur and the exquisite taste and absolute power of the French monarch. After Le Vau's death in 1670, François d'Orbay took over, and more would be done after 1678, notably by Jules Hardouin-Mansart. **CH-M**

Adam Thoroughgood House

Architect: Unknown

Completed: 1680 (begun 1636)

Location: Virginia Beach, near Norfolk, Virginia, United States

Style/Period: English Colonial

When the Adam Thoroughgood House was raised near the Lynnhaven River in the English colony of Virginia, the favored architectural style for domestic buildings was based on houses in the settlers' mother country. Research has established that Adam Thoroughgood arrived in Virginia from Norfolk, England, in 1621, and that he acquired the land on which the house stands in 1636. It is thought that the residence — one of the earliest extant colonial structures — was probably built in around 1680 by one of his grandsons. He must have been relatively prosperous, since it was constructed of brick rather than timber, the cheaper and less durable building material.

A one-and-a-half-story dwelling two rooms wide and one room deep, the Adam Thoroughgood House is almost medieval in its simple appearance, having a centrally placed front door flanked by two windows. On each side a chimney rises above the deep, steeply pitched roof, the northerly one being set actually within the wall, and its southerly counterpart having been added to the exterior. Interesting decorative touches include the use of both English- and Flemish-bond-style brickwork and string courses. The house has been sensitively restored during the past 50 years, and today this National Historic Landmark serves as a museum. **CH-M**

Fort Carré

Architect: Marquis de Vauban

Completed: c. 1680 (begun 1550)

Location: Antibes, France

Style/Period: 18th century Military/Vauban

Elevated some 85 feet (26 m) above sea level to sit astride the rocky Saint Roch peninsula, the guns of Fort Carré command the whole of Port Vauban. The port's name refers to the great Frenchman Sébestian Le Prestre de Vauban, whom Louis XIV commissioned to modernize Antibes' defenses, which dated back to 1565. The foremost military engineer of his age, Vauban was principally a master of attack and the author of various treatises on attacking fortresses with artillery via successive lines of specially dug trenches. His systems recognized that no fortress was impregnable to gunfire, and that the purpose of fixed defenses was to delay an invading enemy and soak up their resources in an assault.

Vauban quickly replaced Antibes' old square towers with a star-shaped citadel whose construction reflected his new scientific methods. The vertical masonry walls were exchanged for sloping ramparts of brick and millstone, which would crumble to powder when hit by cannon balls instead of shattering into lethal shards. The angles of the V-shaped bastions were calculated to counteract the use of ricochet cannon fire, itself a Vauban innovation, while providing the maximum field of fire for the defenders' 18 guns. A monument to the great engineer's private game of cat and mouse, Fort Carré was finally made redundant in 1880, not by technology but by the absorption of Nice into French territory, which robbed the fortress of its strategic border significance. **PC**

Dôme des Invalides

Architect: Jules Hardouin-Mansart

Completed: 1691 (begun 1679)

Location: Paris, France

Style/Period: Baroque

Les invalides means disabled soldiers or pensioners in French, so its name suggests that the Church of the Invalides was dedicated to France's military veterans. This is not entirely the case, however. In 1679, when the dome was begun, the "Invalides" complex (established in Paris by order of King Louis XIV in 1670) already included a retirement home and hospital for *les invalides*, as well as a veterans' chapel, the Église de Saint-Louis-des-Invalides, designed by Libéral Bruant. The Dôme des Invalides was intended as a separate royal chapel, and subsequently it became the burial place of Emperor Napoleon I and other French military heroes.

This monumental baroque stone building — modeled on the St. Peter's Basilica in Rome, Italy (now Vatican City) — was the vision of royal architect Jules Hardouin-Mansart. It is fronted by a symmetrical, classically influenced, two-story facade at the center of which is a double-height portico capped by a pediment. Behind that, a huge ribbed dome soars skyward, elevated above its drum by a high attic. Inside, when viewed from below — through an oculus in the coffered inner dome and with the help of concealed windows — it is possible to marvel at the ornately painted interior of the outer dome (the work of Charles de la Fosse), which renders the chapel unmistakably baroque. **CH-M**

Chapel of the Holy Shroud

Architect: Guarino Guarini

Completed: 1694 (begun 1668)

Location: Turin, Italy

Style/Period: Baroque

One of the northern Italian city of Turin's most prized possessions is the Turin Shroud (*Sindone*), an ancient piece of linen said to bear the imprint of Christ's crucified body. From the late 17th century until 1997, this priceless relic was housed in a reliquary shrine at the center of a chapel rotunda specially designed for it by the Modena-born philosopher, mathematician, and architect Guarino Guarini.

Guarini incorporated his Chapel of the Holy Shoud into the eastern end of Turin's 15th-century Renaissance-style cathedral, or *duomo*, the Cattedrale di San Giovanni Battista. When viewed from the exterior, Guarini's fantastic cone-shaped cupola dominates the lower, longer and simpler original structure. It is reached by means of stairways at the ends of the cathedral's aisles and through a gallery leading to the duke of Savoy's adjoining palace. From the inside, the spatial complexity for which Guarini's work is celebrated was visible in the dome's supportive overlapping and segmented arches, whose span decreased the higher they rose. The overall effect was hailed as a masterpiece in the manipulation of vertical perspective. Further, apparently miraculous, effects were achieved by the ethereal quality of the light that filtered in through grids. The chapel was badly damaged by fire in 1997 and is still undergoing restoration. **CH-M**

William and Mary Wings, Hampton Court Palace

Architect: Sir Christopher Wren

Completed: 1694

Location: Hampton, Surrey, England

Style/Period: English Renaissance

King William III, who was of Dutch origin, and Mary II, the elder daughter of England's James II, came to the British throne in 1689 after a bloodless coup and thereafter ruled jointly. The new monarchs looked for a suitable palace to reflect their status but found only Hampton Court, a royal palace that had been built in Tudor times and which, if nothing else, needed modernizing. Christopher Wren, the Surveyor of the King's Works, was chosen to redesign it. He planned to sweep away the old palace and start from scratch, but financial constraints meant that he could only add two new wings of Portland stone and red brick in the baroque style.

Work began in 1689 and was overseen by two of Wren's acolytes, William Talman and Nicholas Hawksmoor. The new design consisted of both state and private apartments. The south wing, which overlooked the Privy Garden, housed the King's apartments, while the east-facing addition overlooked the Fountain Garden and housed the Queen's Wing. These additions came at a time when baroque was giving ground to newer architectural styles, but Hampton Court later inspired 20th century architect Sir Edwin Lutyens to create a new style, a "Wrenaissance," that was hugely popular and influential. **IW**

18th Century

St. Paul's Cathedral

Architect: Sir Christopher Wren

Completed: 1710

Location: City of London, London, England

Style/Period: Baroque

Wren completed his proposals to renovate the existing medieval cathedral on the site a mere week before it was destroyed in the Great Fire of London in September 1666. The architect immediately returned to the drawing board to devise a wholly new church, and he came up with one in the form of a Greek cross with a central dome. The traditionalist ecclesiastical authorities rejected the idea and demanded that the new building be in the shape of a Latin cross, incorporate a choir that could be shut off so that smaller daily services could be held more easily, and have a plan that would allow the cathedral to rise in stages due to financial constraints.

The result was a building that merged classical features, most notably the huge dome, with those of the Gothic style, particularly the cruciform plan, to satisfy the authorities. Wren was not widely traveled, so he relied on his large collection of books filled with engravings of building designs from France and, above all, Italy for inspiration. He produced a stunning baroque cathedral whose scale is suitably awe-inspiring in the traditional Gothic style but also exquisitely decorated as the baroque fashion demanded. The cathedral's great dome has also come to symbolize London. **IW**

Old Royal Naval College

Architect: Sir Christopher Wren

Completed: 1712

Location: Greenwich, London, England

Style/Period: Baroque

The Old Royal Naval College is the centerpiece of a collection of buildings on the south bank of the River Thames that are not only noteworthy for their architectural elegance, but also for their central role in Britain's, and the world's, maritime history. The college actually began life as the Greenwich Hospital, which was built to house sailors who had been injured fighting in a war against the Dutch. Wren was commissioned by Queen Mary II to design the original hospital, and he was aided by his talented apprentice Nicholas Hawksmoor — and both architects did the work for free.

Greenwich Hospital, it became the Royal Naval College in 1873, consists of four main blocks. They were known as courts and were named after four monarchs — kings Charles and William and queens Mary and Anne. The courts are split by a north-south divide so that the Queen's House, which stands on Greenwich Hill behind the hospital, could still have an uninterrupted view of the Thames. The site is also divided by a road running from east to west. The Old Royal Naval College finally closed in 1998, a year after the entire area had been given World Heritage Site status by UNESCO. **IW**

Old State House

Architect: Unknown

Completed: 1713

Location: Boston, Massachusetts, United States

Style/Period: English Colonial

The elegant colonial-style Old State House — sometimes referred to as the "Towne House" — is not only the oldest surviving public building in the Massachusetts state capital, but it was also the seat of the first elected legislature in the New World. However, its greatest claim to fame came on July 18, 1776, when local people gathered to hear the first public reading of the Declaration of Independence from its small balcony.

In fact, the building had several functions when it was first built. The ground floor was a merchants' exchange, and the basement was used for warehousing. The second floor was largely given over to administrative and political work. The east side contained the council chamber, while the west side housed the courts of Suffolk County and the Massachusetts Supreme Judicial Court. The central section consists of chambers to accommodate the elected Massachusetts Assembly and is the earliest known example of a public gallery in a chamber for elected officials. The red brick building is wonderfully symmetrical and is a fine example of the evolving colonial style. Judging from its architectural influences, it seems most likely that, somewhat ironically, it was designed by a British-trained architect. **IW**

Saint Mary-le-Strand

Architect: James Gibbs

Completed: 1717

Location: The Strand, London, England

Style/Period: Neobaroque

Saint Mary's, which now sits somewhat stranded on a major thoroughfare in the English capital, was the first of several new churches built by a body known as the Commission for Building 50 New Churches, who asked one of their own ex-members, James Gibbs, to design what would be his first public building. Steeped in the Italianesque High baroque style, largely because he had studied in Rome under Carlo Fontana, Gibbs wanted a pure

Italianate church complete with a small bell tower at the west end, but the remaining commissioners subsequently insisted that he add a steeple, using stone purchased for another project.

The architect, who had been removed as a commissioner in 1715, reluctantly complied and took his inspiration from Sir Christopher Wren's works. Somewhat in contrast, the interior of the church is pure high baroque, and the ceiling in particular was inspired by decorative work completed in Rome by Fontana and the painter and architect Pietro da Cortona, another leading figure in the high baroque movement. Despite the project being beset by several problems, Saint Mary's was eventually much lauded, and Gibbs went on to design a number of other churches in London, notably Saint-Martin-in-the-Fields (see page 152). **IW**

Blenheim Palace

Architect: Sir John Vanburgh

Completed: c. 1722

Location: Woodstock, Oxfordshire, England

Style/Period: English Baroque

Blenheim Palace and the surrounding estate was given to John Churchill, the first Duke of Marlborough, by Queen Anne in gratitude for his numerous victories during the War of the Spanish Succession (1701–1714), and it is named after his greatest victory over the French. The queen also chose playwright and architect John Vanburgh to design the new building. This decision did not please the duke's wife, Sara, a close companion of Anne's, who actually wanted a somewhat smaller home and not something akin to a national monument. There was so much

friction between the architect and Sara Churchill, who bitterly resented the cost, that Vanburgh was eventually fired in 1716. Nicholas Hawksmoor saw the project through to completion.

Blenheim clearly celebrates the duke's victories — sculptures, such as a symbolic lion of England attacking the rooster of France, dominated the skyline. There are also sculptural piles of cannonballs and reversed fleurs-de-lis. Vanburgh also created what is generally considered to be one of the finest examples of the baroque style found in England. Blenheim is imposing and monumental in scope, yet it is also highly romantic. **IW**

Upper Schloss Belvedere

Architect: Johann Luckas von Hildebrandt

Completed: 1723

Location: Landstrasse, Vienna, Austria

Style/Period: Baroque

Schloss Belvedere, which lies in a southeastern district of Vienna, was created for Prince Eugene of Savoy and consists of two wings — the earlier single-story Lower Belvedere, which was intended to be no more than a pavilion, and the more architecturally interesting and majestic Upper Belvedere, which consists of three stories and a central attic and was built a decade or so later. The two wings face each other across formal gardens. However, the latter is widely considered to be Hildebrandt's most successful building — he also completed the Lower Belvedere — and is generally credited with introducing the high baroque style with French influences into Austrian architecture.

Hildebrandt was a military engineer and served under the prince during his campaigns in northern Italy, where he most likely developed a taste for baroque buildings, between 1695 and 1701, the year he was made Vienna's court engineer. He had also studied in Rome under Carlo Fontana, who himself had been a pupil of Gian Lorenzo Bernini, the leading light of the Italian baroque movement. The Upper Belvedere shows Hildebrandt at the height of his architectural powers, and it perfectly captures the high baroque style. **IW**

Church of Saint-Martin-in-the-Fields

Architect: James Gibbs

Completed: 1726

Location: Trafalgar Square, London, England

Style/Period: Neobaroque/Palladian

Saint-Martin's is a pivotal piece of ecclesiastical architecture. Scottish-born designer Gibbs created a Palladian building in Portland stone that combined elements of classical architecture (a temple) with elements of the Gothic style (the tower and steeple) for the first time. Gibbs had, in fact, studied in Italy for a time under Swiss-born Carlo Fontana, making him unique among his contemporaries. The frontage is most recognizably inspired by the temples and public buildings of the classical world, while the steeple emulated works completed in London by Sir Christopher Wren. Gibbs, who was both a disciple and friend of Wren, even went to the trouble of escorting the church authorities around a number of Wren's own churches in the capital to gain their approval.

The interior was inspired by Wren, too, but Gibbs was also attuned to the sensibilities of his contemporaries. His *Book of Architecture* contained the drawings for many of his works, including Saint-Martin's, and was published some two years after its construction. It became hugely influential, especially in Britain and North America, where Saint-Martin's-style churches were built in large numbers. **IW**

Zwinger Palace

Architect: Matthäus Daniel Pöppelmann

Completed: 1728 (begun 1710)

Location: Dresden, Germany

Style/Period: Late Baroque/Rococo

The summer palace that Matthäus Daniel Pöppelmann designed for Augustus II, "The Strong," Elector of Saxony and, from 1700, King of Poland, on a bank of the River Elbe in Dresden (Saxony's capital) contributed significantly to Dresden being described as the "Venice of the North" and the "Baroque Florence." *Zwinger* signifies a castle's outer ward in German, and Augustus II intended his to house a fantastic pleasure palace adjacent to his official residence that would also serve as the backdrop to pageants. The combination of the solemn, classically influenced late baroque and the playful, frivolous rococo styles was ideal for the purpose. Pöppelmann initiated (but did not finish) a magnificent edifice of sandstone with two-story pavilions linked by single-story galleries enclosing a central courtyard. The rows of high, arched windows were particularly striking, as were the lavish ornamentation and elaborate sculptures that adorned the walls and gardens, the work of Balthasar Permoser. But the most iconic feature of the *zwinger* remains the vast Polish crown that surmounts the Kronentor (the Crown Gate).

The *zwinger* did not escape the devastation wreaked on Dresden at the end of World War II by the Allied bombing raid and subsequent firestorm of 13–14 February, 1945, but it has since been lovingly restored. **CH-M**

Chiswick House

Architect: Lord Burlington

Completed: 1729 (begun 1725)

Location: Chiswick, London, England

Style/Period: Neopalladian

Perhaps unusually for an aristocrat, Richard Boyle, the third Earl of Burlington, was not only a patron but also an architect. Lord Burlington is, moreover, credited with having introduced Palladianism to England, having been inspired by Colen Campbell's book *Vitruvius Britannicus* (1715) and by the Palladian buildings he had seen in Italy. Chiswick House in west London is exemplary of his work and is modeled on Andrea Palladio's Villa Rotonda (see page 118), albeit with modifications to suit the designer's preferences and the English setting. It was constructed in collaboration with William Kent, who took charge of the interior decoration.

Situated amid spectacularly landscaped and statuary-dotted Italianate grounds, this ornamental neoclassical villa stands out on account of its pale masonry and the purity of its symmetrical design. A dome, with the addition of windows to alleviate the English gloom in the central octagonal saloon below, rises from a shallowly pitched roof, with four chimneys flanking each side, above a square main building. There are three different facades (only the sides are identical), and, when approached from the entrance gates and driveway, twin flights of staircases at each corner of a rusticated ground story lead to a piano nobile (noble floor), at the center of which is a hexastyle Corinthian portico. **CH-M**

Jantar Mantar

Architect: Unknown

Completed: 1733

Location: Jaipur, Rajasthan, India

Style/Period: Indo-Mogul

The Jantar Mantar is a series of architectural astronomical instruments. *Jantar* is the Hindu word for "instrument" and *Mantar* is derived from mantra, meaning "chanting," but these large geometric and highly sculptured forms are actually 14 precise scientific measuring devices. They were created by Maharajah Jai Singh II, the founder of Jaipur and a keen astronomer, and measure, among other things, time. They also predict eclipses, track stars as they make their way across the heavens, fix the declinations of planets and determine the altitudes of celestial bodies.

The Jantar Mantar is the largest of five such sites dotted across India, and all of its instruments are highly accurate. The largest instrument at the site is a 90-foot (27 m) sundial, which is also the largest in the world. It has a face angled at 27 degrees, the same latitude as Jaipur, and the shadow it casts is accurate to two seconds. The sundial is topped by a small domed cupola, which was used to predict eclipses and the onset of the monsoon. Work on the complex, which was built in stone and marble, began in 1728, and it was made a national monument in 1948. Three other complexes survive in Delhi, Ujjain and Varanasi. **IW**

Shirley Plantation House

Architect: Unknown

Completed: 1738

Location: Charles City County, Virginia, United States

Style/Period: Georgian Colonial

Located on the banks of James River, Shirley Plantation House is the oldest plantation in the state of Virginia and the oldest family-owned business anywhere in the United States. The site has been occupied since 1613, but construction work on the present mansion began in 1723, when Elizabeth Hill, daughter of the owner, married John Carter. The so-called "Great House" was completed 15 years later, and it has been handed down through the Carter-Hill family for generations. It is a remarkable example of a building largely preserved in its original form with many of its interior decorations and embellishments still intact.

The mansion has what is known as the Queen Anne Forecourt, the only surviving example of its kind in America. It consists of a two-story kitchen, a laundry house and two barns, one with an ice cellar beneath it. The interior of the mansion also contains several unique features, not least the elegant "flying staircase" that is made out of walnut and appears to have no visible means of support. The plantation house is very much a time capsule of mid-colonial interior design and architectural style, and its uniqueness is unmatched. IW

Leinster House

Architect: Richard Cassels

Completed: 1748

Location: Merrion Street, Dublin, Republic of Ireland

Style/Period: Neoclassical

Leinster House was originally known as Kildare House, named after the peer behind its construction, James Fitzgerald, Earl of Kildare. He was Ireland's senior peer and hatched a plan to build a large Georgian mansion in what was then a highly unfashionable part of south Dublin; the earl dryly noted that fashion would follow wherever he led, and he was proved right. He turned to Richard Cassels (or possibly

Castle), who was born in Germany around 1690, for the design, and work on the residence began in 1745. One facade, which looks toward the city, resembles a town house, while the other, which would originally have looked out over countryside, resembles a country residence. It was renamed Leinster House when Fitzgerald was made the first duke of Leinster in 1766, and since 1922 has been home to the country's parliament.

It is widely believed that Leinster House was the inspiration for the White House in Washington D.C. Its architect, James Hoban, who won the competition to design the White House in 1792, was from Ireland and had studied in Dublin. He appears to have used Leinster House's first and second floors as a model, as well as the cut stone exterior for the original White House's facade. **IW**

Radcliffe Camera

Architect: James Gibbs

Completed: 1749

Location: Oxford, Oxfordshire, England

Style/Period: English Palladian

Although Oxford has been dubbed the "City of Dreaming Spires" and its skyline is largely a forest of towers and steeples, there is one noteworthy exception — the magnificent dome of the Radcliffe Camera. The building was funded through a bequest in the will of Dr. John Radcliffe, a leading physician of considerable wealth. The original concept was by Nicholas Hawksmoor, who drew up plans for a domed rotunda to house the benefactor's library. Gibbs, whose own plans for the site had been rejected, was

subsequently asked to modify Hawksmoor's design, and construction work began in the late 1730s.

Hawksmoor's work was fairly straightforward, but Gibbs gave it an extra dimension, most notably by adding the pairs of columns around the central section, which are matched by the paired urns that sit along the balustrade above them. The interior contains bookcases on two levels and a reading room that is reached by a spiral staircase. The building's beauty is enhanced by its setting in the center of an elegant square made up in part by All Souls and Brasenose Colleges and Oxford Cathedral. The Radcliffe Camera is generally regarded as the most architecturally successful single building in the city. **IW**

Die Wies Pilgrimage Church

Architect: Dominikus Zimmermann
Completed: 1754 (begun 1745)
Location: Steingaden, Bavaria, Germany
Style/Period: Late Baroque/Rococo

After a wooden statue of the scourged Savior (Christ) seemed to start weeping in 1738, a chapel was built at Steingaden Abbey, in the southern German region of Bavaria, to enable Roman Catholic believers to view the figure and pray in front of it. Within a few years the chapel could no longer accommodate those flocking from all over Europe to this rural Alpine spot, which is why a design for a larger pilgrimage church was commissioned from a local architect (and former stuccoist), the Wessobrunn-born Dominikus Zimmermann. And not only is the church that Zimmermann created – Die Wies – now regarded as his masterpiece, it is today a UNESCO World Heritage Site.

Approached from afar, Die Wies appears to be a simple, if large, church, whose oval and oblong ground plan describes a rough cross shape, with an onion-domed bell tower at one end and white-painted walls rising to a steeply pitched roof. Venture inside, however, and the contrast couldn't be more striking: light streams in through the windows, illuminating a riot of color and movement in the form of statuary, painted stuccowork and a frescoed ceiling with spectacular trompe l'oeil effects — the work of Johann Baptist Zimmermann, Dominikus's brother. **CH-M**

Villa Pisani Stable Block

Architect: Girolamo Frigimelica
Completed: c. 1760
Location: Stra, Veneto, Italy
Style/Period: Late Baroque

The Pisani were an influential Venetian family who had made a fortune from trade and business and became hugely influential within the city-state's political circles. Very successful members of Venice's nobility had country villas, with many built along the River Brenta that links Venice with Padua. Traditionally these homes were constructed on a fairly modest scale, but the Pisani family wanted something grander, an imposing villa set in extensive gardens that would reflect their wealth and status.

They turned to Frigimelica, a Padua-born architect, who found inspiration in the Palace of Versailles. He came up with a plan in around 1716 to build a large villa in the late baroque style with a hint of classicism. The main building has a broad facade topped with statuary and an imposing central entrance, and the Pisanis decided to echo this with the villa's stable block, which faces the main building but is separated from it by two long sweeps of lawn divided by a wide artificial water feature. Stables were commonly plain, being purely functional buildings, and often hidden away, but the Pisani family decided to build their block in a prominent position and in the style of the main building, again to demonstrate their spending power. Ironically, the lavish spending on the villa and gardens nearly bankrupted the family. **IW**

Pineapple House

Architect: Unknown

Completed: c. 1761

Location: Dunmore House, Falkirk, Scotland

Style/Period: Gothic/Eclectic

This witty garden folly was created for John Murray, the 4th Earl of Dunmore. He had spent time as the governor of the British-controlled Bahamas, the Caribbean island group with a large number of pineapple plantations. Pineapples were rare and expensive in Europe, so Murray set out to show his own wealth and status by creating a folly to sit on top of an existing hothouse that could function as both a summerhouse and heated greenhouse in which to grow the exotic fruits.

The name of the architect remains a mystery, but some attribute the house to Sir William Chambers. Whatever the case, the house itself is Palladian in influence, with more than just a hint of neoclassicism. More than anything else, the pineapple is a superb example of the stonemason's art — each of the leaves was carved to drain independently, for example — and was well suited to its purpose. Heat from the furnace was channeled through cavities in the walls to heat the interior before escaping from chimneys disguised as large vases. The house was purchased by the National Trust of Scotland and can now be rented as a weekend holiday home through the Landmark Trust. **IW**

The Pagoda

Architect: William Chambers

Completed: 1762 (begun 1761)

Location: Kew Gardens, Kew, Surrey, England

Style/Period: Chinoiserie

At around 164 feet (50 m) tall, the Pagoda (or, as it is also known, the Chinese Pagoda) that stands in the grounds of the Royal Botanic Gardens at Kew is visible from miles around. The gardens were developed starting in 1759 as part of a beautification project sponsored by Princess Augusta, the mother of the future King George III. The Pagoda, which was designed by the Swedish-born William Chambers, Augusta's personal architect from 1757 onward, was built in Chinese style, partly because Chambers had visited China for the Swedish East India Company (his book *Designs of Chinese Buildings* was also published in 1757), and partly because exotic Oriental art forms were then all the rage in Europe, reflecting both increased trade with the Far East and a desire for novelty.

The ornamental Pagoda still appears exotic in its English setting. Its 10 brick stories taper upward, each diminishing in size as they rise toward the apical spike. Together they form an octagonal tower, whose levels are both defined by arched recesses on each side (every other one of which is glazed) and delineated by iron railings above skirted roofs, which once boasted iron dragons — 80 in all — on each edge. **CH-M**

Winter Palace

Architect: Francesco Rastrelli

Completed: 1762

Location: Palace Square, Saint Petersburg, Russia

Style/Period: Late Baroque

Rastrelli was the imperial Russian court architect starting in 1730, and he was commissioned by Empress Elizabeth to build a sumptuous and grandiose palace in central Saint Petersburg, then the Russian capital. The work began in 1754, and the Italian-born architect produced a late baroque style building, but one with certain Russian sensibilities. The block consists of three floors and has a green and white and gold facade that includes a riot of decorative embellishments, including columns, pediments and sculptures. Elizabeth, however, died the same year as the palace's completion.

Rastrelli created a building with around 1,000 rooms, and the interiors were as sumptuous as the exterior, although the original Winter Palace was built in a style that was soon to go out of fashion. Catherine the Great almost loathed it. When it was largely destroyed by fire in 1837, only the so-called Jordan Staircase was restored. The remainder was renovated in different styles, chiefly neoclassical, Greek revival and baroque revival. Today it is part of the internationally renowned Hermitage Museum. **IW**

Palacio Real

Architects: Filippo Juvarra, Giovanni Sacchetti, Ventura Rodriguez and Francisco Sabatini

Completed: 1764

Location: Plaza de Cibeles, Madrid, Spain

Style/Period: Late Baroque/Rococo

By any standard, the official residence of the Spanish royal family, which is now largely used for formal state occasions, is immense. It is the biggest royal palace in Western Europe, with a gigantic floor space and containing 2,800 rooms of various types. The opportunity to build a new palace came when an old Moorish castle on the spot was destroyed by fire in 1734, and

King Philip V ordered a new royal residence. He died in 1746, and the work was actually completed under his successors, Ferdinand VI and Charles III.

The palace owes much to a design created by Gian Bernini, the leading figure of the baroque movement, for the Louvre Palace in Paris that never saw the light of day. A succession of architects worked on the Spanish palace, but the chief ones were fellow Italians, Juvarra — who planned a palace four times the size — and Sacchetti, one of his pupils. They were also aided by Rodriguez and Sabatini. The ornate late baroque building they completed in granite and white Colmenar stone is essentially a quadrilateral with 459-foot (140 m) sides that surrounds a large courtyard. **IW**

Keddleston Hall

Architects: Robert Adam, James Paine and Matthew Brettingham

Completed: 1765

Location: Derby, Derbyshire, England

Style/Period: Neoclassical

In 1759 Sir Nathaniel Curzon commissioned a country house from James Paine and Matthew Brettingham, and they set out to design one in the Palladian style. Curzon, however, became mightily impressed with the work being done by Robert Adam on some decorative temples in the hall's grounds, and he transferred the hall's plans to him. Adam, who had spent several years in Italy absorbing classical influences, modified the original plans. The hall's north facade remains largely Palladian (Adam did manage to add a more imposing portico with six Corinthian columns), but the south facade is in the neoclassical style. Adam pioneered this style, and it became hugely influential across Europe and North America in the late 18th century.

The building is essentially in three parts, with the east and west wings holding the family rooms and the domestic rooms respectively. The center block, which contains the state rooms, is purely neoclassical and is based on the Arch of Constantine in Rome. Adam was also able to rework the interior and add similar flourishes, including creating an atrium. He also transformed the grounds, doing away with the original formal gardens and replacing them with a more naturalistic landscape. Keddleston Hall marked the beginning of a revolution in country house design. **IW**

The Upper Mill

Architect: Richard Arkwright (attrib.)

Completed: 1771

Location: Cromford Mill, Derwent Valley, Derbyshire, England

Style/Period: Georgian Industrial

A wigmaker by profession, Richard Arkwright had spent over 10 years devising a mechanical means of spinning cotton yarn that he hoped would make him his fortune. Perfected with the help of clockmaker John Kay, Arkwright's first spinning-frame was too large to be powered by hand, and it was the expense of using horse-gins that encouraged him to harness Cromford's waters.

Built in 1771, the Upper Mill is a largely conventional Georgian affair, its gritstone walls being lined with brick and spanned by timber beams. What made it revolutionary was its scale and contents. Its 5 stories of 11 bays allowed many spinning machines to be turned by a single waterwheel. Rechristened the "Water-Frame" Arkwright's machines were simple enough to be worked by children, and he actively recruited entire families to relocate to Cromford to live and work within his expanding industrial complex. It was this bringing together of people, power and the means of production in one place that made Cromford's cotton mills the quantum leap from earlier cottage industry. With 208 British imitators in operation by 1788, Cromford was truly the template for the factory age. Protected as a key part of a UNESCO World Heritage Site, the Upper Mill remains a gritty monument to the day the world took off. **PC**

Vierzehnheiligen Pilgrimage Church

Architect: Balthasar Neumann

Completed: 1772 (begun 1743)

Location: Near Bad Staffelstein, Bavaria, Germany

Style/Period: Rococo

Vierzehnheiligen means "14 saints" in German, the 14 saints in question being the " holy helpers" (auxiliary or intercessor saints) to whom the Roman Catholic faithful in need pray inside the pilgrimage church of the same name in Bavaria, southern Germany. There has been a chapel dedicated to the *Vierzehnheiligen* on this site, in a hamlet near Bad Staffelstein, since at least 1448. It was here, in 1445, that a shepherd saw the first of a series of visions instructing him to build a chapel-home for the 14. The magnificent basilica that today stands on the spot dates from 1772, however, when architect Balthasar Neumann completed what has since become one of Bavaria's most celebrated pilgrimage churches.

Two copper-clad onion-domed bell towers constructed of stone flank the central, portico-containing, section of the undulating main facade. Although the exterior appears almost forbidding in its relatively restrained, classically inspired late baroque grandeur, the basilica's light-filled interior is an exuberant rococo fantasy. Here, amid the supportive columns, a complex design of interlinked ovals and circles gives a sense of organic growth — and, in the baldachins, the presence of heaven — with a riot of swirls, statues, paintings and other rococo flourishes providing an impression of energy and movement. **CH-M**

Royal Crescent

Architect: John Wood the Younger

Completed: 1774

Location: Bath, Somerset, England

Style/Period: Georgian

This is arguably the most perfectly realized crescent in Europe. It consists of 30 individual homes that sweep around in a full semiellipse so the houses at the two ends directly face each other. Wood the Younger built in the local gold-colored Bath stone, and his great idea was to create a harmonious frontage but leave the layout of the individual interiors as a matter between the various building contractors and their clients. Work began in 1767.

The architect chose to unify the whole crescent by creating a sumptuously symmetrical Palladian facade that at first-floor level consists of an elegant colonnade of 114 Ionic columns each 20 feet (6 m) high. These columns are displayed singularly except at the crescent's center and ends, which are marked by double columns. To the casual eye it almost appears as if the crescent is a single country house, rather than a collection of family homes — a feeling heightened by the extensive green laid out before the block. It is interesting to note that the rear of the crescent totally rejects the harmony imposed by Wood the Younger on its front elevation, as the various contractors all imposed their individual designs on it. **IW**

Monticello

Architect: Thomas Jefferson

Completed: 1782

Location: Charlottesville, Virginia, United States

Style/Period: Colonial Georgian

Monticello (Italian for "Little Mountain") was a prolonged labor of love by Jefferson (1743–1826), who also found time to be, among other things, a lawyer, a leading figure in the drafting of the Declaration of Independence and the third president of the United States. He was also a keen student of architecture, who had built up an extensive library, including Andrea Palladio's *Quattro Libri dell'Architetura*, which would have a deep impact on his design aesthetics. Work on Monticello, which sits on a grassy rise, began in 1768, and the greater part of the work was completed by the early 1780s, although Jefferson worked on it until his death.

The home is in what is known as the colonial Georgian style, a distinctive U.S. style. It is based on a cross, with most emphasis on the horizontal wings, and it is an undoubtedly understated building — a country mansion that is not domineering, but one that nevertheless exudes power. Although Jefferson took his inspiration from Palladio, he was unafraid to modify the style to accommodate U.S. sensibilities. He also incorporated many innovative features, including disguised closets and both swinging and sliding doors. **IW**

Somerset House

Architect: Sir William Chambers

Completed: 1786

Location: The Strand, London, England

Style/Period: Palladian

Chambers was one of 18th-century Georgian England's leading architects in the popular neoclassical style. As the country was growing in national self-confidence, Chambers, who would become the country's surveyor-general in 1782, was asked to design a grand semipublic building that would function both as offices for the country's growing civil service and the home for various learned bodies, including the Royal Society, the Royal Academy and the Society of Antiquaries. He was fortunate that the site, once home to a palace built for Edward Seymour, 1st Duke of Somerset, was large and overlooking the River Thames.

Construction began in 1776 after the demolition of the original 16th-century Somerset House, and work on Chambers' central block continued after his death, with the work mostly overseen by James Wyatt. The main part of the Embankment building was finished in 1786, and most of the rest of

the building finished by 1809, but records
show that finishing touches were not
completed for another decade. When
completed, Somerset House was not only
England's first purpose-built government
building, but it was also a statement of the
country's burgeoning national pride, not least
because of the quality of its architecture and
the craftsmanship with which it was built. IW

Pavlovsk Palace

Architect: Charles Cameron

Completed: 1787

Location: Pavlovsk, Saint Petersburg, Russia

Style/Period: Neoclassical

This superb example of neoclassical
architecture was created for the heir to the
Russian imperial throne, but the driving
force behind it was the formidable Catherine
the Great. The empress passed the existing
estate, which was little more than dense
forest, to Grand Duke Pavel Petrovich and
his wife in 1777, but little more than a few
unremarkable buildings were built over the
next few years. Matters changed in 1780
when Cameron, Catherine's favorite
designer, was commissioned to create a
wholly new palace and lay out an
appropriately grand park. Work began two
years later.

   Cameron came up with a light and
elegant structure that is Palladian in
inspiration but owes more to the Georgian
style pioneered by Robert Adam, a fellow
Scot. It consists of a central block with two
curving wings that each terminates in a
square pavilion. Scale was added to the
palace by crowning the roof with a large
circular dome that was inspired by the
Pantheon in Rome. Although the exterior is
relatively unembellished, Cameron had
planned a dazzlingly ornate interior but was
fired, with the work going to Vincenzo
Brenna. The palace was badly damaged
during World War II, but subsequently it was
sympathetically restored. IW

Mansion House

Architect: George Washington

Completed: 1787

Location: Mount Vernon, Virginia, United States

Style/Period: Georgian Neoclassical

Washington became increasing involved with the Mount Vernon plantation after the death of the owner, his half-brother Lawrence, in 1752, and he took it over fully following the death of the latter's widow in 1760. He set about extending the plantation, eventually quadrupling its extent, and constructed a fitting central family residence. The house then evolved over the years. Washington extended the existing Mansion House, a humbler affair, by adding an extra story and redecorating the interior. Next came the north and south wings, which were completed just before the beginning of the Revolutionary War in 1776, and the last addition, the Large Dining Room, was completed after its end.

Washington also transformed the exterior using a process known as rustication. The existing wooden planking was removed and replaced by bevel-edged pine blocks that had been coated with a mix of paint and sand to give the appearance of stone. Other embellishments were a grand columned piazza (porch) and a cupola. Washington created a neoclassical mansion that was typical of the period, but colonial sensibilities and materials influenced his design — wood block cladding was never used on country houses in Georgian England. **IW**

Meetinghouse

Architect: Unknown

Completed: 1793

Location: Hancock Shaker Village, near Pittsfield, Massachusetts, United States

Style/Period: Shaker/Dutch Colonial

As its name indicates, Hancock Shaker Village, near Pittsfield in Massachusetts, was once home to a community of Shakers (an offshoot of the Quakers), whose ecstatic mode of worship caused their bodies to shake. The sect was founded in England and was introduced to England's North American colonies by Ann Lee in 1774. Now virtually extinct as a movement, the Shakers are probably best known for their furniture, whose simplicity and utility give it an ageless appeal. The same can be said about Shaker-approved architecture, as exemplified by the buildings preserved at Hancock Shaker Village, which was inhabited between 1790 and 1960, before becoming a museum and a National Historic Landmark.

In Shaker communities, meetinghouses took the place of churches. They were therefore buildings of primary importance, which is why they were typically situated in the center of the village. Hancock Shaker Village's Dutch colonial style wooden meetinghouse is three stories high (the two-sloped gable roof accommodating two stories) and, reflecting the Shakers' emphasis on celibacy, has separate entrances for men and women. The original meetinghouse was demolished in 1939, and the near-identical structure that now stands in its place was moved here in 1962 from Shirley, Massachusetts, where it was originally constructed in 1793. **CH-M**

Georgian House

Architect: Robert Adam

Completed: 1796

Location: Charlotte Square, Edinburgh, Scotland

Style/Period: Georgian Neoclassical

Charlotte Square is one of the Scottish capital's most exclusive residential areas, and the so-called Georgian House, actually No. 7 Charlotte Square in the city's New Town, is one of its most prestigious addresses. Today the upper floors are home to the annually elected leader of the Church of Scotland, but the lower floors are a perfectly preserved time capsule of a fine late-18th-century town house. Robert Adam, a Scot by birth, was the key figure in the evolution of what is now the distinctive Georgian architectural style.

Palladian architecture based on traditional classical proportions and lines was the dominant architectural form of the era, but Adam, who had visited Italy to study Classical buildings, gradually began to develop a style of his own, the neoclassical, in which lightness and elegance counted for as much, and increasingly more, than strictly classical proportions, the hallmark of Palladian architecture. Adam's designs incorporated elements of Byzantine, Greek and Italian Baroque styles. His revolution caught on, and he was closely involved in Scotland's most famous urban renewal project, Edinburgh's New Town, which is now a UNESCO World Heritage Site. **IW**

Jal Mahal

Architect: Unknown

Completed: 1799

Location: Jaipur, Rajasthan, India

Style/Period: Indo-Mogul

Although the name Mahal suggests that this highly ornate building is a royal palace, it is not a permanent royal residence. It was built for nothing more than entertainment, albeit on a spectacular scale. Maharajah Pratap Singh decreed that he needed a structure that could both function as a pleasure garden and as a suitable location for duck-shooting parties for family and friends. As Rajasthan is an extremely dry region, he opted to create a large artificial stretch of water, the Man Sagar Lake, which could be filled during the monsoon season by building a long dam between two hills.

The "palace" is some five stories high, and as the water rises only the top floor actually remains above the level of the lake. The building is reached by a long causeway, and the top floor is largely given over to areas of shade and ornate gardens. The Jal Mahal was neglected for many years, and the lake had become little more than a stinking open sewer, but both are currently undergoing extensive and costly restoration to bring them back to their former glory. **IW**

Hawa Mahal

Architect: Ustad Lal Chand

Completed: 1799

Location: Jaipur, Rajasthan, India

Style/Period: Indo-Mogul

Jaipur was an early example of a planned new city. It was established by Maharajah Jai Singh II (1693–1743), who laid it out in blocks according to concepts set down in an ancient Hindu treatise on architecture, the *Shilpa-Shastra*. The city is renowned for its red sandstone buildings, and the five-story Hawa Mahal ("Palace of the Winds"), which was modeled on the crown of the Hindu god Krishna, is one of the finest. Although it exhibits elements of both Rajput and Mogul architectural aesthetics, it is not actually a palace, but rather an elaborate viewing screen from where the ladies of the court could remain hidden while watching proceedings in the bustling local bazaar below.

Entrance to the palace is to the rear, where there are a series of ramps to the upper floors. The building, however, is not at all deep, and the top three stories are little more than a room wide. Nevertheless, its main facade is an impressive 50 feet (15 m) high and pierced by 953 windows that are beautifully decorated with various designs in white lime wash. The windows protected the viewers' modesty, but they were also an eminently practical way of bringing cooling winds into the often stiflingly hot interiors. **IW**

19th Century 1800–1849

Fort McHenry

Architect: Unknown

Completed: 1802 (begun 1799)

Location: Locust Point, Baltimore, United States

Style/Period: Federal Military

Barely visible from land or sea, the low-lying silhouette of Fort McHenry might seem an improbable piece of "iconic architecture," but its special place in American history lends a double meaning to this well-worn accolade. Built to defend the vital port of Baltimore, the fort's only action began on September 13, 1814, with a punitive attack by 19 Royal Navy warships. Their intent was to destroy a base of American privateers that had been preying upon the British merchant fleet. Frustrated by foul weather and a chain of sunken ships strung across the harbor's entrance, the British turned their guns upon Fort McHenry, launching a barrage of over 1,500 shells and round shot.

Constructed using Vauban's 17th century principals of defense (see page 142), the fort's low earthen ramparts were able to weather this iron storm. When the British commanders gazed through their telescopes the next morning, they were greeted by the sight of an immense American flag flying defiantly in the breeze. Witnessing this scene from the British flagship was an American lawyer named Francis Scott Key, who had gone on board to negotiate the release of an imprisoned family friend. The flag touched a patriotic nerve within Key's creative mind, and, inspired, he penned "The Defence of Fort McHenry," which has since become America's anthem, "The Star-Spangled Banner." Set against such a historic backdrop, it is hard not to view the fort's five-pointed star plan as an inadvertent piece of architectural iconography. **PC**

Gardner-Pingree House

Architect: Samuel McIntire

Completed: 1805 (begun 1804)

Location: 128 Essex Street, Salem, Massachusetts, United States

Style/Period: Federalist/Adam

The United States may have forced Britain to concede the independence of its North American colonies in 1783, but that did not mean the young nation wished to turn its back on Britain altogether. The Federalist style that characterized much of America's architecture between around 1776 and 1800 was influenced by the neoclassical example of the Scottish brothers Robert and James Adam.

One of the leading architects of the early Federalist era was Samuel McIntire of Salem, Massachusetts. He started out as a wood-carver, taught himself the principles of architecture and is consequently described as a craftsman-builder. John Gardner, a prosperous merchant, commissioned McIntire to build a town house in Salem. When work was completed in 1805, the rectangular Gardner residence stood three stories high and was topped with a hipped roof. Modish neoclassical features included an elegantly restrained symmetrical facade and, adding a touch of grandeur to the front door, a portico with columns. McIntire incorporated local elements into this imposing-looking house, too, not least the bricks from which it was constructed and the decorative wooden window shutters. The Gardner-Pingree House, which is now owned by the Essex Institute, is today a National Historic Landmark. **CH-M**

Homewood House

Architect: Charles Carroll Junior

Completed: 1806 (begun 1802)

Location: Baltimore, Maryland, United States

Style/Period: Federal/Early Neoclassical

The cornerstone of any 18th-century gentleman's education, the Grand Tour was designed to introduce wealthy young men to the refinement of the art and architecture of the classical world. The aristocracy of Europe was joined by the sons of America's elite, including a certain Charles Carroll Junior whose father had been one of the signatories of the Declaration of Independence.

Returned from his enlightening cultural expedition, the young Charles was duly wed in 1800 and prepared to assume the dignified role of a country gentleman. His doting father gifted him a 130-acre (52 ha) plot of land along with the funds to transform the farmhouse into a suitable family home. Charles Senior cannot have envisaged how his son's continental travels would translate into an ambitious architectural adventure costing him over $40,000 dollars (about $1 million today). This was due in part to the headstrong boy assuming the role of architect — his constant indecision contributed to the spiraling costs as he ripped out completed work in order to implement his ever-changing ideas.

Despite this ad-hoc approach, the building is an elegant affair. Its mellow red brick exterior is graced by a slender columned white portico, while the interiors are adorned with delicate fan lights and lines of plaster moldings inspired by Robert Adam. His masterpiece complete, the young Charles tragically failed to find a new goal in life and gradually descended into terminal alcoholism. Now a National Historic Landmark, Homewood remains a touching monument to his grand designs. **PC**

ends in a central bay on the floor above.

Today No. 13 holds a museum. Its main architectural attraction is the interior, which is a riotous but delightful maze of rooms packed with Soane's various collections. Some rooms are top-lit to ease viewing, and Soane devised an ingenious space-saving device to show his paintings — a series of folding panels. The museum was opened to the public on Soane's death, as he intended. **IW**

Martello Tower

Architects: General William Twiss and
Captain W.H. Ford
Completed: c. 1812
Location: Aldeburgh, Suffolk, England
Style/Period: Napoleonic/Georgian Military

It is something of an irony that a tower in Napoleon's native Corsica should have provided the blueprint for the British coastal defenses built to resist him. In 1794 a solitary tower on Corsica's Mortella Point successfully fended off two Royal Navy warships. Their round shot made little impression on its thick curved walls. Obliged to laboriously capture it by land, the British were so impressed by the tower's stubborn resistance that they made a detailed survey of its structure and adapted it to their own defensive needs. Only the name failed to translate: the place name "Mortella" being confused with "Torre di Martello," the Italian term for coast-guard tower.

The Martello Tower at Aldeburgh is the only one in the chain of 105 English forts to use a quatrefoil plan, as opposed to the usual single brick drum. This allowed it to mount not one but four heavy guns on revolving pivot mounts whose combined firepower compensated for the tower's exposed position at the most northerly end of the line. Standing on solid rock foundations, its thick brick walls were bonded together with a phenomenally hard "hot lime mortar" made from lime, ash and hot tallow. Completed long after Nelson's victory at Trafalgar sunk Napoleon's dreams of conquest, the tower was periodically called upon to counter new invasion scares before finally being converted into a novel holiday home by the Landmark Trust. **PC**

Sir John Soane's Museum

Architect: Sir John Soane
Completed: 1812
Location: No. 13 Lincoln's Inn Fields, London, England
Style/Period: Neoclassical

John Soane was Georgian England's most celebrated architect and a great exponent of the neoclassical style. His style grew out of his love for the classical world, a passion that led him to amass a huge collection of objects, many from the ancient world. The museum, which was originally his home, grew over time. He began by demolishing and rebuilding the rather plain building at No. 12 Lincoln's Inn Fields between 1792 and 1794. Next came No. 13, which Soane purchased when he was made the professor of design at the Royal College of Art in 1806. Finally, he bought No. 14, which was rebuilt during 1823–1824. The exterior of No. 14 consists of a Portland stone facade that rises from the basement to the second floor and

Château de Rastignac

Architect: Mathurin Salat ("Blanchard")
Completed: 1817 (begun 1812)
Location: La Bachellerie, near Bordeaux, France
Style/Period: Neoclassical

Today the palatial building that the Marquis de Rastignac instructed architect Mathurin Salat (or "Blanchard") to build for him on a hillside at La Bachellerie — not far from Bordeaux in the Dordogne region of southwestern France — is perhaps best known for its remarkable resemblance to the White House (see page 190). Such is the similarity between the two that it is speculated the chateau served as the model for America's most iconic edifice, perhaps at the suggestion of Thomas Jefferson, who once lived in France.

The neoclassical style was fashionable at the time that the Château de Rastignac was planned, which was before 1789, it is thought, although political upheavals in France meant that construction did not take place until 1812–1817. The nobleman's country palace accordingly conformed to this homage to the architecture of ancient Greece and Rome. Fundamentally a simple rectangular, blocklike building constructed of limestone, the symmetrical two-story facade is regularly punctuated by windows, with the most striking feature at the center, a giant-order portico comprising six Ionic columns. Now restored following a catastrophic fire in 1944 that destroyed the interior, the Château de Rastignac has been converted into apartments. **CH-M**

Dulwich Picture Gallery

Architect: Sir John Soane
Completed: 1817
Location: Dulwich, London, England
Style/Period: Neoclassical

This elegant neoclassical building owes its existence to the generosity of the Swiss-born art dealer Sir Francis Bourgeois, who left his private collections of paintings to the public in his 1811 will. He also provided sufficient funds for what would be the country's first public art gallery, a model for those that came after. Bourgeois, who is buried at the gallery, also specified that the task of designing the building should fall to his long-time friend John Soane. Soane was a great collector of antiquarian objects and was particularly attracted to Ancient Egypt, Greece and Rome. His various interests, especially ancient and classical architecture, inspired the gallery's design.

The plan for the gallery was uncomplicated and partly in the style of a Greek temple. It is a collection of interlinking rooms, but Soane's masterstroke was to flood each of them with natural light by placing large skylights in their ceilings. The ceilings are also curved and graded so that, while the light illuminates the rooms for ease of viewing, the sunlight is sufficiently diffused and cannot damage the valuable paintings. **IW**

Baltimore Cathedral

Architect: Benjamin Latrobe

Completed: 1821

Location: Baltimore, Maryland, United States

Style/Period: Neoclassical

British-born Benjamin Latrobe spent much of his youth in Europe, but he returned to England to become an apprentice under John Smeaton, the leading civil engineer of his age. He then worked briefly with Samuel Cockerill, a highly skilled and popular neoclassical architect. Latrobe subsequently immigrated to the United States — his mother was American — in 1796, where he embarked on a career that would see him design an impressive number of major public buildings. Latrobe was appointed Surveyor of the Public Buildings of the United States in 1803, and he spent the better part of the next 14 years working on major projects in the newly emerging capital.

Baltimore Cathedral, or Basilica of the National Shrine of the Assumption of the Blessed Virgin Mary as it is also known, was the first religious building to be constructed after the adoption of the US constitution and is regarded as Latrobe's masterpiece. Begun in 1806, the basilica is a majestic neoclassical edifice built on a Latin cross basilica plan; the facade is a classical Greek portico of ionic columns and two cylindrical towers topped with onion-domes arise behind this. A massive dome covers the crossing point of the Latin cross, and is surrounded by a complex arrangement of barrel vaults. With 24 skylights in the main dome, as well as a series of arched windows in the nave, the interior is airy and flooded with light. Working alongside Thomas Jefferson and Bishop John Carroll, the country's first bishop, Latrobe created an inspirational structure that celebrated the young nation's ambition of religious tolerance. **JM**

All Souls Church

Architect: John Nash

Completed: 1822

Location: Langham Place, London, England

Style/Period: Picturesque/Regency

John Nash was one of the most preeminent architects working in England during the

Regency period (1811–1820) and the Georgian period, which ended with the death of King George IV in 1830. Although All Souls Church, completed in 1822, is technically Georgian, its eclectic style is perhaps more identifiable with Regency characteristics. It is also situated near Regent's Street, which Nash laid out between 1813 and 1820.

Constructed of stone from Bath, All Souls Church — which today has an Anglican Evangelical congregation — comprises an interesting mixture of styles (this being characteristic of the picturesque movement, of which Nash was a master), notably the neo-

classical portico and the Gothic-influenced 17-sided spire rising above it. The giant-order circular portico that dominates the front features Corinthian columns decorated with cherubs inspired by the work of the mannerist master Michelangelo. Behind this is the restrained rectangular body of the church, which was criticized shortly after its dedication in *The Mirror of Literature, Amusement, and Instruction* for its "puny proportions and scantiness of decoration." The church suffered bomb damage during World War II and was subsequently restored. **CH-M**

Royal Pavilion

Architect: John Nash

Completed: 1823

Location: Old Steine, Brighton, England

Style/Period: Exoticism/Anglo-Indian

In 1786 the heir to the British throne, George, Prince of Wales, stayed at a conventional farmhouse in the seaside town of Brighton. The following year he had Henry Holland convert it into a conventional Palladian villa. Various additions were made over the following years as George, later the Prince Regent, acquired the finances to indulge his taste for the opulent and the extravagant. The villa gave way to what can only be described as a unique building, one that marries Gothic and Eastern influences. The architect was John Nash, who remodeled much of late Georgian London and was a favorite of the regent's.

The exterior of the Royal Pavilion is a confection of domes and minarets that take their inspiration from Islamic mosques, while the dazzling interiors were modeled on Chinese and Indian designs. The Banqueting Hall, for example, has a huge chandelier that hangs from the claws of a dragon, while the equally opulent Music Room is lit by nine lotus-shaped chandeliers. Nash was also a pioneer of girders, and cast-iron girders were used to support the new pavilion, which completely concealed Holland's original building. **IW**

University of Virginia

Architect: Thomas Jefferson

Completed: 1826 (begun 1817)

Location: Charlottesville, Virginia, United States

Style/Period: Jeffersonian/Neoclassical

Thomas Jefferson, the third president of the United States, was a man of many talents, being an accomplished politician, diplomat, scientist and architect. He is admired for the neoclassical buildings he designed for his home state of Virginia, notably the Virginia State Capitol in Richmond and his home, Monticello. He also designed the University of Virginia at Charlottesville, the United States' first state university. It was completed in 1826, the year of his death.

Jefferson's inspiration in designing the new university was "an academical village," or a community of students and teachers — what we would today call a campus. He envisioned brick buildings devoted to living and learning situated in close proximity to one another and grouped around a large lawn with a core U-shaped ground plan. The buildings' appearance was typically Jeffersonian, being clearly influenced by such ancient classical models as the Pantheon (in Rome, Italy), on which the circular library — the Rotunda, with its giant-order portico — was based. It stood at the head of the Lawn, which was flanked by two-story professors' dwellings and classrooms housed within 10 pavilions (each offering a visual education in a different classical order). To these buildings were attached student accommodations, all linked by a loggia. **CH-M**

Cumberland Terrace

Architect: John Nash

Completed: 1827 (begun 1826)

Location: London, England

Style/Period: Picturesque/Regency/Neoclassical

If Regent's Park were a clock face, Cumberland Terrace, which runs parallel to the park's Outer Circle, would stand at around 2 o'clock, facing inward, toward this large landscaped area on the northwestern fringes of central London. John Nash, one of the most celebrated architects of the Regency period designed both the park and the terrace of residential houses. The contrast between the natural (if manipulated) green space and the formal built environment is striking. One of many similar terraces, albeit one of the longest, Cumberland Terrace was named in honor of the Duke of Cumberland, the King George IV's younger brother. The actual construction work was entrusted to William Mountford Nurse under the direction of architect James Thomson.

Although it may seem at first sight to be one long building, Cumberland Terrace is in fact a row of attached individual town houses given the appearance of unity by the repetition of their simple, and identical, stuccoed neoclassical facades. Their components may be simple, but the overall effect is one of wealth and grandeur, thanks to the high windows, giant-order Ionic columns spanning the first and second stories, and the grand arches that link the three blocks into which the terrace is apparently divided. **CH-M**

Main Facade, British Museum

Architect: Sir Robert Smirke

Completed: 1827 (begun 1823)

Location: Bloomsbury, London, England

Style/Period: Greek Revival

Although the British Museum first opened its doors at Montagu House in the Bloomsbury district of London in 1759, the iconic facade that makes it instantly recognizable worldwide was not constructed until nearly 70 years later. The architect who designed it was Sir Robert Smirke, who had visited Italy and Greece. The Greek revival style that he settled on was both fashionable and an obvious choice for a museum that housed so many treasures from classical antiquity, including the Elgin Marbles that had once graced the Parthenon in Athens, Greece.

Interior space was already limited when, in 1823, King George IV made a gift to the nation of his father's library, prompting the decision to rebuild the museum. Smirke's main facade at the south front was, in 1827, one of the first of the museum's new components to be completed. Flanked by a pair of projecting colonnaded wings, steps lead up to the elevated octastyle portico, whose Ionic columns are surmounted by a huge ornamented pediment. The remainder of the quadrangular stone building enclosing a central courtyard planned by Smirke was finished by 1852. By 1857 the Rotunda — or Reading Room, designed by Sydney Smirke, Robert's younger brother — had been raised within the central courtyard. **CH-M**

Altes Museum

Architect: Karl Friedrich Schinkel

Completed: 1828

Location: Museuminsel, Berlin, Germany

Style/Period: Neoclassical

The Altes (Old) Museum lies amid a complex of museums and art galleries on an island in the middle of the River Spree, where it runs through the traditional center of the German capital. The plan was initiated by King Frederick Wilhelm III of Prussia. He decided that the, at the time rather scant, collection of royal treasures, especially its paintings, needed a new home so they could be seen by the wider public. Karl Friedrich Schinkel, the state architect, was ordered to build on a marshy piece of land prone to flooding, so he raised the museum on a plinth to protect its contents, and he also altered the course of the river to minimize the risk. Work began in 1825, and the museum was finally opened to the public in 1830.

Schinkel worked from drawings and sketches made by the king, and he produced a superbly balanced neoclassical building in the style of an ancient temple. It has a 285-foot (87 m) facade with a colonnade of 18 Ionic columns. The interior is based on two courtyards linked by a central rotunda, which echoes the Parthenon in Rome. The Altes Museum is arguably the architect's most successful building, and it uses design elements that had previously only been used in palaces and churches. **IW**

The White House

Architect: James Hoban

Completed: 1829 (begun 1792)

Location: 1600 Pennsylvania Avenue, Washington, D.C., United States

Style/Period: Palladian/Neoclassical

There is a theory that a French country house, the Château de Rastignac (see page 180), inspired the neoclassical appearance of the White House's south portico, and the two do look alike. However, the White House is said to have been modeled on Leinster House in Dublin, Ireland, too (see page 158). As the planned official residence of the president of the United States, it was considered important that the building project the dignity of this office but also function as a home. Irish-born architect James Hoban's competition-winning design succeeded in fulfilling both criteria. The four-story building has a practical rectangular footprint softened, on the iconic south-portico side, by a curved giant-order hexastyle portico, which cups the house's central section beneath a balustrade that extends the length of the facade.

Work began on constructing the building from sandstone in the national capital, Washington, D.C., in 1792. It finished in 1799, whereupon President John Adams moved in. In 1814 British troops captured and burned the city, after which, the story goes, the White House was painted white to disguise the damage (this is traditionally the origin of its name). Following reconstruction, the south portico was added in 1824 and the north portico in 1829. **CH-M**

Schloss Charlottenhof

Architects: Karl Friedrich Schinkel and Ludwig Persius

Completed: 1829

Location: Spandauer Damm, Charlottenburg, Berlin

Style/Period: Neoclassical

Prussia's King Frederick William III bought an estate on the western outskirts of Berlin, a little to the south of Sanssouci Park, for his son Crown Prince Frederick William in 1825. The estate came with an old but much-renovated manor house named after Sophie Charlotte, wife of a past monarch. The crown prince opted to remodel the building, and both he and the architect Karl Friedrich Schinkel set about the task. However, the latter was often absent on foreign business once the work began, so it was overseen by one of his assistants, Ludwig Persius.

Money was in short supply, so Schinkel kept as much of the old fabric as possible but added various embellishments — a pediment portico in the Doric style was added to the original centerpiece, for example — to produce a house that epitomized 19th-century neoclassicism. The interiors were redecorated in a simple but elegant style. The crown prince and his architect were also keen to unite house and garden by adding features such as paths, pergolas, seating and steps. The key feature was the Court Gardener's House, which was inspired by recent excavations at Pompeii and has the feel of a Roman villa. **IW**

The Mark Twain Birthplace

Architect: Unknown

Completed: c. 1835

Location: 37352 Shrine Road, Florida, Missouri, United States

Style/Period: Log Cabin

A wooden cabin in the village of Florida, Missouri, is revered as the birthplace of Samuel Langhorne Clemens, the author better known as Mark Twain. It was probably raised in around 1835, the year of the writer's birth. Although it once stood a little north of the Mark Twain Birthplace State Historic Site (in the Mark Twain State Park) to which it was moved for safekeeping, the cabin's original location is still pinpointed by a red-granite monument that marks the spot.

The cabin — rented at the time of Twain's birth — is a simple one-story, timber structure topped by a low roof, above which rises a slightly off-center chimney. It has a centrally placed front door, with a sash window on either side illuminating the structure's two rooms. A central state, Missouri became part of the United States when it was acquired from France in the Louisiana Purchase of 1803. Log cabins like this, which were cheaply and quickly erected, have become symbols of the spirit of the pioneering settlers who ventured ever farther inland. And because so few such old shelters survive, the Mark Twain Birthplace stands for far more than just the place where a great American writer came into the world. **CH-M**

Egyptian House

Architect: John Foulston

Completed: 1836

Location: Penzance, Cornwall, England

Style/Period: Mock Egyptian

When Napoleon Bonaparte campaigned in Egypt between 1798 and 1799, various scientists, archaeologists and artists accompanied his expedition. Few Europeans were familiar with the buildings or artifacts of the Ancient Egyptian world at the time, but all that changed with the gradual publication of a collection of colored engravings collectively known as the *Description d'Egypte* between 1809 and 1828. They sparked a brief but intense fashion for all things Egyptian, even in Regency architectural circles. One of the first such buildings was the Egyptian Hall in London's Piccadilly by Peter Robinson, which opened in 1812.

John Lavin, a Penzance minerologist, commissioned architect John Foulston of Plymouth to build a house where he could also display his mineral collection. Foulston, who had designed the Egyptian-style Classical and Mathematical School in nearby Devonport during 1823, was inspired by engravings of Dendera's Temple of Hathor, an Egyptian goddess who personified the Milky Way. Rather than using stone blocks, he chose to build in Coade, a durable artificial stone manufactured out of ground stone and clay. The Egyptian House is a rare surviving example of the style, and it is now owned by the Landmark Trust, a building conservation charity founded in 1965. **IW**

Arc de Triomphe

Architect: Jean Francois Therese Chalgrin

Completed: 1836

Location: Place Charles de Gaulle, Paris, France

Style/Period: Neoclassical

Emperor Napoleon I was inspired to create this Ashlar stone arch in the center of the French capital the year after winning a great victory at Austerlitz in 1805, an event that made him the master of Europe. The design by Chalgrin was inspired by the Arch of Titus in Rome, but is on a much larger scale and, at 167 feet (51 meters) tall, it is the biggest such arch in the world, which became a template for others. It is a fairly simple piece of neoclassical architecture, consisting of an arch with a vaulted passageway and an attic above the latter.

Each of the arch's four pillars is covered by an allegorical sculpture, while the vault carries the names of 128 battles that either French Republican or Napoleonic forces fought. The inner walls are engraved with the names of 558 famous French generals and the names of those who died in battle are underlined. Thirty shields decorate the attic area and these carry the names of major military victories. This symbolic triumphalism gave way to a sense of patriotic commemoration for those who died in World War I with the entombment of the Unknown Warrior in 1920. An eternal flame now burns under the arch to remember the dead of both world wars. **IW**

Walhalla Temple

Architect: Leo von Klenze

Completed: 1842

Location: Regensburg, Bavaria, Germany

Style/Period: Neoclassical

Ludwig I, the king of Bavaria between 1825 and 1848, spent lavishly on art and personal favorites in his court but especially on large public buildings such as Walhalla. His extravagance provoked popular discontent and eventually led to him being deposed. Walhalla was conceived as a monument at a time when the various German states still felt the humiliation of having been defeated by Napoleonic France, and Ludwig wanted to rekindle their national pride by highlighting great Germanic achievements from the past.

Klenze, Ludwig's neoclassical court architect and, like his master, a keen Hellenist, chose a spot overlooking the River Danube to create the memorial. It was inspired by the Parthenon in Athens and named after the mythical resting place of the souls of the Norse gods. The northern frieze consists of personifications of the German states, while the southern frieze depicts victories in battle. Originally there were also 96 busts and 64 plaques (of individuals whose likeness was not known) commemorating leading figures from all fields of endeavor, including the arts and sciences. Inclusion was on the basis of the subject "being of the German tongue," a broad linguistic category that led to the inclusion of British, Dutch and Russian subjects, among others. **IW**

Albert Dock

Architect: Jesse Hartley

Completed: 1846

Location: River Mersey, Liverpool, England

Style/Period: Industrial Victorian

Albert Dock was designed in the early Victorian period by Jesse Hartley, the Port of Liverpool's dock engineer who also had a background in bridge building. It is considered one of the most innovative examples of mid-19th century industrial architecture. Hartley's experience served him well, as the buildings and wharves combine great practicality with an elegant classical simplicity. His vision consisted of a single large basin and five five-story warehouses that are linked together. Hartley chose to build in brick, sandstone, granite and cast iron.

The warehouses and wharves were eminently practical. All were fireproof, and sandstone was rejected in favor of more resilient granite where friction from mooring ropes and the like was likely to cause damage. Corners at narrow points were curved to prevent a ship's rigging from snagging. At ground level the warehouse facades are supported by large iron columns that use straight lintels and elliptical arches to support the brickwork above, making the transfer of goods from ship to shore to warehouse all the easier. The interior consists of cast-iron supports with vaulted brick ceilings, while the roof is riveted wrought-iron plates on iron trusses. **IW**

Church of St. Giles

Architect: Augustus Pugin

Completed: 1846

Location: Cheadle, Staffordshire, England

Style/Period: Gothic Revival

This masterpiece of religious architecture by Augustus Pugin, the London-born son of a French architectural draftsman, was made possible by the benefice of a wealthy member of the English nobility, the Earl of Shrewsbury. Previous Catholic churches had been relatively modest affairs, but thanks to the earl's deep pockets St. Giles was built on a much grander scale, with a spire rising to 200 feet (61 m). It was a bold statement in Hollington sandstone that announced the rebirth of the Catholic church in England after centuries of retreat.

Pugin, a convert to Catholicism himself, not only created the exterior but also designed everything within, including the stained glass and metalwork. Outside, St. Giles closely resembles a medieval Gothic church from the early 14th century, while the inside is a bold riot of colors, especially gold and red. Pugin considered St. Giles his great masterpiece and his purest work, largely because he was allowed to show his skills to the full without having to compromise on any part of the work since there were no financial constraints. The church also pointed the way for the Gothic revival that Pugin saw as the quintessential Christian architectural style. **IW**

The Palm House

Architects: Decimus Burton and Richard Taylor

Completed: 1848

Location: Kew Gardens, London, England

Style/Period: Victorian Industrial

It took some four years for architect Decimus Burton and engineer Richard Taylor to complete this elegant vision in glass and cast iron to house the botanical garden's world-renowned collection of palms, but its birth was far from easy. Burton's first set of plans was criticized because some thought he used too many internal support columns, but he in turn disliked Taylor's revisions and so modified them. It thus remains a matter of conjecture which of the two designers was ultimately responsible for which part of the building.

It seems that Taylor was behind the structural elements, which were based on shipbuilding techniques, while Burton was responsible for the central section, the detailing and the eastern boiler tower. Whatever the division of labor, they produced a fine curving structure 361 feet (110 m) long and up to 207 feet (63 m) tall, with some 16,000 windowpanes that made use of the recently developed sheet glass manufacturing technology. The Palm House was the first truly large-scale glasshouse to be seen in Britain and inspired many other such structures, not least Joseph Paxton's Crystal Palace for the Great Exhibition of 1851. **IW**

19th Century 1850–1899

Crystal Palace

Architect: Joseph Paxton

Completed: 1851

Location: Hyde Park, London, England

Style/Period: Victorian Industrial

The Crystal Palace was built to host a world's fair, the 1851 Great Exhibition, which was primarily used to reflect and magnify Britain's international prestige during the Victorian era. The challenge to build a suitable building quickly was put out to public tender, but virtually none of the 245 designs submitted fitted the bill. Joseph Paxton submitted a design at the last minute, and it was accepted despite some misgivings.

Paxton had established a reputation as a garden designer with a particular aptitude for large glasshouses while working for the Duke of Devonshire at Chatsworth House in Derbyshire, where he built a 300-foot (91 m) conservatory. For the Great Exhibition he proposed to create a glass hall on a monumental scale, measuring 1,848 feet (563 m) long, 408 feet (124 m) wide and 108 feet (33 m) high. It would require 4,500 tons

(4,082 metric tonnes) of cast-iron framework and 293,000 panes of glass. Paxton's was a seemingly impossible task in the time available, yet the construction was finished in just eight months by 2,000 workers. The secret was that all of the largely standardized components were manufactured off site and then put into position. The Crystal Palace was, therefore, the first true modular prefabricated building of the industrial age. **IW**

The Great Kremlin Palace

Architect: Konstantin Andreyevich Thon

Completed: 1851 (begun 1837)

Location: Moscow, Russia

Style/Period: Russo–Byzantine Revival

"Kremlin" signifies a citadel in any Russian city, with the greatest standing in Moscow, Russia's capital. The Great Kremlin Palace, commonly referred to simply as "the Kremlin," dates back to the 12th century. It has developed into a huge complex over the centuries, which includes churches, palaces and government buildings behind its high

walls. Today a UNESCO World Heritage Site, the Kremlin is also now the official residence of the president of Russia. Before the Russian Revolution, however, it was the Russian tsar's (emperor's) seat, and it was Tsar Nicholas I who ordered the construction of the Great Kremlin Palace in 1837. It was completed in 1851 with the erection of the Kremlin Armory.

Nicholas I intended his new palace to be magnificent and it was. At 410 feet (125 m) long and 148 feet (45 m) high, this monumental stone edifice remains the largest building within the Kremlin's walls. No expense was spared to make the interior rooms — which numbered around 700 and included the imperial apartments and reception rooms — breathtakingly luxurious. Konstantin Andreyevich Thon, the architect who rose to the challenge, employed an eclectic, and patriotic, Russo–Byzantine revival style, which enabled his design to successfully link the existing Terem Palace and Palace of Facets and to incorporate the Resurrection of the Lazarus Church. **CH-M**

King's Cross Station

Architect: Lewis Cubitt

Completed: 1852 (begun 1850)

Location: Euston Road, London, England

Style/Period: Industrial/Railroad

Engineer George Stephenson's completion of the first public railway, running between the English towns of Stockton and Darlington, in 1825 initiated the construction of what would eventually become a dense network of railroads in Britain. This in turn necessitated the building of stations, with major cities — particularly London, England's capital — requiring large terminals that could comfortably accommodate both trains and passengers. It was a new architectural challenge that was often met with ingenuity, notably by Lewis Cubitt. In the mid-19th century he designed King's Cross Station in northeast London, the "gateway" to the north and the east coast.

Cubitt's plan revolved around a dual-vaulted train shed set within a brick building. He made extensive use of glass, which let in light while providing protection against inclement weather. The glazed roofs of the two vaults — which measured 800 feet (244 m) in length and 105 feet (32 m) in width, making it the largest station roof in the world at that time — were supported by skeletal arches that originally comprised laminated timber. These arches were later replaced with steel, which was lighter and more durable. The facade featured a central clock tower, and main glass arches on either side, which had three arches beneath, gave access to the station. **CH-M**

Bodelwyddan Castle

Architects: Joseph Hansom and Edward Welch
Completed: 1852
Location: Bodelwyddan, Denbighshire, Wales
Style/Period: Gothic Revival

Bodelwyddan Castle is something of an architectural mutt. It began life as a manor house in the mid-1400s but has been modified, refurbished and extended on several occasions since. Ownership passed to the Williams family in around 1690, and they continued to live in it for the next 200 years or so. The limestone building that stands today was created not as a castle in the traditional defensive sense, but rather as a mid-19th century Gothic version of one — a practical family home with towers, turrets and parapets as decorative flourishes. This renovation work was undertaken at the behest of Sir John Hay-Williams, the castle's owner, in 1830.

Hay-Williams commissioned two architects, Joseph Hansom and Edward Welch, who had formed a partnership in 1828. Their working relationship actually came to an end in 1834, but work on Bodelwyddan continued. The castle's subsequent history was checkered — it has served as a military hospital and girls' school. After major restoration work it is now part hotel and part Victorian time capsule. Hansom and Welch's radical redesign work has been described by one architectural commentator as "being wildly dramatic and owing nothing to its predecessors." **IW**

Waverly

Architect: Charles Pond
Completed: 1852 (begun 1840s)
Location: Near West Point, Mississippi, United States
Style/Period: Antebellum/Greek Revival /Octagonal

Built for Colonel George Hampton Young of Georgia and today a National Historic Landmark, Waverly (sometimes spelled Waverley) is an antebellum mansion. Construction of this plantation home to the east of West Point, Mississippi, began during the 1840s and was completed in 1852.

It has an elegant, broadly Greek

Revival–style appearance, albeit with a distinctly Southern feel. Two Ionic columns at the center of the rectangular front and rear facades front a shady, recessed porch and are flanked by two windows on each of the two stories of the main structure. An octagonal cupola rises through the middle of the roof, each of whose eight facets is pierced by two windows. Most of these windows are equipped with shutters to keep out the Southern heat. The design also incorporates ingenious feats of design and engineering, such as the curved stairways that lead to the first level of the central four-story atrium that support themselves and the lighting that was once powered by gas generated on site by burning pine knots in a retort. **CH-M**

Paddington Station

Architects: Isambard Kingdom Brunel and Matthew Wyatt

Completed: 1854

Location: Paddington, London, England

Style/Period: Victorian Industrial

The Victorian age saw Britain gradually crisscrossed by a vast rail network, and the Great Western Railway Company, founded in 1833 to link the capital with the west of the country, was at the forefront of this revolution in communications. First came the London-Bristol line, completed in 1841. Then, in late 1850, Isambard Kingdom Brunel, the company's chief engineer, produced an idea for a London terminal and had a detailed scheme completed only a

month later. His work was undoubtedly inspired by the innovative and recently constructed Crystal Palace, and Brunel chose its builders, Fox, Henderson & Company, to undertake construction work using wrought and cast iron and glass.

There were originally three wide vaults of iron and glass, the largest measuring a spectacular 102 feet (31 m) across, which were designed to flood the building with light. Brunel was primarily an engineer, but Paddington is also highly ornate, thanks to Matthew Wyatt, an architect and art historian who devised much of the decorative work. Paddington stands as a testament to the confidence and metaphorically vaulting ambition of industrialized Victorian England. It remains a grand temple celebrating the steam age. **IW**

Round Reading Room, British Museum

Architect: Sydney Smirke

Completed: 1857

Location:Bloomsbury, London, England

Style/Period: Neoclassical

By the early 1850s the British Museum's library was fast running out of shelving space to house its burgeoning collection of books. Sir Antonio Panizzi, then Keeper of Printed Books, had the idea of building a large circular library in the museum's central Great Court, which was being used as a public garden. Panizzi turned to Sydney Smirke, the brother of Sir Robert Smirke, who had designed the Greek revival museum itself, for a design. Smirke had actually completed some of his brother's project and came up with a domed building to fill the courtyard. Building work commenced in 1854 and was completed three years later.

The Round Reading Room was built in cast iron, concrete and glass, and it was at the forefront of mid-19th century technology. It had the latest heating and ventilation systems for the comfort of readers and to help protect the books. The stacks were made in iron to bear the weight of the books and protect them from fire. In all, Smirke included 3 miles (5 km) of cases and 25 miles (40 km) of shelves — sufficient space for an impressive one million books. Large arched windows run around the lower section of the dome to flood the reading area with light, creating an ideal environment for serious study. **IW**

Victoria Mansion

Architect: Henry Austin

Completed: 1860

Location: Portland, Maine, United States

Style/Period: Federal/Victorian

This opulent home remains the United States' finest surviving example of mid-19th century domestic architecture and interior design, and one that acts as something of a time capsule: around 90 percent of its interior fixtures and fittings have survived. The house was built for Ruggles Sylvester Morse and his wife, Olive Ring Merrill Morse. Morse had made a fortune as the owner of luxury hotels in New Orleans and his experience shaped his tastes. He turned to the noted New Haven architect Austin to build his vision and work began in 1858.

Austin created a brownstone Italian villa, a symmetrical building arranged around a four-story tower. When it was completed, the mansion was considered the architect's masterpiece. The interiors were the work of Gustave Herter. They were his earliest commission and the only one that remains largely intact. Aside from the opulent decoration, Herter also filled the mansion with what were then state-of-the-art technologies, including central heating, gas lighting, and hot and cold running water. Morse died in 1893 and the house and contents were sold to a wealthy department store owner, Joseph Ralph Libby, which is why it is sometimes referred to as the Morse-Libby House. **IW**

Red House

Architect: Philip Webb
Completed: 1860
Location: Bexleyheath, Kent, England
Style/Period: Arts and Crafts

Medieval in vision and wholly romantic in spirit, Red House was inspired by and built for William Morris, the founding father of the arts and crafts movement. Architect Philip Webb, a friend of Morris's, designed a building firmly based in the vernacular, but he was inspired to a degree by the Gothic revival as developed by architects such as Augustus Pugin. The guiding principle was one of beauty and utility both within and without. Morris intended for house and garden to be linked, but with the latter having a series of "rooms." Red House is the arts and crafts movement writ large and its most complete and earliest expression.

A number of artists from the movement and members of the associated Pre-Raphaelite Brotherhood, several of them Morris's close friends, worked on the interior. Edward Burne-Jones and Gabriel Dante Rossetti produced the stained glass windows and decorated the walls and furniture, while William De Morgan provided ceramics, and Morris's own company devised the wallpapers. The project inspired Morris to found Morris, Marshall, Faulkner and Company in 1861, a firm that would go on to transform interiors and furniture. **IW**

Oxford University Museum of Natural History

Architects: Thomas Deane and Benjamin Woodward
Completed: 1860
Location: Oxford, Oxfordshire, England
Style/Period: Gothic Revival

The early Victorian era saw a flowering in the sciences, and Oxford University founded its Honour School of Natural Science in 1850. However, the new department had no single home but was scattered across the city among its various colleges. Five years later, the Regius Professor of Medicine, Sir Henry Acland, proposed that the teaching staff and students of several scientific departments, including those of astronomy, mineralogy and chemistry among others, would benefit from being housed under one roof.

Two Irish architects, Thomas Deane and Benjamin Woodward, were commissioned and set about creating a neogothic building wholly inspired by Acland's friend John Ruskin and faithful to his writings, especially his *Seven Lamps of Architecture* (1848) and *The Stones of Venice* (1851–1853). The building is essentially a large square court with a glass roof supported by cast-iron pillars. Cloistered arcades run around the ground and first floors supported by pillars, each made from a different British stone. Ornamentation consists of various organic forms, such as leaves and branches, in the Pre-Raphaelite style. Both elements reflect the museum's original function as a home to scientific enquiry. **IW**

The Capitol

Architects: William Thornton, Benjamin Henry Latrobe,
Charles Bulfinch, Thomas Ustick Walter and others
Completed: 1863 (begun 1793)
Location: Capitol Hill, Washington, D.C., United States
Style/Period: Neoclassical/Greek Revival/Neobaroque

The Capitol was always intended to provide a
suitably dignified place of business for the
United States Congress, and today it remains
a towering symbol of democracy in action. Its
construction took some 70 years, beginning
in 1793 with William Thornton's
competition-winning design. The north and
south wings — the meeting places of the
Senate and the House of Representatives —
had been completed when, in 1814, British
soldiers burned and looted the Capitol.
Benjamin Henry Latrobe then modified the
interior plan during the restoration
program. Charles Bulfinch took over
between 1817 and 1830, and in 1827 he
joined the north and south wings. It was
Thomas Ustick Walter who designed the
neobaroque double dome that today
dominates the skyline atop Capitol Hill, its
immense size having been made possible by
the comparable lightness (to stone at least)
of cast iron, then a relatively new building
material.

The overall effect is extraordinarily
impressive, particularly when viewed from
the west: already on an elevated site, steps
lead higher, to the central section and its
giant-order Corinthian columns, while
extended wings on either side symmetrically
elongate the complex. Above looms the
multitiered dome, and more columns
encircle the lower layer and the lantern, on
whose apex stands a statue representing
freedom. **CH-M**

The Round Barn

Architect: Attributed to Elder William Deming
Completed: 1865 (begun 1826)
Location: Hancock Shaker Village, Massachusetts,
United States
Style/Period: Shaker

The Round Barn embodies the edict of the
Shaker Elder Father Joseph Meacham that

all the brethrens' works "ought to be made according to their order and use." Laid out with diagrammatic clarity, the barn was redesigned after a fire in 1864 to include a 12-sided superstructure whose windows flood the interior with natural light, so reducing the need for lanterns' risky candles. Arranged over three floors, the ground level was filled with radiating stalls for 52 head of cattle that faced inward to eat from a central ring of mangers. Above them ran a circular wooden wagon track accessed through a single door via an external earthen ramp. Wagons laden with hay would enter the barn and circle while distributing their load into the central haymow before exiting. Assisted by gravity, the job of forking down fodder into the stalls below could be performed by one man. A similar basement track ran beneath the stalls, allowing empty wagons to descend and collect the valuable manure, shoveled directly down through the large trapdoors in the floor above.

The whole building was ventilated by a hollow fluelike central column, which drew air through the mountain of hay piled against it, keeping it dry and greatly reducing the chance of spontaneous combustion. Though no longer used for its original purpose, the Round Barn remains one of the Shakers' greatest achievements and an elegant example of architecture as process. **PC**

Bibliothèque Nationale

Architect: Henri Labrouste
Completed: 1868 (begun 1858)
Location: Rue de Richelieu, Paris, France
Style/Period: Rational/Neoclassical

During the mid-19th century, when Henri Labrouste was contemplating the form that France's national library, the Bibliothèque Nationale, should take, cast iron was a relatively new construction material. It was generally considered more suitable for buildings of the new industrial age, such as bridges, mills and railroad stations, than for temples of learning and culture. Yet Labrouste had already used iron to great effect at the Bibliothèque Sainte-Geneviève (the Library of Saint Geneviève), which was

also in Paris, and it was consequently an obvious, if experimental, choice for this influential rationalist architect.

In the Bibiothèque Nationale's reading room, Labrouste again combined beauty and utility through the medium of cast iron. Here 16 lamppostlike cast-iron columns 32 feet (10 m) high and 1 foot (30 cm) in diameter support a canopy comprising nine delicate terra-cotta domes, each of which has

a decorative iron and glass oculus that lets in light. The ceiling of the Salle Ovale (Oval Room) was of glass, again supported by cast iron, as were the ceilings of the stack rooms. Labrouste married material and geometry — cast iron and horizontal and vertical planes — to stylish and practical effect in creating a five-story space within which the books were accessed by means of pierced cast-iron walkways and bridges. **CH-M**

Palace of Westminster

Architects: Sir Charles Barry and Augustus Pugin

Completed: 1870

Location: Parliament Square, London, England

Style/Period: Gothic Revival

Fire swept thought the medieval Palace of Westminster in 1834, destroying much of it, and a commission was appointed to identify a suitable architect to build its replacement. The only stipulation was that the new palace had to be in either the Elizabethan or Gothic revival style. After reviewing 97 proposals, the commissioners chose the plans submitted by Charles Barry and Augustus Pugin, both of whom opted for the latter style. Pugin completed the drawings for the competition, and Barry oversaw the actual building work while Pugin concentrated on its sumptuous interiors.

Work began in 1840, and the materials were metals and sand-colored Anston limestone, a stone that has proven to be highly vulnerable to pollution. The building is largely symmetrical, although the Victoria Tower and the Clock Tower give it a degree of asymmetry. Its two main elements, the House of Lords and the House of Commons, were completed in 1847 and 1852 respectively. The palace was built on a monumental scale — there are more than 1,100 rooms, 100 staircases and 3 miles (5 km) of corridors — and this imposing statement ensured that Gothic revival was the dominant architectural style in England for decades to come. **IW**

Royal Albert Hall of Arts and Science

Architects: Captain Francis Fowke and Lieutenant-Colonel Henry Scott

Completed: 1871

Location: Kensington Gore, London, England

Style/Period: Classical Revival

Queen Victoria's husband, Prince Albert, proposed that an area of London's South Kensington should be given over to various museums, but when he died in 1861 it was instead decided to build a public concert hall in his name. Fowke, an Anglo-Irish military engineer who was subsequently appointed as an architect and engineer to the government's Department of Science and Art, was given the commission. He designed the 8,000-seat building but died before it was completed, and Henry Scott, who came from a similar background, stepped in.

The hall, which is in the classical revival style, is a large-scale elliptical building some 219 feet (67 m) across at its greatest extent. It is reminiscent of a Roman amphitheater but possesses a domed roof some 135 feet (41 m) high, which was created by engineer Rowland Ordish. The chief building materials were Fareham red brick, wrought iron, glass and terra-cotta. The hall is unmistakably a temple of culture, a fact emphasized by the terra-cotta frieze, entitled *The Triumph of Arts and Science*, that runs around its exterior. The frieze has 16 subjects, ranging from music and architecture to engineering, pottery and glassmaking. **IW**

Grand Opera

Architect: Charles Garnier

Completed: 1874

Location: Avenue de la Opera, Paris, France

Style/Period: Neo-Baroque

Charles Garnier was a relatively unknown architect when he won a competition to design a new theater in 1861, but his design came to symbolize the flamboyance that typified France during the period known as the Second Empire, when Napoleon III was on the throne (1852–1870). Garnier had, in fact, spent five years studying in Rome and was inspired by what he referred to as the "pageantry of [ancient] Roman society." He incorporated his love of spectacle into his creation, building a theater that defined what he called the "Style Napoleon III."

Work began in 1862 and progress was far from easy as the site was swampy and an underground lake had to be painstakingly drained. Further problems followed during the politically turbulent early 1870s, but the theater was eventually completed. It is in the Neo-Baroque style and is a monumental creation, one capable of seating an audience of some 2,200. Large, wide staircases and rich decorative flourishes, including many statues and busts of both deities of the classical world and leading lights in various performing arts, typify the interior. There are also multicolored marble friezes and an exuberance of gold decoration. **IW**

Midland Grand Hotel

Architect: Sir George Gilbert Scott

Completed: 1876

Location: St. Pancras, London, England

Style/Period: Gothic Revival

St. Pancras was the London terminal of the Midland Railway Company. The station, which opened in 1868 with a 243-foot (74 m) vaulted roof designed by the company's engineer-in-chief W.H. Barlow, is an architectural treasure. It was the biggest open space on the planet for a time, and when it was felt that an associated hotel of great luxury would add to its luster, the company turned to George Gilbert Scott, a renowned advocate of the gothic revival style. Scott was also exploring different architectural forms, and he produced a very ambitious design that the company accepted on a slightly reduced scale.

Nevertheless, it was a huge undertaking. The 300-room hotel required some 60 million Nottingham bricks and 900 tons (816 metric tones) of iron. Both the interior and exterior were highly ornate — Scott was influenced by the work of Augustus Pugin and used 14 different types of polished granite and limestone for his pillars. Scott also incorporated new technologies, such as hydraulic "ascending chambers" (early elevators), fireproof floors and revolving doors. The hotel opened in 1873 and was completed in 1876, a true cathedral to the industrial revolution and the age of steam. **IW**

Keble College

Architect: William Butterfield
Completed: 1876
Location: Oxford, England
Style/Period: Gothic Revival

The college was named in honor of John Keble, a leading Christian theologian and poet of the first half of the 19th century. When it was opened it was as a shrine "to sober living and high culture of the mind." It was originally known as a "new foundation" that was linked to the university but was not a full member of it, and the construction was financed by the wealthy Gibbs family from Bristol. Their aim was to provide young men from less wealthy but church-going backgrounds with a comparatively affordable Church of England education. Construction work on Butterfield's design began in 1868, the first student arrived in 1870, and the final building, the monumental chapel, was completed six years later

Gothic revival Keble was in many ways unique for its time. It was built in polychrome brick rather than the usual limestone associated with Oxford buildings, its student accommodation was based on corridors rather than the more traditional staircases, and the two quadrangles were sunk, supposedly to prevent unruly student behavior. Unlike the older, more sober colleges, Keble is a riot of color, and Butterfield made extensive use of decorative glass, mosaics, tiles, and vivid paints throughout. **IW**

Galleria Vittorio Emanuele

Architect: Giuseppe Mengoni
Completed: 1877
Location: Piazza del Duomo, Milan, Italy
Style/Period: Neoclassical/Baroque

Mengoni's Galleria Vittorio Emanuele appears at first sight to be a highly decorated temple to consumerism. This classical revival work consists of four five-story stone arcades running at right angles to each other that meet in a central octagon with a domed roof. The arcades' arching glass and cast-iron framework roofs keep the weather out and allow light to flood through, as does the octagon's dome. The flooring is an intricate pattern of colored tiles. The decoration is

lavish, even theatrical, with pilasters and balconies topped by caryatids, above which appear lunettes filled with mosaics. The original plan appeared in 1861, but construction work did not begin until 1865.

The Galleria is not only a precursor of today's ubiquitous shopping malls, but it was also an exuberant celebration of political freedom, Milan and the rest of Lombardy having gained their independence from Austria's House of Savoy in 1859. Vittorio Emanuele II, king of Sardinia at the time but ruler of a newly unified Italy from 1861, was the leading figure in the battle for freedom. The gallery also became a place to meet and talk, and it is now affectionately known as *il Salotto di Milano* ("Milan's drawing room"). **IW**

Solent Forts

Architects: Captain E. Stewert, Captain Inglis, Lieutenant English and Sir John Hawkshaw
Completed: 1880
Location: The Solent, off Portsmouth, England
Style/Period: Victorian Military

These four forts — Horse Sands (below), No Man's Land, Saint Helen's and Spitbank — were built to protect Portsmouth, a large natural harbor and major naval base in southern England, from attack through the Solent seaway that leads into the English Channel. They were a response to the development of ironclad warships and improved rifled artillery. Because of their relative invulnerability, ironclad ships could sail to comparatively close range to bombard a target, and the greater destructive power of the new artillery gave them a means to reduce a traditional masonry fort to rubble.

The circular forts, which were hugely expensive and difficult to build, never actually fired a shot in anger, but they did mark the transition from masonry defenses to those of iron, steel and concrete. They consisted of a masonry foundation and central core surrounded by an iron framework with a concrete roof. The outer face was wholly or partially clad in three layers of laminated iron plating. The go-ahead was given for the construction work in 1860, but the last of the four forts was not completed for two decades. **IW**

Natural History Museum

Architect: Alfred Waterhouse

Completed: 1880

Location: South Kensington, London, England

Style/Period: Gothic Revival

The Natural History Museum was paid for out of the profits generated by the Great Exhibition of 1851, but it had a long gestation. A building was first designed by Captain Francis Fowke in 1859, but he died before contruction started, and it was not until a year later that a commission reconsidered the project. It was finally given the green light in 1870. Alfred Waterhouse was chosen as the new architect. He produced a new design in brick and iron and began construction work three years later. The commission was, however, rather thrifty — the museum's side wings and rear were planned but never built — and Waterhouse had to fight to complete his vision.

Waterhouse built in the German-Romanesque style and combined function with beauty. The Great Hall is flooded with natural light, largely because gas lighting was considered too dangerous as so many exhibits were preserved in distillated spirits. Its beautiful roofline was also partly a response to the need to hide the museum's many water tanks. Waterhouse also proved a master of groundbreaking decorative terra-cotta work, and his designs, executed by Farmer & Brindley, depict the creatures both living and extinct that can be found in the museum's collections. **IW**

Sever Hall, Harvard University

Architect: Henry Hobson Richardson

Completed: 1880 (begun 1878)

Location: Cambridge, Massachusetts, United States

Style/Period: Richardsonian Romanesque

Such is the architectural importance of Sever Hall — a building designed for the purpose of teaching and learning at Harvard University in Cambridge, Massachusetts — that it has been elevated to the status of a National Historic Landmark. A substantial donation from Anne Sever, in memory of her husband, James Warren Sever, prompted the erection of Sever Hall. However, its significance lies in the choice of architect and in the style of the building that Henry Hobson Richardson (whose alma mater was Harvard) designed and constructed between 1878 and 1880. This style was so idiosyncratic that it was named after him.

This Richardson Romanesque building is essentially rectangular and measures 176 feet (54 m) in length, 74 feet (23 m) in width and 80 feet (24 m) in height. Three window-lined stories, delineated by molded-brick string courses, are visible when the symmetrical facades are viewed from a distance, and a fourth is set above the cornice, within the roof space. The roof is hipped and, on the western and eastern sides, incorporates two projections that appear to be the turrets of two towers. These "towers" are, in fact, hemispherical bays. Entry from the west is via a deeply recessed Romanesque archway and through a rectangular pediment-topped doorway from the east. **CH-M**

OMNIA VINCIT AMOR ET NOS CEDAMVS AMORI

Cardiff Castle

Architect: William Burges
Completed: 1881 (begun 1868)
Location: Cardiff, Wales
Style/Period: Gothic Revival

Although there has been a fortification on the site where Cardiff Castle stands since Roman times, only traces of that structure survive. Far more visible, however, are the Norman keep and the Victorian Gothic Revival–style additions designed by William Burgess, notably the Clock Tower. In fact, Cardiff Castle's coal-enriched owner at that time, John Patrick Crichton-Stuart, the third Marquis of Bute, was so involved in the work that it can almost be considered a collaboration between two enthusiastic medievalists, both working toward the realization of their shared vision, supported by a team of designers and craftsmen.

As a result, from the outside, the skyline resembles a medieval town. As work progressed the four-walled Clock Tower was joined by the Tank Tower, the Guest Tower, the Herbert Tower and the Bute Tower, while the existing Octagon Tower received a timber spire. Inside the palace the attention to detail and lavish decorative touches for which Burges is renowned are evident in, for instance, the carvings around the stone fireplaces, the eccentric murals that enliven the walls and the themed appearance of such chambers as the Banqueting Hall, the Winter and Summer Smoking Rooms, the Arabic Room, the Chaucer Room and the Roof Garden. **CH-M**

Palais de Justice

Architect: Joseph Poelaert
Completed: 1883
Location: Poelaert Square, Brussels, Belgium
Style/Period: Baroque Revival

The Belgian Palais de Justice (Palace of Justice) is breathtakingly immense and was the largest building erected anywhere in the world during the 19th century. It has some 30,000 square yards (25,000 sq. m) of floor space divided between 27 assembly rooms, 245 smaller rooms and a towering entrance hall. Its Great Hall is crowned by a 333-foot (104 m) dome that looms especially large over the city, thanks in part to the whole edifice being built on a piece of high ground formerly known as Gallows Hill.

The design was the subject of an international competition instigated by King Leopold II in 1860 but, when no one won, his minister of justice gave the commission to the relatively obscure local architect Joseph Poelaert the following year. Work finally began in 1866. Poelaert opted for an overblown stone building that reflected various classic architectural styles from late antiquity, which largely defy a simple categorization but can be best described as baroque revival. The project was troubled from start to finish — it suffered innumerable delays, vastly overran its original budget and Poelaert died before it was completed, allegedly being driven mad by the project. **IW**

Stoughton House

Architect: Henry Hobson Richardson

Completed: 1883 (begun 1882)

Location: 90 Brattle Street, Cambridge,
Massachusetts, United States

Style/Period: Shingle/Richardsonian

Although many buildings designed by the American architect Henry Hobson Richardson during the second half of the 19th century are categorized as "Richardsonian Romanesque," Stoughton House (also sometimes called M. F. Stoughton House) is not one of them. Richardsonian it may be, but it is also a shingle-style residence and, therefore, conforms to a more general trend in house-building that largely prevailed in New England between 1880 and 1900 (and the Stoughton House accordingly dates from 1883). The rustic, informal and organic appearance of shingle-style houses reflects their origins in the New England seashore. However, the style soon became popular inland, and Stoughton House stands on a suburban street in Cambridge, Massachusetts.

The essential characteristics of a shingle-style house were, of course, the wooden shingles that covered the entire wood-framed building (roof apart), and the wildly original Stoughton House is regarded as one of the most outstanding examples of this design. Two stories high, the asymmetrical frontage of the large single-family home includes a round tower, a turret and a gallery. These, somewhat incongruously romantic, old-world touches are set within an emphatically new-world situation and constructed of basic local materials. Yet the unlikely fusion works, and the disparate architectural elements appear unified by their covering of shingles. **CH-M**

Papplewick Pumping Station

Architect: Marriott Ogle Tarbotton

Completed: 1884

Location: Nottingham, England

Style/Period: Victorian Gothic/Industrial

Blessed by geology, Nottingham stands on a sprawling bed of red bunter sandstone whose honeycombed strata acts as a sponge and filter, absorbing the surrounding groundwater and cleansing it for human consumption. It was this natural resource that Papplewick Pumping Station was designed to tap. The pumping rods of its two impressive beam engines rhythmically plunged up and down a 200-foot (61 m) well cut deep into the aquifer. Thought to be the last products of the famous firm of James Watt & Co, the two 140-horsepower engines ran almost continuously for 85 years before finally being replaced by more mundane electric pumps.

Wonderful works of craftsmanship, Watt's machines are almost upstaged by the lavish engine house that wraps around them. Built from the ubiquitous red sandstone, the building's solid Gothic exterior frames many large stained-glass windows that hint at the wealth of exuberant decoration within. Four white and green cast-iron columns support the engines' pivot point, their surfaces embellished with delicate brass friezes of aquatic life filled with bulrushes, lilies and little carp and pike. Each column is topped by a capital of four gilded ibises, which stare haughtily down from their lofty perches to survey the scene. Only the proud engineers of the Victorian age would lavish such attention on a workspace that was never designed for public viewing, quietly creating a little palace of industry to quench the thirst of a midland town. **PC**

Schloss Neuschwanstein

Architects: Christian Jank, Eduard Riedel and Georg
Dollmann
Completed: 1886
Location: Hohenschwangau, Bavaria, Germany
Style/Period: Neogothic /Romantic

King Ludwig II of Bavaria was a wildly
enthusiastic patron of composer Richard
Wagner, and Schloss Neuschwanstein ("New
Swan Stone Castle") was to be built in
homage to Wagner's opera *Lohengrin* (the
"Swan Knight"), who was the eponymous
hero of a medieval Nordic saga. Ludwig II
publicly asked for a building in the
"authentic style of the old German knights'
castles," but what he got — and really wanted
— was a fairy-tale castle with an exterior in
the Romanesque style and an interior that is
a mishmash of Byzantine, Romanesque and
Gothic influences.

The outcome was hardly surprising, as
Ludwig had asked Christian Jank, a theatrical
set designer, to devise the plans — although
they were seen through by two architects,
Eduard Riedel and Georg Dollmann. Yet
Ludwig was more than a romantic dreamer,
and the castle includes much state-of-the-art
technology, including steam engines,
electricity, venting systems and heating pipes.
Construction began in 1869, but the king was
declared insane, on possibly dubious
grounds, in 1886 and died in mysterious
circumstances the same year. This and other
similar projects nearly bankrupted the
Bavarian royal family, but Neuschwanstein,
one of Germany's most popular attractions,
did have one lasting legacy — it inspired the
various Sleeping Beauty castles in Disney
parks around the world. **IW**

Eiffel Tower

Architects: Gustave Eiffel and Maurice Koechlin

Completed: 1889

Location: Champ de Mars, Paris, France

Style/Period: Industrial

The 1,062-foot (325 m) Eiffel Tower is arguably the world's most iconic tower, yet it might never have been built in Paris. Gustave Eiffel originally submitted his plans to the Spanish authorities in Barcelona, only to have them rejected. He then entered a French competition to design an entrance arch for the forthcoming Exposition Universelle, a world fair, to be held in 1889, the centenary of the French Revolution. Eiffel was just one of 700 entries and, although he won, a 300-name petition was signed objecting to the tower's construction.

Work began in 1887, involving 200 steelworkers who used some 2.5 million rivets to hold together around 18,000 pieces of especially strong puddle iron. The structure's elegant shape was largely determined not by aesthetic considerations but by the need to minimize the impact of wind resistance. Structural engineer Maurice Koechlin undertook this work. When the construction ended, the tower was the tallest structure in the world and would remain so until 1930. Although now known as a tourist attraction, it has had more practical functions, serving as a radio transmitter, a base for scientific experiments and even as a billboard for a French car manufacturer. **IW**

Central Station

Architects: Petrus Cuypers and Adolf van Gendt

Location: Stationsplein, Amsterdam, Netherlands

Completed: 1889

Style/Period: Flemish Gothic Revival

Amsterdam's Central Station was a new gateway into a commercial city that had grown around maritime trade, and whose fate had rested, metaphorically and literally, on water. The two men tasked with creating the station had recent experience of large-scale building in difficult circumstances. Cuypers had designed the vast Rijksmuseum (1885), while Van Gendt was the architect behind the city's main concert hall, the Concertgebouw (1881).

Construction work began with the creation of three artificial islands — 8,687

wooden pilings supported the largely red brick neorenaissance building. When finished, its imposing central section comprised a pair of towers flanking the main entrance that together suggest a triumphal arch. The station was completed at a time when the Dutch were rediscovering their sense of national pride, but it also reflects a break with the past. The station obscured the dock complex beyond and literally turned its back to it, as the entrance is on the opposite side, suggesting a country ready to move forward to embrace the modern world. The architects did not, however, entirely forget the old sailing ships that brought the country great wealth. One of the towers has a "clock," that actually shows wind direction. **IW**

Madras High Court

Architect: Henry Irwin
Completed: 1892 (begun 1862)
Location: Madras (now Chennai), India
Style/Period: Indo-Saracenic/Indo-Gothic

If the Madras High Court in Chennai looks somewhat European, it is because India was part of the British Empire at the time of its construction. Because Britain ruled India, the instruments and symbols of imperial rule tended to conform to British models. That said, a composite, Indo-Saracenic style eventually evolved that mixed Hindu, Saracenic (Muslim) and British elements (which is why its alternative name is Indo-Gothic, for Gothic revival architecture was all the rage in Britain at the time).

Although the Madras High Court as a jurisdictional authority was established in 1862, the building of the same name was not completed until 1892. It was largely the work of the Irish-born architect Henry Irwin, who made his name in British India with his Indo-Saracenic buildings. The Madras High Court was constructed of red sandstone and was notable for its minarets, one of which, at 175 feet (53 m) above sea level, was used as a lighthouse. Inside, high ceilings and long corridors ensured a cool and spacious interior, while beauty and interest were provided by a host of decorative features in the form of stained glass, fretted and carved woodwork, ironwork and tiling. **CH-M**

Monadnock Building

Architects: Burnham & Root and Holabird & Roche
Completed: 1893
Location: Chicago, Illinois, United States
Style/Period: Richardsonian

Named after a New Hampshire mountain, the Monadnock Building is a prototype skyscraper that was built in two distinct phases for Peter Brooks, a Boston-based developer who, unusually for the time, wanted a building with little ornamentation. The first phase of construction work began in 1889 using plans produced by Daniel Burnham and John Root. They produced what is now the 16-story northern half of the building. It remains one of the world's largest masonry load-bearing buildings. The walls are a massive 6 feet (2 m) thick at the base, but even so the structure sank under its own weight, necessitating the building of steps.

The second phase of work, the 17-story southern half, began in 1891 and was based on work done by William Holabird and Martin Roche. They opted to use the comparatively new technique of steel-frame construction — a structural advance that would lead to taller and taller buildings. Lighter and stronger, the steel frame also allowed them to have narrow pillars and larger windows. The Monadnock, briefly the world's tallest building, marks a key turning point in architectural history between two building techniques. **IW**

Bradbury Building

Architect: George H. Wyman
Completed: 1893 (begun 1889)
Location: 304 South Broadway, Los Angeles, California, United States
Style/Period: Commercial Romanesque/Italian Renaissance Revival

Although it is over a century old (and is officially a U.S. National Historic Landmark), the Bradbury Building has a number of futuristic associations. It featured, for instance, in the stylish science-fiction movie *Blade Runner* (1982) and was inspired by *Looking Backward* (1887), a utopian novel by Edward Bellamy that envisaged life in the year 2000.

The Bradbury Building bears the name of the man who commissioned it. Lewis Bradbury, a millionaire real-estate developer, dreamed of erecting a grand edifice that would be regarded as a monument to his commercial acumen and influence. The architect to whom it eventually fell to translate this dream into reality was George H. Wyman, and, thanks to his boldness, the Bradbury Building (which still functions as an office space) has indeed become a renowned monument. With its four levels of windows (those on the top floor displaying Roman arches) and giant-order pilasters, the sandstone, brick and terra-cotta exterior of the five-story building is reminiscent of Italian Renaissance architecture. The real glories lie within, however, not least the center court, or atrium, which is spectacularly illuminated by a skylight five stories above, and by the wrought-iron cagelike elevators and decorative railings that border the balconies and appear to channel the stairs upward. **CH-M**

Wightwick Manor

Architect: Edward Ould
Completed: 1893 (begun 1887)
Location: Wightwick Bank, Wolverhampton, England
Style/Period: Arts and Crafts

Wightwick Manor's elaborately half-timbered exterior may look Tudor at first sight but, in fact, dates from the late Victorian period. It is a testament to the desire of the then fashionable arts and crafts movement's leading lights to evoke a simpler age's vernacular traditions and styles. Attaining such an effect did not come cheap, however, and only wealthy patrons — in this case the industrialist Theodore Mander — could afford to commission a country residence like this one.

In designing Wightwick Manor (whose main part dates from 1887, with the Great Parlour/Dining Room/Billiard Room east wing being completed in 1893), architect Edward Ould's intention was to evoke a 16th-century English manor house. Steep roofs and gables surmount a three-story building with ranks of red brick chimneys towering above. Yet, so artlessly higgledy-piggledy is

the mixture of features, styles and materials (sandstone, brick, timber and tile, for instance) that it appears to have grown almost organically over centuries, rather than over mere years. Wightwick Manor is set within fine English gardens, reflecting the domestic revival's emphasis on unifying

buildings and their natural surroundings as organically as possible. The arts and crafts theme is spectacularly reinforced inside, with wood paneling, stained glass in the leaded windows and William Morris & Co. fabrics and wallpapers. **CH-M**

Tower Bridge

Architects: Sir Horace Jones and Sir John Wolfe-Barry

Completed: 1894

Location: River Thames, London, England

Style/Period: Gothic Revival

The 19th century saw a vast expansion in the trade passing through London's docks and a large increase in the population of the East End that surrounded them, yet there were no bridges across the River Thames in the vicinity. In 1876 the Corporation of the City of London formed the Special Bridge or Subway Committee, and it instituted a public competition to find an appropriate design to remedy the problem. More than 500 plans were produced, but it was not until 1885 that a suitable winner, a low-level bascule bridge, was found. It had been devised by Horace Jones, the Architect and Surveyor for the corporation.

Work began two years later, but Jones died the same year. Civil engineer John Wolfe-Barry took his place. The bridge consists of two huge piers sunk into the riverbed, which support some 10,000 tons (9,070 metric tonnes) of steel framework clad in Cornish granite and Portland stone. The granite and stone protected the metalwork and gave it a more — as was fashionable at the time — conventional Gothic revival look. When completed it was the largest and most sophisticated bascule bridge in the world, and its arms can be raised to their maximum 86 degrees in less than a minute. **IW**

Heian Jingo Shrine

Architect: Unknown

Completed: 1895

Location: Japan

Style/period: Shinto

Built to mark the 1100th anniversary of Kyoto (originally Heiankyo), the Heian Jingo Shinto shrine is dedicated to Emperor Kanmu (737–806), who made Kyoto the country's capital city in 794, and Emperor Komei (1831–1867), the last emperor to have Kyoto as capital before the honor moved to Tokyo. The shrine's design is a model of the Daigoku-den (Palace of the Hall of State), the Imperial Palace of Japan from 710 to 784, but is two-thirds of the original's size.

The concrete *torii* (traditional gateway) at the entrance to the shrine is one of the largest in Japan, standing 79 feet (24 m) high with a top rail over 108 feet (33 m) long. The buildings are predominantly orange, green and white, and they include the *Ote-mon* (main gateway), the *Hon-den* (east and west main halls), the Daigoku-den and the spirit hall. Near to the main halls are two Chinese-style towers known as the *Byakko-ro* ("white tiger") and the *Soryu-ro* ("blue dragon"). The Daigoku-den building was rebuilt in 1979 after a fire and now measures 108 x 39 feet (33 x 12 m), rising to a height of 54 feet (16.5 m). Outside are three beautiful stroll gardens to the east, west and north of the shrine. **EW**

Sezessionhaus

Architect: Josef Olbrich

Completed: 1898

Location: Freidrichstrasse, Vienna, Austria

Style/Period: Art Nouveau/Secession

In 1897 the German-born Josef Olbrich — together with 18 others, including the renowned Austrian artist Gustav Klimt — formed an antitraditionalist art group, a branch of the art nouveau movement known as the secessionists, in Vienna. They took their inspiration, to a degree, from the work of the Scottish architect and designer Charles Rennie Mackintosh, and their aim was to create a new art that bore no relationship to the past. The Sezessionhaus was the temple and home to their new art form, and the pylonlike entrance carried the movement's motto, "To every age its art. To every art its freedom."

The building, which was created as an exhibition hall to display secessionist works, combines imposing monumentality with delicate detailing. It consists of simple geometric forms relieved by fine embellishments, not least on the front facade, which is partly covered by a tendril-like design in gold that was the movement's chosen motif. There are the heads of the three Gorgons above the main door, which

symbolize architecture, sculpture and painting — the art forms that the secessionists wanted to bring together. A delicate fretwork cupola of golden laurel leaves tops the building. **IW**

Carson, Pirie, Scott and Company Department Store

Architect: Louis Sullivan

Completed: 1899

Location: 1 South State Street, Chicago, Illinois, United States

Style/Period: Chicago School

The Carson, Pirie, Scott and Company Department Store was a pioneering commercial building that blazed an innovative trail as the old century gave way to the new. Not only did it use a fundamentally novel structural technique — based on a strong, light, fireproof and rapidly raised steel-frame skeleton — but this technique in turn enabled the creation of a new type of building: the department store. This U.S. National Historic Landmark was commissioned in 1899 from architect Louis Sullivan by Schlesinger and Mayer, a Chicago dry-goods merchant. However, it was bought after completion in 1904 by Carson, Pirie, Scott and Company. In the meantime, Sullivan had erected a nine-story building into which a 12-story annex was subsequently incorporated.

Although it followed a groundbreaking design, the Carson, Pirie, Scott and Company Department Store was also of its time, as manifested in the sinuous, organic, densely detailed art-nouveau style of the cast-iron "frames" that appear to encase the windows of the first two stories. Above the storefront elements, however, the terra-cotta-clad facade, which encompasses the serried horizontal ranks of windows in the multiple upper stories, is defined by the steel-frame skeleton. This treatment is characteristic of the Chicago School of architecture, of which Sullivan was an innovative member. **CH-M**

Hvitträsk

Architects: Eliel Saarinen, Armas Lindgren and Herman Gesellius

Completed: 1901

Location: Hvitträskintie 166, Luoma, Finland

Style/Period: Finnish National Romantic/Arts and Crafts/*Jugendstil*

Hvitträsk's purpose — a commune-anticipating complex of beautifully designed living spaces and workspaces — and style — Finnish National Romantic, incorporating elements inspired by *Jugendstil*, the Northern European version of art nouveau — may be regarded as chasing an ideal, but the ideal became a reality. Its creators, Eliel Saarinen, Armas Lindgren and Herman Gesellius, had founded their own architectural firm in 1896, and in 1901 they decided to move their individual homes and collective practice from Helsinki, the Finnish capital city, to the countryside. Hvitträsk was accordingly constructed on a hill above the forest-fringed Lake Vitträsk. It incorporated living spaces, design studios and workshops where domestic objects were crafted.

The major inspiration underpinning Hvitträsk's style was Finnish national Romanticism, a movement that had been kick-started by the publication, in 1835, of Elias Lönnrot's epic poem *Kalevala*. This popular interpretation of Finnish folktales generated a fervent interest in Finland's history and traditions that, in the arts, was sustained by ideals borrowed from the English arts and crafts ethos. This is why the complex was built primarily from local logs and stone, as well as plaster and shingles, why it includes medieval-looking traditional Finnish elements like snow-repelling steeply pitched roofs, and why it blends so sympathetically with the surrounding landscape. **CH-M**

Haus Behrens

Architect: Peter Behrens

Completed: 1901 (begun 1899)

Location: Mathildenhöhe, Darmstadt, Germany

Style/Period: *Jugendstil*

The Haus Behrens, or Behrens House, is the residence that German architect Peter Behrens built for himself on a hill named Mathildenhöhe outside Darmstadt. He had moved from Munich (where he had been a founding member of both the Munich secession and the Vereinigte Werkstätten) at the invitation of Grand Duke Ernst Ludwig of Hesse-Darmstadt in 1899. The grand duke's intention was to establish an artists' colony with the help of such increasingly acclaimed architects as Josef Maria Olbrich and Behrens.

Perhaps it was because it was his own home, and partly because an atmosphere of innovative creativity inevitably pervaded Mathildenhöhe, that the highly unusual Haus Behrens can be considered a statement building both inside and out. Behrens designed the furniture and fittings, too, and the building may be considered a "total work of art." The stucco facade of the three-story house is dominated by a bullet-shaped gable, above which soars a steeply pitched triangular roof. Although it includes a number of *Jugendstil* (the German variation of art nouveau) touches, such as the decoration applied to the high double doors leading into the house, the overall effect simultaneously pays homage to aspects of traditional German vernacular architecture and, in its austerity, anticipates modernism. **CH-M**

Fuller Building (The Flatiron)

Architect: Daniel Burnham

Completed 1902 (begun 1901)

Location: New York City, United States

Style/Period: Beaux Arts/Chicago Early Modern

Originally called the Fuller Building (after George A. Fuller, the Chicago contractor who financed the project), this iconic building is now universally known as the Flatiron. It sits on an awkwardly narrow triangular plot at 175 Fifth Avenue at the intersection of Fifth with 23rd and Broadway. Designed in Beaux-Arts style by Chicago architect Daniel Burnham, it was one of the first buildings to be constructed using a steel skeleton and, accordingly, one of the first New York skyscrapers. The steel was deliberately over-specified to withstand the strong winds that presented a danger to the building's particularly narrow profile. Theoretically, it would fall over intact before it failed. The public was skeptical and called the building "Burnham's Folly."

Built to house offices for the Fuller Construction Company, it is 285 feet (87 m) high, has 22-stories and is split into three distinct horizontal sections. It is clad in non-load-bearing carved limestone and gray-colored terra-cotta panels. Based on the principals of a classical Greek column, the base is of rusticated limestone with copper-clad windows; the central section is of pale colored bricks and terra-cotta, while the top (the capital) has a heavily overhanging triangular cornice, which runs around the entire building, under a flat balustraded roof. The apex is only 6.5 feet (2 m) wide at the top. The entire facade is elaborately decorated with designs and motifs reminiscent of French and Italian Renaissance architecture. The Flatiron has been a National Historic Monument since 1989. **SF**

Parliament House, Budapest

Architect: Imre Steindl

Completed: 1902 (begun 1885)

Location: Budapest, Hungary

Style/Period: Neogothic

When Hungary achieved independence from Austria, Emperor Franz Joseph I and Prime Minister Kálmán Tisza announced an architectural competition to design the new parliament building (Országház) on the embankment of the River Danube. The winner was Hungarian architect Imre Steindl, who was in part inspired by the Houses of Parliament in London. Unfortunately he died soon after the building's completion.

Although intended to celebrate the millennium of the Magyars' founding of Hungary in 1896, the building was far from finished but was inaugurated nevertheless. It was not completed for a further six years. When finally finished, the Országház was 880 feet (268 m) long and 388 feet (118 m) wide with a 226-foot (69 m) high central dome. The facade features statues of Hungarian emperors, Transylvanian leaders and famous military heroes, and above the windows are the armorial bearings of the Hungarian monarchy and aristocracy. Inside were 10 courtyards surrounded by 691 rooms connected by around 12 miles (20 km) of passages, 29 staircases and 13 elevators. An estimated 1,000 construction workers toiled there, placing the 40 million bricks. The magnificent central hall is 16 sided (hexadecagonal) and elaborately decorated. The decor includes half a million precious stones, numerous frescoes and stained-glass windows and 88 pounds (40 kg) of gold. At the time it was the largest parliament building in the world; it remains the third largest and is now used as the seat of the National Assembly of Hungary. **SF**

Maison Horta

Architect: Victor Horta

Location: Brussels, Belgium

Completed: 1902 (begun 1898)

Style/Period: Art Nouveau

The leading architect of the short-lived art nouveau period was Belgian genius Victor Horta, whose work enormously influenced many of his younger contemporaries. One of his many extraordinary projects was Maison Horta, his private house and attached studio. The elaborate cut-stone facade, with its large windows, is less exuberant than some of his other works, but the interior is sinuous and extravagant. One of Horta's great innovations was the design of the open-plan central hall around which all the rooms lead off. This handsome hall is clad with black- and gray-veined white marble, and from here the stairs — edged with a metal and wood balustrade in a beautifully curved whiplash motif (a favorite of Horta's) — rise to the reception rooms and the internal entrance to Horta's studio. Another important innovation was the extensive roof glazing, which floods natural light into the stairwell and principal rooms.

Ostensibly finished in 1902, Horta changed and extended his masterpiece before finally selling it in 1919. Maison Horta was opened as the Musée Horta, dedicated to Victor Horta's life and works, in 1969. In 2000 it became a UNESCO World Heritage Site, cited for its pioneering stylistic architecture. It is one of four Horta town houses in Brussels recognized by UNESCO. **SF**

Little Thakeham

Architect: Sir Edwin Lutyens

Completed: 1903 (begun 1902)

Location: Storrington, West Sussex, England

Style/Period: Arts and Crafts

This grand English manor house was designed by Edwin Lutyens for the railroad and Madeira tycoon Ernest Blackburn, and it is set among the rolling hills, woods and orchards of West Sussex. Blackburn bought the site for £16,000 (around U.S.$30,000) and then spent a further £24,000 (around

$50,000) on the construction. Thanks to the large workforce — numerous bricklayers, masons and carpenters — construction took only 18 months.

Edwin Lutyens designed in the arts and crafts style, a movement that emphasized the old-fashioned virtues of craftsmanship and quality materials. Consequently, his buildings characteristically have architectural references to the past — typically, as here, the Elizabethan style. Designed on an E-shaped plan, the house walls are $2^1/_2$ feet (75 cm) thick. The exterior looks late Tudor, but the interior contains classical mannerist elements.

The architecture is pure theater: the

entrance is through a heavy oak door into a low-ceilinged towered porch, which leads to a long and relatively narrow low-ceilinged entrance passage, which suddenly opens up into a magnificent double-height hall. The hall contains a handsome baroque-style stone screen and impressive oak staircase, which are illuminated by a huge double-height oriole window. Lutyens described Little Thakeham as the "best of the bunch" of his manor houses. Among the great glories of the building are the magnificent gardens, of which there are seven — one for each of Blackburn's children. **SF**

Hill House

Architect: Charles Rennie Mackintosh

Completed: 1903 (begun 1902)

Location: Helensburgh, Scotland

Style/Period: Art Nouveau

Hill House is the largest and finest of Charles Rennie Mackintosh's domestic buildings. It was commissioned by the Glasgow publisher Walter Blackie. Designed in the Scottish baronial tradition with a corner tower, a few arrow-slit windows and a parapet, all with a distinctly arts and crafts cast, it is built on a hill from local sandstone and rendered, as specified by Mr. Blackie, with gray roughcast on the exterior walls. The client knew what he wanted and rejected Mackintosh's first design on the basis of excessive cost and too much decoration or, as he described it, "adventitious ornament."

All the principal rooms are light and bright since they face south and overlook the spectacular Firth of Clyde. Typically, Mackintosh's attention to detail saw him designing almost all of the furniture and fittings for the principal rooms — fitted wardrobes, fireplaces, even the pewter fire tongs and poker. For the decor he specified mostly white walls decorated with pink, silver and pale green stencilwork, although in the wide hall, dark wooden panels contrast with pale wallpaper.

No expense was spared on the necessities: the bathroom had the latest and best plumbing, including the recently invented shower. Mackintosh also designed the initial formal landscaping around the house, giving precise instructions as to the positioning of the hedges and the shaping of the trees. **SF**

The Stock Exchange

Architect: Hendrik Petrus Berlage

Completed: 1903 (begun 1898)

Location: Amsterdam, Netherlands

Style/Period: Amsterdam School

Founded by the Dutch East India Company in 1602, the Amsterdam Stock Exchange, or Beurs, is probably the oldest such institution in the world. The Stock exchange (or Beurs van Berlage) was one of the first modern buildings in the Netherlands. It was constructed on land reclaimed from the River Amstel.

This huge building was designer Hendrik Petrus Berlage's first big commission. Berlage rose to the challenge, producing a spectacular building of simplicity and clarity with no extraneous detail. Instead, he varied its silhouette with towers of different heights and shapes and different windows and elevations to give the impression of great architectural variety but unified by the same building materials: red brickwork with natural stone details. The clock on the main tower traditionally tolled at 1:30 in the afternoon to signal the start of the day's trading, and it bears the advice "Bide your time" and "Await your hour." The main trading hall rises 72 feet (22 m) and is roofed over with double-glass panes. Arches pierce the walls, which are decorated with various carved reliefs by Lambertus Zijl, and a statue of Mercury, the god of trade and thieves, stands by the main balcony. By 1912 the building was already too small, and some Beurs traders moved out to the current stock exchange building at Beursplein 5. In 1988 the Beurs became home to the Dutch Philharmonic Orchestra. **SF**

Sanatorium Purkersdorf

Architect: Josef Hoffmann
Completed: 1905 (begun 1904)
Location: Purkersdorf, near Vienna, Austria
Style/Period: Wiener Werkstätte

When, in 1903, the Austrian industrialist Victor Zuckerkandl bought a "mineral spa with cure-park" at Purkersdorf, on the outskirts of Vienna (the capital of the then Austrian-Hungarian Empire), he was determined to attract a wealthy clientele to his new investment. To this end, he commissioned one of Vienna's most talked-about architects to design a new sanitorium building — a health spa cum hotel.

Josef Hoffman was a founding member of the Wiener Sezession, or Vienna secession, a movement that had seceded from the Viennese Academy of Fine Arts in 1897. Although *Sezessionstil* (secession style) was a variation of art nouveau, Hoffmann's designs tended toward the clean and rectilinear — many were almost industrial looking — and the Sanitorium Purkersdorf accordingly followed these simple, angular lines. Monotony, however, was avoided by means of numerous projections, giving the four-story facade an elegant modular appearance. This practicality was avant-garde in comparison to the prevailing architecture of the time, but it entirely suited a sanatorium and spa. Another feature of the Wiener Sezession was its emphasis on an arts-and-crafts-type fusion of art, architecture, crafts and furnishings. The fixtures and fittings within the sanatorium were consequently designed and created by the Wiener Werkstätte (Vienna Workshops), which were established in 1903. Again, Hoffmann was a founding member. **CH-M**

Grand Hotel Europa (Evropa)

Architects: Bedřich Bendelmayer and Alois Dryák,

Location: Wenceslas Square, Prague, Czech Republic

Completed: 1905 (begun 1903)

Style/Period: Art Nouveau

Also known as the Grand Šoubek and the Grand Hotel Evropa, the hotel was originally built in 1889 as *U Arcivévody Stepana* ("At the Archduke Stephen"), but it was completely rebuilt in the early 20th century, in the art nouveau style that was current at the time, during an architectural revival in Prague.

Entrusted with the project were Bedřich Bendelmayer and Alois Dryák, well-known Czech architects, who were celebrated for their style. The magnificent mustard yellow art nouveau facade — one of the best preserved in Prague — looks out over famous Wenceslas Square, the main square in the city. Meanwhile, the incredible interior — as showcased in many movies, notably *Mission Impossible* — was designed by Bohumil Hübschman, Jan Letzel and architectural sculptor Ladislav Šaloun (his work is also seen on the front facade). Lavishly designed and decorated, the principal rooms are laden with mosaics, decorative metalwork and elaborate light fixtures. The stunning art nouveau restaurant, called the Titanic Restaurant, is one of the grandest dining rooms in the whole of Prague. **SF**

Scotland Street Primary School

Architect: Charles Rennie Mackintosh

Completed 1906 (begun 1903)

Location: Glasgow, Scotland

Style/Period: Arts and Crafts

Scotland Street Primary School was Charles Rennie Mackintosh's last major commission in his hometown of Glasgow and his second commission for a school (the first was Martyr's Public School, also in Glasgow, completed in 1895). His brief was to design a school for 1,250 students for the district of Kingston, but Mackintosh frequently clashed with the school governors as they tried to cut down on expenses — principally the detailing for which Mackintosh was famous. When the building was eventually finished it came in at 25 percent over budget at a cost of £34,291 ($70,000).

The school board wanted a standard layout with separate entrances for boys and girls; instead, Mackintosh produced two Scottish baronial towers — which contain the stairs and are extravagantly glazed, almost top to bottom, with leaded-glass windows — and finished off with molded stonework at the top. These are the entrance halls and are magnificently tiled light-filled areas. The rear elevation looks more conventional, but upon closer inspection reveals molded window detailing that features stylized Scottish thistles and Trees of Life. Even the metal railings surrounding the school bear Mackintosh's trademark styling, again using thistle heads that symbolize the Scottish school children who grow with knowledge as they attend school. The building now serves as the Scotland Street School Museum, presenting the history of education in Scotland. **SF**

GIRLS

Larkin Administration Building

Architect: Frank Lloyd Wright

Completed: 1906 (begun 1904) (Demolished 1950)

Location: Buffalo, New York, United States

Style/Period: Early Modern

The Larkin Company, a successful mail-order retailer of general domestic goods, decided to spend a lavish $4 million on a new headquarters to be built across the road from their main factory in Buffalo, New York. Frank Lloyd Wright was commissioned and designed a radically innovative office building that was huge and made the most of natural light. Typical of Wright, every detail was specified: from his own design for an air-conditioning system — the first office to have one — to the hermetically sealed double-paned windows, electrical fittings and metal office furniture. Constructed with dark red bricks and pink-tinted mortar, the five-story main building was linked to a three-story annex. It was designed to last and made from 10-inch (25 cm) thick reinforced concrete in slabs 34 x 17 feet (10 x 5 m) with floors supported by 24-inch (60 cm) steel beams. The austere entrance was decorated with bas-reliefs by Richard W. Bock and two waterfall-like fountains. The building opened up into a central court containing office desks and surrounded by balconies, which increased the natural light. To bounce back even more light Wright used hard semi-vitreous cream-colored brick on the internal walls. The upper stories contained the kitchen and bakery, a refectory, dining rooms, restrooms and classrooms, as well as a branch of the Buffalo Public Library and a conservatory. The roof itself held a roof garden and was bricked out as a recreation area for staff and guests. **SF**

Casa Batlló

Architect: Antoni Gaudí

Completed: 1906 (begun 1904)

Location: Barcelona, Spain

Style/Period: Expressionism/Art Nouveau

One of the architectural highlights of Barcelona is Casa Batlló, designed by Catalan genius Antoni Gaudí for the wealthy businessman Josef Batlló. Gaudí was approached to modernize an existing apartment building (built in 1877), but what he did was remodel the interior by moving the walls around, creating a much bigger internal light well. He also completely altered the facade into a continuous, sinuous, flowing building, which to many eyes resembles a skeleton or some sort of organic creature. Local people call it *Casa dels ossos*, the "House of Bones."

There does not appear to be a straight line in the entire building: the lower floors have huge irregular oval windows of differing sizes that flood the interior with natural light. The exterior is built of carved and shaped sandstone and concrete studded with colorful glass and ceramic pieces (called *trencadís*), mostly in golden oranges and shades of blue and turquoise. Yet another layer of elaboration is added by the decorative metalwork, in particular the balcony railings. The double-story attic roof is tiled in such a way as to look like a lizard's skin, and it is often likened to a dragon, with its ribbed and arched "skeletal" ridge and weird chimney stacks. **SF**

Villa Ruggeri

Architect: Giuseppe Brega

Completed: 1907 (begun 1902)

Location: Pesaro, Italy

Style/Period: Art Nouveau/Stile Floreale
(Villino Ruggeri)

Commissioned by rich Italian ceramics businessman and industrialist Oreste Ruggeri and his wife as their summer retreat, this small villa overlooks the Adriatic Sea on the Marche coast in the then fashionable holiday resort of Pesaro, northern Italy. They wanted their villa to be in the latest style, which was generally labeled art nouveau. The extravagant and sinuous decoration was also known as *stile Inglese* or *stile Liberty* — the style of the English, in homage to Liberty, the Regent Street store in London and quintessential purveyor of the arts and crafts style.

Italian architect Giuseppe Brega was commissioned for the project and produced a design with a mixture of stylistic influences and elements, part Oriental and part Western. The pagoda-shaped roof is clad with red tiles, and the town-side elevation has a fairy-tale semicircular tower at first floor level, complete with a pointed spire in the middle. The beige-colored exterior walls are enlivened by flamboyant white stucco floral ornamentation around every window and across all the architectural elements. All the balconies and the railings surrounding the house have typical art nouveau sinuous patterns. Built on a relatively small scale to accommodate just one family, internally the villa is much more conventional in execution. SF

Samaritaine Department Store

Architects: Frantz Jourdain and Henri Sauvage

Completed: 1907 (Store 2) and 1910 (Store 1)

Location: Paris

Style/Period: Art Nouveau/Art Deco

One of the biggest and most impressive department stores in Paris is the Samaritaine, which sits in the First Arrondissement on the right bank of the Seine overlooking Pont Neuf. It gets its name from the hydraulic pump that provided the area with water from 1609 until 1813: the pump had a bas-relief of the Good Samaritan on its face. The original store was first opened in 1869 by Ernest Cognacq, but by the turn of the century a bigger building was needed, and in 1904 architect Frantz Jourdain started work on a building in the art nouveau style. Business expanded, and an even larger store was needed. This time Henri Sauvage was approached for an art deco extension to be designed in collaboration with Frantz Jourdain.

This latter expansion, made out of steel in four rising stages, surrounds a vast internal court, which is overlooked from the upper shopping levels. The entire building is thick with cast-iron ribs, girders and decorative railings, all topped by a magnificent glass ceiling. Francis Jourdain, the architect's wife, designed the external art nouveau decorations in conjunction with the

painter Eugene Grasset, the ceramicist
Alexandre Bigot and the ironworker
Edouard Schenck.

The building was further expanded
between 1926 and 1928, at which time the
city planners requested that, for aesthetic
reasons, the steel frame be hidden
underneath cream stone cladding. A third
building was added in 1930 using the same
two architects. **SF**

Unity Temple

Architect: Frank Lloyd Wright
Completed: 1908 (begun 1906)
Location: Oak Park, Illinois, United States
Style/Period: Cubist

Unity Temple, built for the Unitarian
Universalist congregation of Illinois, is the
only public building still in use from Frank
Lloyd Wright's early works. It was also one of
his favorite projects. As a member of the
congregation who lived only a few blocks
away, he was the obvious choice as architect
when the original church burnt down after a
lightning strike in 1905.

Wright's innovative design was one of the
first public buildings to be built using
shuttering and poured concrete with metal
reinforcements. He did this for reasons of
economy, as well as for aesthetics. Inspired by
ancient temples and the solemnity of
worship, he also insisted that it be called a
temple rather than a mere church. Unity
Temple was built on a narrow lot beside a
noisy street, so Wright devised solid walls to
cut out the noise. He kept the facade simple,
only enlivening them with an integral series
of ornamented columns that support the
huge projecting slab roof. The main
entrance is behind an enclosing wall on the
side of the building to preserve a sense of
intimacy and privacy. The deliberately dark
and somber interior is lit from high amber-
colored slit windows that run in ribbons
around the building. What Wright termed
his "jewel box" is rimmed with balconies on
three sides and only holds a congregation of
about 400 souls. The decor is simple but
elegant, and much of the internal decoration
is made of wood. **SF**

Glasgow School of Art

Architect: Charles Rennie Mackintosh

Completed: 1909 (begun 1896)

Location: Glasgow, Scotland

Style/Period: Arts and Crafts/Art Nouveau

Although at the time only a lowly assistant at the Glasgow architectural firm of Honeyman & Keppie, Charles Rennie Mackintosh won the (limited to 12 contenders) competition to design the new premises for the prestigious Glasgow School of Art in 1897. The brief was for a plain building, and, although it was his first commission, many consider it to be his greatest building.

The school is based on an elongated E-shaped plan and fills an entire block along the side of a steeply sloping and narrow south facing hill. The slightly off-center entrance lies up a short flight of steps and under an art nouveau iron arch. Long corridors link the large studio spaces that are illuminated by huge braced windows that make the most of the light, and the offices and smaller rooms are located behind. The building strongly reflects the Scottish baronial tradition, with its volumes of heavy masonry and brickwork relieved by the large windows, the lighter floral and geometric motifs of art nouveau in the decoration and detailing, the wrought iron used for structural features and the colorful tiles. Mackintosh designed the art nouveau interiors in collaboration with his wife, Margaret Macdonald, including the carpets, fireplaces, light fixtures, bookcases, tables and chairs and even the dishes. The building costs were funded mainly by private donation, and the project was completed in two stages, 1897 and then 1909. **SF**

Gamble House

Architect: Greene & Greene

Completed: 1909 (begun 1908)

Location: Pasadena, California, United States

Style/Period: American Arts and Crafts

Architect brothers Charles Sumner Greene and Henry Mather Greene — better known as Greene & Greene — were commissioned by wealthy Cincinnati clients David and Mary Gamble (of the Procter and Gamble Company) to design their retirement home in Pasadena, California. Greatly influenced by Japanese architecture and the importance of nature in relation to their work, the brothers developed a unique architectural aesthetic that reached its apogee with their "ultimate bungalows," of which Gamble House is perhaps the best example.

The architects and their clients collaborated closely over the plans to design and decorate the house. Once the ground was broken in February 1908, construction continued apace. The building was completed within 10 months and the custom-made furniture — built-in cupboards, paneling, art glass, lighting, carvings and rugs — was moved in. Every element, down to the smallest switch and peg, had been carefully thought out, designed and made. Gamble House was quickly recognized as a masterpiece — an inspired piece of design that merged the best elements of Californian and Japanese architecture that fitted seamlessly and elegantly into the landscape in true arts and crafts style. Internally, the impression is of wide, open rooms and rich craftsmanship, which is emphasized by the extensive use of wood. Gamble House is a National Historic Landmark. **SF**

Great Mosque of Djenné

Architect: Ismaila Traoré
Completed: 1909 (started 1907)
Location: Djenné, Mali
Style/Period: Sudano-Sahelian

The largest adobe building in the world today, the Great Mosque in Djenné is the successor to other similar structures built from mud bricks in this location. The first mosque was built here in 1240, when Mali converted to Islam. Demolished when the country was conquered by Amadou Lobbo in 1834 and later rebuilt, the rebuild was torn down to make way for the present structure in 1906.

The mosque was built on a site carefully chosen by Ismaila Traoré, the head of Djenné's masons guild, to protect it from flooding by the River Bani. Its adobe walls — some 16 to 24 inches (40 to 60 cm) thick and strengthened with deleb palm wood — are coated with mud plaster to make them smooth. The thickness of the walls acts as insulation against the heat of the African day and yet retains enough of the heat to keep the mosque warm at night. Designated a World Heritage Site by UNESCO in 1988, along with the Old Towns of Djenné, the Great Mosque is one of the great achievements of adobe architecture. The mosque is dominated by its three large minarets, whose prominent spires hark back to the pre-Islamic spires that represented the protective spirits of ancestors, giving the mosque a strongly African character. **SF**

A.E.G. Turbine Hall

Architect: Peter Behrens
Completed: 1910 (begun 1908)
Location: Moabit, Berlin, Germany
Style/Period: Industrial

The architect and designer Peter Behrens had been working with A.E.G. (or, to give it its full name, Allgemeine Elektrizitäts Gesellschaft) as a consultant for two years when, in 1908, he was commissioned to design a turbine hall for this Berlin-based general-electrical company's headquarters in the German capital. Behrens's subsequent design has been hailed as a masterpiece of form and functionality, being both arrestingly modern (in terms of its appearance as well as the materials used) and perfectly suited to the building's purpose: accommodating huge turbines.

Massive reinforced-concrete corners curved around the less visible elements of the steel-frame skeleton that supported this essentially rectangular structure (a modular two-story annex projected from one side). Vast windows also dominated the walls, letting in as much light as possible,
particularly along the street facade. An arched, subtly faceted roof covered the building, whose German name – A.E.G. Turbinenfabrik — was incised in the concrete at the gable end in a clean sans-serif typeface (Behrens was responsible for developing a corporate identity and house style for A.E.G. that extended to its logotype). The effect, particularly from the inside, was strongly reminiscent of a church or cathedral, giving the impression that the A.E.G. Turbine Hall was a hymn — in glass, concrete and steel — to industry. **CH-M**

Frederick C. Robie House

Architect: Frank Lloyd Wright
Completed: 1910 (started 1909)
Location: Chicago, Illinois, United States
Style/Period: Prairie

A quintessential example of Wright's prairie house style, the Robie House sums up America's love affair with its greatest architect. Designed from Wright's Oak Park home and studio in 1910, it was built in 1909–1910 by H.B. Barnard of Chicago. The
Robie family had to sell the house in 1912, and when the site was eventually purchased in 1926 the house was slated for demolition. It was saved from this fate first by economic circumstances — the Great Depression — then by World War II and finally by William Zeckendorf, who bought it in 1958 and later donated it to Chicago University.

The 1950s and 1960s saw a revival in interest in both Frank Lloyd Wright's architecture and the preservation of America's architectural heritage. The Robie House was designated a National Historic Landmark on November 27, 1963, and a Registered Historic Place in Chicago when the register started in 1966. In 1997 the Robie reached the safety of the Frank Lloyd Wright Preservation Trust, which in 2002 started an $8-million restoration.

Architectural critics and historians noticed Wright's practice of using natural materials and making his creations blend in with their environment. They coined the term prairie style to describe the practice, and the Robie House, with its low horizontal profile that appears to spread over the prairie, is one of the best examples. **SF**

Palais Stoclet Palace (Stocletpaleis)

Architect: Josef Hoffmann

Completed: 1911 (begun 1905)

Location: Avenue de Tervueren, Brussels, Belgium

Style/Period: *Jugendstil*/Art Nouveau

Fine-art collector, wealthy banker and railroad financier Adolphe Stoclet wanted an impressive private mansion in the Avenue de Tervueren in Brussels, and he commissioned the Austrian architect and leader of the Vienna secession, Josef Hoffman, for the project. The brief was to produce a building that was an artwork in itself. No expense was to be spared, and only the best and most precious materials were used. Additionally, Stoclet insisted that only the very best craftsmen and artists work on the project.

Hoffmann engaged the Weiner Werkstätte (Viennese Workshop), a collective of craftsmen, designers, artisans, painters, architects and sculptors, of which he was a cofounder. Accordingly, the house has a totality of ensemble between the exterior, based on a series of cubic shapes, the interior and all the decor and furnishings. The simple Norwegian Turili-marble-clad facade with regularly shaped and spaced windows anticipates the linear austerity of modernism, and it can certainly be classified as early art deco, particularly the top of the tower, which is crowned by four copper male nude figures by the German sculptor Franz Metzner. The somewhat austere facade is relieved by decorative metal railings and thin molded friezes that surround the windows, along with occasional sculptures and carved ornaments. The magnificent double-storied intricately parquet-floored entrance hall contains a fountain surrounded by marble pillars and pilasters. Throughout, the sumptuous interior has walls clad in yellow-brown Italian Paonazzo marble and contains various artworks, including a specially commissioned frieze by Gustav Klimt. **SF**

Michelin Building

Architect: Francois Espinasse

Completed: 1911

Location: Chelsea, London, England

Style/Period: Art Nouveau/Art Deco

Historic commercial buildings are frequently bursting with character, unlike many of their dreary modern equivalents. The lavishly decorated Michelin Building is a literal example, its design revolving around the rotund figure of its former occupant's friendly logo. Designed in 1898 by artist Marius Rossillon, the portly white figure of Bibendum is known worldwide as the "Michelin Man." One of the earliest registered trademarks, Bibendum allegedly owes his existence to Édouard Michelin, who saw anthropomorphic potential in a stacked display of his company's pneumatic tires. With his brother André, Édouard built up a Gallic business empire that subsequently expanded into the British market. Their purpose-built headquarters in London's fashionable Chelsea district is a monument to the walking pile of tires, with bulbous glowing lanterns flanking the front elevation and three immense stained glass windows depicting "Bib" in his original cigar-smoking incarnation.

Though dripping with hand-made glazed tiles and art nouveau signage, the underlying structure was progressively modern. It was constructed using François Hennebique's reinforced-concrete system, which supports the large uninterrupted expanse of the service forecourt. Its fire-retardant properties were useful insurance, given that some

30,000 flammable tires were housed in the basement below. Michelin departed Chelsea in 1985. They sold their building to Terence Conran and Paul Hamlyn, who restored many original features while converting the building for a mixture of new uses. Given Michelin's gourmet association, it is fitting that one of these is the Bibendum restaurant, whose hearty French cuisine can still help patrons acquire a spare tire. **PC**

Austrian Post Office Savings Bank

Architect: Otto Wagner

Completed: 1912 (begun 1904)

Location: Geog-Coch-Platz 2, Vienna, Austria

Style/Period: Early Modernism

The design entered by Otto Wagner, a professor of architecture at the Viennese Academy of Fine Arts, into a competition soliciting plans for the new Österreichische Postsparkasse (Austrian Post Office Savings Bank) building in Vienna in 1903 proved itself a prize winner, albeit a controversial one. That the finished building is still held up as an outstanding example of pre–World War I avant-garde architecture confirms the wisdom of the judges' choice. The structure itself was erected in two stages: from 1904 to 1906 and from 1910 to 1912.

That practicality was one of the criteria at the forefront of Wagner's mind is evident from the numerous ingenious features that he incorporated into a building whose solid-looking brick facade was calculated to inspire confidence in those who entrusted their money to the Austrian Post Office Savings Bank. Thus, durable and easy-clean marble tiles were decoratively riveted with aluminum bolts to clad the eight-story exterior, whose many windows helped to illuminate the interior. Natural light also brightened the central *Kassenhalle*, or transactions hall, on the first floor, thanks to the glazed barrel-vaulted ceiling, and glass tiles set into the floor enabled light to filter through to the story below. In addition, none of the interior walls was load bearing, allowing for their future removal or rearrangement. **CH-M**

Casa Milà

Architect: Antoni Gaudí
Completed: 1912 (started 1906)
Location: Barcelona, Spain
Style/Period: Expressionism

Better known as *La Pedrera* (Catalan for "the quarry"), so nicknamed because of its size and shape, Casa Milà is the last secular building Gaudí constructed before devoting all his energies to the Sagrada Familia (see page 506). Commissioned by Pedro Milá i Camps, a rich businessman who was impressed by the Casa Battló, today it is part of the "Works of Antoni Gaudí" UNESCO World Heritage Site.

With its wavy façade, Casa Milà is reminiscent of a cliff peppered with caves and hollows. As with all of Gaudí's works, it is unusual and unconventional with few straight lines. The use of a steel frame meant that the walls were not load bearing, and so they could be a part of the sinuous design that is so well complemented by Josep Maria Jujol's wrought-iron balconies. Casa Milà is built around two courtyards that act as light wells and is crowned by a remarkable roof terrace with spectacularly surreal chimneys. It has completely irregular floor plans, with pillars and ceilings at different heights, and rooms that are a mixture of art nouveau — the style in vogue at the time of its construction — and expressionism. **SF**

Folly Farm

Architect: Sir Edwin Lutyens
Completed: 1912
Location: Sulhamstead, Berkshire, England
Style/Period: Arts and Crafts

This fine arts and crafts house is one of the most celebrated collaborations between the architect Edwin Lutyens and the garden designer Gertrude Jekyll. The oldest part of the house dates from around the time of Queen Anne (1702–1714), but in 1906 the new owner, H.H. Cochrane, commissioned the fashionable country house architect Edwin Lutyens to enlarge the house. He added a gray and red brick hipped roof and a William and Mary–style symmetrical wing at right angles to the farmhouse.

Six years later Folly Farm was bought by wealthy mine owner Zachary Merton, who again engaged Lutyens, this time to add a west wing. For this new addition Lutyens reverted to his more familiar Surrey arts and crafts style, with red brick and clay tiles on the roof and some elevations, small dormer windows and a weather-boarded gable end. Above a new cloister Lutyens placed a first floor sleeping balcony, which surrounded a large pool. Elsewhere he built a mews courtyard, some cottages and a circular dairy, and he extended the garden with a formal Dutch canal and sunken rose garden. The finished ensemble bears Lutyens' unmistakable trademark style: solid brickwork interspersed with large windows, pillars and arches overlaid with huge hipped roofs. When Merton died in 1915 his widow invited Lutyens to live at Folly Farm through the summer of 1915; it was the first time he had spent any length of time in one of his own houses. Folly Farm remains a private house. **SF**

Grand Central Station

Architect: Warren & Wetmore and Reed & Stem

Completed: 1913 (started 1904)

Location: New York, New York, United States

Style/Period: Neoclassical

Saved in 1967 from the wrecker's ball by the Landmarks Preservation Commission, Grand Central Terminal is a historic jewel in New York's architectural heritage. From the cavernous beauty of its concourse to its star-studded ceiling and grand 42nd Street facade — which boasts the world's largest example of Tiffany glass and Jules-Felix Coutan's huge sculptural group — Grand Central Terminal is one of the best-known stations in the world and the largest by number of lines and platforms.

Today's building replaced Grand Central Station (a name by which the terminal is still sometimes known). The station was a fantastic steel and glass edifice whose train shed measured 100 x 650 feet (30 x 200 m). But as the days of the steam locomotive drew to a close and building space on Manhattan became even more expensive, railways no longer needed aboveground open rail yards. Grand Central Station was slated for demolition and its replacement would be primarily underground. The "air rights" above the tracks were to be sold to developers. The winners of the competition to construct the new station were the Saint Paul firm of Reed and Stem — the fact that Reed's sister was married to the vice president in charge of construction surely being a coincidence.

However, another firm of architects — Warren and Wetmore — submitted a late proposal. Warren was a cousin of New York Central Chairman William Vanderbilt, and the two companies signed an agreement to work together in February 1904. Its success was staggering: in 1947 over 65 million passengers passed through the station. But the 1950s saw the end of long distance rail travel, and by the 1960s Grand Central was close to demolition. Saved, restored and revitalized, it was rededicated in 1998. **SF**

Woolworth Building

Architect: Cass Gilbert

Completed: 1913

Location: New York, New York, United States

Style/Period: Neogothic

Commissioned in 1910 to provide the F.W. Woolworth Company with a corporate headquarters on Broadway, the "Cathedral of Commerce" was the tallest tower in the world for nearly 20 years, until the arrival of the Bank of Manhattan Tower and the Chrysler Building in 1930 (see page 284). Designed around a steel frame that is supported on massive caissons, engineers Gunvald Aus and Kort Berle turned Cass Gilbert's gothic tower into a reality, including arches, spires, flying buttresses and gargoyles.

The interiors are as dramatic as the exterior. Heineicke and Bowen were responsible for the stained-glass dome over the marble staircase and the lavish decorations, which include caricatures of the men who were involved in the building's construction in the lobby. Inside, there are barrel-vaulted mosaics filled with flowers and birds, as well as other ornaments based on early Christian mosaics from Ravenna, Italy. Also of note are the elevators, which were numerous and high-speed for the time. Famously catering to the "five and dime" market, it is ironic that Woolworth paid the $13.5-million cost of the building in cash. The headquarters only occupied a couple of floors in the building, which financed itself with rentals — including the Irving Trust bank and Columbia Records. Woolworth's relinquished the tower in 1998 when they — by that time called the Venator Group — sold the building to the Witkoff Group for $155 million. **SF**

Hala Stulecia

Architect: Max Berg

Completed: 1913 (begun 1911)

Location: Breslau (now Wroclaw), Poland

Style/Period: Modernism

Hala Stulecia (Centennial Hall) was commissioned by the then German city of Breslau to house an exhibition in 1913 to commemorate the 100th anniversary of the *Völkerschlacht bei Leipzig* ("Battle of the Nations"), as the Germans call it but known elsewhere as the Battle of Leipzig, when Napoleon Bonaparte was beaten by a coalition of European forces.

German architect, and Breslau city planner and chief architect, Max Berg was charged with the important project. He produced a pioneering work of engineering, technology and a design that made the most of his modernist ideas. He produced a vast quatrefoil-shaped building with a large central circular space that could seat 6,000 people. The huge reinforced concrete cupola is 138 feet (42 m) high with an inner diameter of 75 yards (69 m) and is topped by a steel and glass dome 75 feet (23 m) high. In volume, Hala Stulecia contains almost 10.5 million square feet (975,000 sq. m), and when it was built it was the largest building of its type in the world. Following the memorial events, the building was used for various recreational and cultural uses, as it continues to be today. Hala Stulecia became a World Heritage Site in 2006 for its importance in the development of reinforced-concrete structures. **SF**

Scheepvaarthuis

Architect: J.M. van der Mey
Completed: 1916
Location: Amsterdam, Netherlands
Style/Period: Amsterdam School

Designed by J.M. van der Mey, the Scheepvaarthuis (Shipping House) stands on the corner of Prins Hendrikkade and Binnenkant in Amsterdam's former harbor. It is one of the most famous buildings in the city. Van der Mey was one of the leading figures of the Amsterdam School of architecture that developed in the Netherlands in the early part of the 20th century. The Scheepvaarthuis, commissioned in 1912 and on which van der Mey collaborated with the other two leaders of the style, Michel de Klerk and Piet Kramer, is considered the first building designed in the pure Amsterdam School style.

Reflecting the Netherlands' rich shipping tradition and built between 1912 and 1916 as an office building for six Amsterdam shipping companies, the stone building's decorative masonry, wrought ironwork and sculptures, both inside and out, reinforce the influence of the sea. Seahorses, anchors, shells and dolphins abound, and the Mediterranean Sea and Atlantic, Pacific and Indian oceans are represented around the entrance, as is Neptune, the Roman god of the sea. The last of the shipping companies vacated the building in 1981, and the Scheepvaarthuis has been used as a luxury hotel since 2007. **EW**

78 Derngate

Architect: Charles Rennie Mackintosh
Completed: 1917
Location: Northampton, England
Style/Period: Art Nouveau

Completed 10 years before his death, the renovation of 78 Derngate in Northampton is considered one of the most significant examples of Charles Rennie Mackintosh's work. It was also his only commission outside Scotland. A Georgian town house, 78 Derngate had been bought by businessman Wenman Joseph Bassett-Lowke, founder of a renowned toy company that bore his name and specialized in model railways. In 1916 he commissioned Mackintosh to supervise the renovation of the house, and it is the remodeled interior in the art nouveau style for which the house is famous.

Somewhat surprisingly, it does not appear that Mackintosh ever actually visited the house while the main renovations were taking place. Yet his influence, and that of the progressive Bassett-Lowke, on the visual impact of the interior is clear. In addition to the cohesive design that featured trademark Mackintosh characteristics, such as simple but striking decorative motifs, 78 Derngate was a very modern house with central heating, indoor plumbing and a plethora of kitchen gadgets. Functional yet beautiful, the Northampton house drew on Mackintosh's work in the library at Glasgow's School of Art, utilizing dark wood and strong geometric lines and exploiting natural light. After years of service as a girls' school, the house was transformed into a museum in 2003. **EW**

Carl Larsson's House

Architect: Carl Larsson
Completed: 1919 (begun 1899)
Location: Sundborn, Sweden
Style/period: Arts and Crafts

Now a major tourist attraction, the two-story home of Swedish painter Carl Larsson in Sundborn, originally built in 1837, was a gift to him and his wife Karin from his father-in-law. Larsson described the house, called "Lilla Hyttnäs," as "a very small, unpretentious, rather ugly, insignificant building" but his alterations to it made it a much-loved family home. "I wanted the house my way," he wrote, "or else I would not feel at home in it, and then my work would suffer."

Perhaps the most famous of the rooms is the drawing room, which, with its wall paneling, simple furniture and plain floors, is a prime example of Swedish interior design. By contrast, the strong reds and greens of the dining room, which were ahead of their time, exude warmth and intimacy. The bedrooms, particularly of Carl Larsson himself, show ingenuity and an original approach. Larsson's relatively small room is dominated by a multifunctional central bed, while the one used by his wife and children is a charming, open room with bright green and red detail set against a white background. Larsson painted many pictures of his family life with Karin and their children at Lilla Hyttnäs, ensuring the house a place in artistic history. **EW**

Helsinki Station

Architect: Eliel Saarinen

Completed: 1919

Location: Helsinki, Finland

Style/Period: Romantic/Rationalist

Wary travelers approach the ticket hall of Helsinki's grand railway terminal under the stern gaze of four stone sentries who stand with arms outstretched, clasping glowing orbs of light. These theatrical pieces of figurative sculpture belong to a building that lies on the very cusp of the modernist world, marking its architect's transition from fairy-tale Romanticism toward his own unique brand of expressionism.

Eliel Saarinen had originally won the 1904 competition for Helsinki Station with a design that played to Finnish preoccupations with national architectural identity. Its massive rubble walls and rustic stone finishes, surmounted with numerous turrets and no less than eight stone bears, followed the formula of his highly popular National Museum of Finland, which had helped bring Finnish Romanticism to the fore in 1902. This time, however, Saarinen faced an unexpected backlash led by architects Sigurd Frosterus and Gustaf Strenell. His colleagues publicly called for "a style of iron and common sense," in place of what they deemed to be picturesque excess. The force of their argument led Saarinen to rethink his scheme.

Following a tour of new rationalist German railway stations, Saarinen stripped his design of its quasi-medieval trappings to create a composition of austere granite walls capped in restrained copper details and surmounted by an almost streamlined 164-foot (50 m) clock tower. This hard, muscular aesthetic became the new model for much modern railway architecture, its monumental stonework finding favor in Britain and the United States, where Saarinen himself immigrated to in 1923. **PC**

Royal Palace

Architect: Unknown

Completed: 1919 (begun 1886)

Location: Phnom Penh, Cambodia

Style/Period: Cambodian

Built in 1866 by King Norodom when he moved the royal court from Oudong to Phnom Penh, the spectacular royal palace has been used by the Cambodian monarchy ever since (apart from the murderous years of Khmer Rouge rule, 1975–1993).

All of the buildings face east. While some have been modified or rebuilt over the years, the complex of the Throne Hall, Silver Pagoda, Khemarin Palace (the royal residence), along with several other structures, remains a stunning example of Cambodian architecture. Perhaps most interesting is the Silver Pagoda, named after its floor of 5,329 silver tiles. The building exhibits an astonishing collection of national treasures, such as a 198-pound (90 kg) gold Buddha encrusted with 9,584 diamonds, including a 25-carat diamond in the crown; a 17th-century baccarat-crystal Buddha; and the Wat Phnom Mondap, which contains Buddha's footprint. The cross-shaped Throne Hall, still used today for ceremonial occasions, incorporates a 194-foot (59 m) central spire topped with a white four-faced head of Brahma, the Hindu god of creation. Within the grounds, the Chan Chhaya Pavilion is most easily visible from outside the palace precincts, and it is still used for both open-air displays of traditional Khmer dance and royal appearances on state occasions. **EW**

The Ship

Architect: Michel de Klerk

Completed: 1921

Location: Spaarndammerbuurt, Amsterdam, Netherlands

Style/Period: Amsterdam School

A leading figure in the Amsterdam School of architecture that developed in the Netherlands in the early part of the 20th century, Michel de Klerk's legacy lives on in the housing blocks he designed between 1913 and 1921 in the Spaarndammerbuurt district of northwestern Amsterdam, the third of which is nicknamed "the Ship" (Het Scheep).

The Ship is built on a triangular site of some 113,000 square feet (10,500 sq. m) and comprises 102 homes in 18 different designs, a meeting hall, a communal garden, a school and a post office. Its uniqueness lies in de Klerk's ability to make all these separate entities look and feel like individual parts of a unified whole — in this case, a ship. Much of the architectural and decorative features resonate with a maritime influence, including the gently waving line above the doors and the sculpted post office set at the Ship's "prow." The somewhat mastlike spire at one end of the block serves no function beyond the aesthetic. Considered by some local politicians at the time as too luxurious for public-funded housing, the Ship has become one of the most important examples of the socialism-inspired Amsterdam School. **EW**

Einstein Tower

Architect: Erich Mendelsohn

Completed: 1921 (begun 1919)

Location: Wissenschaftspark Albert Einstein, Potsdam, Berlin, Germany

Style/Period: Expressionism

Today part of the Astrophysikalisches Institut Potsdam (the Potsdam Astrophysical Institute), the Einstein Tower, which stands in the Wissenschaftspark Albert Einstein (Albert Einstein Science Park), has been used for solar research since the 1920s. But that is not its only claim to fame. Erich Mendelsohn's unique structure is itself an object of fascination on account of its experimental futuristic appearance and streamlined sculptural curves. Perhaps one of the most extraordinary aspects of the project is the way in which Mendelsohn strove to interpret and express through architecture Einstein's relativity theories. Einstein was then the director of Berlin's Kaiser Wilhelm Institute for Physics and won the Nobel Prize for Physics of 1921, the same year in which the tower named in his honor was completed.

The Einstein Tower, which was commissioned by astronomer Erwin Finlay-Freundlich, comprises two main components: the tower itself, which houses a telescope beneath a dome at the top, and the irregularly shaped three-story laboratory from which it rises. A sense of unity is created by the molded, white-painted rendering that encases much of the concrete-and-brick structure and by the scooped-out appearance of the door and window recesses. The overall impression is of an organic, yet immensely sophisticated, construction that is utterly timeless. **CH-M**

Lincoln Memorial

Architect: Henry Bacon

Completed: 1922

Location: Washington, D.C., United States

Style/Period: Neoclassical

Dedicated on Memorial Day (May 30), 1922, 57 years after the death of America's 16th president, Abraham Lincoln, the Lincoln Memorial in Washington D.C.'s National Mall is one of the most iconic structures in the United States. The classic, rather stark design includes 36 Greek Doric–style columns representing the states in the Union at the time of Lincoln's death. The Memorial itself measures 190 feet (62 m) long by 119 feet (40.5 m) wide and 100 feet (27 m) high. It was built using materials native to the United States: the floor is pink marble from Tennessee, the walls are limestone from Indiana, the ceiling is marble from Alabama and the external facade is white marble from Colorado.

Inside is the famous 20-foot (6 m) high statue of Lincoln created by American sculptor Daniel Chester French out of 28 blocks of Georgian white marble. Behind the statue is the inscription "In this temple, as in the hearts of the people for whom he saved the Union, the memory of Abraham Lincoln is enshrined forever." On either side are two separate chambers; Lincoln's Gettysburg Address is inscribed on the wall of one and his second inaugural address is inscribed on the other. **EW**

Victor Emmanuel II Monument

Architect: Guiseppe Sacconi

Completed: 1922

Location: Rome, Italy

Style/Period: Neoclassical

King Victor Emmanuel II of Sardinia joined forces with Garibaldi and assumed the title of king of Italy on February 18, 1861. A tribute to Victor Emmanuel II's triumph as the first king of a united Italy, work on this white marble monument designed by Guiseppe Sacconi began in 1885. Also known as *Il Vittoriano* ("the victory celebration"), the monument sits between the Piazza Venezia and the Capitoline Hill in Rome. One of Italy's most derided landmarks, its location created some controversy because ancient Roman ruins and medieval churches were demolished to make way for what some have nicknamed "the wedding cake" and others "the typewriter." Others have complained that the bright white of the marble sits uneasily among the ancient buildings around it.

Standing 443 feet (135 m) wide and 230 feet (70 m) high, the monument includes a flight of steps to what is known as the "Alter of the Nation," where a huge 39-foot (12 m) long equestrian sculpture of Victor Emmanuel II dominates. Behind is a corridor of 49-foot (15 m) high Corinthian columns topped by two bronze quadrigae holding statues of Victoria, the Roman goddess of victory. The monument was inaugurated in 1911, 50 years after the creation of the new kingdom. In 1921 the Tomb of the Unknown Soldier was dedicated within the monument. Military guards stand watch over its eternal flame. **EW**

Stockholm City Hall

Architect: Ragnar Östberg

Completed: 1923 (begun 1911)

Location: Stockholm, Sweden

Style/Period: National Romanticism

With its mass of monumental brickwork dominating Stockholm's skyline, the famous Stockholm City Hall remains one of the 20th century's most influential buildings. Begun in 1911, Östberg's seamless blend of stylized regional vernacular, Venetian palazzo and columned medieval guildhall produced a remarkable building that managed to absorb a host of historical lessons while remaining resolutely modern. Raised upon a promontory on the island of Kungsholmen, the hall is best viewed from across the harbor's glittering waters, enjoying an enviable site that perhaps only the Sydney Opera House can rival.

There is a clean and elegant simplicity to the bare expanses of red brick (all 8 million of them), their color perfectly complemented by the weathered green verdigris of the high-pitched copper roofs. The solid 348-foot (106 m) tower is surmounted by a rather more delicate copper lantern. Cleverly evolved from other, smaller buildings that can be seen across the city, the hall subliminally suggests that it is part of a natural process of local evolution. Already loaded with national symbolism, the hall's patriotic silhouette is completed by the lantern's gilded *Tre Kronor*, Sweden's national symbol of three crowns. Royal connections continue to this day, with the king of Sweden visiting the hall to present the Nobel Prizes each December. Much admired in the Netherlands, Britain and America, the hall set a precedent for large-scale brick structures, including the art deco factories, libraries and power stations of Giles Gilbert Scott. **PC**

Fiat Factory

Architect: Giacomo Mattè-Trucco

Completed: 1923

Location: Lingotto, Turin, Italy

Style/Period: Modernism

The enormous former Fiat factory in Lingotto, Turin, was completed in 1923, and it is a striking example of early reinforced-concrete industrial architecture. At the time, it was the largest car factory in the world, and it was designed so that managers could drive throughout the plant to oversee progress without leaving their vehicles. It was set over five floors, with a carefully designed production line: raw materials entered on the ground floor and finished vehicles departed five floors later via the celebrated rooftop test track. Told by Fiat founder Giovanni Agnelli, that he "must have no aesthetic concerns," architect Mattè-Trucco produced a pioneering concrete structure that quickly became one of Italy's most famous landmarks. Le Corbusier described the building as "one of the most impressive sights in industry" and used an illustration of it in his seminal work, *Vers une architecture* ("Toward a new architecture"),

published in 1923.

The factory closed in 1983, presenting a real challenge to planners for the future of what had become a potent symbol in Turin. It was decided to redevelop the site, under the guidance of Renzo Piano, into a civic, commercial and arts center. Only the inside has been remodeled, and the external structure, including the famous floor-to-ceiling windows, have been left intact. Above, however, sits the new 400-ton (363 metric tonnes) steel and glass *Scrigno* ("treasure chest"), topped with an oversized flat roof nicknamed the "flying carpet." **EW**

Storer House

Architect: Frank Lloyd Wright

Completed: 1923

Location: 8161 Hollywood Boulevard, Los Angeles, California, United States

Style/Period: Early Modernism/Textile Block

In 1923 Frank Lloyd Wright experimented with a new building process he called the textile block system, in which he constructed buildings from precast concrete blocks with

decorated surfaces. The Storer House was the second home to be built in this way, and it was unique in that Wright used four different designs on the blocks. It presents an almost brutal mass of blockwork, yet the formidable exterior, inspired by Mayan architecture, is alleviated by the decorative detail and panel of two-story windows that open onto terraces at both the front and back.

The construction was supervised by Wright's son, Lloyd Wright, who landscaped the steep hillside site. When it was first built, the house had a far more stark appearance than it does today; mature foliage now softens the severe lines, giving the illusion of a building barely visible through a verdant jungle. It would seem that neither architect nor owner were entirely satisfied with their creation. Wright commented to his son that it "lacked joy" and called it "a tragedy from my standpoint." Storer sold the house in 1927, but subsequent owners were fortunately more appreciative of its merits. In 1931, tenant Pauline Schindler wrote, "The room in which I sit writing is a form so superb that I am constantly conscious of an immense obligation to Mr. Wright." **JM**

Notre Dame Le Raincy

Architect: Auguste Perret

Completed: 1923

Location: Le Raincy, France

Style/Period: Modernism

Auguste Perret is often regarded as a transition architect — a John the Baptist to Le Corbusier's Messiah (who worked in Perret's studio) — but his work deserves acclaim in its own right. The son of a Belgian builder, Perret joined the family construction firm and began to experiment with reinforced concrete as a building material. His first project, the 1903 apartment building in the Rue Franklin, Paris, proved that concrete, previously regarded as an industrial material, could be used to produce beautiful buildings.

Notre Dame Le Raincy was the product of several years of experimentation, but it was erected quickly in 1922–1923. The graceful church fused Gothic influences with modern materials and showed that concrete could be used artistically. The 164-foot (56 m) long nave is supported by slim columns, which are linked by concrete walls of tracery decoration. These walls are not load bearing, so they could be filled with glass, suggesting a delicate filigree effect. The interior is a simple 185-by-63-foot (56 x 20 m) rectangle surmounted by a concrete barrel vault, which is supported by four rows of 28 unadorned circular columns.

As a result of the concrete-molding process, the columns are ridged, which makes them seem elegantly fluted. The 145-foot (44 m) bell tower at the front of the church is square and rises in stages to a cross at the apex. **JM**

Schröder House

Architect: Gerrit Rietveld

Completed: 1924

Location: Utrecht, Netherlands

Style/Period: Modernism

The Schröder House was designed by Gerrit Rietveld in 1924 for the widow Truus Schröder-Schräder, who specified that she wanted a building to be designed, as far as possible, without walls. While the De Stijl group of artists and architects had manifested their unique style in paintings and furniture, the Schröder House was the first time their theories were applied in an architectural setting. Measuring about 23 x 30 feet (7 x 9 m), the house has two stories and a central spiral staircase. The upper floor is a single large space with rooms "created" by moveable partitions. The exterior presents a collection of clean lines and planes that seem to slot together.

Rietveld had a studio in the house until 1932, and he moved in permanently in 1958. After Rietveld's death, Schröder established

the Rietveld Schröderhuis Foundation, and it was under its auspices that the exterior of the house was restored to its original state in 1974, including the original De Stijl color scheme of red, blue and yellow. The interior and original furniture were restored in 1985–1987, after Schröder's death, and the building is now a museum. In 2000 the Rietveld Schröder House was declared a UNESCO World Heritage Site. It was described as "a manifesto of the ideals of the De Stijl group of artists and architects in the Netherlands in the 1920s, and … considered one of the icons of the modern movement in architecture." **EW**

Selfridges Department Store

Architect: Daniel Burnham

Completed: 1926

Location: Oxford Street, London, England

Style/Period: Neoclassical

Opened on March 15, 1909, in London, England, Selfridges is the largest store on Oxford Street and the second largest in the United Kingdom. Designed by Daniel Burnham, at the time one of the foremost architects in the United States, Selfridges department store was one of the first buildings to use a steel-frame construction, which is hidden behind the masonry

columns. Originally, the store comprised only nine and a half bays; the art deco main entrance, above which stands a statue of the Queen of Time, and all the remaining building to the left were added about 17 years later. Today it covers over 150,000 square feet (14,000 sq. m).

The store's American founder, Harry Gordon Selfridge, was an innovative retailer. He displayed the goods in the best possible way, displaying the most popular items in the most accessible places. Equally innovative was his use of public exhibitions to encourage more people into the store. These displays included the tiny monoplane used by Louis Blériot for the first cross-Channel flight in 1909 and the first demonstration of the television by John Logie Baird in 1925. Not all of those who came through the majestic front doors were welcome, however: on the day the store opened, a shoplifter was arrested for trying to remove an umbrella and a walking stick. **EW**

The Bauhaus

Architect: Walter Gropius

Completed: 1926 (begun 1925)

Location: Dessau, Germany

Style/Period: Modernism

When the Bauhaus — an avant-garde German school of arts, crafts and architecture — moved from Weimar to Dessau in 1925, it required new accommodation. It fell to its director, Walter Gropius, to design it. In accordance with the practical Bauhaus ethos and its increasing emphasis on function-alism, cubist forms and industrial design, the complex whose construction Gropius supervised combined living and working spaces in the form of classrooms, workrooms and modular housing for students and teachers.

Gropius's plan described two interconnected buildings that were roughly L-shaped. One L comprised classrooms and a connecting bridge (whose two levels were used as office space), which spanned the road to Dessau and lead to workshops situated in a block on the right and students' rooms located in a block on the left. Symmetrical the design was not, but its pinwheel-like form, reminiscent of an airplane's propeller, suggested dynamism and modernism, this latter quality under-lined by the glass, steel and reinforced-concrete used in its construction. While its clean lines, unornamented facades, asphalt-tiled flat roofs and bands of large windows acted as unifying elements, variety was provided in, for example, the contrast between the horizontal and vertical blocks. The influential Bauhaus buildings in Weimar and Dessau are now UNESCO World Heritage Sites. **CH-M**

Stockholm Stadsbibliotek

Architect: Gunnar Asplund

Completed: 1928

Location: Observatoriekullen, Stockholm, Sweden

Style/Period: Scandinavian Modernism

When Gunnar Asplund won the commission to build a public library in the Observatoriekullen (Observatory Hill) area of the Swedish capital in the 1920s, it was to form part of a new administrative and cultural quarter within the city. However, he had no experience of such projects, so he traveled to the United States for inspiration. When he returned, Asplund drew up plans for a building that was largely based on the monumental neoclassical style of the 19th century with which he was familiar. This was despite the fact that the modernist style was fast becoming mainstream.

Work began in 1924, and upon its completion Stockholm had a library that was a three-story U-shaped box containing a large cylinder. The building was accessed though a large entrance, and access to the cylinder, which was the reading room, was by an internal staircase. Interior detail was kept to a minimum, largely due to budgetary constraints, and the library actually has the pure functionality of a modernist building despite its neoclassical exterior. Asplund actually became a firm proponent of modernism in the last decade of his life. **IW**

German Pavilion

Architect: Ludwig Mies van der Rohe

Completed: 1929

Location: Montjuic, Barcelona, Spain

Style/Period: Modernism/International

This pavilion was built by the German-born U.S. architect Ludwig Mies van der Rohe for the Barcelona International Exhibition. He was a leading member of the Modernist movement — he had been director of the Bauhaus in Dessau, Germany, between 1930 and 1933 — and this work is arguably his greatest masterpiece. The basic design is elegantly simple and consists of a flat reinforced-concrete roof supported by cross-shaped steel pillars. The base is travertine, and the partitions are constructed from marble and onyx — all materials with which Mies van der Rohe would have been familiar, as his father was a master mason. Floor to ceiling tinted glass completed the construction materials used in the project

The pavilion was groundbreaking for its use of the unusual materials at a time when the movement's leitmotif was white-painted plaster. However, its most innovative feature is the way the internal space, despite its minimal structure, can be reconfigured by moving partitions, which offers great flexibility. Equally, these partitions can be moved to divide the space without fully segregating it. Despite the building's now iconic status, the original was actually demolished in 1930. A facsimile was constructed on the site during the 1980s. **IW**

Lovell House

Architect: Richard Neutra
Completed: 1929
Location: Los Angeles, California, United States
Style/Period: Modernism

This Modernist building was hugely innovative when it was built. It was designed for Philip Lovell, a physician, by the Austrian-born Richard Neutra, some six years after he had immigrated to the United States. The European *Lebensreform* movement that stressed the importance of a healthy environment influenced both men, and Lovell was a strong advocate of a sensible diet and regular exercise as a form of preventative medicine. He wanted a "healthy" house, and the building is sometimes referred to as the Lovell Health House. Neutra worked in concrete, steel and glass, and all of the components were manufactured off site and then erected in situ. Work began in 1927.

The house was the first building in the United States to have a steel frame, which was regarded as healthier than traditional frame materials, as well as being stronger. It was made in sections but took only 40 hours to erect. Neutra made good use of the steep hillside location by spreading the building out and terracing the garden. Among its healthy amenities are a gym, swimming pool and outdoor sleeping areas. The large areas of glass are designed to flood the comfortable interior with sunlight, which helps to raise the body's vitamin D levels. **IW**

Chrysler Building

Architect: William van Alen
Completed: 1930
Location: New York, New York, United States
Style/Period: Art Deco

American zeitgeist made silvery solid, the Chrysler Building is the pinnacle of corporate Art Deco. The penultimate act in New York's interwar skyscraper saga, it embodies the ambitions of Walter P. Chrysler and his architect William van Alen. The tower's reach for the sky was given extra impetus by Alen's fierce rivalry with his former business partner, H. Craig Severance, who was engaged to build the neighboring Bank of Manhattan. Had Alen stuck to his original 925-foot (282- m) plan, Severance's bank would have claimed the title of "Tallest Building in the World" by a margin of just 2 feet (0.6 m). Not content with second-best, Alen secretly designed a slender needle for the Chrysler's spire. Prefabricated in sections then hidden in the upper stories, it was only winched aloft once Severance had completed his bank. Having slyly topped out at 1,046 feet (319 m) to take the coveted title, the Chrysler was unceremoniously dethroned within months by the far less flamboyant Empire State Building.

With its facades packed with automotive references, Alen's masterpiece still remained a potent advertisement for Chrysler's products, as well as those of German manufacturers Krupps, whose "Nirosta" stainless-steel alloy was used to clad the crown of overlapping "starburst" hubcaps. In a final twist, Alen was obliged to successfully sue Chrysler for his fees after being falsely accused of corrupt practices with contractors.
PC

Tugendhat House

Architect: Ludwig Mies van der Rohe

Completed: 1930

Location: Brno, Czech Republic

Style/Period: Modernism

Mies van der Rohe designed this superlative example of early modernism as a home for a wealthy young couple, Greta and Fritz Tugendhat, but his early studies were interrupted when he was asked to create what became the German Pavilion for the Barcelona International Exhibition of 1930. When he returned to work on the house, he incorporated several of the experimental pavilion's features into the Tugendhat project. Most obviously, he used similar materials, such as travertine for the floor, onyx for a partition and cross-shaped steel columns.

The steel-framed Tugendhat House was built on a sloping site, so the entrance and service areas are at a higher level than the living spaces. Van der Rohe was able to reproduce the pavilion's slab roof supported by columns, and he also used partitions to divide rooms. However, he had to compromise on the pavilion's purity for the sake of domesticity, and he included staircases and private areas. The architect also designed all of the house's furniture. The finished family home brilliantly turned an experimental design into a wholly practical one. It was named a UNESCO World Heritage Site in 2001. **IW**

Castle Drogo

Architect: Sir Edwin Lutyens

Completed: 1930

Location: Drewsteignton, Devon, England

Style/Period: Arts and Crafts

Sir Edwin Lutyens was at the height of his popularity when Sir Julius Drewe, a self-made millionaire, asked him to design a modern Edwardian take on a traditional, if very grand, family seat. The architect had made his name by designing idyllic houses for the newly moneyed class. However, Castle Drogo was altogether more foreboding, as it looks out to the rugged uplands of Dartmoor and rises hundreds of feet above the valley of the River Teign. Lutyens built in hard-wearing granite and topped the building with decorative battlements and turrets. The castle also has thick mullioned windows in homage to earlier Tudor styles.

The interior of Castle Drogo, which is spread over several floors, is almost as austere as the exterior, with granite walls and floors and wood-paneled rooms. The layout echoes that of a stately home, with servants' quarters below large function and reception rooms. The foundation stone was laid in 1911, and it took two decades to complete the construction work, but at the end Drewe had his somewhat kitsch faux-medieval castle — the last one of its type to be built in England. **IW**

Institut d'Art et d'Archéologie

Architect: Paul Bigot

Completed: 1930 (begun 1925)

Location: 3 Rue Michelet, Paris, France

Style/Period: Eclecticism

The year 1925 was a momentous one for the French architect Paul Bigot. It marked his appointment as a professor at the respected École National Supérieure des Beaux-Arts in Paris and the start of the construction of the Institut d'Art et d'Archéologie on the Rue Michelet, also in Paris. Bigot had won a competition organized by the University of Paris in 1922 to find a suitable design for a building in which to house its "Institute of Art and Archeology." When you look at the realization of his vision, which was completed in 1930, it is not surprising that his submission caught the eye of the judges.

Constructed of concrete around a central courtyard but clad in heavily and diversely textured red brick, the exterior of Bigot's Institut d'Art et d'Archéologie presents an astonishingly bold and eclectic combination of styles to passers-by. A terra-cotta frieze at ground level is reminiscent of ancient Greco–Roman reliefs, for instance, while flame-shaped battlements at the top recall both Moorish style and medieval architecture, other elements being borrowed from Mesopotamia and Byzantium. Now officially listed as a French historical monument, Bigot's extraordinary-looking building continues to accommodate researchers, teachers and students of art and archeology as part of the Université Paris Sorbonne-Paris IV. **CH-M**

Pantages Theater

Architect: B. Marcus Priteca

Completed: 1930 (begun 1929)

Location: 6233 Hollywood Boulevard, Hollywood, California, United States

Style/Period: Art Deco

Hollywood's Pantages Theater is, perhaps, best known as the venue for the Oscars ceremonies hosted by the American Academy of Motion Pictures between 1949 and 1959, but it also merits a page in the history books in its own right, its Art Deco glamour having made it a Hollywood landmark.

Theater impresario Alexander Pantages ordered construction of the "Hollywood Pantages," and his chosen designer was his "house" architect since 1910, B. Marcus Priteca. It may have been the last of a string of movie and vaudeville theaters (collectively known as the Pantages Theater Circuit) in Pantages's entertainment empire, but its location in Hollywood — the center of the movie industry — made it special.

On its completion, the exterior of the long and low horizontal building conformed to the then fashionable streamline variation of the art deco style, and decorative external elements were based on simple, elegant geometric forms. The Wall Street crash of 1929 sidelined a planned adjoining 10-story office tower, but the stylish, stylized gilded decor created by Tony Heinsbergen encouraged patrons to leave their troubles at the door and enter an opulent fantasy world. With its seating capacity of around 2,700, this theater really was a palace of mass escapism. **CH-M**

Villa Savoye

Architect: Le Corbusier (Charles-Édouard Jeanneret)
Completed: 1930
Location: Poissy, Paris, France
Style/Period: Early Modernism

Villa Savoye remains Le Corbusier's most famous domestic building — it's actually a weekend country retreat — and it is a manifesto for future living in the international style. It was based on his own "Five Points": the tenets for a revolutionary new architectural aesthetic that he postulated in 1927 in response to the opportunities offered by reinforced concrete. Le Corbusier created a building that rises on slender columns (one of the five points), which do away with the need for load-bearing walls. The design allowed for a flexible floor plan that was not dictated by the position of walls, permitting large horizontal windows that flood the interior with light. The columns are also set back and so allow for a free, uncluttered facade.

Work on the villa, which was undertaken in concrete, steel and glass, was largely completed by 1929, but the building was not without its problems — the owners tried to sue Le Corbusier as the flat roof leaked. However, its iconic status remains undeniable, not least because of its setting, within which the pure white exterior finish can shine. The building fell into a parlous state, but it was subsequently renovated. It is no longer occupied and most of the rooms are empty of furnishing. **IW**

Hilversum Town Hall

Architect: William Marinus Dudok

Completed: 1931 (begun 1927)

Location: Hilversum, Utrecht, Netherlands

Style/Period: Modernism

At first glance the hard, angular aesthetics of Hilversum Town Hall suggest an affinity with the famous De Stijl group and the abstract rectilinear paintings of Piet Mondrian. However, Dudok's lasting monument is a direct product of his practical training at the Royal Military Academy in Breda, tempered by a lasting admiration for the prairie-style houses of Frank Lloyd Wright. Dudok's service as an engineer gave him a thorough grounding in the use of brick, which was employed extensively (and without ornament) in the fortifications of the day. Leaving the army in 1913, he began his civilian career as Temporary Director of Public Work in Leiden, before becoming the City Architect for the small town of Hilversum in 1928.

Given free reign, Dudok designed many new public buildings, and even entire neighborhoods, before he tackled the prominent structure of the town hall itself. In his hands the utilitarian expanses of martial brickwork were transformed into elegant asymmetrical compositions, which were cut with dark shadows and edged in black tiles. He lavished his attention on every element, from the tower's blue glazed clock to the council chairman's hammer. Even the hall's 680,000 distinctive yellow bricks were made to his own design. Widely influential, echoes of Dudok's masterpiece can be found in many British and American equivalents. **PC**

Viceroy's House

Architect: Sir Edwin Lutyens

Completed: 1931

Location: Raisina Hill, New Delhi, India

Style/Period: Indian-Colonial

In the latter days of the Raj, the British authorities in India decided to create a new imperial city by moving the functions of state from Calcutta to Delhi, the former capital of Mogul India. The rare task of creating a modern administrative city, New Delhi, from scratch fell to architects Sir Herbert Baker and Sir Edwin Lutyens, who had an increasingly difficult working relationship. Nevertheless, Lutyens produced a masterpiece in the Viceroy's House by blending European, Classical and Indian designs. Work began in 1912 and was largely completed in 1929. The palace formally opened two year later.

The house is on a massive scale and covers 4½ acres (1.8 ha). Entrance is by way of 32 wide steps that lead into the palatial circular Durbar Hall. Four wings, which contain apartments, bedrooms, offices and the kitchen, lead off this central block, which is crowned by an Indian-inspired copper dome some 177 feet (54 m) high. Lutyens worked in stone: the upper part is a creamy sandstone, and the lower parts are deep red with a thin red stone line around the parapets. Today the building is known as the Rashtrapati Bhavan, the official home of the now independent country's president. **IW**

Empire State Building

Architects: Shreve, Lamb and Harmon Associates

Completed: 1931

Location: New York, New York, United States

Style/Period: Art Deco/Modernism

The Empire State Building was about pride and bragging rights — a clash between two wealthy motor manufacturing chief executives. Walter Chrysler of the Chrysler Corporation and John Raskob of General Motors went head to head to see who could erect the city's tallest structure. Chrysler called in Shreve, Lamb and Harmon Associates, showed them a pencil on its end and asked, "How high can you build it so that it won't fall down?"

By the time construction began in 1930, the Wall Street crash of 1929 had hit hard, and the subsequent Great Depression forced Chrysler to tighten his purse strings. The graceful art deco skyscraper was now to cost as little as possible, and work had to be finished in a mere 18 months. The architects built in preformed steel, some 60,000 tons (54,431 metric tonnes) in all, to produce a frame that went up rapidly, sometimes more than four floors per week. The building was then clad in stone. It took the workers a mere 12 months and 45 days to complete the job and, at 1,252 feet (381 m), it lauded it over the already completed Chrysler Building by 204 feet (61 m), which was also constructed to rival a GM building. And so, what had started out as little more than a private bet had produced two iconic buildings born out of big business that defined not only New York's skyline, but also the city itself. **IW**

Church of the Sacred Heart of Our Lord

Architect: Joze Plecnik

Completed: 1932

Location: Vinohrady, Prague, Czech Republic

Style/Period: Neoclassical/Arts and Crafts

This astonishing Catholic church, originally designed to be just one element of a set of buildings, lies in one of the suburbs of the Czech Republic's capital, and its architectural style defies any easy classification. Slovenian-born Plecnik, himself a devout Catholic, had clearly been inspired by elements of early Christian basilicas, but other elements found in his design are drawn from modernism, as well as Byzantine and even Slovenian vernacular styles. Some two-thirds of the exterior comprises dark brown brickwork interspersed with klinker, which is twice-fired brick. Squares of granite and artificial stone also appear. The whole is dominated by the unusually immense 138-foot (32-m) clock tower that is pierced by two large windows and topped by a copper cupola.

The interior mirrors the exterior to some degree, and the entrance opens onto the main hall, which is a 125-foot (38 m) long rectangular space. This open nave has brick walls, its floor is a stone mosaic pattern and the ceiling is of polished coffered timber. The church's most sacred space lies below — the simple crypt consists of a hemispherical tunnel that leads the devout to a plain altar. **IW**

Daily Express Building

Architects: Owen Williams with Ellis & Clarke

Completed: 1932

Location: 121–128 Fleet Street, London, England

Style/Period: Art Deco

Before new technology dictated a move from central London, Fleet Street was the home of Britain's biggest-selling national newspapers, and to the journalists, editors, proofreaders, typesetters and printers who put them together each day. Competition was fierce, production could always be improved and modernity was all the rage. And so it was that Lord Beaverbrook, the *Daily Express's* proprietor, commissioned "Britain's most modern building for Britain's most modern newspaper," as the eventual edifice was hailed on its completion in 1932.

The "in" style of the early 1930s being art deco, it was its streamlined vocabulary that architect Owen Williams, working with Ellis & Clarke, referenced for the project. When it was completed, the curtain wall that sleekly enveloped the exterior was striking on account of its curved corner and the smooth,

striped effect created by the alternating black Vitrolite cladding and glass windows, the horizontal bands being smartly delineated by chromium strips. On entering the lobby, visitors came face to face with elaborate mural panels, a huge stylized pendant lamp and other flashy, modish details designed by Robert Atkinson. Not only did the details elevate it to the epitome of glamour, but the building was also functional, with a large basement area (enabled by the concrete skeleton) accommodating the all-important printing presses. **CH-M**

Arnos Grove Underground Station

Architect: Charles Holden

Completed: 1932

Location: Arnos Grove, London, England

Style/Period: Modernism

Arnos Grove in northeast London lies close to the end of the subway's Piccadilly Line, which runs through the center of the capital before heading westward toward Heathrow

Airport. Charles Holden, who was fully aware of traditional architectural styles but was more concerned with practical matters and functionality, devised the station. He stated that architecture should "throw off its mantle of deceits; its cornices, pilasters, moldings." He had a long relationship with Frank Pick, the managing director of London Transport, for whom he produced several buildings. He was commissioned to design 18 new stations when the Piccadilly Line was extended between 1930 and 1933.

Holden chose a welcoming modernist style that was adopted to a British setting, and he relied on simple forms — cylinders, curves and rectangles — built in brick, concrete and glass. While the stations' exteriors were largely unadorned, interiors were a riot of colored tiles. Holden took care of every detail, from lighting and seating to ticket machines and garbage cans. Arnos Grove is generally considered one of his best stations and was, along with several others, designated as having "special architectural interest" in 1971 by the British heritage authorities. **IW**

La Maison de Verre

Architects: Pierre Chareau and Bernard Bijvoët
Completed: 1932 (begun 1927)
Location: 13 Rue St.-Guillaume, Paris, France
Style/Period: International/Modernism

Designing La Maison de Verre (French for "The House of Glass") presented a number of problems to architects Pierre Chareau (also a noted interior designer) and Bernard Bijvoët. Not only was it to be the home of Dr. Jean Dalsace and his wife, Annie, but it would also act as this Parisian gynecologist's clinic. And if that weren't a demanding enough brief, the top-story tenant of the existing house bought by Dr. Dalsace refused to allow its demolition. This is why Chareau and Bijvoët's L-shaped, glass construction appears framed by a conventional building looming above and behind it. But the contrast between the two also serves to emphasize both the modernity of La Maison de Verre — an early example of the international style — and its designers' innovative use of materials.

The most visible material used in La Maison de Verre was, of course, glass, with windows seeming to have been mostly dispensed with in favor of walls made from glass blocks slotted into a steel skeleton frame. The ingenuity continued inside the three-story building, with sliding walls and doors offering versatility in the arrangement of the internal space, for instance, and movable traps in the glass-cube walls providing ventilation. **CH-M**

Stormont Parliament Building

Architect: Sir Arnold Thornley
Completed: 1932
Location: Stormont, Belfast, Northern Ireland
Style/Period: Neoclassical

Stormont, which lies some 6 miles (10 km) to the east of Belfast, was the home of the government of Northern Ireland until it was suspended by the British government in 1972. It is now home to the Northern Ireland Assembly. The need for a separate parliament came with the creation of the province after the passing of the

Government of Ireland Act of 1920. The original plans called for a large-domed classical Greek building, in Portland Stone on a Mourne granite plinth, with two subsidiary side buildings that together could house all three branches of the new government — legislative, executive and judicial.

However, these ambitious plans by Sir Arnold Thornley had to be shelved due to financial considerations after the Wall Street crash in 1929, and only a smaller main building went ahead, without the dome. Completed in 1932, its main areas are the larger green-leather-benched House of Commons of Northern Ireland, the red-benched Senate of Northern Ireland and the Great Hall. Stormont was built with a sense of political purpose and solidity that was sadly lacking in Northern Ireland before and during the decades-long Troubles that split the Protestant and Catholic communities. **IW**

Boots Pharmaceutical Factory

Architect: Owen Williams

Completed: 1932 (begun 1930)

Location: Beeston, near Nottingham, Nottinghamshire, England

Style/Period: Modernism

Still Britain's biggest homegrown chain of commercial drug stores and pharmacies, Boots was founded in Nottingham, in central England, in 1849. By 1927, when the company acquired a 30-acre (121,410 sq. m) greenfield site at Beeston, near Nottingham, it was under American ownership. The business-boosting plan was to create a headquarters complex for Boots that would offer office accommodation as well as manufacturing and warehousing capacity. Sir Owen Williams was commissioned to design the factory part of the complex, which was

completed in 1932 and opened in 1933.

D10, or "Wets," as the Boots Pharmaceutical Factory is also called, turned out to be an outstanding example of the stylishly simple international style, which was in turn eminently suited to industrial buildings, being both practical and functional. (Indeed, so successful was Williams's design that efficiency rose rapidly, and the factory remains in use by Boots decades later.) Williams based the rectangular ground plan on two atria, which housed the production processes. Galleries on four levels overlooked the factory floor, and overhead lighting was provided by a glazed ceiling. Supported by mushroom columns, the four-story reinforced-concrete building was enveloped by a sleek curtain wall of glass and steel. **CH-M**

Paimio Sanatorium

Architect: Alvar Aalto

Location: Paimio, Finland

Completed: 1932

Style/Period: Modernism

Alvar Aalto won the 1929 competition to design this complex of buildings. With its whitewashed walls and ribbon windows, it clearly takes its aesthetics from the international style as pioneered by Le Corbusier. Aalto was, above all, concerned that Paimio be fit for its designated purpose, and he went to considerable lengths to ensure that it was a fully functioning sanatorium. He consulted with both doctors and other medical practitioners to understand their needs and those of their patients at a time when the only way to deal with tuberculosis was long-term isolation with plenty of rest and fresh air.

The sanatorium, which was built between 1929 and 1932, consists of four principal wings, and Aalto gave each a specific function. The six-story range created to house the patients, for example, was positioned on a southwest axis so that the rooms faced southeast to catch the early morning sun. Aalto also added cantilevered terraces so the patients could enjoy the sun for most of the day. He also developed much of the furniture — the Paimio chair, which was designed to ease a patient's breathing, and a sink that lessened the noise generated by splashing water. **IW**

Isokon Building (Lawn Road Flats)

Architect: Wells Coates

Completed: 1934

Location: Belsize Park, London, England

Style/Period: Modernism

While the Chrysler and Hoover buildings were simply presenting the public with the face of corporate modernity, the avant-garde apartments commissioned by Isokon took the concept of architecture as brand extension to its logical conclusion. Returning from a European tour as a salesman for the Venesta Plywood Company, Jack Pritchard was inspired to form his own design-led firm after meeting with leading modernists, such as Le Corbusier and Walter Gropius. (The name "Isokon" is a contraction of "Isometric Unit Construction" that alludes to Russian constructivism.) In 1933 Jack and his wife, Molly, engaged the talented but untried architect Wells Coates to design a family home for them. However, they soon changed their brief to a block of apartments through which they might implement and promote their shared ideas on modern living.

Often compared to a land-locked ocean liner, the Isokon's cabinlike apartments were extensively furnished with the company's own plywood products, including sliding wooden dividers and large pieces of built-in furniture. Aimed squarely at mobile middle-class professionals with few material possessions, the Isokon functioned like a hotel, with meals being provided by a centrally run kitchen. Residents would meet and drink at the Isobar downstairs, which became a focal point for leading Hampstead artists and writers such as Barbara Hepworth and Ben Nicolson. The Isokon's "passenger list" eventually included such luminaries as Agatha Christie, Marcel Breuer and even Walter Gropius himself, briefly helping to fulfill the Pritchards' communal vision of a progressive intellectual lifestyle. **PC**

Penguin Pool

Architect: Berthold Lubetkin/Tecton

Completed: 1934 (begun 1933)

Location: London Zoo, Regent's Park, London, England

Style/Period: Modernism

The single-most memorable piece of interwar modernism in Britain, the intertwining spiral ramps of London Zoo's Penguin Pool conclusively proved that there was poetry to be found in concrete. Lubetkin's tour de force was made structurally feasible by the work of a young Danish engineer called Ove Arup, whose blossoming talent would later take him to Australia to wrestle with the complex geometry of the Sydney Opera House. The delicately descending ramps may appear to lean lightly against the pool's edges, but even their slender forms generate considerable lateral forces, each being capable of supporting the weight of 24 zookeepers, or 240 pounds per linear foot (35.7 kg/l m). It is a testament to Arup's skill that the massive abutments needed to contain those curves were incorporated so unobtrusively into the nesting boxes on the pool's perimeter.

Lubetkin's design successfully turned the pool into a natural piece of theater. The penguins could preen themselves before their viewing public before diving off the ramps to demonstrate their swimming skills in the long elliptical tank. The color scheme is almost nautical, with polar white concrete surfaces wrapping around red-oxide decks that frame the glass-mosaic-tiled pool of a brilliant blue. Now no longer considered compatible with penguins' feet or courting rituals, the beautifully restored pool has played host to a succession of tenants, from alligators to porcupines, in the zoo's quest to find a new function for its radical form. **PC**

Hornsey Town Hall

Architect: Reginald Harold Uren

Completed: 1935 (begun 1934)

Location: Crouch End, London, England

Style/Period: Art Deco/Modernism

Flanked by its escorts of gas and water utilities, Hornsey Town Hall is a textbook model of progressive local government in the 1930s. One of no less than 26 interwar town halls in London, it was the first to abandon historical pastiche and express the arrival of the modern age in terms of both form and function. A competition-winning design by the 27-year-old New Zealand architect Reginald Harold Uren, the hall combines council chamber, meeting rooms, offices and a public auditorium that later played host to both *Queen* and *the Kinks*. Continental influences can be discerned, most notably in the tall tower and the choice of brick construction, which recall both Stockholm City Hall and Dudok's town hall in Hilversum (see pages 272 and 293).

However, Uren added something new to this typology with his logical separation of the building's different functions into distinct volumes. He softened Dudok's quasi-military brickwork along the way with an abundance of high-quality art deco sculptures, which he specially commissioned from artist A.J. Ayres. The clean lines of the interiors smack of quiet civic efficiency, but their rich marble finishes betray more than a hint of wealthy middle-class civic pride. The well-figured exotic veneers of the plentiful wood paneling possess an aura of transatlantic luxury akin to Cunard's ship *Queen Mary*. In comparison with the sterile government offices of today, Hornsey is truly a palace for the people. **PC**

De La Warr Pavilion

Architects: Serge Chermayeff and Eric Mendelsohn
Completed: 1935
Location: Bexhill-on-Sea, England
Style/Period: Modernism

The breezy, faded charm of an English seaside town would seem an unlikely backdrop to one of the most seminal international modernist structures. This apparent anomaly is thanks to Britain's role as refuge for a talented architectural avant-garde fleeing the tide of European Fascism. As a German Jew, the prominent architect Eric Mendelsohn was on a collision course with the Nazi party. He wisely chose to immigrate to England in 1933, buying a 55 percent stake in the small architectural practice of his Russian-born friend Serge Chermayeff. Their brief but brilliant partnership lasted just three years.

Mendelsohn and Chermayeff immediately won the competition to design a cultural pavilion in Bexhill-on-Sea, which was instigated by its mayor, the 9th Earl De La Warr. An aristocrat with a socialist agenda, the earl had campaigned for the town to fund a unique tourist attraction dedicated to the public's education and entertainment, going so far as to supply the land himself.

Cutting-edge in its day, the slender cantilevered lines of the De La Warr Pavilion were something foreign and exciting in a largely conservative environment. The first building in Britain to be constructed around a welded steel frame, it was engineered by Austrian-born Felix Samuely, who had previously helped Mendelsohn create revolutionary department stores in Germany. The frame and concrete floor-plates permitted the non-load-bearing walls to be made entirely of glass, flooding the interior with sun and sea air. Now beautifully restored, the pavilion is a constant reminder of how immigrant talent can enrich a country's architectural heritage. **PC**

Hoover Building

Architects: Wallis, Gilbert & Partners

Completed: 1935

Location: Western Avenue, Perivale, England

Style/Period: Art Deco/Modernism

An art deco fanfare heralding your arrival into London, the Hoover Building stands alongside a main arterial road, basking in the floodlights that formed part of its original decorative scheme. One of the most famous products of the partnership between American construction firm Kahncrete and British architect Thomas Wallis, the structure marries a vast reinforced concrete factory with a very public frontage, which acted as a permanent billboard for its owners.

The exterior decoration borrows heavily from the stylized forms of Ancient Egypt, in common with much art deco produced in the decade following the discovery of Tutankhamen's tomb. Regal precedents aside, Wallis always intended the factory to be a modern palace of industry. Its airy workspaces were flooded with natural light that streamed in from the tall windows that fill the facade.

The long, symmetrical frontage is punctuated at regular intervals by columns topped with green and black tiled capitals, which step back to connect with the lines of the green metal windows. These, in turn, are framed by a continuous line of red faience above and a plinth of indigo blue and black beneath. The prominent lettering that is such an integral part of the front elevation was altered from the original "Hoover Limited" to the more familiar "Hoover Building." It was a small concession to the new occupants, grocery-store chain Tesco, who stepped in to fill the vacuum left by Hoover's departure in 1982 and restored this now listed building to its former glory. **PC**

Fallingwater

Architect: Frank Lloyd Wright

Completed: 1936

Location: Bear Run, Pennsylvania, United States

Style/Period: Usonian

Fallingwater is one of the world's most instantly recognizable architectural icons, and it is the most renowned work by the most famous U.S. architect of the 20th century. It is the prime example of Wright's prairie style of design: a long, low building constructed of natural materials with roofs that appear to the uninitiated to be floating unsupported over the living areas. Wright was commissioned by Edgar Kaufmann, a wealthy department store owner, who wanted a weekend retreat for his family in Pennsylvania's mountainous southwest.

Kaufmann specified that the house had to be built in a forested area at a point where a stream, Bear Run, flows over a waterfall. Wright went one better, suggesting the sandstone and concrete house be built over the falls so that it became part of the scenery itself. The plan caused many tricky engineering problems, not least the positioning of huge horizontal cantilevered concrete terraces over the stream some 30 feet (9 m) below. Fallingwater sits beautifully in its surrounds — Wright even used boulders recovered from the site to build the fireplace hearth, and one group of boulders actually protrudes slightly through the floor. **IW**

Gatwick Airport Terminal Building

Architects: Hoar, Marlow & Lovett

Completed: 1936 (begun 1935)

Location: Gatwick, East Sussex, England

Style/Period: Modernism

The potential of powered flight was rapidly developed following the Wright brothers' pioneering breakthrough at Kitty Hawk, North Carolina, in 1903. U.S. aviator Charles Lindbergh became the first person to fly solo and nonstop across the Atlantic Ocean in 1927. Biplanes were followed by monoplanes, and by the 1930s flying was becoming increasingly available to wealthier citizens.

Greater public accessibility meant that buildings — airports — were required to service this new mode of transport, such as the airport terminal that was built at Gatwick, southeast of London, on what was originally a private airfield.

The competition-winning design submitted by the student trio Hoar, Marlow & Lovett was ingenious. Nicknamed "The Beehive," the Gatwick Airport Terminal Building resembled a wheel when viewed from the air. Its central hub housed immigration and departure lounges, and six "spokes" — covered walkways — lead to an outer "rim," or circular runway, on which airplanes landed and took off. The design also incorporated a subway connecting the terminal to Gatwick's railroad station, where trains took passengers to (or received them from) London. The Beehive's limitations soon became evident, however, and the airport was redeveloped during the 1950s.

The Beehive can still be admired on the airport's southern perimeter, where it serves as a helicopter terminal. **CH-M**

Cavalier Hotel

Architect: Roy F. France
Completed: 1936
Location: 1320 Ocean Drive, South Beach, Miami, Florida, United States
Style/Period: Art Deco/Modernism

Such was the craze for constructing buildings in the art deco style in Miami, Florida, during the 1920s and 1930s that the area in which they are clustered is today known as the Art Deco District (or Miami Beach Architectural District) and is listed on the U.S. National Register of Historic Places. The Cavalier Hotel is one of many hotels situated on Ocean Drive, South Beach, that were

built to accommodate the vacationers that were encouraged to visit this "tropical playground" during the interwar years. The hot, sunny climate and relaxed, leisurely atmosphere of a vacation spot no doubt had much to do with the bright colors and ice-creamlike pastels that decorated these homes-away-from-home.

Designed by Roy F. France, the Cavalier Hotel was completed in 1936 and today offers its guests a choice of 45 rooms. Many other glass, concrete and plaster examples of the "MiMo" style (short for "Miami moderne" or "Miami modern") referenced ocean liners, and alternative names for the type of art deco that prevailed in Miami include art moderne, streamline moderne and, its offshoot, nautical moderne. The Cavalier, however, is more purist in its emphasis on clean, rectangular shapes. **CH-M**

Gropius House

Architect: Walter Gropius

Completed: 1938

Location: Lincoln, Massachusetts, United States

Style/Period: Modernism

This radical building was almost single-handedly responsible for introducing the international style of modernism to the United States, and it caused a sensation when it was unveiled in the late 1930s. German-born Walter Gropius was the founding father of the radical Bauhaus design movement, but he immigrated to the United States, by way of a three-year stint in England, in 1937 to avoid Nazi persecution. He became a professor of architecture at Harvard University's Graduate School of Design, and he was given a site in nearby Lincoln on which to build his house by the wife of a one James Storrow.

Gropius was content to mix aspects of the New England architectural style and locally sourced materials with those of the internationalist movement. The building, which is positioned amid a sizeable apple orchard, rests on a wooden post-and-beam frame and is covered in vertical tongue-and-groove planking. Thus it was built, in part, from traditional materials like wood, brick and fieldstone, but Gropius also used metals and glass blocks to complete his vision, which was executed on the basis of simplicity and maximum efficiency. Much of the interior furniture was designed by fellow Bauhaus member and Harvard colleague Marcel Breuer. **IW**

Wingspread (Herbert F. Johnson House)

Architect: Frank Lloyd Wright

Completed: 1938

Location: Wind Point, near Racine, Wisconsin, United States

Style/Period: Prairie/Organic

Shortly after commissioning Frank Lloyd Wright to construct an administration building for the family firm (the Johnson Wax Building, see page 324), Herbert F. Johnson asked the Wisconsin-based architect to build him a family home at Wind Point, on Lake Michigan's western shore. Wright responded with an organic-looking long, horizontal building of red brick, limestone, wood and stucco that not only blended sympathetically with its natural surroundings but appeared to have sprung up and sprouted spontaneously.

Wingspread's ground plan resembled a pinwheel in shape, with four wings extending from a central hub whose height and shape prompted Wright to call it a "wigwam." While communal, delineated living spaces were accommodated within the open-plan "wigwam," the four wings, or "zones," were respectively intended to house a kitchen (the south wing), guests and automobiles (the west wing), the master bedroom (the north wing, and the only zone to have a second story) and the children's rooms (the east wing). At the heart of the "wigwam" was a 30-foot (9 m) high chimney, with five fireplaces ranged around it to warm the octagonal Great Hall. Light flooded in through three levels of clerestory windows and through the large, brick-bounded glazed doors and windows that made up the walls. **CH-M**

Mayakovskaya Metro Station

Architect: Aleksei Nikolayevich Dushkin

Completed: 1938 (begun 1937)

Location: Moscow, Russia

Style/Period: Stalinist/Socialist Realist/Art Deco

Aleksei Nikolayevich Duskin had already completed the Kropotkinskaya Station for the Moscow Metro (subway) system when, in 1937, he began work on the Mayakovskaya Metro Station, which was situated about 108 feet (33 m) below ground and named after a futurist poet. Lighting was a crucial consideration, and Dushkin's solution was effective and decorative: a row of large, circular recesses, ringed with electric lights, each set within a section of the ceiling between vaults formed by connecting columns standing opposite one another. Arches, forming a pair of colonnades on each side of the platform, linked adjacent columns.

Although the Mayakovskaya's style was predominantly Stalinist (as emphasized by the 35 mosaics within the ceiling recesses created by Alexander Deineka, collectively entitled *A Day in the Soviet Sky*), it also had a distinctly art deco flavor, particularly in the striking use of materials and color. Reflective stainless steel was contrasted with rhodonite (a pinkish-brown mineral) for the cladding of the columns, for instance, and four hues of marble and granite were incorporated into the floor and walls. The overall effect was elegant and palatial, and in 1939 the Mayakovskaya Metro Station won a grand prize at the New York's World Fair. Two years later, it was serving as a bomb shelter. **CH-M**

Neue Reichskanzlei

Architect: Albert Speer

Completed: 1939 (begun 1938)

Location: Voßstraße 6, Berlin, Germany

Style/Period: Totaliarianist/Nazi

Adolf Hitler, the *Führer* (leader) of the totalitarian Nazi regime that governed Germany's Third Reich between 1933 and 1945, had grandiose plans for his "Thousand-year Reich," including a new capital city called Germania. He therefore commissioned Albert Speer, his favorite architect, to draw up plans for his pet project, which he based on the Pantheon of ancient Rome. Only one building was completed, however: the Neue Reichskanzlei, or New Reich Chancellery, on Voßstraße, in the central, government district of Berlin.

Given the scale of Hitler's ego and ambition, his new headquarters was appropriately monumental and intimidating. Important visitors approached the long, horizontal, classically inspired red marble facade through huge gates that opened onto the Ehrenhof ("Court of Honor"). Inside, a gallery 476 feet (145 m) in length led to Hitler's office, which measured 4,306 square feet (400 sq. m). During the last days of

World War II, and with the Allies closing in, Hitler retreated to a bunker beneath the bomb-damaged New Reich Chancellery, eventually committing suicide there. Today no trace of the New Reich Chancellery, the symbol of a dictator's megalomania, remains — deliberately so, lest it become a focal point of neo-Nazi veneration. **CH-M**

2 Willow Road

Architect: Ernö Goldfinger
Completed: 1939 (begun 1937)
Location: Hampstead, London, England
Style/Period: International/ Modernism

Although Ernö Goldfinger was born in Hungary, he trained as an architect in Paris, France, before marrying an Englishwoman and moving to London. And it was to accommodate their growing family that they acquired a terrace of four cottages in Willow Road, in the north London suburb of Hampstead.

In Paris, Goldfinger had become enthused by the work in reinforced concrete of Le Corbusier and Auguste Perret, and their influence is evident in the trio of new houses that he designed for Willow Road. The three connected houses (1, 2 and 3 Willow Road) each took up a vertically divided section (2 Willow Road, the Goldfingers' home, was the largest) of a horizontal and rectangular module constructed of reinforced concrete and clad in red brick. Garages and a hallway occupied the ground floor, while the communal living space was on the second and the bedrooms were on the third, beneath the flat roof. Inside, open-plan arrangements and the huge band of glass along the facade on the second floor ensured that the rooms were spacious and light. Such custom-made features as built-in closets and the spiral staircase designed by Ove Arup made this a modernist house both inside and out and, consequently, an extremely controversial domestic building at the time of its construction. **CH-M**

Battersea Power Station

Architect: Sir Giles Gilbert Scott

Completed: 1939 (designed 1933)

Location: Battersea, London, England

Style/Period: Art Deco/Moderne

Faced with the threat of collective nationalization, London's private electricity generators preempted government intervention by amalgamating to form the London Power Company in 1925. One of its first actions was to accept the government's own proposals to replace the existing patchwork of small capacity generators with a series of larger power stations, beginning with this 400,000-kilowatt "super station" alongside the Thames at Battersea. Anticipating that such a mammoth industrial project might well inflame local opinion, London Power astutely employed the services of one the country's most distinguished architects, Sir Giles Gilbert Scott, then the

Royal Institute of British Architects' president-elect. The designer of both Liverpool's Anglican Cathedral and Britain's ubiquitous red telephone box, Scott's ability with monumental forms and track record of applying historical details to public utilities made him the perfect person for the job.

He proceeded to clothe the turbine hall's massive steel frame with brick, relieving its mass with his trademark "jazz-modern" details and transforming its tall chimneys into heroic fluted columns on stepped brick pedestals. Completed in two stages, the station's familiar four-chimney silhouette did not emerge until 1953, when Station "A" gained its identical twin "B," boosting the station's capacity to 509 megawatts in the process. Finally decommissioned in 1983, Battersea remains imposing even in its semi-derelict state. The vast shell now stands empty and silent, waiting to be brought back to life once more. **PC**

Maginot Line

Architects: Section Technique du Génie, CORF

Completed: 1939

Location: France

Style/Period: Interwar Military

Much maligned for its failure to protect France from German attack in 1940, the famous Maginot Line has been badly served by history. It owes its existence to the oratory skill of André Maginot, the French Minister for War who was convinced that the Treaty of Versailles had sown the seeds for future conflict and campaigned tirelessly for France to defend its border with Germany. Conscious that a "great wall" of traditional ramparts would be prohibitively expensive, he advocated for a more flexible design approach based on the dual principles of "taking full advantage of the terrain and establishing a continuous line of fire everywhere." His perseverance and

eloquence paid off, and the French parliament grudgingly voted him funds of 3,300 million French francs ($132 million) in 1929.

Taking "full advantage of the terrain" often meant burrowing beneath it. The defensive line quickly became a warren of reinforced concrete bunkers, tunnels linked by underground railways and subterranean barracks for entire regiments, which were supported by an arsenal of cunningly positioned mortars, howitzers and machine guns. The formidable weaponry of these linear forts, or *ouvrages*, was intended to compensate for Germany having nearly twice France's manpower, discourage surprise attacks and buy the valuable three weeks the French army needed to mobilize. All this it achieved, obliging the German army to deploy a large decoy assault force along the border before attacking through the "back door" of neutral Holland and Belgium. **PC**

Rockefeller Center

Architects: Reinhard & Hofmeister; Corbett, Harrison &
MacMurray; Hood, Godley & Fouilhoux

Completed: 1940

Location: New York, New York, United States

Period/Style: Art Deco

This business center was the vision of Nelson
Rockefeller, one of the United States' wealth-
iest industrialists. He had the confidence to
build New York's only major commercial
complex of the Depression era: a group of
buildings with gardens and a sunken plaza at
street level that remains the largest privately
run building project of the modern era.
Rockefeller put together a team of architects
for the project, but they largely worked under
the direction of Raymond Hood. He envisaged
a public-private space that included 19 commercial buildings of various forms and heights
on a 22-acre (9 ha) site. Work began in 1930.

Fourteen of the tower blocks were in the
art deco style, and 13 of them are slightly
smaller than the 14th, the 70-story and 872-
foot (266 m) GE Building, which was
originally known as the RCA Building. It has
been suggested that the first 13 buildings
represent the original 13 colonies, while the
RCA Building stands for the authority and
preeminence of the federal state. Whatever
the case, Hood designed an ensemble of
buildings that testify to the power of capitalism,
yet he still managed to involve ordinary
people, with the much-used public spaces. **IW**

Grundtvigkirke

Architect: Peder Jensen-Klint

Completed: 1940

Location: Bispebjerg, Copenhagen, Denmark

Period/Style: Expressionist

This extraordinary church in the Danish
capital is a towering example of expressionist
ecclesiastical architecture that owes a debt to
the medieval Gothic style of Europe and
Denmark's homegrown national Romantic
movement. It was the result of a competition
to build a tangible memorial to Nikolaj
Grundtvig, a popular writer of hymns. The
site chosen was a residential suburb to the
north of the city center. Jensen-Klint won the
competition in 1913, but construction work
did not begin until 1921. The church was
consecrated on the 150th anniversary of
Grundtvig's birth in 1933. Jensen-Klint died
before construction was complete, but his son,
Kaara saw it through to conclusion in 1940.

Its most striking feature is the immense
triple-gabled frontage, its stepped gables
reminiscent of a ziggurat. These quint-
essentially expressionist motifs are echoed on
the gables that run down the side of the
church, which are interspersed with windows.
The high-ceiling interior is clearly a modern
take on the Gothic style, with a long nave
and pointed arcades. It took some six million
bricks to complete it; decoration takes the
form of projecting and receding brickwork,
rather than Gothic-inspired carvings. **IW**

The National Gallery of Art, West Building

Architect: John Russell Pope

Completed: 1941 (begun 1939)

Location: National Mall, Washington, D.C., United States

Style/Period: Neoclassical/Italian Renaissance Revival

The National Gallery of Art may have come into being as the result of a resolution by the U.S. Congress in 1938, but much of the credit for its establishment must go to Andrew W. Mellon. This rich collector of art left his statues and pictures to the nation on his death in 1937, along with funds with which to construct a suitable home for his collection. Little time was lost in commissioning architect John Russell Pope (who was also responsible for the Jefferson Memorial), and what is today known as the West Building (the East Building was added in 1978) was formally opened in Washington, D.C., in 1941.

Given the importance of its purpose — a palace of beauty and education for the American people — its location in the capital and the debt the visual arts owe to ancient Greco-Roman culture, it is not surprising that Pope designed a handsome and imposing neoclassical building. An octastyle portico of Ionic columns constructed, appropriately, in seven different hues of pink marble (albeit from Tennessee rather than Italy), dominates the facade, fronting an enormous building with symmetrical extended wings and a central rotunda. In 1941 it was the largest marble construction in the world. **CH-M**

Pope-Leighey House

Architect: Frank Lloyd Wright

Completed: 1941 (begun 1939)

Location: 9000 Richmond Highway, Woodlawn Plantation, Alexandria, Virginia, United States

Style/Period: Usonian

The Pope-Leighey House conformed to a style in which American architect Frank Lloyd Wright began building during the 1930s. The name that he gave to such houses was "Usonian," a contraction of "United

States of North American," and a description intended to apply to a uniquely North American architectural style. Usonian houses were aimed at ordinary Americans, many of whom were struggling to make ends meet during the Depression. In all, the 1,200-squarefoot (111 sq. m) Pope-Leighey House cost the Pope family $7,000 to commission, build and furnish (it was sold in 1946 to the Leighey family for $17,000).

Although mass production and simple components kept construction costs down, design standards were not compromised. An open-plan living room, flat roof, large windows, carport and radiant-heating elements embedded in the concrete-slab foundations were modern features, but such cozy touches as a central fireplace and the warm colors of natural materials, like brick and tidewater red cypress, gave it a homely feel. And while democratic Usonian homes were humbler than many other Wright creations, they were still designed to organically blend with their surroundings. The Pope-Leighey House was originally raised in East Falls Church, but it was moved to Woodlawn Plantation in 1964. **CH-M**

Casa Malaparte

Architects: Curzio Malaparte and Adalberto Libera

Completed: 1942 (begun 1937)

Location: Near Cape Massullo, Capri, Italy

Style/Period: Italian Rationalist

Casa Malaparte means "House of Malaparte" in Italian, the Malaparte in question being Curzio Malaparte, a writer, one-time Fascist, later a Communist and general colorful character. He was also the owner and creator of an idiosyncratic house on Capri, the Italian island at the southern entrance to the Bay of Naples that is famed for its beauty and climate.

That Curzio Malaparte was blessed with both self-awareness and a lack of modesty was reflected in his nickname for his unique house, "Casa Come Me," Italian for "House Like Me." Indeed, Casa Malaparte was neither a conventional nor a subtle addition to Capri's landscape. Having been unimpressed by the plans initially proposed by Italian rationalist architect Adalberto

Libera, Malaparte instructed the local stonemasons and builders himself as they labored on a narrow point 105 feet (32 m) above sea level, which afforded spectacular marine views. The result was a two-story oblong building, painted Pompeian red, that followed the line of the cliff. The flat roof

served as a sun terrace and featured a curved white wall that sloped upward to shield the sunbathing Malaparte from the intrusive stares of those sailing past. A funnel-shaped staircase led up to the roof from the landward side. **CH-M**

Palazzo della Civiltà

Architects: Giovanni Guerrini, Ernesto Bruno La Padula
and Mario Romano
Completed: 1942 (begun 1938)
Location: Rome, Italy
Style/Period: Italian Rationalist/Italian Fascist

Not only was the Palazzo della Civiltà, or Palace of Italian Civilization, constructed when Italy was enduring the Fascist dictatorship of Benito Mussolini, it was also erected during World War II. This edifice was therefore intended to send a heartening message to the Italian people — and, indeed, the wider world — namely that no matter what the current difficulties and setbacks, the Italian genius would ultimately prevail. This message was spelled out by a legend inscribed at the top of the facade, which referred to Italian poets, artist, heroes, saints, thinkers, scientists, navigators and voyagers.

The centerpiece of the Roman Esposizione Universale di Roma district (EUR, E.42 or Universal Exposition of Rome district), the Palazzo della Civiltà was designed by Giovanni Guerrini, Ernesto Bruno La Padula and Mario Romano. Its popular name, *Il Collosseo Quadrato* or "The Square Colosseum," aptly describes its appearance and evokes a truly iconic structure. That this building of four equal, Travertine-marble-clad sides, with its row upon row of nine Roman-arched windows (six loggias in all), invited comparison with the ancient Roman Colosseum equated Mussolini's regime with one of history's mightiest empires. The overall effect was less impressive, however, being a mundane mixture of classical and modernist styles. **CH-M**

Pentagon

Architect: George Bergstrom
Completed: 1943
Location: Arlington, Virginia, United States
Style: Neoclassical

The Pentagon is currently home to the U.S. Department of Defense and the Joint Chiefs of Staff, but the original idea was developed shortly before the country was plunged into World War II. The design — five sides with five floors above ground, two basement levels and a central plaza — was by Bergstrom, but the actual construction, which began in September 1941, was overseen by John McShain, the "Man Who Built Washington." Because of wartime shortages, little steel was used, but 650,000 tons (589, 670 metric tonnes) of sand were dredged from the

nearby Potomac River for reinforced concrete, and Indiana limestone was brought in to face the structure. The building was inaugurated after just 16 months.

The Pentagon's shape was determined by the original site chosen for it, an intersection where two roads met at roughly 108 degrees, the angle of a regular pentagon. It was moved so as to leave an uninterrupted view between Washington D.C. and Arlington National Cemetery. As befits the headquarters of a military superpower, the Pentagon is huge — it has 17.5 miles (28 km) of corridors alone — and some 26,000 people are employed there. It also has the largest floor space of any building in the world. **IW**

Kaufmann Desert House

Architect: Richard Neutra
Completed: 1946
Location: Palm Springs, California, United States
Style: Modernism

Neutra's Californian building is widely regarded as one of the top-five examples of a modernist domestic building of the 20th century. It was built for the successful Pennsylvanian department store owner Edgar Kaufmann Sr., who was something of a fan of modernist architecture and had commissioned Frank Lloyd Wright for the Fallingwater project. Overall, the international-style house is in the shape of a cross with wings running off a central living area at the cardinal points of a compass. There is an overhanging flat roof and vast sliding glass windows that make the most of the exterior desert landscape, but the house, with its manicured gardens, is not really part of the environment.

Neutra's bold move was to put an essentially suburban house in an extreme context, making a statement about man's ability to control or overcome a harsh environment — the Sonora Desert in this case — and elements of the house reflect this notion. There is an upper story with three sides with movable vertical fins that offer protection against the intense heat and occasional sandstorms, while the precinct is protected from the elements by substantial drystone walls. **IW**

Case Study House No.8 (Eames House)

Architects: Charles Eames and Ray Eames

Completed: 1949

Location: Pacific Palisades, California, United States

Style: Modernism

The Eames House was one of 25 experimental buildings that formed the Case Study Home Program that took place from the mid-1940s to the early 1960s, and it is widely regarded as the most successful of them. The idea for the program came from John Entenza, the publisher of the influential *Arts and Architecture* magazine, and his rationale was to design and furnish homes that would best suit a modern lifestyle, using materials and techniques developed during World War II. Charles Eames and his wife Ray opted to devise an international-style house for a married couple who were apartment dwellers working in design and the graphic arts, namely themselves, using off-the-shelf components.

Concrete, steel frame (erected in just 16 hours by five workers) and glass were the main materials. Inspiration came from chicken wire, which appeared on the cover of Entenza's magazine in June 1950, and the brightly colored and rigidly geometric paintings of Dutch artist Piet Mondrian. The house took little time to build and sits comfortably on a hillside surrounded by eucalyptus trees. Its internal space includes two spacious and light live-work areas. The Eameses moved in during December 1949 and lived there for the rest of their lives. **IW**

Glass House

Architect: Philip Johnson

Completed: 1949

Location: New Canaan, Connecticut, United States

Style: Modernism

This iconic and minimalist modernist house was designed by Philip Johnson as a country retreat for himself. It lies approximately one hour's drive north of New York, where Johnson worked, in a town that is something of a showcase for modernist architecture. It is located in its own 45-acre (18 ha) grounds on a small wooded bluff. The estate not only contains the Glass House but also 11 other buildings that Johnson either refurnished or built from scratch. The house is an essay in minimalism and consists of just three building materials — steel frame, glass windows and an interior brick cylinder.

There are no partitions within, save for the cylinder, which not only defines the living, dining, sleeping and study areas but also contains a bathroom on one side and an open hearth on the other. The latter gives sense to the living area, which otherwise was merely defined by a large rug and an easel-mounted painting by the 17th century French artist Nicolas Poussin. The vast expanse of glass allows light and a superb view of the natural gardens to pour into the house, yet it retains a measure of privacy. Johnson died in the house, and it is now in the care of the National Trust for Historic Preservation. **IW**

Johnson Wax Building/
S.C. Johnson & Son
Administration Building

Architect: Frank Lloyd Wright

Completed: 1950

Location: 14th and Franklin Street, Racine, Wisconsin, United States

Style/Period: Organic

The building that Frank Lloyd Wright designed to act as the administration offices of S.C. Johnson & Son attracted considerable attention following its opening in 1939, and it continues to be hailed as a landmark of corporate architecture, just as it remains this international company's headquarters. A taller laboratory tower was constructed between 1944 and 1950.

In his use of natural materials and forms, Wright demonstrated that a building dedicated to business need not feel boring, uniform or inhuman. Thus it was primarily constructed from Cherokee red-colored bricks molded into hundreds of different forms, enabling a mixture of curves and angles, as incorporated into the circular mezzanines and square floors. The brick sections were alternated with narrower bands of Pyrex-glass tubing, which let in light but did not offer distracting views, unlike more ordinary windows. Glass also featured prominently in the roof of the open-plan Great Workroom, which was supported by cream-colored reinforced-concrete internal columns with mushroom-shaped tops, which have also been described as dendriform (treelike) or as resembling lily pads. Wright designed the office furnishings, too, so that while the building's sleek exterior looks relatively featureless, there is much for the desk-bound office-worker to enjoy inside, not least the sense of not being confined within a conventional corporate box. CH-M

Rose Seidler House

Architect: Harry Seidler
Completed: 1950
Location: Wahroonga, New South Wales, Australia
Style/Period: Modernism

This uncompromisingly modernist home in the international style would not have been out of place on the East Coast of the United States, but it was a a jolting wake-up call for Australian architects. Austrian-born Canadian Harry Seidler had studied under Walter Gropius and Marcel Breuer in New York, worked in the latter's studio for a time and then studied under Oscar Niemeyer in Brazil, so he was steeped in the aesthetics of modernism. Seidler designed this Bauhaus-influenced house for his parents, Max and Rose, in a Sydney suburb, and it is fundamentally an open square with separate living and sleeping areas linked by a family room.

It was built in concrete and timber. It overlooks a valley in a public reserve, and Seidler makes the most of the spectacular views. It is open on all sides and there is a central terrace that is reached by a ramp. The architect chose his colors carefully — the light interior is dominated by cool colors and textures, while the exterior of the terrace has a large mural in blues, reds and yellows that are picked up elsewhere in the furnishings and on the predominantly white walls. **IW**

Farnsworth House

Architect: Ludwig Mies van der Rohe

Completed: 1951

Location: Plano, Illinois, United States

Style/Period: International/Modernism

This pristine white pavilion, set within a naturalistic green landscape, embodies a romantic architectural ideal stretching back to the 18th century. Returning from their grand cultural tours, Europe's nobility eagerly transformed their estates into artificial vistas of lakes and hills, complete with facsimiles of the ancient ruins they had visited. Though differing greatly in form to its neoclassical forebears, the house Ludwig Mies van der Rohe designed for Dr. Edith Farnsworth shares a common belief — that an unashamedly manmade structure can still enhance its natural surroundings.

Touching lightly upon the landscape, the house floats $5^{1}/_{4}$ feet (1.6 m) above the Fox River's floodplain, perched upon eight slender steel I beams. Reducing the home to its purest abstract components, Mies laid a flat roof above an identical floor slab then wrapped them with a continuous curtain of glass to enclose the space in between. The transparency of Mies' design blurs the distinction between inside and out, admitting vast amounts of natural light, though at the expense of the residents' privacy. A little modesty is preserved by the wooden core that contains the bathroom, toilets and services. The simplicity of the structure belies its expense, the final bill standing at $74,000 dollars (around $1 million today). This resulted in a bitter lawsuit between architect and patron, possibly exacerbated by the souring of a rumored romantic liaison. Beautifully restored as a National Historic Landmark, the house's 57-year relationship with its environment is showing no such signs of decay. **PC**

Unitarian Meeting House

Architect: Frank Lloyd Wright

Completed: 1951 (begun 1947)

Location: 900 University Bay Drive, Madison,
Wisconsin, United States

Style/Period: Modernism

When the First Unitarian Society (FUS) of
Madison decided that it needed a new
meetinghouse in 1946, it commissioned
Frank Lloyd Wright, a member of its
congregation, to design it. Five years later,
the FUS was the proud possessor of such an
extraordinary-looking church complex that it
has since been declared a U.S. National
Historic Landmark.

The most striking feature of the single-
story limestone-and-oak Unitarian Meeting
House — where the recurring motif was an
equilateral triangle — was the steeply
pitched copper-clad roof, which extended
almost to the ground and whose apical ridge
formed such a sharp point that the overall
effect was like an arrowhead or prow. Underneath its overhanging eave, the entire wall was
constructed of glass divided into horizontal
bands, which flooded the meetinghouse's
auditorium with light; warmth was provided
by the red concrete floor in which heating
pipes were embedded. Accessed though an
entrance and lobby situated to the eastern
side, the auditorium's shape described one
half of a rough diamond, with the other,
lower half — the hearth room — housing a
fireplace and providing a venue for social
gatherings. Extending to the west was the
Loggia, with classrooms and a library
running alongside it, which led directly to
the west living room. **CH-M**

Royal Festival Hall

Architect: LCC Architects' Department

Completed: 1951 (begun 1949)

Location: South Bank, London, England

Style/Period: Modernism

The Royal Festival Hall — a concert hall on
the South Bank of London's River Thames
— was built as part of the Festival of Britain
of 1951. This festival looked back to the
famous Great Exhibition of 1851 but, more

importantly, encouraged a nation that still bore the scars of World War II to look forward to a brighter future. The festival's central South Bank site was a significant choice, since not only did it occupy a prime position in Britain's capital, but it had also suffered severe bomb damage. Constructing a public building dedicated to music here consequently symbolized both Britain's regeneration and its civilized values.

The modernist style of the building designed by Leslie Martin, Peter Moro and Robert Matthew, of the London County Council's (LCC) Architects' Department, similarly conveyed a sense of putting the past to rest. Martin compared his architectural team's creation to "an egg in a box," the egg being the auditorium (designed according to acoustical principles), and the box being the surrounding structure, starting with the open-plan foyers and meeting places. Outside, the long, low limestone-and-glass riverside facade was composed of horizontal and vertical oblong shapes softened by a few curves. The Royal Festival Hall later underwent major alterations, completed in 1964 and in 2007. **CH-M**

Lomonosov Moscow State University

Architect: Lev Vladimirovich Rudnev
Completed: 1952 (begun 1947)
Location: Vorobyovy Hills, Moscow, Russia
Style/Period: Totalitarian/Stalinist Gothic

If the Lomonosov University building's 787-foot (240 m) tall tower looks slightly reminiscent of those built a few decades earlier in the United States, that may be because Joseph Stalin covertly dispatched architects to the U.S. to study skyscrapers so that lessons learned there could be applied in the Soviet Union. When World War II ended, the Soviet dictator was free to focus on consolidating his grip on the Union of Soviet Socialist Republics (USSR) and glorifying the Bolshevik regime. To this end, he decided to erect seven skyscrapers (popularly called the "Seven Sisters") in Moscow, the Soviet capital, one of which was earmarked for occupation by the Moscow State University.

An example of Stalinist Gothic, architecture professor Lev Vladimirovich Rudnev's design was a monumental proclamation of Soviet might. It was made even more imposing by its elevated site on the Vorobyovy Hills above the River Moskva, to the southwest of central Moscow. The central tower, which contained 36 stories, was divided into three levels that described a rough pyramid and supported a spike bearing a Soviet star. Offices and teaching rooms were situated within this tower, while students, lecturers and researchers were accommodated and otherwise catered for in the four long wings that extended from the sides. **CH-M**

long, 66 feet (20 m) wide and 200 feet (61 m) tall, and is raised up on piloti (stilts) by 23 feet (7 m). Aside from the apartments, which are reached by elevators, there is a street of shops on the fifth floor, a hotel, medical and educational facilities, and a private recreational area on the roof hidden behind tall parapets. This space includes children's play zones, seating areas, a garden, and a swimming pool. The unit became the blueprint for other such developments across Europe and elsewhere. **IW**

Säynätsalo Town Hall

Architect: Alvar Aalto
Completed: 1952 (begun 1950)
Location: Säynätsalo, Finland
Style/Period: Functionalist

In the town hall, or civic center, that he created for the community of Säynätsalo, Finland, architect Alvar Aalto combined traditional Finnish materials with a modern design, giving a building that was used for day-to-day civic matters a far from mundane appearance. Aalto constructed the town hall's various components, including a library, a council chamber, offices and accommodation, around a central courtyard that was open to the elements. He adopted this centuries-old ground plan but gave it a unique twist by ensuring that none of the four surrounding wings looked the same, punctuating some with steps leading to the inner courtyard.

The main construction material used was red brick, which, during the cold, dark Finnish winters suggested an element of warmth. The pitched roofs discouraged snow from settling. And yet the presence of nature was welcomed, not least in the form of the raised grassy courtyard that the building enclosed and by the floor-to-ceiling glass windows ranged around it, which both let in light and created a sense of harmony with the natural environment. The generally two-story civic center's tallest, and most outstanding, component was the council chamber, whose sloping ceiling was supported by a sunburst-style arrangement of wooden rafters. **CH-M**

Unité d'Habitation

Architect: Le Corbusier (Charles-Édouard Jeanneret)
Completed: 1952
Location: Marseilles, France
Style/Period: Modernist

The Unité d'Habitation ("Housing Unit" or "Housing Unity") was a groundbreaking design by Swiss-born French architect Le Corbusier, as it was the Modernist movement's first effort to create a public residential block. It also gives full expression to many of the arch-Modernist's architectural tenets in that, among other elements, it used modern materials including concrete, and was built upward surrounded by large open spaces, thereby increasing dwelling densities but without compromising on outside areas for recreation and play. Le Corbusier strove to create a fully-fledged community in the sky and thus provided the 12-story, 337-apartment buildings with various amenities.

The building is some 450 feet (137 m)

United Nations Headquarters

Architect: Le Corbusier, Oscar Niemeyer, Wallace K.
Harrison and Others
Completed: 1953 (begun 1947)
Location: First Avenue at 46th Street, New York, New
York, United States
Style/Period: International Modernism

The United Nations (UN) was created in the aftermath of World War II, its purpose to ensure that peace would, in future, prevail through international cooperation. It having been decided that the UN's headquarters would be based in New York, construction began on an 18-acre (72,846 sq. m) plot alongside the East River — which is officially international, not U.S., territory — in 1947. Completed in 1953, this mammoth under-taking was directed by an international team of architects, initially working to an overall design by the Swiss-born Le Corbusier.

The most eye-catching element of the United Nations Headquarters — which, in conforming to the international modern style, evoked the future rather than the unhappy recent past — was inevitably the towering, oblong, slablike Secretariat building. Based on a reinforced–concrete skeleton, the two longer sides received a green-tinted-thermopane-glass curtain wall, while the two shorter white-marble-faced end walls remained without windows. At the top of this 39-story, 544-foot-tall (166 m) skyscraper was an aluminum grille that concealed necessary equipment from view, while two windowless floors lower down created horizontal bands in the glass curtain wall. Other components of the United Nations Headquarters' complex were the General Assembly and Conference buildings and the Dag Hammarskjöld Library. **CH-M**

Biblioteca Central, Universidad Nacional Autónoma de México (UNAM)

Architect: Juan O'Gorman

Completed: 1953 (begun 1950)

Location: Cuidad Universitaria, near Mexico City, Mexico

Style/Period: International Modernism with pre-Hispanic detailing

Mexican-Irish architect Juan O'Gorman's Central Library building for the National Autonomous University of Mexico (UNAM) was part of the planned *Cuidad Universitaria* ("University City"), or the huge campus that came into being during the early 1950s on an area measuring 173 acres (70 ha) outside Mexico City. Le Corbusier's influence on O'Gorman's work at this stage in his career was evident in the Central Library's fundamentally modernist and functionalist style. The 10-story, rectangular building's design was perfectly suited to its purpose as a stackroom tower (a place where books are stored and accessed).

The immense and intricate mosaics that decorated the exterior, covering a surface area of 43,057 feet (4,000 sq. m), made the Central Library unique, injecting interest into a potentially dull, windowless facade and conveying something of the exuberant color and pre-Hispanic traditions of Mexican art. (While the building was raised from local volcanic rock, the tesserae used in the mosaics came from all over Mexico.) Juan O'Gorman's artistry can be seen in the images he created for the Central Library's walls, which illustrate themes drawn from Mexico's history. The campus is now included on the UNESCO's list of World Heritage Sites. **CH-M**

Beth Sholom Synagogue

Architect: Frank Lloyd Wright

Completed: 1954

Location: 8231 Old York Road, Elkins Park, Pennsylvania, United States

Style/Period: Eclectic Modernism

That Frank Lloyd Wright strove to give each of his constructions a unique quality is evident in the synagogue that he designed for the Beth Sholom congregation in Elkins Park, a suburb of Philadelphia, Pennsylvania. And while the architectural merits of this remarkable synagogue have earned it a place on the list of U.S. National Historic Landmarks, the care that Wright took to heed the advice of Rabbi Mortimer J. Cohen resulted in a building whose religious references have profound sacred significance to the Jewish congregation that still gathers there.

At first sight, the synagogue resembles a flat-topped pyramid with three ridges (adorned with menorah-style decorations). This is quite deliberate, since the pyramid may be likened to Mount Sinai, as well as to the tents and tabernacles used by the early nomadic Jews. The hexagonal base with two side extensions, on which the canopied roof rests, recalls a pair of cupped hands enclosing those within. At night, light illuminates the pyramid's glass-and-plastic roof — supported by steel beams 115 feet (35 m) long — causing it to glow. The auditorium that is situated directly below can seat over a thousand people. The floor beneath the auditorium, or prayer hall, contains the entrance lobby, gathering places, bridal suites and a smaller place of prayer. **CH-M**

Notre Dame du Haut

Architect: Le Corbusier (Charles-Édouard Jeanneret)
Completed: 1955
Location: Ronchamp, Franche-Comté, France
Style/Period: Late Modernism

When Canon Lucian Ledeur approached Le Corbusier with this building proposition, he could offer the architect little financial inducement, but he did have a stunning setting and set no limits to the building's look. The hilltop site was of deep religious significance, having been the location of a pagan temple before becoming a Christian sanctuary in the 4th century CE. The previous chapel had been destroyed during World War II. Le Corbusier took up the challenge, using some of the old chapel's stone, and he created both a place of worship and a piece of monumental sculpture that looked nothing like his previous, largely angular, boxlike civil or public, works.

The chapel breaks all the rules of traditional ecclesiastical architecture in that it is a swooping vision of both convex and concave curves, rather than the traditional angular form. The materials, largely rendered concrete, are also far from traditional, and the colors — white walls and a raw, unrendered concrete roof — are equally modernist. Yet Le Corbusier infused the building with religious power. Various stained-glass windows cut through the walls and send shafts of light into the interior, giving it a feeling of great spirituality. **IW**

Kundert Medical Clinic

Architect: Frank Lloyd Wright

Completed: 1955

Location: 1106 Pacific Street, San Luis Obispo,

California, United States

Style/Period: Modernism

Not only is the site of the Kundert Medical Clinic prone to seismic activity, it is also situated alongside the San Luis Obispo Creek. Frank Lloyd Wright's design for this healthcare facility in a small, coastal central Californian town took account of both potentially destructive natural forces by incorporating an L-shaped concrete slab that linked a wall to the riverbed behind. And in typical Wright style, the architect also ensured that the clinic complemented its natural surroundings rather than act as a blot on the landscape.

There are no windows as such set into the front-facade walls of the red brick structure, which is essentially horizontal, although a smaller rectangular level rises above the main building. However, a triple-layered band of glazing runs underneath the projecting edges of the flat roof. This innovative use of glass, which is protected and enlivened by a repeating, superimposed cutout design, lets light into the open-plan waiting area, where seating for patients and a reception desk stand amid exposed brick and wood. Glazed wooden floor-to-ceiling doors open up to provide access to a patio area at the back, which is enclosed by a low wall that backs onto the creek. **CH-M**

Sleeping Beauty Castle

Architect: Herb Ryman

Completed: 1955

Location: Main Street, Walt Disney World, near

Orlando, Florida, United States

Style/Period: Modernism/Gothic Pastiche

Even those who have not been to a Disney theme park — be it in Florida or elsewhere in the world — probably recognize the turreted towers and soaring spires of Sleeping Beauty's Castle, whose image and outline is ubiquitous in relation to the Disney brand and logo. And if it reminds some of Neuschwanstein, "Mad" King Ludwig of Bavaria's castle in Germany, it is because Disney "Imagineer" Herb Ryman deliberately based his design on that archetypal fairytale castle (itself a 19th-century Romantic fantasy, see page 226).

Excited young visitors to Walt Disney World in Florida have been approaching Sleeping Beauty's Castle, at the end of Main Street and the entrance to Fantasyland, since its completion in 1955. A bridge over a moat leads to a lowered (working) drawbridge, which in turn gives way to an archway that provides access to Fantasyland. All of the towers — the tallest of which rises to a height of 77 feet (23 m) — are different in style, but they all look medieval, while the castle (which was constructed of timber and stone) resembles a European fortress of the same period. Snow White's Grotto is situated under the castle, on the right-hand side. **CH-M**

High Court

Architect: Le Corbusier (Charles-Édouard Jeanneret)

Location: Chandigarh, Punjab, India

Completed: 1955

Style/Period: Modernism

Chandigarh became the capital city of the newly created Indian state of Punjab when India gained its independence from Britain and was partitioned in 1947. The previous capital, Lahore, was ceded to Pakistan. Le Corbusier had been invited to build the new city after one of the original town planners/ architects died and the other withdrew from the project. He completely revised their work according to certain ideas laid down by the CIAM (*Congres Internationaux d'Architecture Moderne*/International Congress of Modern Architecture), of which he was cofounder. It called for "honesty of materials," particularly brick, stone and concrete, and a pure functionality in which straight lines predominated.

Le Corbusier's buildings, largely administrative, are concentrated in Sector I, where the High Court is also found. It is a blocklike structure of reinforced concrete with an arched roof that shades the entire building and a large main entrance comprising three imposing 59-foot (18 m) vertical concrete slabs in red, yellow and green. The building has nine courts and associated offices, each with its own entrance. The High Court, the first of the architect's designs to be completed, is an essay in the possibilities of working with reinforced concrete. **IW**

Annunciation Greek Orthodox Church

Architect: Frank Lloyd Wright

Completed: 1956

Location: 9400 West Congress Street, Wauwatosa, Milwaukee, Wisconsin, United States

Style/Period: Eclectic Modernism

Although Frank Lloyd Wright designed the Annunciation Greek Orthodox Church in Wauwatosa, a suburb of Milwaukee, the venerable architect did not live long enough to attend its dedication ceremony in 1961.

Like most of Wright's sacred structures, the Annunciation Greek Orthodox Church has been hailed as a masterpiece in its original combination of ancient conventions and concepts with modern materials and methods. Although his creation was tiny in comparison, Wright called it his "Little Sofia," naming his inspiration as the Byzantine-era Hagia Sofia in Istanbul, Turkey (see page 52), and there are subtle similarities, not least in the domed roof. Constructed of concrete, Little Sofia's dome measures 106 feet (32 m) in diameter. While the exterior is circular, the ground plan inside is based on the shape of a Greek cross. This cross-within-a-circle motif appears in microcosm in such decorative details as the icon screen (of anodized aluminum but incorporating the gold that is such a striking feature of traditional Greek Orthodox art forms). Steps lead up to the entrance doors, which are set into a long, low arched recess, with stained-glass panels on either side. This bow shape is repeated for the recessed stained-glass windows that ring the building in a band beneath the dome. **C H-M**

Case Study House No. 21 (Bailey House)

Architect: Pierre Koenig

Completed: 1958 (begun 1956)

Location: 9036 Wonderland Park Avenue, Los Angeles, California, United States

Style/Period: SoCal Modernism

The reason Case Study House No. 21 (otherwise known as the Bailey House) has such an uninspiring name is because it was one of 36 prototype buildings erected in southern California ("SoCal") between 1945 and 1966. The intention was for these show homes to introduce postwar Californians to low-cost modernism as interpreted by different architects. Pierre Koenig took charge of two: No. 21 and No. 22. Both of Koenig's case-study residences demonstrate his gift for using such modern materials as glass and steel in avant-garde structures that, for all of their futuristic appearance, somehow suit their surroundings. They were also practical to live in and economical to construct ($20,000 in this case), thanks to their prefabricated structural elements.

From the outside, the single-story, L-shaped, flat-roofed Case Study House No. 21 appeared starkly simple against its hillside setting. Supported by prefabricated steel frames, the huge windows of the glazed north and south walls (those on the east and west were solid) allowed the bright Californian light to stream into the house. They also provided spectacular reflective effects for the pools that encircled the house, which was reached via brick terracing. Inside, the house was simply divided into a living room, two bedrooms and a kitchen, and there was also an integral carport. **CH-M**

Palazzetto dello Sport

Architect: Annibale Vitellozzi and Pier Luigi Nervi
Completed: 1958
Location: Piazza Apollodoro, Rome, Italy
Style/Period: Modernism

The 5,000-seat Palazzetto dello Sport was the smaller of two arenas built by Nervi for the 1960 Olympic Games and, although a modernist architect was involved in the project, the vision and execution of the arena was all Nervi's. He was an engineer and contractor par excellence, one who had been a professor of engineering at Rome University from 1946 until 1961. His mastery of engineering — he had a reputation for speed, quality and keeping to budget — allowed him to bring geometry and sophisticated prefabrication techniques to bear on architectural issues and still produce elegant buildings.

The Palazzetto dello Sport is an unadorned but strikingly elegant circular design topped by a beautiful dome with a diameter of 194 feet (60 m). The latter is so finely engineered that it is remarkably light-weight: concrete was simply poured over a thin wire mesh supported by diagonal ribbing. It is also rigid, and because the lower section is not load bearing (a job done by exterior leaning columns shaped like a letter "Y"), Nervi was able to incorporate a ribbon of windows along the entire length of the arena. Nervi was, of course, on time, and the Palazzetto was officially opened in 1959. **IW**

Atomium

Architect: André Waterkeyn
Completed: 1958
Location: Boulevard du Centenaire/Eeuwfeestlaan, Brussels, Belgium
Style/Period: High-Tech/Metabolic

The Atomium was a futuristic vision brought about by the hope and optimism that sprung up as the memories of World War II receded during the dawn of the atomic and space ages. It was designed by André Waterkeyn, an engineer by training and director of a metallurgical company, for the 1958 World's Fair. It was intended to encourage young

people to seek careers in science. Its bizarre shape is based on the atomic structure of an iron molecule — but one enlarged to around 165 billion times its actual size. To ensure it would not topple over, a large-scale model with three "bipods" (pylons) was successfully tested in a wind tunnel.

The Atomium was originally clad in aluminum over a steel frame.It consists of nine 59-foot (18 m) diameter spheres connected by diagonal tubes 75 feet (29 m) long and 11 feet (3 m) wide. The tubes contain escalators, which were the longest in Europe when the attraction opened. Within the spheres were displays relating to scientific and medical subjects, while the top-most sphere offers today's tourists panoramic views of Brussels. Waterkeyn's worthy hope now seems to belong to a less cynical and less fearful age. **IW**

Seagram Building

Architect: Ludwig Mies van der Rohe

Completed: 1958

Location: Park Avenue, New York, New York, United States

Style/Period: International/Modernism

Much copied but never bettered, the Seagram Building has been the inspiration for many, often taller, international-style skyscrapers since it opened. Mies van der Rohe began experimenting with similar designs in the 1920s, and the 38-story Seagram became the tangible expression of his wish to build a monument in structural steel and tinted glass. He also eschewed conventional detailing and decoration to produce a pure symmetry that itself was the beauty he was striving to achieve.

Mies van der Rohe also took a brave step that has rarely been repeated since; the building is set back and does not occupy the whole site — a raised granite plaza fronting onto Park Avenue. It was a bold suggestion given the eye-watering land values in New York, but the business tycoon who commissioned the architect, Samuel Bronfman, agreed. Work began in 1954, and the 1,776-foot (541 m) building was completed in four years. Mies van der Rohe had to make one compromise to his vision —

the steel had to be clad because of fire regulations. Concrete was the usual option, but he chose bronze beams that only added

to the beauty of this modernist monument to corporate wealth. **IW**

Solomon R. Guggenheim Museum

Architect: Frank Lloyd Wright

Completed: 1959

Location: New York, New York, United States

Style/Period: Expressionism/Late Modernism/Organic

As much a work of art as the priceless collection it contains, the Solomon R. Guggenheim Museum remains a monument to Wright's sculptural ingenuity, the subtle details of his composition having a subliminal effect on the unsuspecting viewer. Inspired by the spiraling ziggurats of the Middle East, Wright proceeded to invert their forms, creating a drumlike tower whose overhanging stories hide continuous clerestory windows (long since blocked out by overzealous curators). The unconventional gallery space within takes the form of a continuous curving ramp that tapers inward as it rises, distorting the atrium's perspective to exaggerate its height. The pure, uninterrupted white line of its winding parapet gives the illusion of being self-supporting, but closer inspection reveals 12 slender columns radiating out from the walls. Set back from the parapet's edge, these columns act as partitions, dividing the slope into a procession of individual bays, before

finally arching up to become the glazing bars of the circular skylight. The flow of one element into another typifies Wright's concept of "organic" architecture, emulating the inherent structure found within natural forms.

Wright's self-absorbed design approach produced a seminal building, but it presented curators and their public with the unenviable task of hanging and viewing largely rectilinear art on curving walls around sloping floors. Though visitors are today directed to take the elevator to the ramp's summit and begin a gradual descent toward the exit, Wright may well have intended the reverse. In either event, visiting the Guggenheim remains a unique experience. **PC**

House on the Klong (Jim Thompson House)

Architect: Jim Thompson

Completed: 1959

Location: Bangkok, Thailand

Style/Period: Traditional Thai

The Delaware-born architect Jim Thompson fell in love with Bangkok when he joined the

U.S. Army and was posted to Thailand. Following his discharge, he returned to this Asian country, set up the Jim Thompson Thai Silk Company and constructed himself a house in Bangkok. He lived there until 1967, when he disappeared while on vacation in Malaysia.

It may seem strange that an American entrepreneur's house should have become a popular destination for tourists visiting Bangkok, but it is as much an old and traditional Thai dwelling as it is a foreigner's fantasy. Having acquired a plot of land alongside a *klong*, or canal, Thompson scoured the country for beautiful old Thai houses. Six 19th-century structures were eventually purchased, dismantled and transported to the *klong*-side site by barge. Local carpenters, working under the supervision of a Thai architect, reassembled the structures according to Thompson's design. The result was a large teak house situated alongside the canal and set within lush grounds, which also contained smaller pavilions. The two-story house itself was roughly rectangular, with much of its charm arising from the assemblage of steeply pitched, curved roofs, each of which was decorated with upward-curving *naga*-head (snake-head) finials. **CH-M**

National Congress

Architect: Oscar Niemeyer

Completed: 1960 (begun 1956)

Location: Monumental Axis, Brasília, Brazil

Style/Period: International Modernism

When, during the 1950s, Brasília was designated the new capital of Brazil, the prospect of building an entirely new city created a unique architectural opportunity. The work of urban planner Lucio Costa having found favor, it fell to Oscar Niemeyer, Costa's young associate, to act as chief architect and shape Brasília's development. In so doing, he evolved a design that was an eye-catching fusion of the international style and the bold Brazilian spirit.

Twin elements are evident in the building that Niemeyer designed to house the two-chamber Congresso Nacional (National Congress), and appropriately so, since the Brazilian parliament comprises both an upper house (the Senado Federal, or Federal Senate) and a lower house (the Câmera dos Deputados, or Chamber of Deputies). These chambers meet in separate assembly halls on either side of a pair of twin skyscrapers (which are connected by a covered walkway around halfway up) that provide office space. Both parliament buildings are housed within a long one-story edifice that rises above an artificial lake. Apparently perched on the rectangular structure's flat roof, the convex dome of the Federal Senate resembles an overturned bowl, while the concave roof of the Chamber of Deputies looks like a saucer. The whole brilliant-white complex appears clean and modern against the blue Brazilian sky. **CH-M**

U.S. Embassy London Chancery Building

Architect: Eero Saarinen

Completed: 1960 (begun 1955)

Location: Grosvenor Square, London, England

Style/Period: Modernism/Expressionism

Designing a new home for the embassy of the United States of America, situated on the entire west side of Grosvenor Square in London, Britain's capital, was a challenge, and not only on account of such practical considerations as how best to accommodate about 750 diplomats and support staff. Almost as important as these practicalities was conveying the might and dignity of the United States and ensuring the new embassy would harmonize with the old buildings that surrounded it. Not only did the Finnish-born U.S. architect Eero Saarinen meet all of these demands, he also created an architectural landmark.

Saarinen's design was based on a large, rectangular and flat-roofed building constructed of reinforced concrete clad in Portland stone. Although it had nine stories, three of these were below ground, so only six were visible to passers-by, and the first two were recessed and ringed by concrete pillars. Despite the detailing that Saarinen used for the facade being distinctly modern, the proportions of the levels delineating each story, as well as the symmetry and repetition of the prevailing checkered pattern, made this a sympathetic addition to the Georgian-era neighborhood. The huge gilded-aluminum bald eagle affixed to the center of the fascia, which measures 35 feet (11 m) from wing tip to wing tip, has come to symbolize the embassy. **CH-M**

Malin Residence

Architect: John Lautner

Completed: 1960

Location: West Hollywood, California, United States

Style/Period: Late Modernism

This modernist house, which also goes under the name of Chemosphere, was commissioned by Leonard Malin, an aerospace engineer. He had chosen (or rather, been given by his father-in-law) a difficult spot to build upon — a precipitously steep hillside in the Hollywood Hills in a notorious earthquake zone. Lautner, who had worked under Frank Lloyd Wright, came up with an ingenious solution that was as much about structural engineering as architecture and aesthetics.

The 2,200-square-foot (200 sq. m) octagonal living area consists of a wooden-beam frame that is fixed to a steel compression ring, which in turn is fixed to a central cast-concrete column some 30 feet (9 m) high from which eight steel beams rise to support each of the octagon's vertices. The wooden beams also allow for a circle of windows around the living area, and they support the roof, which terminates in a central skylight. Access to the building is by a funicular up the slope and a bridge across the gap. The home is a unique solution to a problem site and has proved sufficiently robust to survive several earthquakes. **IW**

Trans World Airlines (TWA) Terminal

Architect: Eero Saarinen

Completed: 1962

Location: Idlewild Airport (now John F. Kennedy Airport), New York, New York, United States

Style/Period: Expressionism/Modernism

Given that mass-aviation is now a daily reality for countless millions, it is hard to imagine how impossibly glamorous the concept of transcontinental air travel was to the first generation of jet-setters. Back in the late 1950s, instead of a mind-numbing assault course of security check-ins and baggage carousels, passengers enjoyed a level of exclusivity and service that made boarding the early airliners akin to catching the Orient Express. TWA recognized that their point of departure demanded a similar sense of occasion, and they commissioned architect Eero Saarinen to create a distinctive transport hub that could be used as a concrete form of corporate identity.

Saarinen's response came closer to capturing the essence of flight than any building before or since, and it was a consummate demonstration of his unique synthesis of art and engineering. Four leaping concrete shells, their cantilevered peaks echoing the tail fins and wingtips of the planes they served, converge on a central hall some 50 feet (15 m) high and 315 feet (96 m) long. The rough boards used as shuttering left the concrete with a richly textured surface — a warm, handmade finish that catches the light. The interior is equally organic, with floors merging seamlessly into walls before morphing into flying footbridges or wide flights of steps. Gazing through its full-height glazing, the waiting passengers found themselves with ringside seats from which to watch the silver planes perform the miracle of flight. **PC**

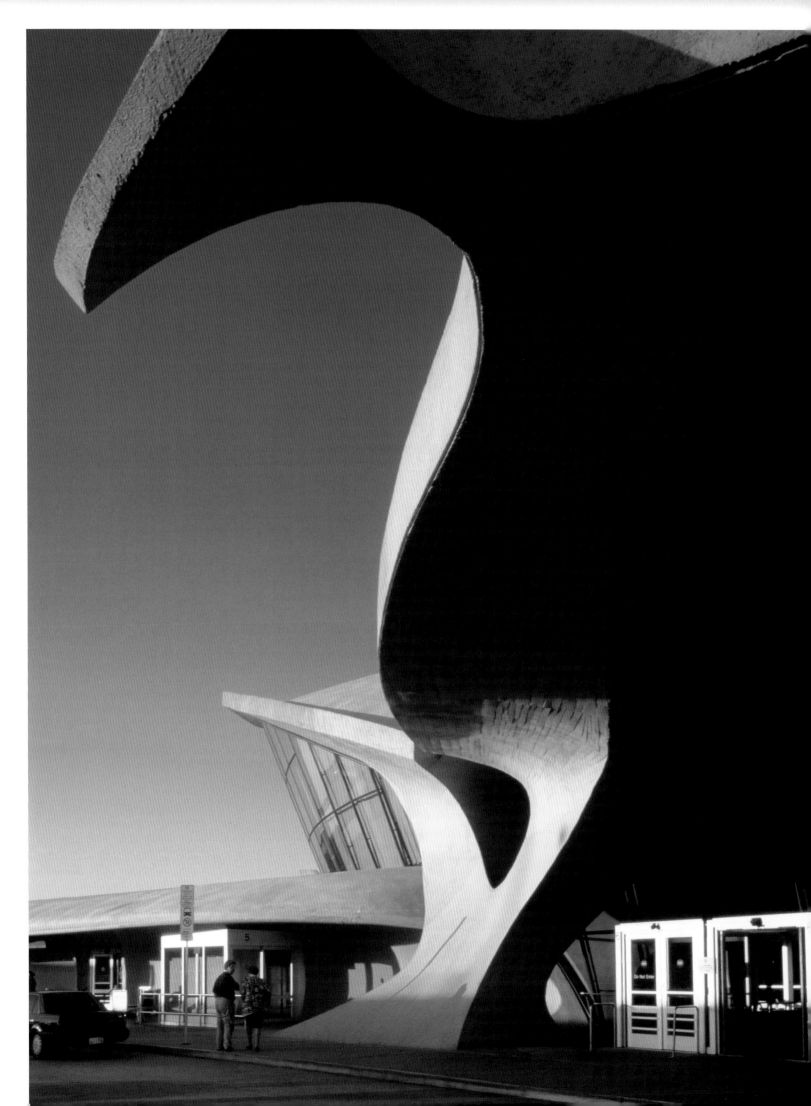

Coventry Cathedral

Architect: Sir Basil Spence

Completed: 1962 (begun 1956)

Location: Coventry, West Midlands, England

Style/Period: Modernism

On the fateful night of November 14, 1940, a vicious storm of German incendiaries rained down on medieval Coventry, unleashing a firestorm that consumed the 14th century cathedral of Saint Michael. The next morning a devastated city resolved to rebuild its spiritual centerpiece as an act of faith and hope for the future. An open competition in 1950 attracted some 219 entries, from which Basil Spence's daringly modern design was selected. Though radical, Spence's scheme retained the old cathedral's ruins as the backdrop for a quiet garden of remembrance. Leading on from this hallowed ground, he laid out a long nave bordered by zigzagging red sandstone walls, whose stepped edges are filled with thick stained-glass blocks that direct the sun's rays to illuminate the alter. The shallow roof is supported by a fine lattice of concrete ribs, which spread out from delicate tapered columns that balance lightly on their narrow bases.

Spence commissioned Britain's finest artists and sculptors to enrich the building inside and out, keeping the tradition of ecclesiastical patronage alive in the 20th century. Graham Sutherland's immense tapestry *Christ in Glory*, Jacob Epstein's bronze *St. Michael and the Devil* and John Piper's baptistery window form part of an art collection worthy of the finest galleries. But perhaps the most symbolic act of modernity was the installation of the cathedral's prefabricated metal spire, dramatically lowered into place by an RAF Belvedere helicopter on April 16, 1962. Aviation ultimately played a part both in the cathedral's inception and completion. **PC**

National Library of the Argentine Republic

Architect: Clorindo Testa

Completed: 1962 (begun 1961)

Location: Recoleta, Buenos Aires, Argentina

Style/Period: Brutalism/Argentinian Modernism

Although Argentina had had a national library since the early 19th century, a century and a half later, it was clear that it had outgrown its original home. A plot measuring 7 acres (30,000 sq. m) in the Recoleta barrio (area) of Buenos Aires, Argentina's capital city, was accordingly earmarked for a new library in 1960. Construction of the building designed by Clorindo Testa began a year later and was completed in 1962. (The national library was not, however, inaugurated until 1992.)

Testa's Biblioteca Nacional de la República Argentina is an arresting six-story edifice that looks like a squared-off mushroom atop an oblong stalk with a few rectangular projections sprouting from its flat roof or a monolithic viewing platform. Testa's building turned traditional library design topsy-turvy by situating the stack rooms (in which an estimated 2 million books were stored) underground and the reading rooms on the top floors, so readers who wearied of looking at text could feast their eyes on views of the surrounding area. There was also an auditorium on the first floor. The concrete with which the library was erected was left exposed, in true *béton brut* ("raw concrete") brutalist style, but the subtle detailing and juxtaposition of rectangular shapes added life and interest. **CH-M**

Bankside Power Station

Architect: Sir Giles Gilbert Scott
Completed: 1963
Location: Bankside, London, England
Style/Period: Art Deco/Moderne

Accepting the commission for Bankside Power Station represented an awkward public U-turn for the illustrious Sir Giles Gilbert Scott, who had previously opposed the use of central city sites for heavy industry. Despite his earlier calls for town planners to prioritize civic and social functions, the tempting prospect of implementing ideas he had harbored since he designed Battersea (see page 314) proved simply irresistible.

Rapidly designed in 1947 to resolve an energy crisis, Bankside began generating in 1952 and was finally completed 11 years later. Involved from the outset, Scott was able to break away from the Battersea model and collect all four chimneys together in a single soaring tower, whose lines recall his work on Liverpool's Anglican Cathedral. It rises a restrained 325 feet (99 m) into the sky in respectful deference to the taller dome of St. Paul's Cathedral on the opposite bank. Even more impressive is the single cavernous

turbine hall, measuring 115 feet (35 m) high and 500 feet (152 m) long. Like Battersea before it, the station's underlying steel structure was disguised behind a sparingly decorated facade, reputed to have absorbed some 4,200,000 bricks in its construction. Though built to last, Bankside enjoyed only a short operational life, closing in 1981 after the escalating cost of oil had made it uneconomical. Saved from demolition at the eleventh hour, its subsequent conversion into the cultural success of the Tate Modern art gallery has proved a more than adequate penance for Scott's momentary lapse of resolve. **PC**

Spaceship House

Architect: Eugene Van Grecken
Completed: 1963
Location: Bayview, Sydney, Australia
Style/Period: Modernism/Expressionism

The inherent drama of Australia's natural landscape allows it to upstage any man-made objects placed within it. Recognizing this unequal struggle, enlightened architects have evolved forms that attempt to embrace their surroundings by breaking down the

barriers between inside and out. Completed a full 10 years before the complex concrete shells of the Sydney Opera House, the home of maverick architect Eugene Van Grecken was at the time the largest free-form concrete structure in the southern hemisphere.

Spaceship House derives its name from the daring elliptical domed roof, some 83 feet (25 m) wide by 68 feet (20 m) across, supported by 11 boomerang-shaped pillars. Amazingly, this colossal carapace is held on only by gravity, its edges resting on 2-inch (5 cm) thick neoprene pads covering the pillars' tips. These allow the monolithic roof to slide back and forth as it expands and contracts in the fierce heat of the Australian sun. Two rings of circular skylights illuminate the open-plan interiors, whose new 1-inch (25 mm) panes provide better protection from the elements than Van Grecken's 1960s originals. Approached from the cliff-top path, the house's saucerlike canopy appears ready to break free from its moorings and launch itself out into the void. Beneath its rim, the curving fully glazed walls frame the panoramic views out over Bayview, allowing residents to gaze directly down the precipitous cliff side at the sailing boats bobbing some 502 feet (153 m) below. **PC**

Engineering Faculty Building

Architects: James Stirling and James Gowan

Completed: 1963 (begun 1959)

Location: Leicester University, Leicester, England

Style/Period: Functionalist/Brutalist

The British architectural pairing of James Stirling and James Gowan put itself on the map with the Engineering Faculty Building for Leicester University, the likes of which had never been seen on a campus before. Yet despite its unconventional form — the massing together of diverse shapes, materials and levels — functionality was the guiding principle behind the building's design.

A notable innovation was the setting of glass roof panels at an angle of 45 degrees, a feature that provided indirect illumination while also maximizing the amount of natural light that filtered through during daylight hours. Two adjacent, different-sized towers rose above this roof to one side; these towers accommodated offices, lecture halls and laboratories. The smaller rectangular structure comprised alternating horizontal bands of orange-red brick and glass, while the larger, slimmer oblong tower, which was partly supported by stilts, was enveloped by a glass curtain wall for most of its height. Between them stood a thinner structure, like the spine of a book, that housed stairwells and elevator shafts. Different-sized and -shaped decks protruded from both towers about a quarter of the way up, beneath which, in the case of the larger tower, stretched a triangular wall. A huge workshop area at ground level accommodated heavy machinery. **CH-M**

Marina City

Architect: Bertrand Goldberg

Completed: 1964 (begun 1959)

Location: State Street, Chicago, Illinois, United States

Style/Period: Modernism

Ever since its completion in 1964, Bertrand Goldberg's Marina City has served as a model for both urban regeneration and big mixed-use complexes. This "city within a city" used 3 acres (12,141 sq. m) of land on the Chicago River's north bank that had once served as a railroad route. It provided housing for people and cars, as well as office space, stores, restaurants and entertainment facilities, including a marina — all in spectacular-looking fashion.

The most visible elements of this concrete-and-glass complex are the two 65-story circular towers — officially called Marina City I and II but nicknamed "corncobs" thanks to their balconies — that rise to a height of 587 feet (179 m), which, in 1964, made these high-rise residences the world's tallest reinforced-concrete buildings. They are perched on a raised two-story platform that also supports a 16-story rectangular building (used as an office and a hotel) and a saddle-shaped structure that serves as an auditorium. At the base of the "corncobs" are 19 floors of parking lots; the 20th story is dedicated to laundry; apartments occupy the 21st to 60th floors; and the top five levels house elevator and plant machinery. At the center of each tower is a concrete elevator core measuring 35 feet (11 m) in diameter. **CH-M**

National Gymnasia

Architect: Kenzo Tange

Completed: 1964

Location: Yoyogi Park, Tokyo, Japan

Style/Period: Modernism

Kenzo Tange, who was inspired by the work of Le Corbusier but later developed his own style, built these two sports halls for the 1964 Summer Olympics, the first to be held in an Asian country. He arguably produced not only the two most beautiful public buildings devised by a modernist architect, but also ones that elegantly fused modernist design aesthetics and materials with elements of traditional Japanese building styles, notably with regard to their roof lines. The larger stadium seats around 15,000 spectators and the smaller a more modest 4,000, but the crowning features of both are their spectacular roofs, which flow majestically down from huge supporting pylons to the stadiums' load-bearing walls and are supported by high-tension cables.

Although this solution to producing a large suspension roof is ingenious, the two halls are aesthetic triumphs as well. Tange avoided any extraneous detailing or decoration to produce two beautifully refined statements in reinforced concrete and steel that are a pure expression of modernism. His citation for winning the international Pritzker Prize for architecture in 1987 rightly stated that the halls were "among the most beautiful buildings of the 20th century." **IW**

NASA Vehicle Assembly Building

Architects: Max Urbahn and Robert Schaefer

Completed: 1966 (begun 1963)

Location: Kennedy Space Center, Cape Canaveral, Florida, United States

Style/Period: High-Tech

The NASA Vehicle Assembly Building (V.A.B.) was constructed during a pioneering phase in space exploration: although the "space race" between the Soviet Union and the United States was well under way, humankind would not land on the Moon until 1969. Similarly, the National Aeronautics and Space Administration (NASA), the U.S. government agency for space research, was only five years old when construction of the Vehicle Assembly Building began at the Kennedy Space Center on Merritt Island, near Cape Canaveral (then Cape Kennedy), where the United States' space vehicles were launched.

Vehicles such as Saturn rockets were of necessity huge, which is why the steel-and-concrete hangar that was constructed to shelter them while they and their components were being vertically assembled or stored was even larger. Its mind-bogglingly massive dimensions — 525 feet (160 m) tall, 716 feet (218 m) long and 518 feet (158 m) wide — make it one of the biggest structures in the world. Its ground plan comprises four equal-sized high bays within a rectangular building, to the front of which is attached the low-bay area, whose simple stepped-pyramidal design gives it a somewhat art deco appearance. Each of the high-bay doors of this eminently functional structure measures 456 feet (139 m) in height. **CH-M**

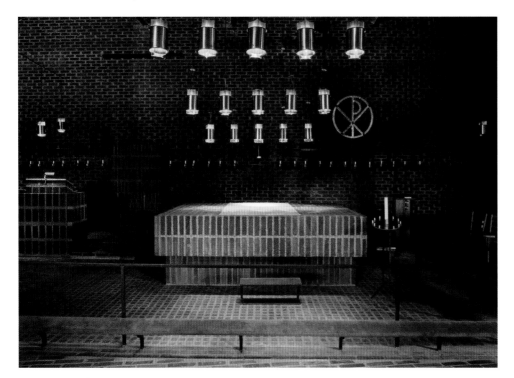

Saint Peter's Church

Architect: Sigurd Lewerentz

Completed: 1966

Location: Klippan, Skane, Sweden

Style/Period: Modernism

This remarkable church in the south of Sweden effortlessly combines cutting-edge design principles and aesthetics with traditional sensibilities. It is all the more remarkable because Sigurd Lewerentz, who was in his 80s at the time of its development and construction, was battling depression. Lewerentz, who is widely considered one of Sweden's two best 20th century modernist architects, had designed several ecclesiastical buildings, but Saint Peter's is the best of his smaller works.

The church is of purple brick and steel, with the latter being misshapen rejects that required irregular mortar joints. The complex is entered through a parish office that gives entrance into the church itself, which has a deliberately low ceiling. The floor is also brick, but they are laid out in different shapes to emphasize functional divisions within the space. The altar is again brick, but the font is actually a large shell, and excess water escapes through a simple hole in the floor. The windows, simply panes of glass hung to the outside of the buildings, appear fragile compared to the large areas of solid brickwork. The church is overall a simple space, but one beautifully executed to impart a deep sense of Christian spirituality among the congregation. **IW**

Whitney Museum of American Art

Architect: Marcel Breuer

Completed: 1966

Location: Madison Avenue, New York, New York, United States

Style/Period: Modernism

Hungarian-born Marcel Breuer, who was to become one of the great modernist architects working in the United States, was made the professor of the furniture workshop of the German-based Bauhaus design school in 1924. After a spell in

England, he immigrated to his adopted country in 1937, worked at Harvard University and then set up his own practice in 1947. The Whitney (Breuer's was the third museum so named) was one of his final projects and was named after wealthy philanthropist Gertrude Whitney, who had established a museum to house her collection of modern art in 1931.

Breuer created something of a brutalist building in concrete, stone and glass. The front facade has the appearance of an inverted ziggurat that climbs out of the street below, and its granite walls have no embellishment save for a jutting trapezoidal window. The other walls have more windows but are equally stark. The design can hardly be called welcoming and is, in truth, rather intimidating, but it makes excellent use of what was a small site (hence the extension over the street). At the very least it remains a serious and uncompromising architectural vision. **IW**

Salk Institute for Biological Studies

Architect: Louis Kahn

Completed: 1966 (begun 1959)

Location: 10010 North Torrey Pines Road, La Jolla, California, United States

Style/Period: Modernism

The U.S. microbiologist Dr. Jonas Salk is famous for having developed the first polio vaccine, but his name is also celebrated in architectural circles because of his association with an innovative campus building – the Salk Institute for Biological Studies, part of the University of San Diego – designed by Louis Kahn at La Jolla, California. In his brief, Salk charged Kahn with creating a versatile complex that would be easy to maintain, capable of changing with the times and "worthy of a visit by Picasso." Kahn met the challenge magnificently.

Although it was made up of 29 modular structures, the Salk Institute's ground plan fundamentally comprised two buildings standing opposite one another across a marble-floored plaza. Each six-story building accommodated three alternating laboratory

stories, and the stories between each were used for service equipment. Two stories were underground, but light wells provided illumination, and glass walls maximized the amount of light entering the upper levels. The eastern and western ends were used for service systems and office space, while

geometrical towers jutting out into the courtyard (which was open on two sides, affording a spectacular view of the Pacific Ocean) were allocated to the professors. The choice of pink reinforced concrete, steel, glass and teak ensured that little maintenance would be required. **CH-M**

Fuente de los Amantes

Architect: Luis Barragán
Completed: 1966 (begun 1963)
Location: Los Clubes, Mexico City, Mexico
Style/Period: Mexican Modernism/Landscape
Architecture

Deciding whether to describe Luis Barragán's Fuente de los Amantes ("Lovers' Fountain") as a construction, sculpture or, indeed, a fountain — as well as a feat of engineering — is not straightforward, and it illustrates the self-taught architect's unique style of "landscape architecture," as he himself called it. The Fuente de los Amantes is an integral part of the Los Clubes residential development in Mexico City, which was constructed between 1961 and 1972. It may have been a modern housing complex, and Barragán may originally have been an engineer struck by the modernist architecture he had encountered in Spain and France, but he was also profoundly influenced by his native country's indigenous traditions, spirit and appearance.

The Fuente de los Amantes appears to be a simple structure comprising an L-shaped block turned on its side, with its longer side resting on a rectangle set at right angles to it. Both the "L" and the rectangle rise from a pool of water (a symbol of femininity), which is the source of the stream of liquid that gushes from the end of the "L." The forms may be modern and minimal, but the structure's deep reddish brown color recalls the Mexican earth, while the inclusion of a soothing, refreshing fountain in a housing complex is in absolute accordance with Mexican pueblo (village) tradition. **CH-M**

Creek Vean

Architects: Team 4
Completed: 1967 (begun 1964)
Location: Feock, near Truro, Cornwall, England
Style/Period: Modernism

Two young members of Team 4 — Norman Foster and Richard Rogers — would later become superstars of the design world, but in the mid-1960s they were fresh from architecture school at Yale. When Marcus and Rene Brumwell, the parents of another Team 4 member, Rogers's wife, Su, commissioned a house from them in 1964, they put much of what they had learned in the United States into practice on a steep hillside location above the River Fal in Feock, near Truro, in the southwestern English county of Cornwall.

When it was completed in 1967, it was clear that Creek Vean's design owed a large debt to Fallingwater, the house that U.S. architect Frank Lloyd Wright had constructed at Bear Run, Pennsylvania, in 1936 (see page 308). Both looked uncompromisingly modern yet blended sympathetically into the surrounding landscape. They also shared the same horizontal lines and asymmetric, organic design. Built from concrete, which was left exposed, the two-story Creek Vean had slate floors and walls of frameless plate-glass windows at the front to make the most of the views overlooking the creek. This is also why the living room was on the top floor and the kitchen and dining room below, with a long, low gallery-corridor leading off at an angle to the bedrooms. **CH-M**

Habitat Housing

Architect: Moshe Safdie

Completed: 1967

Location: 2600 Pierre Dupuy Avenue, Montreal,

Quebec, Canada

Style/Period: Modernism

The extraordinary-looking Habitat Housing provoked much debate when it was exhibited at Expo 67 in Montreal, Canada. Simply described, it comprised 354 prefabricated reinforced-concrete modules, or "boxes," that appeared to have been assembled in higgledy-piggledy fashion. The thinking behind it was not at all random, however, as Habitat Housing grew out of Israeli-Canadian architect Moshe Safdie's long-term study into the reconciliation of family and urban living.

The logic behind Habitat Housing was compelling: prefabrication kept costs down and ensured uniformly high standards, while the apparently arbitrary assembly lent life and interest to a housing complex that could otherwise have seemed regimented. Similarly, although the "boxes" were manufactured to a set specification, there were 15 different types, ensuring that the 158 family dwellings created here varied. The "boxes," which were attached to a supportive three-sectioned "spine" and accessed by walkways and elevator shafts, were connected to one another by means of steel rods and cables. They were furthermore arranged in such a way that each residence had a balcony area — the flat roof of the module in front of it — and retained some privacy. The apartments at Habitat Housing ranged in size from one- to four-bedroom units, measuring between 600 and 1,700 square feet (183 to 518 sq. m). **CH-M**

Metropolitan Cathedral of Christ the King

Architect: Sir Frederick Gibberd

Completed: 1967

Location: Brownlow Hill, Liverpool, England

Style/Period: Modernism

This Catholic cathedral in the north of England had a prolonged gestation, and there had been five other proposals over the years before the present building was approved. Sir Edwin Lutyens, who conceived of a huge structure positioned over a crypt to rival the nearby Protestant cathedral, initiated the fifth concept. Due to financial problems, only the crypt was finished after World War II, but fresh impetus came with the appointment of Cardinal John Heenan. He held a competition in 1960 to design a cathedral, but he stipulated that the new building had to come in on a tight budget and take no more than five years to construct. Frederick Gibberd, one of 300 entrants, won.

He produced a modernist building on a suitably cathedral-sized scale with exterior load-bearing struts mimicking medieval flying buttresses. Inside, Gibberd created a circular nave flanked by 16 side chapels and anterooms topped by a dome. The dome gives way to a high lantern of multicolored glass that, along with floor-to-ceiling glass panels, floods the interior with light. The interior space was largely determined by the new religious thinking that the congregation should be more closely integrated into liturgical ceremonies. **IW**

Biosphere

Architects: Richard Buckminster Fuller and Shoji Sadao

Completed: 1967

Location: Saint Helen's Island, Montreal, Quebec, Canada

Style/Period: Modernism/Early High Tech

The U.S. Information Agency commissioned Fuller to design a cutting-edge structure that would serve as the American Pavilion at Expo 67, the world's fair held in Montreal. Fuller was something of a polymath. He was, among other things, an author, inventor, poet and designer, and he had also become interested in the possibilities of the geodesic dome. It was a spatial structure based on a latticework of great circles (geodesics) lying on the surface of a sphere. Such domes had the highest ratio of enclosed volume to their weight, making them lightweight and, despite their fragile appearance, strong.

Fuller created a geodesic dome that was 200 feet (61 m) high with a diameter of 250 feet (76 m). It was roughly 75 percent of a complete sphere and consisted of a delicate two-layer latticework of steel piping (the outer triangular and the inner hexagonal), which supported some 1,900 molded acrylic panels. Excessive interior temperatures were controlled by a complex system of shades. Fuller's was not the first attempt at a geodesic dome, but his captured the public's imagination more than its predecessors and became the benchmark for the aesthetics of high-tech structural design. **IW**

Halls of Residence

Architect: Sir Denys Lasdun

Completed: 1968

Location: University of East Anglia, Norwich, England

Style/Period: Brutalism/Modernism

Denys Lasdun was an uncompromising modernist who was greatly influenced by the writings of both Le Corbusier and Ludwig Mies van de Rohe, and he designed some of the most monumental reinforced-concrete-slab buildings seen in Britain. They were essays in brutalism at its most uncompromising.

The British government initiated its New Universities program at the beginning of the 1960s, and the University of East Anglia was one of the first of the new institutions to be commissioned. It was designed as a campus university and was sited on a large former golf course in the southern suburbs of Norwich, in eastern England. Lasdun designed the core of the new buildings, including the students' residential blocks, and work got underway in 1962. These halls consist of an east-west orientated block with Lasdun's trademark cubic towers and sharply jutting forms, in this case ones styled like a ziggurat. While the halls of residence are brutalism personified and have undoubted architectural merit, they have not always been appreciated by those who live and work in them — some people feel that they are too domineering and impersonal. **IW**

Marin County Civic Center

Architect: Frank Lloyd Wright

Completed: 1969 (begun 1957)

Location: North San Pedro Road at U.S. Route 101,

San Rafael, California, United States

Style/Period: Modernism/Futurism

The Marin County Civic Center was commissioned from Frank Lloyd Wright in 1957. Wright died in 1959 so never saw his Californian space-age vision realized, but those who continued his work ensured that it conformed to his plans (although not all of the buildings envisaged were constructed). Wright may have been 88 years old when he designed the Marin County Civic Center, but his thought processes and imagination remained as ingenious and innovative as ever. For instance, rather than leveling the three existing hills on the construction site north of San Rafael, he worked around them, linking their crowns with his unique, forward-looking civic-government complex, whose arched facades echoed the hilly landscape.

The diverse forms of the sand-colored and blue-roofed steel-and-concrete buildings that make up the Marin County Civic Center reflect their different purposes. The Administration Building (completed in 1962), which houses offices, is a four-story horizontal structure measuring 584 feet (178 m) in length. A library is situated on the fourth floor under the flattened dome — 80 feet (24 m) in diameter — which is one of the complex's most eye-catching features, alongside the 172-foot (52 m) tall spirelike tower that contains radio and television antennae. The Hall of Justice building (finished in 1969) measures 880 feet (268 m) in length and contains circular courtrooms. **CH-M**

Taivallahit Church (Church of the Rock)

Architects: Timo and Tumamo Suomalainen

Completed: 1969

Location: Helsinki, Finland

Style/Period: Modernism

Persecution by pagan Rome obliged the early Christians to worship in secret subterranean chapels, but it was a belief in civic amenities,

rather than fear of reprisals, that led parishioners in 1960s Helsinki to burrow underground. Dominated by a rocky outcrop rising to 43 feet (13 m) high, Temppeliaukio Square had long been a place of communal recreation for residents of the surrounding apartment blocks. Not wishing to deprive them of this precious open space, the Suomalainen brothers' competition-winning design placed the bulk of the new church beneath the rock. It reused the quarried stone in a low circular curtain wall that insulates religious services below from the noisy urban activity above.

The inner walls were left rough-hewn to emphasize the raw, natural geology of the setting, creating a deliberate contrast with the man-made insertions in copper and concrete. The irregular profile of the walls required each of the roof's 180 prestressed concrete beams to be a different length, coming together to support a domed ceiling some 79 feet (24 m) in diameter. The narrow strips of glazing held between the beams' fingers create a halo of light above the assembled congregation, who stand in the warm reflected glow of the ceiling's copper-strip cladding. Paradoxically, the architects' orientation of the altar to receive direct sunlight during morning worship seems to echo another stone circle, one whose pagan rituals took place long before the birth of Christ. **PC**

John Hancock Center

Architect: Bruce Graham (of Skidmore, Owings & Merrill)
Completed: 1969 (begun 1965)
Location: 875 North Michigan Avenue, Chicago, Illinois, United States
Style/Period: Modernism

When it was completed in 1969, the skyscraper that the Bangladeshi-American structural engineer Fazlur Khan — working with Bruce Graham for the firm of Skidmore, Owings & Merrill (SOM) — created for the John Hancock insurance company towered over Chicago. At 1,127 feet (344 m) high (1,500 feet/457 m if the pair of antennae fixed to the roof is included), it was one of the tallest buildings anywhere in the world at

the time. An important factor in enabling this extreme height was the cross-bracing that contributes to the John Hancock Center's distinctive appearance, along with its bronze-tinted glass and black aluminum cladding. This cross-bracing provides vital additional support by reinforcing the strength of the steel-tube frame.

Essentially a tapering rectangular structure, the John Hancock Center has 100 stories, which are used for a number of

purposes: for commercial outlets, as parking lots and office space, for restaurants and leisure facilities and as residential accommodation. There is also an observation deck on the 94th story that looks out over the city and Lake Michigan. Running around the top of the building is a narrow band of lights that are illuminated at night, while an elliptical plaza at the skyscraper's foot features a waterfall amid well-tended gardens. **CH-M**

Catedral Metropolitana Nossa Senhora Aparecida

Architect: Oscar Niemeyer

Completed: 1970 (begun 1958)

Location: Monumental Axis, Brasília, Brazil

Style/Period: Modernism

Just as the apical points of pyramids and church spires point toward heaven, as if poised to communicate directly with the divine, so the cathedral that Oscar Niemeyer designed for Brasília, the new capital of predominantly Roman Catholic Brazil, appears both to indicate and commune with God. This metropolitan cathedral (also called Cathedral of Brasília), which is situated on the southern side of Brasília's Monumental Axis, is dedicated to Our Lady of Aparecida, the patron saint of Brasília. With its 16 exposed-concrete elliptical "ribs," this extraordinarily graceful-looking modern cathedral is a striking example of a hyperboloid structure. The 16 ribs are arranged so that they form a circle 230 feet (70 m) in diameter. The space between them is filled with fiberglass that is stained blue, white and golden brown in parts. The roof is also of glass, which means that the congregation below is washed with natural light during daylight hours. The nave is actually below ground level and is reached by a dark corridor, so that when worshipers pass from here into the sunlit cathedral, or the symbolic "light of God," the contrast is dramatic and, thanks to the white marble floors, frequently also dazzling. A futuristic bell tower, roughly resembling a fork but echoing the cathedral's white curves, stands alongside it. **CH-M**

Phillips Exeter Academy Library

Architect: Louis Kahn

Completed: 1971 (begun 1965)

Location: Exeter, New Hampshire, United States

Style/Period: International Modernism

When the Phillips Exeter Academy, a coeducational boarding school for 9th- to 12th-graders, commissioned a new library building for its campus in Exeter, New Hampshire, in 1965, it could not have foreseen the momentous consequences. Indeed, not only is it still the largest school library of its type in the United States, but in 1997 the building (which was named the Class of 1945 Library in 1995) won the American Institute of Architects' 25-Year Award.

The book repository that architect Louis Kahn constructed for the academy was an outstanding structure that incorporated various ingenious touches. At the center of the reinforced-concrete library is a glass-roofed atrium that rises for five stories, allowing natural light to illuminate the interior.

The boundaries of this square atrium are defined by vast screen walls, each comprising a huge cutout circle through which the bookcases and reading areas that line each balcony level can be seen. Viewed from the outside, the brick-clad building is punctuated by regular rectangular openings: a loggia on the ground floor, windows on the next three stories (two for each: one at eye level with a sliding wooden shutter and a larger one above) and unglazed openings rising above roof level. The four corners appear to have been shorn off at an angle. **CH-M**

Azadi Tower

Architect: Hossein Amanat

Completed: 1971

Location: Tehran, Iran

Style/Period: Modernism with Islamic influences

The striking "gateway into Iran" constructed by Iranian architect Hossein Amanat in Tehran, Iran's capital city, was originally called the Shahyad Tower. However, it was renamed the Azadi Tower (*azadi* means "freedom" in Farsi) following the Iranian Revolution of 1979, when Muhammad Reza Pahlavi, the shah (king) of Iran, went into exile and a fundamentalist Islamic regime was instituted. But in 1971 Iran was still being governed by this modernizing, pro-Western shah, and the structure he commissioned to mark the entrance to Tehran as a visible symbol of the 2,500th anniversary of the foundation of the Persian Empire, and a celebration of the shahs' rule, was accordingly given the name "Remembrance of the Shahs."

Throughout the political upheaval and name change that followed, the Azadi Tower has stood tall and apparently aloof in the center of Azadi Square. Constructed from 8,000 blocks of white marble quarried in Iran's Isfahan region, the tower soars to a height of 148 feet (45 m), with the vault beneath leaving 69 feet (21 m) of clear space. Although it appears a starkly modern structure at first sight, elements of traditional Sassanian and Islamic architecture become evident on closer inspection — in, for example, the points of the integral smaller arches and the breathtaking use of geometry. **CH-M**

Nakagin Capsule Tower

Architect: Kisho Kurokawa

Completed: 1972

Location: Shimbashi, Tokyo, Japan

Style: Metabolist

Kurokawa aimed to put all of the essentials (and some of the inessentials) of modern apartment living into the smallest space possible and, in doing so, built the original capsule tower in a city where space is at a premium. This modernist building is unremarkable at ground level, being merely an undercroft and conventional first floor supported on a series of square concrete pillars. However, Kurokawa's real achievement then begins: 11 stories of modular concrete capsules that were built off site and simply inserted into a steel framework and held in place by four high-tension bolts for ease of removal and replacement.

The individual capsules measure 7 ½ feet (2.25 m) by 12 feet (4 m) by 7 feet (2 m) and are not for the claustrophobic, not least because the only natural light comes from a 3-foot (1-meter) porthole. Creature comforts are centered on a plastic console wall that contains various storage units, drop-down multipurpose tables, telephone, tape recorder and television. There is also a molded plastic shower, sink and toilet unit. The capsules were expected to have a 25-year lifespan and, although they need updating, are still used as living and working spaces. **IW**

Olympiastadion München

Architect: Günter Behnisch and Frei Otto

Completed: 1972 (begun 1968)

Location: Munich, Bavaria, Germany

Style/Period: High Tech/Modern Expressionist

Sadly, the main reason the summer Olympic Games of 1972 — held in Munich, the capital of the southern German region of Bavaria — are remembered is on account of the shocking murder of a number of Israeli athletes. However, among many aficionados of building design, it is architect Günter Behnisch and engineer Frei Otto's Olympiastadion München (Munich Olympic Stadium), at the heart of the Olympiapark, that springs to mind — particularly the technically astounding canopies that protected spectators from the elements. Otto was something of a pioneering specialist in the tensile field, and rapid advances in what were then state-of-the-art materials resulted in an undulating perimeter roof that functioned as effectively as it looked eye-catching (rather like space-age tents or the nearby Alpine mountains).

This extraordinary roof, which was constructed of 915,000 square feet (278,822 sq. m) of transparent acrylic glass and PVC-coated polyester suspended from hangers and supported by steel cables, was ultimately held in place by steel pillars 249 feet (76 m) long. The stadium itself was constructed within a basin, at the center of which was a rectangular grass pitch enclosed by an oval running track. Tiers of seats for the spectators (there was room for up to 80,000) surrounded the track, and the roof covered only one side of the stadium. **CH-M**

The World Trade Center

Architect: Minoru Yamasaki
Completed: 1973 (begun 1966)
Location: New York, New York, United States
Style/Period: Modernism

Although U.S. architect Minoru Yamasaki was aware that his twin towers at the World Trade Center (WTC) were (briefly) the tallest buildings in the world on their completion in 1973, he could not foresee that they would become world famous for a horrifying reason. Ironically, given the terrorist attack by airplane that would cause these strong structures to crumble to the ground on September 11, 2001, Yamasaki had proclaimed them "a living symbol of man's dedication to world peace," as well as representative of the global economy.

At 1,368 and 1,362 feet (417 and 415 m) high, the near-identical silvery-aluminum-alloy-clad towers (called One World Trade Center or the north tower, and Two World Trade Center or the south tower) dominated New York City's skyline. Owned by the Port Authority of New York and New Jersey, each stood on a footprint measuring 208 x 208 feet (63 x 63 m) in lower Manhattan and sat next to a plaza covering 5 acres (20,235 sq. m) that was ringed by five further buildings belonging to the WTC complex. The twin towers' steel-lattice-framed-tube skeletons accommodated 110 stories, seven of which were underground; floors were delineated by concrete slabs on prefabricated steel trusses surrounding a reinforced-steel core. The twin towers accommodated office space (open plan with no interior columns), stores, services, parking and two subway stations. **CH-M**

Sydney Opera House

Architect: Jorn Utzon

Completed: 1973

Location: Circular Quay, Sydney, Australia

Style/Period: Modernism

The origins of the opera house stretched back to 1955 when the state government of New South Wales set aside funds for its construction and opened a competition to find a suitably iconic building that would symbolize Australia's transition from a remote backwater into a fresh and vibrant country with global ambitions. The winner was the little-known Danish architect Jorn Utzon, whose work to date had largely been on domestic projects. His eye-catching design was so radical that it took several years of thought before the large, shell-like precast concrete roofs could be made. Covered in creamy white tiles that stand out against the blue antipodean sky, the opera house is one of the most iconic buildings of the 20th century.

Work finally got underway, but the building was beset by delays and cost overruns. Matters came to a head in 1966 when the state's new minister of works tried to simplify Utzon's design in order to reduce costs. A few days later Utzon left Australia and has never returned. When the opera house was finally completed, it was years behind schedule and a staggering 14 times over budget, yet Utzon's vision was truly remarkable and might have been even more so if his plans for the interior had been realized. He was awarded the Pritzker Prize, architecture's highest award, in 2003 and the opera house was named a UNESCO World Heritage Site four years later. **IW**

National Assembly Complex

Architect: Louis Khan
Completed: 1975
Location: Sher-e-Bangla Nagar, Dhaka, Bangladesh
Style: Modernism

The National Assembly complex (Jatiyo Sangshad Bhaban) in Bangladesh's capital was the last work designed by Louis Khan, but he did not live to see his monumental homage to brutalism completed. Between 1957 and 1974 Khan, who was originally born Itze-Leib Schmuilowsky in Estonia but later became a U.S. citizen, was a professor of architecture at the University of Pennsylvania's School of Design. He had spent time in Italy during the early 1950s and came into contact with various ancient Egyptian, Greek and Roman buildings. These structures impacted on his largely modernist sensibilities to bring about a new, less rigid style of design.

The Dhaka complex was inspired by such ancient buildings, and Khan set to work to create a huge monolithic structure that hid neither its means of construction nor the modern materials used, which were chiefly concrete but also the more traditional marble. The National Assembly comprises eight blocks placed around a central octagonal building, but the blocks are linked so that the elegant but harsh fortresslike complex appears as a single entity. The bleakness of the structure is relieved by a series of geometric devices that allow light to flood into the interior. **IW**

Willis Faber Dumas Building

Architects: Foster Associates
Completed: 1975 (begun 1970)
Location: Ipswich, Suffolk, England
Style/Period: High Tech

Ipswich is a small river port in a rural eastern English county, and the construction of this pioneering high-tech glass building in 1975 was then considered shockingly modern and somewhat astonishing. Today it is regarded as an architectural icon.

The office building was commissioned from Norman Foster's Foster Associates by

Willis Faber & Dumas to serve as the insurance company's headquarters. The site was challenging in being surrounded by immovable roads and a Unitarian Meeting House, which resulted in an irregular footprint. Foster's design overcame this potential problem with great style, however, not least by swathing the exterior with a curved and faceted bronze-tinted-glass curtain wall. (Technically innovative features included bolted glass panels, connective patch fittings and vertical, wind-repelling glass fins.)

The three-story building's skeleton comprised reinforced-concrete pillars and cantilevered concrete floor slabs. Situated in the center of the building, in an airy atrium, was a moving staircase that transported staff to a restaurant on the turfed roof. Here, in the midst of an elevated garden, they could relax and admire the views; there was also a swimming pool on the ground floor — for its time, these people-cherishing touches were

revolutionary. The offices were open plan, offering future-proofed flexibility, while heating was provided by natural gas, taking fluctuating oil prices out of the equation. **CH-M**

Taalmonument

Architect: Jan van Wijk
Completed: 1975
Location: Paarl, West Cape Province, South Africa
Style/Period: Structural Expressionism

Paarl's Boer history is evident in this South African town's very name, which means "Pearl" in Afrikaans, a language that evolved from the Dutch spoken by its European settlers. The reason this settlement that sprang up alongside a wagon track leading to Cape Town was named Paarl can be ascribed to the Paarl Mountain that looms above it, whose granite boulders assume a pearl-like

luster when washed with rain. And it was on this mountain, overlooking the Berg River Valley, that the Taalmonument, or the Afrikaans Language Monument, was unveiled in 1975, marking the 100th anniversary of the foundation of the Genootskap van Regte Afrikaners (GRA, or the Society of True Afrikaners).

Architect Jan van Wijk's design includes three concrete columns, each of which symbolizes an element that contributed to the Afrikaans tongue. It complements the landscape and is said to have been inspired by the work of Afrikaans writers C.J. Langenhoven and N.P. van Wyk Louw. A low wall curves between the columns and a hollow spire soars to a height of 187 feet (57 m) and represents Afrikaans — the implication being that they are not only linked to this language but have also contributed to its greater glory. A smaller, adjacent, canoe-shaped pillar denotes the Republic of South Africa. **CH-M**

National Theatre

Architect: Sir Denys Lasdun
Completed: 1977
Location: South Bank, London, England
Style: Modernism

There was a postwar consensus that Britain needed a national cultural center that would bring the wider public into contact with the world of the arts. The location chosen was an area on the south bank of the River Thames where a complex of public buildings was slowly emerging, which would eventually comprise three concert halls, a trio of theaters, an art gallery and movie theaters. The National Theatre was to be the South Bank's centerpiece and, although parliamentary approval for the scheme was gained in 1949, it took years of discussion between the modernist Denys Lasdun, who had never designed a theater before, and various others to settle on a suitable design.

Unfortunately, work began at a time of industrial unrest in 1969 and proceeded slowly. The brutalist exterior of reinforced concrete is somewhat unusual in that it has been given a decorative effect by forming the various slabs in molds with roughened sides. Inside, there are three theaters of varying sizes that radiate off the main foyer, which consists of various levels and terraces. The building work dragged on into the second half of the 1970s, and the three theaters were opened successively. IW

Sainsbury Centre for Visual Arts

Architects: Foster Associates
Completed: 1977
Location: University of East Anglia, Norwich, England
Style: High Tech

When Sir Robert and Lady Sainsbury donated their 300-piece collection of artwork and other objects to the University of East Anglia, the new owners set about finding an architect to create a suitable building to house them. They chose Norman Foster to undertake the design, and the work began in 1974. Foster had spent time in America and came up with a high-tech design that was

virtually unknown in England at the time. He produced a cubelike box structure with a tubular-steel frame that was largely clad in aluminum sheeting except for one end that was glazed and another that was louvered.

The interior appears to be no more than an endless, flexible open space that can be reconfigured to hold both the center's ever-growing permanent collection and the regular temporary exhibitions that it hosts. Foster's design is wholly uncluttered so as not to distract visitors' attention away from the exhibits. All the usual clutter — such as cabling and services — are hidden away, either in the triangular steel frames or in the spaces between the interior and exterior cladding. **IW**

Centre Georges Pompidou

Architects: Richard Rogers and Renzo Piano
Completed: 1977
Location: Place Georges Pompidou, Paris, France
Style: High Tech

This groundbreaking public building was a late entry into a competition to provide a multifunctional cultural center on the site of what had been Les Halles, one of Paris's largest markets. The area was run-down, and it was hoped that the center would spearhead a renaissance of its fortunes. It was originally named the Centre Beaubourg, but its name was changed in honor of Georges Pompidou, president of France from 1969 to 1974. Two architects, England's Richard

Rogers and Italian-born Renzo Piano, were aided by two structural engineers , Peter Rice and Edmund Happold, employed by Ove Arup and Partners. Together they came up with a colorful design that is both highly functional and witty.

The high-tech center was inspired by many styles, but it was architecturally groundbreaking in its use of a huge steel exoskeleton that left the usually hidden "guts" visible to the public. It is a building that is inside out, but in doing this Rogers and Piano freed up a huge internal space, some 1 million square feet (93,000 sq. m) in total. The central message is that art does not have to be entirely serious and elitist — it can be welcoming and populist. **IW**

Santa Maria Assunta Church

Architect: Alvar Aalto

Completed: 1978 (begun 1975)

Location: Riola di Vergato, near Bologna, Italy

Style/Period: Scandinavian Modernism/Functionalism

Although he designed (in 1966) the Roman Catholic church that was constructed at Riola di Vergato, near the Italian town of Bologna, between 1975 and 1978, the Finnish architect Alvar Aalto did not live to see his vision become reality, since he died in 1976, aged 78. The church can therefore be said to be one of the last examples of this unique architect's mature style, and it is a bold and original reinterpretation of the components of traditional church architecture. And had his plans not been significantly truncated due to funding difficulties, the result would have been even more unusual.

The concrete, wood and copper-embellished church's exterior lines are curved but completely asymmetrical when viewed from the side — in cross-section, as it were — with one half describing an arc and the other a rough three-peaked rectangle. Set into the sides of these peaks are bands of glass, which illuminate the basilicalike space below, especially the altar area. Inside, the six reinforced-concrete arches that act as the structure's supportive ribs have been left exposed; perhaps the most extraordinary aspect of this vaulting scheme is its asymmetrical shape, which recalls Aalto's famous bentwood furniture. A tall three-planed concrete bell tower was erected alongside the church in 1994. **CH-M**

Brion Cemetery

Architect: Carlo Scarpa

Completed: 1978

Location: San Vito d'Altivole, Treviso, Italy

Style/Period: Eclectic/Postmodernism

On the outskirts of sleepy San Vito d'Altivole lies the cemetery commissioned by Onorina Brion for her late husband Giuseppe, the cofounder of Brionvega, the progressive Italian electronics company. In his last great work, Carlo Scarpa rejected the customary marble-columned mausoleums of the elite in favor of a truly modern necropolis, successfully combining the mass and solidity of Ancient Egypt with details drawn from Mayan civilization, echoing the forms evolved by his idol, Frank Lloyd Wright.

Encircling the cemetery with a leaning concrete rampart, Scarpa provided the inner space with the seclusion it required. Within these walls he placed three main elements: a chapel, a water pavilion and the Brions' own tomb. Sited at the corners of the L-shaped plot, the three are linked by a composition of narrow water channels and carefully framed lines of sight. The central component is the canopy that arches over the couple's two sarcophagi, which Scarpa referred to as the *Arcosolium*, a Latin term from early Christian times that describes the niches in the catacombs where important persons and martyrs were interred. The white marble bases and black stone tops of the sarcophagi are both heavily carved with his distinctive stepped reliefs, but elsewhere the hard geometry is deliberately softened by the creeping foliage allowed to trail across the concrete. Weathered by the elements to resemble the ruins of a lost civilization, the Brion Cemetery offers a timeless place for quiet reflection. **PC**

Liverpool Anglican Cathedral

Architect: Giles Gilbert Scott
Completed: 1978 (begun 1904)
Location: St. James' Mount, Liverpool, England
Style/Period: Neogothic

Giles Gilbert Scott's design for the Cathedral Church of Christ in the northwestern English city of Liverpool — or Liverpool Anglican Cathedral, as it is also known (to distinguish it from Liverpool's Roman Catholic cathedral) — was a competition winner. The competition was held in 1903, but it took another 75 years before Scott's design (which he modified in 1910 to make it less Gothic) was entirely realized, which was actually a trifling amount of time in comparison to many other European cathedrals. That said, world wars intervened, and the main body of the cathedral was consecrated in 1924; services were first conducted in 1940, and work slowly but steadily continued until the structure was finally completed in 1978.

Constructed as it was from local sandstone on an elevated site (St. James' Mount) in the city center, the Cathedral Church of Christ is visible for miles around. Its ground plan describes the shape of a Latin cross with a tower rising from the center to a height of 331 feet (101 m). The cathedral itself measures 619 feet (189 m) from end to end. The tower is a bell tower, and the 13 bells that it accommodates at the 217-foot (66 m) level are believed to be the world's highest (and heaviest) ringing peal. **CH-M**

Gehry House

Architect: Frank Gehry
Completed: 1978
Location: Santa Monica, California, United States
Style/Period: Deconstruction

This was the building that kick-started the career of U.S.-based Canadian-born Frank Gehry, arguably the most sought-after architect of the modern era. Prior to this he was a paper architect — one who experimented with folded paper but had not actually produced a finished piece of work. The original building was a standard Cape Cod, New England, clapperboard house that was spotted by his wife. Gehry effectively added a second skin that cut through parts of the original to create a firmly postmodern house, although Gehry himself denies adherence to any particular architectural style.

The addition was primarily made from comparatively cheap materials, including corrugated metal sheeting, chain link, plywood and glass, and at first glance seems to lack any order or discipline. Yet, on closer inspection the finished residence is a visual, almost playful, delight and, rather than being a chaotic mishmash, was designed down to the tiniest detail. Highly controversial and virtually uncategorizable when first built, the house set the scene for the many larger public commissions that have followed. Gehry returned to it in the early 1990s to add a few finishing touches. **IW**

Kuwait Towers

Architects: Sune Lindström and Malene Björn

Completed: 1979 (begun 1975)

Location: Arabian Gulf Street, Kuwait City, Kuwait

Style/Period: Islamic Modernism

They may look like futuristic space-age fantasies, but the three Kuwait Towers that were constructed in Kuwait City, capital of the Gulf state of Kuwait, serve eminently practical purposes. Designed by Sune Lindström and Malene Björn, they were commissioned by the Ministry for Power and Water Management of Kuwait and were erected on a waterfront site between 1975 and 1979. Although all are constructed from reinforced concrete, each tower is different in appearance — and performs a different function — and yet, when viewed from afar, they make a harmonious-looking grouping that has become a symbol of Kuwait.

The tallest tower measures 614 feet (187 m) from top to bottom and incorporates two bulbous aluminum-clad spheres. Half of the top sphere operates as a glazed revolving observation deck, and the lower sphere is home to a restaurant and also stores water, as does the second-tallest tower. It has a single concrete sphere and rises to a height of 571 feet (174 m). The third tower, which is 371 feet (113 m) tall, has a needlelike shape and serves on the one hand as a control tower for the provision of electricity to Kuwait City and, on the other, as a source of illumination for its two fellows. **CH-M**

New Zealand Parliament Extension

Architect: Sir Basil Spence

Completed: 1979 (begun 1969)

Location: Wellington, New Zealand

Style/Period: Modernism

The newly knighted Sir Basil Spence was busily delivering the Chancellor's Lectures at Victoria University when he was asked for advice on extending New Zealand's seat of government. Having outgrown the neoclassical halls of Parliament House, the country's executive was in desperate need of more generous accommodation. Spence's radical solution called for a 236-foot (72 m) high tower of 10 cylindrical stories stacked like automotive gears, whose rows of brise soleil sun shades hint at the machinery of government within. Shocking to some, the architect's rationale for the scheme was that the circle was both a symbol of unity and the best shape to resist the force of New Zealand's not infrequent earthquakes.

Like a diagram of the democratic process, the building obeys a strict vertical hierarchy, beginning with the cabinet room under its copper-sheathed roof, below which is the prime minister's spacious office. The subsequent levels are divided radially to provide space for senior ministers and junior colleagues in that order. The double-height first floor holds the staff cafeteria and a semicircular banqueting hall capable of hosting grand state dinners for 300 guests. Aware of the need to blend the old with the new, Spence carefully aligned the top of the banqueting hall's drum with the cornice of the existing Parliament House to maintain a unifying sense of scale. The extension's popular moniker, "The Beehive," is an apt description of its outward appearance, but it might equally express voters' unity with their hard-working representatives within, or a certain cynicism about the political system as a whole. **PC**

Garden Grove Community Church

Architects: Philip Johnson and John Burgee

Completed: 1980

Location: Garden Grove, California, United States

Style/Period: Modernism

Although there has been a long tradition of church building on a grand scale in the United States, it reached its apogee in the 1980s. This particular church by Johnson and Burgee, which is popularly known as the Crystal Cathedral, inspired the church-building boom and certainly fits the bill in terms of scale, as it seats up to 2,890 worshippers. The church was built for Dr. Robert Schuller, and the religious television program he founded is still broadcast from it.

Johnson was no stranger to large-scale design in which glass predominates, having worked on the Seagram glass skyscraper in New York (see page 345). The heart of the church is a huge area that rises up to 128 feet (39 m) and is made from more than 10,000 panes of tempered silver-coated glass supported on a steel frame shaped like a star. The glass reflects back more than 90 percent of the fierce sunlight hitting the building so that the congregation keeps cool. The Crystal Cathedral is a modernist building in terms of the materials used, but it plays with the movement's strictness of form for a more free-flowing approach that is more typical of the postmodernist era. **IW**

Sri Lankan Parliament

Architect: Geoffrey Bawa

Completed: 1981 (begun 1979)

Location: Kotte, near Colombo, Sri Lanka

Style/Period: Sri Lankan Modernist

Once a colony of the British Empire (when this Indian Ocean island nation was known as Ceylon), Sri Lanka achieved its independence in 1948 but remained a British dominion. During the 1970s, constitutional amendments saw Ceylon changing its name to Sri Lanka and changing its instruments of government, too, so that the head of state is now a powerful president, while its single-chamber parliament is based on the British model.

Since 1982 the Sri Lankan Parliament, or National State Assembly, has been accommodated in an island complex on Kotte, 10 miles (16 km) east of the Sri Lankan capital of Colombo. This island was created by flooding the Diyavanna Oya Valley, leaving a knoll — the construction site — rising above the lake. Although Geoffrey Bawa's design is modern, it includes many references to Sri Lanka's architectural past, such as the Kandyan-inspired copper-clad roofs that create a sense of unity and tented community. The parliament building comprises a collection of six low pavilions constructed on concrete plinths. The debating chamber is housed in the four-story central pavilion, with five further pavilions ranged asymmetrically around it. These pavilions are respectively used as a meeting hall, the main entry point for the public, offices, a service building and a cafeteria for the members of parliament. **CH-M**

Bely Dom

Architects: Dmitry Chechulin and P. Shteller
Completed: 1981 (begun 1965)
Location: Krasnopresnenskaya Naberezhnaya 2,
Moscow, Russia
Style/Period: Stalinist Modernism

Although it shares a name — and a predominant color — with the president of the United States of America's official residence in Washington, D.C. (see page 190), Moscow's White House (Bely Dom in Russian) is far more monumental, and more modern, in appearance. Now a government building, during the days of the Soviet Union it served as the home of the Russian Soviet Federal Socialist Republic's Congress of People's Deputies and Supreme Soviet. It has twice taken center stage in the history of Russia's turbulent politics: first in 1991, when Boris Yeltsin, president of the Russian Republic, led a protest here against an attempted coup d'état, and, secondly, in 1993 when, angered by uncooperative parliamentarians, Yeltsin himself ordered the building shelled.

It may have been constructed between 1965 and 1981, but the white-marble building's design can be traced back to 1934 and architect Dmitry Chechulin's design for the Aeroflot Building, which was never built. This explains why the high-rise part of the Bely Dom, with its curved sides, has the streamlined, art deco look that is so typical of the 1930s. This, the most visible element of the building, rises above the squat, column-lined U-shaped section in front of it, through which the Bely Dom is entered. **CH-M**

Arch of Triumph

Architect: Unknown
Completed: 1982
Location: Pyongyang, North Korea
Style/Period: Totalitarian Pastiche

At the end of World War II, the eastern Asian country of Korea was left divided into two parts: North Korea and South Korea. North Korea became the Democratic People's Republic of Korea, a Soviet-style state officially governed by the Communist

Workers' Party of Korea, but, in fact, ruled by Kim Il-Sung, the "Great Leader." He was initially the general secretary of the Workers' Party, but he eventually became North Korea's "eternal president."

Kim Il-Sung was born on April 15, 1912, and in 1982 his birthday present from the North Korean nation was the Arch of Triumph that was erected in Pyongyang, North Korea's capital city. The triumph refers to the vanquishing of Japan, Korea's one-time occupier, in 1945, and specifically to Kim Il-Sung's personal role in this victory. Although it was modeled on the 19th-century Arc de Triomphe in Paris, France, at 197 feet (60 m) high, 164 feet (50 m) wide and 118 feet (36 m) deep, Pyongyang's edifice is said to be the largest such arch in the world. It houses elevators, rooms and viewing platforms. Constructed of white granite with a three-tiered roof, decorative motifs on the Arch of Triumph's facade include the dates "1925" and "1945" and characters spelling out the "Song of General Kim Il-Sung." **CH-M**

Barbican Centre

Architects: Chamberlain, Powell & Bon
Completed: 1982
Location: City of London, London, England
Style: Brutalism/Modernism

Large parts of central London were flattened by German bombing raids during World War II, and much of the postwar reconstruction work was overseen by the local government authority, the London County Council. It had a large site that was ripe for redevelopment in the Barbican area to the east of the city center and put the work out to commission. The chosen company first completed 13 high-density medium- to high-rise residential blocks, the Barbican Estate, in 1975, and they then went on to develop the Barbican Centre as a venue for various performing arts and exhibitions.

The architects had never designed such a complex before, but they came up with a large-scale and, frankly, difficult to access brutalist design in concrete that was destined to become Europe's biggest multi-arts center, although critics complained that it was not entirely welcoming to the public.

Work began in 1971, and when completed it had a concert hall, two theaters, a pair of art galleries and three movie theaters, as well as various function rooms, restaurants and the

like. Although the center is a popular venue, it is not really loved and has been voted the ugliest building in the capital. **IW**

PA Technology Center

Architect: Richard Rogers

Completed: 1982

Location: Princeton, New Jersey, United States

Style/Period: High Tech

The high-tech style of British architect Richard Rogers and the needs of PA Management Consultants Ltd., a high-tech company, found their perfect — and striking — combined expression in the PA Technology Center (PATCenter for short), which Rogers designed for an industrial-park site in Princeton, New Jersey.

All of the assisted-span-tension structure's components were prefabricated, which kept costs down and enabled the PATCenter to be speedily erected. Rogers future-proofed the single-story, 40,000 square-foot (12,192 sq m) PATCenter — which was to be used as a research-and-development (R&D) laboratory — by including only a few partitions within the large, low steel-framed building, also ensuring that these partitions were moveable. The suspended steel-framed roof, whose exposed components caused it to resemble a skeleton roof, signaled the futuristic, technological nature of PATCenter's business, as well as its unique corporate outlook. And positioning elements of the air-conditioning system on the flat roof, between the masts that made up the A-frame, literally demonstrated thinking "outside the box." The building's facade comprised aluminum-framed clear-glass panels and translucent-fiberglass panels, the former acting as windows and the latter providing diffused illumination by day and enabling the PATCenter to glow against the dark sky at night. Inside, research laboratories were supplemented by offices and a staff cafeteria. CH-M

Xanadu House

Architects: Roy Mason and Bob Masters

Completed: 1983

Location: Kissimmee, Florida, United States

Style/Period: Blobotecture/Futuristic

Bob Masters, a pioneer in house building in polyurethane, devised an architectural

project, the Xanadu Houses, in the late 1970s. His plan was to construct experimental, quick-to-build space-age homes that would be ergonomically efficient and make full use of computers and automation to make the residents' lives as easy as possible. Three were built in the early 1980s at Wisconsin Dells, Wisconsin, Gatlinburg, Tennessee, and the largest, and most visited, one at Kissimmee, Florida. The designer was Roy Mason, and construction involved laying a large concrete base and then inflating a balloon over it. The interior was then sprayed with quick-hardening polyurethane insulation foam. When it had hardened, the balloon was deflated and porthole windows and doorways could simply be cut through.

Kissimmee, which was effectively a showcase "house for the future," covered some 6,000 square feet (560 sq. m) of living space and had a plain white exterior. The interior, which consisted of several rooms running off a central living area, had pale green floors and cream walls. The Xanadu House at Kissimmee was a popular tourist attraction, if not much liked by other architects, but interest soon waned. The designs, which were cramped, had low ceilings and were prone to mold, never caught on. All were eventually closed and demolished, with Kissimmee being the last to go in 2005. **IW**

Neue Staatsgalerie

Architects: Stirling & Wilford Partnership

Completed: 1984

Location: Konrad-Adanauer-Strasse, Stuttgart, Germany

Style/Period: Postmodern

The Neue Staatsgalerie (New State Gallery) wears its postmodern credentials on its sleeve. It is arguably the finest piece of architecture produced by Sir James Stirling, with the aid of Michael Wilford. Their commission was to enhance Stuttgart's cultural quarter by designing a building that could be bolted onto the mid-19th-century neoclassical Altes Staatsgalerie (Old State Gallery) and linked to other cultural centers, such as the nearby History Museum, which can be accessed by way of a terrace.

The new gallery was primarily built to house modern art in a series of interlinked rooms, but it is in fact multifunctional — in addition to the interior and exterior exhibition areas, it also houses a theater, library and music school, as well as administrative facilities. The building itself is geometric, but irregularly so. While stone (travertine marble and sandstone), steel and glass predominate, the architects injected hints of neoclassicism with the stone facade of the central rotunda. They also added a lighter postmodern note, both literally and metaphorically, by their use of bright colors. The reception area has a green rubber floor and pink and purple handrails, for example. **IW**

Kubuswoningen

Architect: Piet Blom

Completed: 1984

Location: Overblaak, Rotterdam, Netherlands

Style/Period: Postmodernism/Deconstructionism

The Kubuswoningen (Dutch for "Cubic Houses") that architect Piet Blom designed for the towns of Helmond and Rotterdam in the Netherlands are also called the Paalwoningen, or "Pole Houses," indicating that these are cubic houses built on poles, which is indeed the case. Each house comprises a cube tilted at an angle of 45 degrees, so that a diamond shape is formed, which is then slotted onto a hexagonal supportive pylon. If many such houses are assembled together, the effect is extraordinary. Blom compared each dwelling to a tree and the Cubic House complex to a forest, but with their brightly colored facades, geometrical shapes and the use of repetition, they also look rather like a giant child's building blocks. White cladding on their steeply pitched roofs means that they resemble snow-capped mountain peaks when viewed from above.

Thirty-two Cubic Houses are connected to each other at Overblaak, a street in Rotterdam, and are supported by a pre-existing pedestrian bridge that incorporates stores. Each tilted concrete-and-wood, zinc-clad cube contains three levels. The triangular bottom section houses a living room and kitchen, the middle level accommodates a bedroom and bathroom and the top triangle offers additional space. The windows are double-glazed, and the concrete pylon beneath contains a staircase leading outside. **CH-M**

AT&T Building

Architects: Philip Johnson and John Burgee

Completed: 1984 (begun 1978)

Location: 550 Madison Avenue, New York, New York, United States

Style/Period: Postmodernism

Today the postmodern skyscraper that Philip Johnson, working with John Burgee, built on New York City's Madison Avenue is called the Sony Building, but when it was completed it bore the name of the company that had commissioned it: AT&T. And the AT&T Building won almost instant fame as a symbol of the newly emerging postmodernist movement, which is an eclectic, iconoclastic style that combines all manner of historical stylistic references with modern materials and methods.

Although he followed the usual international style, or modernist, conventions that had, by now, come to apply to skyscraper construction — the AT&T Building is 647 feet (197 m) tall — such as a reinforced-steel skeleton, Johnson embellished his design with a number of postmodernist twists. These

details included surmounting the 37-floor tower with a neoclassical-style (or "Chippendale-type") pediment. Similarly, at the center of the entrance level he placed a giant-order Roman arch flanked by straight columns — neoclassical touches that recalled New York City's Municipal Building. Another link with older New York architecture can be seen in the pinkish gray granite with which the building is clad, which matches that used for the Grand Central Station's facade. Inside, a seven-story high atrium initially accommodated a huge AT&T corporate statue. **CH-M**

Spiral Building

Architects: Fumihiko Maki Associates

Completed: 1985

Location: Tokyo, Japan

Style/Period: Postmodernism

From the outside, in the midst of Tokyo's crowded urban landscape, the Spiral Building appears anything but curvilinear, being characterized instead by blocks of glass

and aluminum. Commissioned by the lingerie company Wacoal as a cultural hub, the Spiral Building, also known as the Wacoal Art Center, incorporates shops, bars, restaurants, and gallery space. It is one of the few spots in Tokyo where visitors can sit, relax, and watch the world go by.

Maki employed his favorite building materials to construct a radical edifice that has multiple uses, yet has a cohesion of purpose. The façade of the building demonstrates Maki's fondness for collage and fragmentary composition, as asymmetric panels of aluminum sit next to squares of glass. This evokes the layered spaces of traditional Japanese architecture and gardens, but also references 20th century Cubist design. Inside, a dramatic spiral ramp 49 feet (15 m) in diameter appears to float through the rear gallery space up to the second floor. Naturally lit from a semicircular skylight at the top of the building, the ramp is set slightly away from the white marble wall, allowing the light to fall straight down to the ground and providing the illusion of floating. **JM**

Nehru Centre

Architects: Kadri Consultants Pvt. Ltd.

Completed: 1986 (begun 1972)

Location: Dr. Annie Besant Road, Worli, Mumbai, India

Style/Period: Indian Modernism

The Nehru Centre was named in honor of Jawaharlal Nehru, India's first prime minister following the granting of its independence from Britain in 1947. Fittingly, it was Nehru's daughter, Indira Gandhi — who had followed in her father's footsteps to become India's premier — who laid the foundation stone at the 6-acre (24,282 sq. m) site that had been set aside in the Worli district of Mumbai (then called Bombay) in 1972.

The first part of this cultural complex to be completed in 1977 was the planetarium, whose hemispherical roof protrudes from the center of a four-sided two-story structure. Although the planetarium's dome is distinctive, it is the Discovery of India Building that has really become a Mumbai landmark. Constructed between 1973 and 1986 to a design by I.M. Kadri's architectural firm, Kadri Consultants, the cylindrical tower is notable for its fretworklike, latticed or crosshatched cladding, causing it to bear a resemblance to a sturdy beeswax candle. This tower soars upward from a moundlike structure whose sloping, turfed roof supports a flight of steps leading to the facilities within. The interior space houses an auditorium that seats nearly 1,000 people, a library, an art gallery and other exhibition rooms, a restaurant, the permanent Discovery of India Exposition and administration offices. **CH-M**

Hong Kong and Shanghai Bank Main Building

Architects: Foster Associates

Completed: 1986

Location: Queen's Road Central, Hong Kong

Style/Period: High Tech

Although this skyscraper owes something to earlier "inside out" high-tech buildings, it is nevertheless a brilliant example of, not only modern architecture, but also structural engineering. The site on the crowded island was so tight that the various prefabricated steel and glass sections were manufactured elsewhere and then put into position. The building, which soars to 47 stories and has a magnificent 170-foot (52 m) atrium on the 11th floor lit by giant mirrors, has no internal load-bearing frame. Foster (1933–) instead used eight groups of four vertical supports, each in the shape of a ladder linked together by cross bracing.

Five levels of suspension trusses held up by the ladders that support the floors and all elevators, staircases and other service features are banished to the block's east and west wings. The building also takes into account the beliefs and sensitivities of the local people, especially that of feng shui. Foster made sure that it faces water, did not have too many sharp edges and also set two bronze statues in position to guard its entrance. Such attention to detail and experimental structural work came at a price, however. The bank was the most expensive building in the world when it opened. **IW**

Lloyds Building

Architects: Richard Rogers Partnership

Completed: 1986

Location: Lime Street, London, England

Style/Period: High-Tech

The 1980s was a boom time for the British financial sector, which has its home in the City of London. The board of Lloyds, one of the country's main financial institutions, had decided in the late 1970s that they needed a new headquarters and so commissioned Rogers. He produced an inside-out high-tech design that was clearly inspired by his work on the Centre Georges Pompidou in Paris. British financial institutions, mostly conservative by instinct, were not generally known as supporters of radical architecture in which the guts of a building cover its exterior, but Lloyds gave Rogers' scheme the go-ahead. Work began in 1979.

The structure comprises three main and three service towers that cluster around a central area. The centerpiece is the Underwriting Room — a large space that is overlooked by the galleries that make up the 200-foot (60 m) atrium, which is lit by natural light through a barrel-vaulted glass roof. In all, the building is some 250 feet (76 m) tall and has 14 stories. Although it is undeniably modern, it contains elements that reflect Lloyds' long history, including the Lutine Bell, which is rung whenever a ship is lost, and on the 11th floor there is a complete 18th-century dining room that was housed in a previous Lloyds Building. **IW**

The Baha'í House of Worship

Architect: Fariborz Sahba

Completed: 1986

Location: Delhi, India

Style/Period: Modernist/Expressionism

In a modern multicultural world, where different religions must coexist, the tolerant teachings of the Baha'í faith have struck a chord with almost 6 million souls. At its core lie three principles: the unity of God, the unity of religion and the unity of mankind. Recognizing most of the major figures in the world's great religions as divine messengers, or manifestations of God, Baha'í regard these faiths as the successive revisions of His will for mankind and, therefore, as equally valid. It is from this theological perspective that the anchor of Baha'í unity, commonly called the Lotus Temple, on the vast Indian subcontinent was designed. Here amongst a sea of Hindus, Muslims and Buddhists a marble lotus flower has bloomed, its form relating to the iconography of all those faiths.

Built without the luxury of sophisticated Western equipment, the temple absorbed the creative energies of 40 engineers and over 700 laborers during its six-year construction. Using the nine-sided geometry prescribed by Baha'í scripture, the single great hall is wrapped in 27 concrete leaves rising 131 feet (40 m) high which are arranged in clusters of three and clad in sheets of white Greek marble. Nine doors open out in all directions to welcome followers of every faith who have arrived in their millions to meditate and pray within its walls. Expressing unity through architecture is an ancient concept, but rarely is the result as successful as the Lotus Temple. **PC**

Hallgrimskirkja

Architect: Gudjon Samuelsson

Completed: 1986

Location: Reykjavik, Iceland

Style/Period: Expressionism

This massive expressionist ecclesiastical building has been imbued with a monumental religious sensibility and symbolically captures the essence of the country and its people. Gudjon Samuelsson was the country's state architect, and the church is dedicated to Hallgrimur Petursson, a famous writer of hymns from the 17th century. Samuelsson was commissioned to design the church in 1937, but the work did not begin until 1945, and the tower was only the first major element of the prolonged build to be completed.

The church soars over the Icelandic capital, not least because its tower is 250 feet (88 m) tall, and it stands on a hill. Its scale is also heightened by the vertical rows of descending concrete pillars fixed to each corner. Although the building is concrete, hardly a natural material, the church does capture some of the country's natural essence. The bright white concrete reflects its snowfields and icy glaciers, while the concrete pillars can be seen as facsimiles of basaltic lava outcrops. The statue of Leif Ericsson, who is believed to have discovered North America, that stands before the church provides a reminder of Icelandic culture and history. **IW**

Kidosaki House

Architect: Tadao Ando

Completed: 1986 (begun 1982)

Location: Setaguya, Tokyo, Japan

Style/Period: Critical Regionalism

Japanese architect Tadao Ando's Kidosaki House, which was constructed in a Tokyo suburb between 1982 and 1986, takes careful account of ancient Japanese living conventions and accommodates them within a minimalist, modern-looking structure. And it is the exquisitely planned combination of bold, geometrical lines, simple construction materials and their interweaving with natural elements that makes this house a triumph of understated elegance.

Designed to accommodate an extended family — specifically a married couple and their respective parents and, consequently, three family units for two people each — the Kidosaki House is three stories high and comprises communal living spaces as well as private areas. The layout differs on each level, but the light and airy, minimally furnished interiors generally accord with centuries-old Japanese stylistic preferences. While the materials used are such 20th-century staples as glass and exposed concrete, the windows are situated in positions that cause the light admitted to wash the walls with ever-changing patterns. Further controlled natural touches are evident in the shrubs planted in the garden zones, which are demarcated by concrete walls. The house and incorporated garden areas are enclosed by a wall that forms a rectangle on three sides and an arc on the fourth, which curves around a corner of Kidosaki House's front elevation, indicating the entrance. **CH-M**

Musée d'Orsay

Architects: Victor Laloux, ACT Partnership, Gae Aulenti
Completed: 1987
Location: Rue de Lille, Paris, France
Style/Period: Modernism

The Musée d'Orsay on the left bank of the River Seine in Paris began life as a mainline railway station and hotel, the Gare d'Orsay. The station was largely designed in the Beaux Arts–classical tradition by Victor Laloux in a mere two years as part of the preparations for the 1900 Exposition Universelle. The station gradually declined. It first became a mere terminal for suburban trains and was then closed after its platforms proved too small for the longer trains coming into service. It remained mostly unused until 1977, when the president, Valery Giscard D'Estaing, made the decision to convert it into a museum to house art largely from 1848–1914.

The ACT Partnership worked on the exterior, while Italian Gae Aulenti headed the team that transformed the interior. They came up with a design that respected the building's history and integrity — the station's cast-iron pillars and decorative stucco were left intact, for example, but Aulenti also produced a three-tier modernist design. The ground level consists of several galleries that lead off a central zone. On the second level is a terrace that gives way to an auditorium, bookshop, more galleries and a restaurant housed in the station's former dining room. **IW**

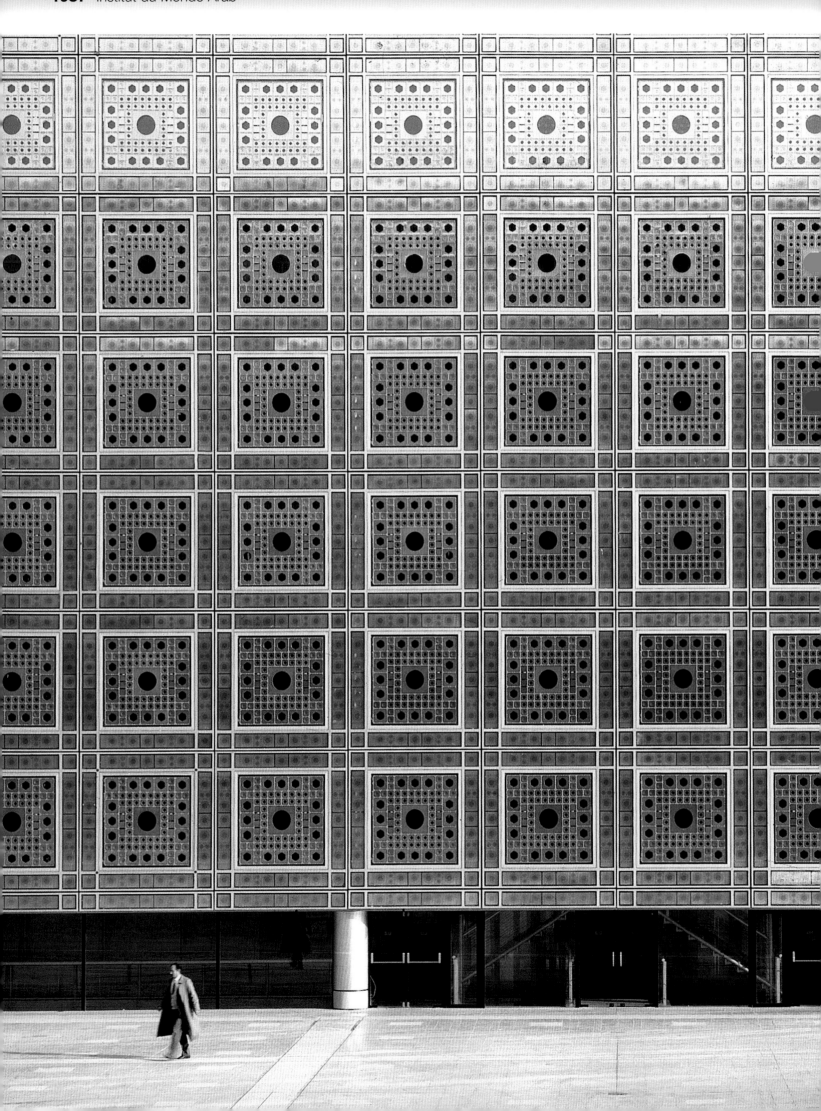

Institut du Monde Arab

Architect: Jean Nouvel

Completed: 1987

Location: Paris, France

Style/Period: High Tech

The delicate wooden *mashrabiya* of Arabia are among the most beautiful architectural elements of the Islamic world. Constructed from carved or turned components, these geometric lattice screens enhance many a facade, their closely spaced bars controlling solar gain and preserving the privacy of those within. Conversely, it was publicity, rather than privacy, that the Institute du Monde Arab (IMA or Arab Institute) was seeking in 1981, when it announced a competition to design its high-profile Parisian headquarters.

The winning French architect, Jean Nouvel, designed a building that houses a library, auditorium and exhibition spaces that collectively support the IMA's agenda of disseminating information on the values of the Arab world to Western audiences. Occupying a triangular site next to the River Seine, the north facade is wrapped in a suspended wall of glass that mirrors its surroundings, while the south facade reflects a high-tech take on the traditional *mashrabiya*. Executed in steel and glass, it presents a tapestry of over 240 grid squares, each incorporating 57 photosensitive mechanical oculars. These oculars open and close like camera apertures in response to changing light conditions, thereby controlling the internal temperature and glare. For his stunning success in synthesizing Muslim decoration with modern technology, Nouvel received the 1989 Aga Khan Award for Architecture, the largest prize in the architectural world, which effectively heralded his arrival on the international stage. **PC**

Lippo Centre/Bond Centre

Architect: Paul Rudolph

Completed: 1988 (begun 1987)

Location: 89 Queensway, Admiralty, Hong Kong Island, Hong Kong

Style/Period: Postmodernism

The Lippo Centre was constructed on reclaimed waterfront land in Hong Kong Island's Admiralty district. On its completion in 1988, however, it had a different name: the Bond Centre, which proclaimed its developer as being the Bond Corporation. The Bond Corporation was an Australian company, which is one of the reasons why the Bond Centre was nicknamed the "Koala Tree," another being that the two adjacent towers that make up the complex look as though columns of koala bears are climbing them, clinging on tightly with their arms and legs.

Built to a design by U.S. architect Paul Rudolph, the two towers — used for office space — that make the Bond Centre so memorable were erected on a four-story podium section (which accommodates restaurants and stores). Respectively referred to as Lippo Centre 1 and Lippo Centre 2, Lippo Centre 1 is the smallest, at 564 feet (172 m) in height with 44 stories, while Lippo Centre 2 measures 610 feet (186 m) and has 48 floors. Although the Bond Centre was constructed using conventional materials for high-rise buildings — notably reinforced concrete, steel and glass — Rudolph added interest with his koala-effect motif, which was created by incorporating protruding rectangular sections into the exterior walls, which were then clad with glass. **CH-M**

Bicentennial Conservatory

Architect: Guy Maron
Completed: 1988
Location: Adelaide, South Australia, Australia
Style/Period: Modernism

Located in the northeast of South Australia's state capital, the Adelaide Botanical Gardens are home to one of the country's finest late modernist buildings: a conservatory erected to commemorate the 200th anniversary of the establishment of the first permanent white settlement. The design work was given to a local architect, and he produced a curvilinear structure that is some 328 feet (100 m) long, 154 feet (47 m) wide and 89 feet (27 m) high — dimensions that make it the largest single span conservatory in the southern hemisphere. Building commenced in 1987.

The building consists of a steel structure that supports some 7,986 square feet (2,434 sq. m) of toughened glass, which makes up the greater part of its roof, walls and door. The unusual shape — it's known to the locals as "the Pasty," a reference to the ubiquitous Australian handheld meat pie — was dictated by the need to house endangered tropical trees and palms from the rainforests of the southwest Pacific up to 65 feet (20 m) tall. The interior has two walkways: one at ground level and the other at tree-canopy height. Temperature and humidity are regulated by state-of-the-art computer and sensor systems, while various predators and parasites control any pests that might threaten the collection. **IW**

Canadian Museum of Civilization

Architects: Douglas Cardinal
Completed: 1988
Location: Gatineau, Quebec, Canada
Style/Period: Postmodern

Douglas Cardinal is one of Canada's foremost architects, his signature curvilinear style influenced by the landscape around his buildings. One of the first Canadian architects to utilize computer-aided-design (CAD), he was a natural choice when, in 1982, the Trudeau government announced that what was then known as the Museum of Man would move to its own site, across the Ottawa River in Gatineau, Quebec. Renamed in 1986, the Museum of Civilization opened in 1989 amid some controversy, not least because the original budget of $80 million had risen to $340 million. Today, the museum is one of Canada's most popular attractions and is rightly considered one of the most important architectural landmarks in the country.

The curves of the 1 million-square foot (93,000-sq. m) building hug the landscape, sinuously curving along the banks of the Ottawa River. The dramatic picture window (367 x 49 feet/112 x 15 meters) in the museum's Grand Hall is the architectural focus of the interior, and looks out on to a magnificent view of the spires and towers of the Neogothic parliament building atop Ottawa's rocky cliffs. The two buildings complement each other perfectly, providing a fusion between Canada's past and future. **JM**

Pumping Station

Architect: John Outram
Completed: 1988 (begun 1987)
Location: Stewart Street, Isle of Dogs, Docklands, London, England
Style/Period: Postmodernism

The Pumping Station at Stewart Street on the Isle of Dogs in London's East End serves a vital, if unglamorous, purpose within a building whose design has been lauded as a postmodernist masterpiece. It was commissioned by the London Docklands Development Corporation (LDDC) — which had been set up at the start of the 1980s to redevelop and inject new life into London's traditional, but rundown and poverty-stricken, Docklands area — and Thames Water, the utility company responsible for water supply and waste-water treatment in London.

Architect John Outram's design is both eye-catching and functional. The functional section of the building comprises an underground pump room measuring 43 x 36 feet (13 x 11 m). It contains two dry-weather pumps and 10 storm-condition pumps, which pump surface and storm water into a surge tank, which is expelled from there directly into the River Thames that runs alongside it. The low, rectangular building that rises above the pump room has been described as reminiscent of ancient Egyptian architecture in style. A circular instrument at the center of the pediment that crowns the facade may look decorative, but it is actually a huge fan that disperses any methane gas that builds up inside. The short columns that stand on either side of the entrance house ventilation ducts. **CH-M**

Vitra Design Museum

Architect: Frank Gehry

Completed: 1989

Location: Charles-Eames-Strasse, Weil-am-Rhein, Germany

Style/Period: Deconstructionism

Vitra is a Swiss-based furniture-making company of German origin that was founded in 1950 by Willi Fehlbaum. In the early 1980s the director, Rolf Fehlbaum, began collecting the furniture of named designers such as husband-and-wife team Charles and Ray Eames, George Nelson and Alvar Alto, and it soon became apparent he needed a private building to display these pieces. In 1987 he contacted Frank Gehry and also met Alexander von Vegesack, later the museum's director, and the idea for a museum open to the public gradually emerged.

The museum was Gehry's first work in Europe, and he also built a more functional production hall and gateway at the company's nearby factory. He stuck with his sculptural deconstructionist architectural hallmark for the design museum, but he unusually permitted curves to break out of his more usual angular forms. He also limited himself to a few building materials, just titanium-zinc alloy and plaster, for the fabric. The latter is painted plain white, possibly in homage to Le Corbusier's Notre Dame du Haut chapel (see page 336), which lies nearby across the border with France. Weil-am-Rhein is the location of several other cutting-edge buildings, built largely thanks to Vitra's almost obsessive interest in modern architectural styles. **IW**

Pyramide, Le Grand Louvre

Architect: I.M. Pei

Completed: 1989

Location: Palais du Louvre, Paris, France

Style/Period: Modernism/High Tech

President François Mitterand intended to leave an architectural legacy in the French capital and initiated several building schemes in the 1980s that were collectively known as "Les Grands Projets" ("the Big Projects"). The overwhelming majority were built by French architects, but Pei, Chinese-born and U.S.-based, was chosen to design a new entrance to the Louvre museum. The commission itself was almost as controversial as the radical pyramidal structures that he designed, and Pei, unlike the other French architects, was never presented with an award for his work.

The Louvre's existing entrance could not cope with the volume of visitors, was confusing and had few facilities. Pei decided to dig down in the large courtyard to build a bigger entrance hall, unite the separate wings of the museum and provide space for stores and other facilities. The high-tech modernist pyramid built in glass and steel was an elegant solution to major problems — how to avoid blocking the vistas across the courtyard to the various wings of the Louvre and how to flood the interior with natural light (three small pyramids were built for the same reason). Pei was also successful in harmonizing two wholly distinctive architectural styles by creating a simulacrum of a classic French garden around the pyramid to link the old and new together. **IW**

Fawley House (facade)

Architect: Quinlan Terry

Completed: 1989

Location: Fawley, Oxfordshire, England

Style/Period: Neoclassical

Strictly speaking, 20th-century British architect Quinlan Terry was not responsible for all of Fawley House, since its shell dates from the mid-18th century, when it was built near Henley-on-Thames, Oxfordshire, to serve as a parsonage. Original bricks still accommodate two stories and an attic and form a decorative checker pattern on the garden facade, but the Georgian building underwent a dramatic facelift and remodeling in the 1980s, during the residency of David McAlpine, a scion of the British building firm Sir Robert McAlpine.

Terry's striking contribution is the front facade, which was fashioned from Portland stone and flint and is exuberantly neoclassical in style, particularly at roof level — so much so that architectural authorities generally describe it as baroque. Beneath the central pediment are Ionic-style stone pilasters on the second floor, which are separated from the plainer Tuscan-style pilasters on the ground floor by a knapped-flint course. Four knapped-flint blind arched windows also feature on each level, alternating on either side of two rectangular sash windows that flank the glazed arched window above the front door, which has an arched fanlight. The flint used so extensively both echoes the rusticated surround that encloses the French doors set into the garden facade and contrasts sympathetically with the lighter Portland stone. **CH-M**

Price House

Architect: Bart Prince

Completed: 1989

Location: Corona Del Mar, California, United States

Style/Period: Organic

America boasts a fine tradition of truly organic architecture, stretching back to the 1930s when Frank Lloyd Wright studied the *Staghorn cholla* cacti before designing the slender columns of the Johnson Wax

Building. Finding natural solutions to his clients' requirements, architect Bart Prince has made several notable contributions to the organic canon, including the Price House. It was built for the same family of wealthy patrons who had previously commissioned Wright's one and only skyscraper, the Price Tower.

The Price House begins with a street facade of cedar shingles layered 10 to 15 deep to form a three-dimensional contoured surface. This writhing mass partially envelops three semicircular living "pods," which are nested together on a group of columns that resemble a grove of trees. Each rooted in a separate concrete floor pad, these "trees" are able to sway independently in the event of an earthquake, reducing potential damage. Constructed from laminated strips of fir, they branch out then up to form the pods' floors and walls before twisting back to carry the roof. Additional support is supplied by stainless steel knee joints, whose substantial bolt heads are protected from the corrosive sea air by large turned wooden stoppers, producing a Victorian sci-fi aesthetic that would be at home in a Jules Verne novel. Filled with tangible components clearly expressing the forces they bear, the Price House is a logical, if novel, application of natural forms to modern living. **PC**

Church of the Light

Architect: Tadao Ando
Completed: 1989 (begun 1988)
Location: Ibaraki Kasugaoka Church, Ibaraki, Osaka
Prefecture, Japan
Style/Period: Critical Regionalism

"I am the light of the world: he that followeth me shall not walk in darkness, but shall have the light of life" (Gospel of Saint John 8:12). Christians are familiar with Christ's self-identification with light, just as they recognize the sign of the cross as a symbol of his self-sacrifice for the redemption of humankind. And in his design for the Church of the Light in the Japanese city of Ibaraki, Japanese architect Tadao Ando combined these two profound concepts, setting them center stage in the most simple, yet dazzling, manner.

The cross of light is formed by a cruciform 8-inch (20 cm) gap that divides the reinforced-concrete wall behind the altar, which is 15 inches (38 cm) thick, into four sections. This wall is oriented toward the east, causing light to penetrate the gap, illuminating the cross shape; the effect is dramatic, particularly since the church's interior is both gloomy and plainly

furnished. This wall stands at one end of the modest church building — 19 feet (6 m) high, 19 feet (6 m) wide and 58 feet (18 m) long — whose concrete walls were cast in situ, including a freestanding wall that slices through the rectangular structure at an angle of 15 degrees to create a separate entrance lobby. **CH-M**

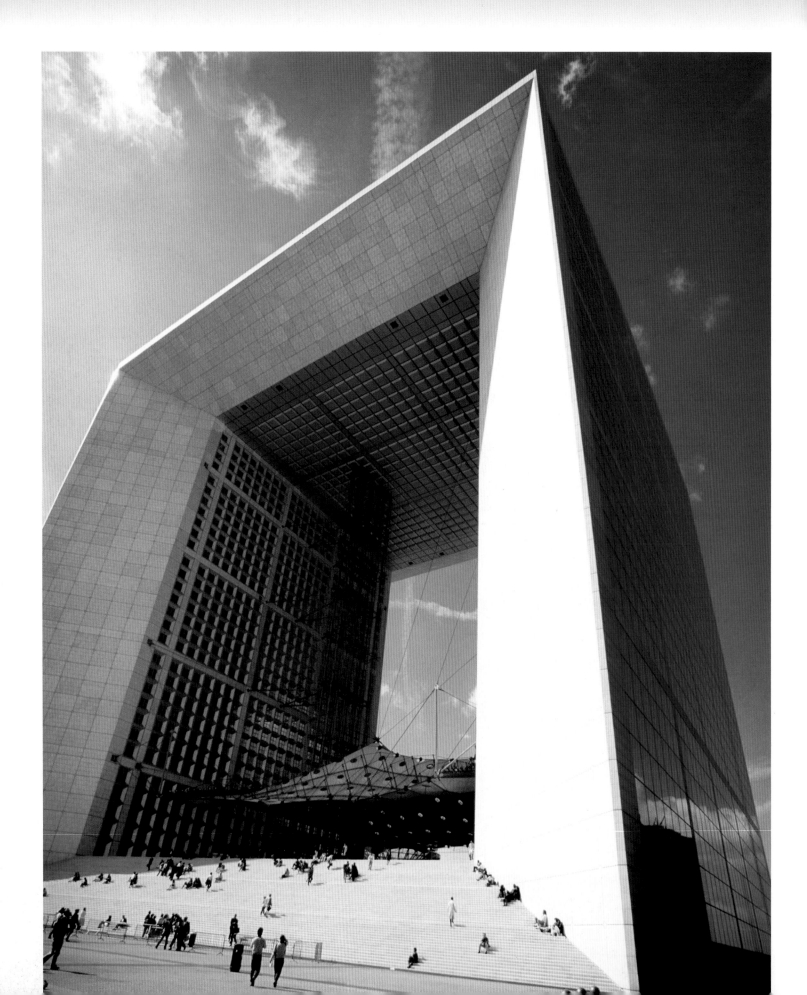

La Grande Arche de la Fraternité

Architect: Johann von Spreckelsen
Completed: 1990
Location: La Defense, Paris, France
Style/Period: High Tech

This great arch, also known as L'Arche de la Defense, was one of President François Mitterand's "grands projets," his architectural legacy for the French capital. Danish architect Johann von Spreckelsen won the commission, and came up with a modern 20th century take on the Arc de Triomphe, a grand arch dedicated to humanity and humanitarian ideals. His design is almost a perfect cube, with a height of 361 feet (110 m), a depth of 368 feet (112 m) and a width of 354 feet (108 m). The building has a concrete frame covered in granite, Italian Carrara marble, and glass. Spreckelsen did not live to see the arch completed, but the final work was overseen by the French architect, Paul Andreu.

The arch is one part of what is known as the "Axe historique" (historic axis), which runs down the Champs Elysées, linking some of the capital's iconic landmarks, including the Louvre and the Arc de Triomphe. However, it is set at a slight angle to the dead-straight axis, as its foundations circumvent two subway stations and a freeway. The arch is also a functional building, in that two sides house government offices, and its roof, accessible by external elevator, offers tourists panoramic views of Paris. **IW**

Villa Neuendorf

Architects: John Pawson and Claudio Silvestrin
Completed: 1990
Location: Majorca, Spain
Style/Period: Minimalism

A spectacular example of the collaboration between the British architect John Pawson and his Italian colleague Claudio Silvestrin stands on the Spanish island of Majorca, the largest of the Balearic Islands. It was here, in 1990, that they constructed a remarkable vacation home for Hans Neuendorf, a German art dealer, and his family. Although many of the elements that feature in the Villa Neuendorf's design are local and traditional, Pawson and Silvestrin combined these with a modern, minimalist ethos to create a unique building.

With its high, unadorned walls, the Villa Neuendorf rises like a latter-day fortress above a grove of almond trees. A stepped path running parallel to a garden wall leads directly to the entrance: a rectangular aperture set into a long, windowless facade, whose only other notable feature is a cutout mirror-image rectangle above it, which disturbs the line of the roof like a single crenellation. On entering, visitors find themselves in a courtyard-type atrium. The exterior brick walls are rendered in a reddish plaster that, having been mixed with local earth, blends with the landscape, while inside, Majorcan limestone lines the floors. The villa's small and carefully positioned windows maximize the impact of a particular view, rather like picture frames. A swimming pool extends from the terrace. **CH-M**

Westin Regina Hotel

Architect: Javier Sordo Madaleno
Completed: 1990
Location: San Jose del Cabo, Baja California, Mexico
Style/Period: Modern Mexican

Those vacationers who travel to San Jose del Cabo, at the tip of Mexico's Baja California, are in for a real treat, and not just on account of the sun, sea and sand. For here they can admire Mexican architect Javier Sordo Madaleno's ingenious design for the Westin Regina Hotel, which, apart from supplying an upscale hotel's usual amenities, has been a striking addition to the local land- and seascape since 1990.

The Westin Regina Hotel both stands out from and harmonizes with its desert surroundings and beach-front situation — its rectangular, curve-softened planes and the red color of the local stone from which it was built echo the former, and its curving line (which also contributes to guests' privacy) follows that of the coastline. Another remarkable feature of this eight-story hotel is the huge rectangular archway that appears to have been cut out of the first four stories of part of the structure, which provides a postcardlike view of the white sands, blue skies and turquoise Pacific Ocean and Sea of Cortés beyond. More colors stimulate the eyes in the form of bright yellow, pink and green paint accents, which, in combination with the exotic flowers and foliage growing in the hotel's gardens, increase the sense of being in a tropical paradise. **CH-M**

Casa Hernández

Architect: Agustín Hérnandez
Completed: 1990 (begun 1988)
Location: Bosques De Las Lomas, Mexico City, Mexico
Style/Period: Postmodernism

With a population in excess of 19 million, Greater Mexico City is the largest metropolitan area in the western hemisphere, its urban density placing a high premium on conventional level building plots. Confronted by an affordable but precipitous 65-degree slope, Agustín Hérnandez had to perform an act of

architectural gymnastics in order to use the full depth of his site.

Approached from the winding hillside road the house appears only lightly moored to the rocky gradient, as if preparing to launch itself out into the void. Its two vertical uprights stand 115 feet (35 m) high, clasping four corrugated prisms that contain the living spaces. Held captive within circular apertures and supported by massive steel beams, these prisms appear to be in the act of sliding past each other, imparting a kinetic quality to the structure. As a result of this frozen motion, the house gains a projecting balcony out front and a covered parking space to the rear. The interior is dominated by a seam of glazing that runs up the full height of the facade, emphasizing the four-prism construction while offering panoramic views of the city spread out below. Greatly moved by his act of creation, the architect composed a poem in which he described geometry as "my religion!" With its rectilinear slabs, sliding prisms and circular openings, the Hernández House is almost a private shrine to the pure mathematical forms he holds so dear. **PC**

Sainsbury Wing, National Gallery

Architects: Robert Venturi and Denise Scott-Brown

Completed: 1991 (begun 1987)

Location: Trafalgar Square, London, England

Style/Period: Postmodernism

How exactly, and even whether, Britain's National Gallery in London's Trafalgar Square should be extended to provide much-needed extra space was the subject of a fierce debate during the 1980s, with Prince Charles memorably condemning one proposal as a "monstrous carbuncle." The postmodernist design submitted by the U.S. husband-and-wife architectural team of Robert Venturi and Denise Scott-Brown was better received, however. This was in part because, in echoing elements of the existing edifice, it created a sympathetic compromise solution to the problem of whether to cause controversy with the shockingly new or simply ape the original model, in which case the accusation would be a lack of originality

and boldness. (The prototype was a neoclassical building designed by William Wilkins, which was opened in 1838.)

Although Venturi and Scott-Brown's Sainsbury Wing (named in honor of its funders) was separate from the National Gallery, it was clad in the same Portland stone, and its facade incorporated similar giant-order columns. In addition, it was

lower and smaller than its "parent" building, to which it was linked by means of a circular bridge, consequently complementing rather than dominating it. Inside, notable features included an impressive staircase, gallery spaces (in which were hung paintings from the gallery's early Renaissance collection), a book-store, restaurant and auditorium. **CH-M**

Chiat/Day Headquarters

Architects: Frank Gehry, Claes Oldenburg and Coosje
van Bruggen
Completed: 1991 (begun 1985)
Location: Main Street, Venice, Santa Monica,
California, United States
Style/Period: Deconstructionism

When, during the 1980s, the ambitious
Chiat/Day U.S. advertising agency decided
that it needed a new West Coast
headquarters, it hired local architect Frank
Gehry. The bureaucratic frustrations that
subsequently plagued its construction must
have been forgotten when, in 1991, Gehry's
Chiat/Day Headquarters became an
architectural sensation. Its Main Street
facade remains a startling sight.

Venice's planning restrictions dictated
the Chiat/Day Headquarters' dimensions,
and the result was a building covering 75,000
square feet (6,968 sq. m), with three
underground parking levels and three
aboveground stories. The Chiat/Day
Headquarters comprises one L-shaped
building, but when viewed from Main Street,
the facade gives the impression of four
separate elements. Firstly, there is a white,
streamline-moderne art deco–style three-
story structure in curving concrete and glass.
Secondly, next to that is a pair of 45-foot
(14 m) tall dark gray binoculars (designed
with the help of U.S. pop artist Claes
Oldenburg and his wife, Coosje van Bruggen).
The shafts accommodate office space, the
eyepieces are actually glazed skylights and
visitors gain access to the building and
parking lots through the arch between the
cylinders. And then, thirdly, is a reddish
building that can be glimpsed behind, which
is linked to, fourthly, a copper-clad section
that is part sculpture and part structure and
resembles a deconstructed forest. **CH-M**

One Canada Square

Architect: César Pelli
Completed: 1991 (begun 1988)
Location: Canary Wharf, Docklands, London, England
Style/Period: Postmodernism

Developed by the Canadian company
Olympia & York and promoted by the
London Docklands Development
Corporation (LDDC) as the crowning glory
of the redevelopment of London's
Docklands area, the skyscraper that
Argentine-American architect César Pelli
designed for the Canary Wharf section of the
former West India Docks was once hugely
controversial. One Canada Square — or
Canary Wharf Tower, as it is popularly called
— was criticized mainly on account of its
height and its perceived symbolism, with
many regarding this towering office block as
representing the brash confidence and cold,
greed-driven culture of corporate capitalism.
Such objections have faded, however, and for
the many who today occupy its 6.6 million
square feet (20.1 million sq. m) it is simply a
place to work.

At 771 feet (235 m) tall, One Canada
Square was Britain's highest building on its
completion in 1991, and the apical flashing
red light that warns off passing aircraft can
be seen from many miles away. Fifty stories,
some of them below ground, are
accommodated within the square tower,
whose pointed, pyramid-shaped roof section
gives it the appearance of a giant obelisk.
Clad as it is in stainless steel and glass, the
building glistens or glows according to the
prevailing quality of the sunlight. **CH-M**

Tokyo City Hall

Architect: Kenzo Tange
Completed: 1991
Location: Shinjuku, Tokyo, Japan
Style/Period: Metabolist/High Tech

Construction of Japanese architect Kenzo Tange's second design for Tokyo City Hall (his first dated back to the 1950s) was completed in 1991, but its extraordinary, futuristic appearance suggests that it was erected a century ahead of its time. As such, it reflects the preoccupations of the Japanese metabolist architectural movement, of which Tange was a leading member. The metabolist school combined elements of traditional Japanese style with a growing belief that rapid advances in technology would increasingly blur the boundaries between home and work, so that the high-tech scenarios envisaged in science fiction would soon become a reality.

The glass-and-steel, subtly contoured structure that was erected in Tokyo's Shinjuku district to serve as the new home of the Tokyo Metropolitan Government describes a rough "U" shape, with the towers that form the two arms towering above the city. Tower 1 is higher, at 797 feet (243 m) and 48 stories; Tower 2 is 535 feet (163 m) and 34 stories tall. Both accommodate government offices and support staff, with Tower 1 being dedicated to Tokyo's governor, although observation decks at the top of Tower 1 are open to the public. The seven-story "infill" structure between the two towers is 135 feet (41 m) tall and houses the assembly building and associated offices. **CH-M**

London Ark

Architect: Ralph Erskine
Completed: 1992
Location: Hammersmith, London, England
Style/Period: High Tech/Modernism

Although Ralph Erskine was born and raised in England, he spent most of his working life in Sweden. He was attracted there for two main reasons: he admired the country's lavish social welfare system, which chimed with his socialism and strong Quaker faith, and he also much admired the work of Sweden's functionalist architects and designers, such as Sven Marhelius and Sigurd Lewerentz. Functionalism, which developed in the 1930s following the publication of the manifesto *Acceptera* ("Accept") at the beginning of the decade, held that architects should design buildings based on the building's function.

Erskine returned to England to build the steel-and-brick ark, arguably one of the most distinctive buildings in the country. It sits on a confined site in West London and, as is suggested by its title, does somewhat resemble a ship, especially as the brown glass might pass for a wooden hull. The 250-foot (76 m) 10-story building, which is made bright and airy with a top-lit floor-to-roof atrium, is given over to open-plan offices with communal meeting places, and it incorporates a novel cooling system in the ceiling that removes the need for the more usual ducting system. **IW**

Supreme Court Building

Architects: Ram Karmi and Ada Karmi-Melamede

Completed: 1992 (begun 1986)

Location: Jerusalem, Israel

Style/Period: Modernism

Recurrent motifs at Israel's Supreme Court Building, which was created by Ram Karmi and Ada Karmi-Melamede, sibling architects from Tel Aviv, include the circle and the line, which, in this context, respectively represent justice and humankind. The prize-winning design, which was completed in 1992, is a uniquely Israeli combination of traditional Jewish references (and building materials), a white modernist appearance and functional areas that cover 250,000 square feet (76,200 sq. m).

If visitors are arriving by car, they first come to a square parking area, set at an angle to the Supreme Court Building, which describes a rough "T." A copper-clad pyramid (which recalls Zechariah's tomb) that rises from the roof of the T-shape's left-hand wing indicates the location of the entrance, or gatehouse; this section also accommodates a three-story law library. The right-hand side of the "T" houses the justices' chambers, the core of this part being the Courtyard of the Arches, through the center of which runs a symbolic channel of water. And while administrative offices are situated along the left-hand side of the "T's" spine, five court-rooms extend from the right. Of different sizes (seating between 40 and 150 onlookers), each courtroom is constructed in the shape of a Roman basilica, also recalling a Talmudic synagogue, and each is lit by windows running along both long sides. **CH-M**

Vauxhall Cross

Architects: Terry Farrell & Company

Completed: 1993 (begun 1988)

Location: 85 Albert Embankment, Vauxhall, London, England

Style/Period: Postmodernism

Standing on the north bank, it is impossible to overlook the huge and extraordinary, white-and-green ziggurat-style building that the British architectural firm Terry Farrell & Company constructed on the south bank of London's River Thames, near Vauxhall Bridge, between 1988 and 1993. It is rather ironic, given that Vauxhall Cross — the building in question, on the Albert Embankment — was commissioned to house the offices of Britain's Secret Intelligence Service (SIS), or Military Intelligence, Section Six (MI6), hence its alternative names: the SIS Building and the M16 Building. It does, however, help to explain why few details about Vauxhall Cross have been made public and justifiably so, given that it was the target of a rocket attack by suspected terrorists in 2000.

The ziggurat, or stepped-pyramid, effect was achieved by setting three long, rectangular blocks one behind the other in a terracelike formation. These blocks are graduated in height from low rise (the riverside elevation) to medium rise, with a maximum of nine stories. Glazed atria and courtyards between the blocks provide spacious areas flooded with natural light, and there are also landscaped gardens and river views for civil servants to enjoy. The total floor area comprises 460,000 square feet (42,734 sq. m) and accommodates refreshment and sports areas, as well as offices. **CH-M**

so that the worshippers can see the ocean. It was also built to withstand earthquakes, has heated flooring, electronic doors and a sliding roof.

The mosque covers an area of 22 acres (9 ha), which makes it the second biggest in the world, and its 689-foot (210 m) minaret is the tallest anywhere; at night it shines a laser beam in the direction of Mecca. Aside from the mosque and courtyard, which together can accommodate 125,000 worshippers, the complex contains a school, a library and a parking lot. The lavishly decorated and ornate interiors, with their beautiful calligraphy and mosaics, were produced by some 6,000 craftsmen. **IW**

Vitra Fire Station

Architect: Zaha Hadid
Completed: 1993
Location: Weil Am Rheim, Germany
Style/Period: Deconstructionism

An institution within the furniture industry, Vitra has amassed a product portfolio that reads like a history of 20th century design. A host of iconic pieces by Charles Eames, Verner Panton and George Nelson grace the Vitra showrooms alongside stylish new works by emerging young talent. Following a destructive factory fire in 1981, Vitra's new owner, Rolf Fehlbaum, chose to extend the company's design patronage to the field of architecture, commissioning prominent architects for each new element. This transformed the Vitra site into an outdoor gallery of the avant-garde, with the most notable structures being Frank Gehy's Vitra Design Museum (1989) and the famous fire station by Zaha Hadid.

Constructed almost entirely from crisply cast reinforced concrete, the deftly jutting planes and angular surfaces of Hadid's design marked the first physical incarnation of a style she had evolved through countless freehand sketches and atmospheric paintings. This process accounts for the overall aesthetic, the station presenting an accretion of graphic elements combined into a single elongated form. A slight bend at its middle divides the structure into two wings containing quarters for the firemen and a

Great Mosque Hassan II

Architect: Michel Pinseau
Completed: 1993
Location: Casablanca, Morocco
Style/Period: Modern Islamic

This monumental structure was commissioned by King Hassan II, who had something of a mania for building mosques.

He chose his favorite architect, Michel Pinseau, to undertake the work. A site was chosen on a small cliff, but much of the mosque actually lies over water. Work began in 1986, and the finished mosque owes much to traditional Moorish architecture, even though Hassan insisted that Pinseau incorporate a number of very modern features. For example, it is built out over the Atlantic and part of the floor is glass covered garage with a clear span of 105 feet (32 m). Most dramatic of all is the cantilevered garage door canopy: a jagged shard that stretches out 39 feet (12 m) from its slender steel supports. Rendered redundant when a new municipal fire station was built nearby, Hadid's contribution to Vitra's design credentials now serves as an iconic gallery for its landmark collection of 100 classic chairs. **PC**

Hôtel du Département des Bouches-du-Rhône

Architects: William Alsop and Jan Störmer

Completed: 1994 (begun 1990)

Location: 52 Avenue St. Just, Marseilles, Bouches-du-Rhône, France

Style/Period: High Tech

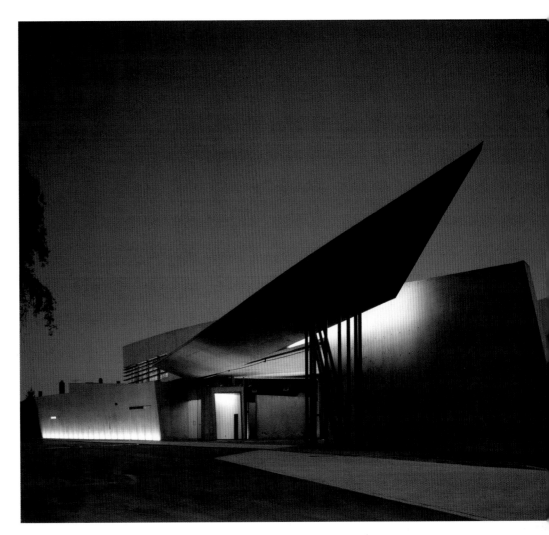

It is not difficult to grasp the reasons behind the nicknames given by the locals to the Hôtel du Département des Bouches-du-Rhône (the local-government headquarters of the Bouches-du-Rhône region), a prize-winning concrete, glass and steel building that was erected in the eastern part of the southern French town of Marseilles between 1990 and 1994. The building, designed and constructed as a result of the collaboration between the Anglo-German architects William Alsop and Jan Störmer, can indeed readily be described as "Le Grand Bleu" ("the big blue thing"), and parts of this administrative complex also clearly resemble a "Bateau Bleu" (blue boat) or "Vaisseau Bleu" (blue vessel), as well as a "Baleine" (whale).

The Hôtel du Département des Bouches-du-Rhône basically comprises two long, rectangular buildings standing alongside one another. These steel-framed structures are connected at certain points by means of tubelike walkways and bridges. An adjacent cigar-shaped construction set on legs invites the whale comparisons. Not only is the blue-tinted glass — a "light-sucking blue," as Alsop described it — that clads the building truly striking, but it also evokes the sea that is so crucial to this Mediterranean port's economy. It serves a functional purpose, too, in deflecting the glare of the sun so that those inside are not dazzled. **CH-M**

Saint-Exupéry TGV Station

Architect: Santiago Calatrava

Completed: 1994

Location: Lyon, France

Style/Period: Expressionism

This striking expressionist building came about because three different bodies had a mutual interest in creating a new station at what was then known as the Gare de Satolas in Lyon, France. The French national railway company SNCF wanted a new station to show off their high-speed TGV trains traveling between Paris and Marseilles, the regional authority of Rhône-Alpes wanted an iconic building to greet visitors and the Lyon Board of Trade and Industry wanted improved links between the airport and station, both of which lie some 12 miles (20 km) from the city's center. The commission was given to Spanish architect Santiago Calatrava (1951–), who had considerable experience in designing public buildings of various types.

He undoubtedly created an elegant building that solved a practical problem. Its centerpiece is the main hall, which is built in curving steel, glass and concrete, and from where platform wings lead off either side of the main concourse and run out over the railway track below. To reach the airport, the visitor ascends an escalator and then along an elevated pier. From the outside the station has a skeletonlike quality, and from above it has been described as having the look of a bird with outstretched wings. **IW**

Passenger Terminal, Kansai International Airport

Architect: Renzo Piano Workshop

Completed: 1994

Location: Osaka, Japan

Style/Period: High-Tech

It took some 20 years for this building to be given the go-ahead and the commission was given to a design team that produced an exceptionally elegant but functional building that also had to be strong enough to survive the earthquakes and typhoons to which the region is prone. The work began in 1987 by building a large artificial island some 2.5 miles (4 km) long by 1.5 miles (2.5 km) wide out into Osaka Bay. Land around the old airport was in short supply and siting the terminal off-shore helped to minimize the air and noise pollution that were plaguing the lives of local people. The terminus has a length of one mile (1.7 km) and is one of the longest such buildings in the world. The exterior is clad with stainless steel panels and darkened glass.

The interior space is perfectly designed for its purpose. Arrival and departure facilities lie under the beautiful curved roof, and the architecture team used sinuous outlines on trussed supports as a visual way to take passengers to the terminus's key points. The heart of the structure is the light and airy full-height atrium that works beautifully as a meeting point. **IW**

Église Sainte-Trinité

Architect: Ugo Brunoni

Completed: 1994 (begun 1984)

Location: 67/69 Rue de Lausanne, Geneva, Switzerland

Style/Period: Postmodernism

At first sight, the Église Sainte-Trinité, or Church of the Holy Trinity, that stands in Geneva's Rue de Lausanne bears an incongruous resemblance to the round bomb, complete with fuse, that often featured in 20th-century cartoons. In fact, Ugo Brunoni, the Swiss architect responsible

for this Christian church's design, intended his spherical house of worship to represent an orb, which in turn symbolizes the globe. This is an apt choice since Geneva, in neutral Switzerland, houses the headquarters of many global organizations, including the International Red Cross and a number of the United Nations' intergovernmental agencies. Set as it is within an artificial pool amid a jungle of modern office and apartment blocks, the church appears a self-contained island of separateness and spirituality.

The Church of the Holy Trinity measures 66 feet (20 m) in diameter. Its curved exterior is clad in pink granite, and one enters it through a portico lined with fin-shaped concrete columns. Four chimneylike structures arranged as a square protrude from the roof; their glass tops enable daylight to filter into the body of the church below, specifically to illuminate the altar. Twelve small, round windows glazed with different-colored glass ring the church, each representing one of Christ's apostles. Rectangular windows lower down illuminate the crypt area. **CH-M**

Évry Cathedral

Architect: Mario Botta

Completed: 1995 (begun 1992)

Location: Évry, Île-de-France, France

Style/Period: Postmodernism

After Évry, which is situated just south of Paris in the Île-de-France region of northern France, became a "new town" (Évry Ville Nouvelle) in 1965, there was an increasing demand for certain types of communal buildings to serve the needs of the growing population, including, in this predominantly Roman Catholic country, a cathedral. Thus it was that in 1992 the Swiss architect Mario Botta was commissioned to design such a place of worship, which was to be dedicated to Saint Corbinien.

Although some have unkindly likened it to a blast furnace, Évry Cathedral is both rich in symbolism and entirely suited in style to its new-town setting. The cathedral building is constructed in the form of a cylinder — 125 feet (38 m) in diameter — with a roof that slopes upward to a height of 112 feet (34 m) while following a diagonal slant, rather like an integral and asymmetrical spire. Planted around the edge of the roof in a circle are 24 living lime trees, which symbolize life and time. A skeletal-steel bell tower projects from the side of the cathedral like an upright handle. Red bricks, arranged to form a variety of geometrical patterns, clad the walls both inside and out. A low, arched stained-glass window is situated behind the altar, opposite the entrance. **CH-M**

Bonnefanten Museum

Architect: Aldo Rossi

Completed: 1995 (begun 1992)

Location: Avenue Ceramique, Maastricht, Limburg, Netherlands

Style/Period: Postmodernism

The Bonnefanten Museum — which was constructed alongside the River Maas, in Maastricht, Netherlands, between 1992 and 1995 — may look aggressively modern, but was, in fact, designed by Italian architect Aldo Rossi to complement the Dutch town's past. This is an industrial city (the

Bonnefanten Museum stands in the former ceramic-making district) with a rich artistic tradition, which is why Rossi was commissioned to create an appropriate setting for the region's collection of Old Masters and contemporary art.

The main museum building was constructed in an approximate "E" shape before being faced with a mixture of red brick, red trachyte and Irish freestone. At the end of the four-story central wing, overlooking the Maas in which its zinc cladding is reflected, is the museum's most striking element: a tall bullet-shaped tower (the "Cupola," or dome), which rises to a height of 92 feet (28 m), with a viewing platform encircling the top. Rossi included this eye-catching element partly to make a link with classical and neoclassical architecture and partly to act as a landmark in homage to the Netherlands' seafaring history. The visitor enters the museum through the telescope-shaped *Lichtraum*

("light room"), and once inside, a typically Dutch wooden stairway, measuring 115 feet (35 m) in length, provides access to the various wings and stories. **CH-M**

San Francisco Museum of Modern Art

Architect: Mario Botta

Completed: 1995 (begun 1989)

Location: 151 Third Street, San Francisco, California, United States

Style/Period: Neorationalism

In 1995, the San Francisco Museum of Modern Art (SFMOMA) celebrated the 60th anniversary of its establishment by moving from its previous home in the War Memorial Veterans Building to a new building on Third Street that it had commissioned from Swiss architect Mario Botta in 1989. Eye-catching on the outside and eye-pleasing on

the inside, Botta had designed a museum that both served its purpose perfectly and merited the critical acclaim it received.

The new SFMOMA building is large, at 225,000 square feet (68,580 sq. m), and rises to a height of five stories at the back. Constructed of precast concrete but clad in elegantly textured and patterned red brick, two stepped-pyramidal forms flank a central cylindrical tower faced with black-and-white-striped stone that rises between them. Not only is this tower a striking decorative addition to the Third Street facade, but its diagonal roof, which slants toward the viewer, is glazed, which means that it acts as a giant skylight illuminating the central atrium area below. Inside, a staircase leads visitors from the atrium to the galleries that are accommodated in the four stories above. SFMOMA also contains a theater, a café, a store, an education center, a study area and library, as well as an art-conservation center and administration offices. **CH-M**

Oriental Pearl Tower

Architect: Jia Huan Cheng

Completed: 1995

Location: Pudong, Shanghai, China

Style/Period: Postmodern

This remarkable postmodern concrete-and-steel structure is part of the ongoing project to enhance Shanghai's reputation as one of the world's leading economic powerhouses, and it is a tangible expression of China's new-found confidence and self-belief. The architect, a member of the Shanghai Modern Architectural Design Company Limited, designed a tower that, at 1,576 feet (468 m), is the tallest such structure in Asia and the third tallest in the world. Construction began in 1991, and it was completed four years later, instantly becoming one of the city's major landmarks.

The structure consists of 11 spheres of various sizes, the largest of which is 164 feet (50 m) in diameter. They are linked and supported by three columns that are each 30 feet (9 m) in diameter. The tower has three main observation levels, which are known as the Space Module, the Sightseeing Floor and Space City, and a revolving restaurant at 876 feet (267 m). It also contains various exhibition facilities, a number of other restaurants, a shopping mall and the 20-room Space Hotel. The look of the tower is symbolic and was inspired by a Tang Dynasty poem that talks of a string of pearls dropping onto a jade plate. **IW**

Dancing House

Architects: Vlado Milunic and Frank Gehry

Completed: 1996

Location: Prague, Czech Republic

Style/Period: Deconstructionism

The construction of this extraordinary building was backed by Vaclav Havel, the country's first president after the peaceful Velvet Revolution of 1989. Havel had lived in an apartment opposite the empty site, which was flattened by a bomb in World War II, and wanted to build a top-class piece of modern architecture on it. He first turned to a local designer, Vlado Milunic, but a Dutch company owned the site and wanted a foreign architect to work on the project, so Frank Gehry was brought on board.

The plan was drawn up using computer software originally created for aircraft and industrial design. The postmodern structure, which is nicknamed "Fred and Ginger" after the Hollywood movie stars Fred Astaire and Ginger Rogers, consisted of a flared glass tower on concrete pillars, "Ginger," that leans into a second concrete-clad tower, "Fred," which is topped by a twisted and perforated sphere constructed in metal sheeting. Their form was partly dictated by the site, as part of it had been lost due to road widening, and the flared look recaptures some of the lost space. The building is largely given over to offices, but there is also a rooftop restaurant. **IW**

Tokyo International Forum

Architect: Rafael Viñoly

Completed: 1996 (begun 1989)

Location: 5–1 Marunouchi 3-chome, Chiyoda-ku, Tokyo, Japan

Style/Period: High Tech

It is not surprising that South American architect Rafael Viñoly's design for this civic complex in Tokyo won a prestigious competition; it successfully addresses the multiple problems of how best to cater for a variety of cultural and business needs on a difficult site and in a practical and aesthetically pleasing manner.

The shape of the complex was dictated by the train stations to the north and south and the railroad track running alongside the 7-acre (28,329 sq. m) site to the east. Viñoly conceived three separate components for the complex. On the west side a long, thin rectangular slab element connects four roughly cubic structures that are graduated in size, with the smallest at the southern end. These structures are used as performance, exhibition and conference halls. Separated from these four halls by a central public plaza is an eye-shaped building, whose eastern side follows the curve of the adjacent railroad track. The 190-foot (58 m) high and 738-foot (225 m) long glazed Glass Hall is supported by two concrete pillars and, mainly, an intricate truss-and-tension system of reinforced-steel beams and cables. The main entrance lobby is connected to the four halls (which also have their own individual entrances) by means of elevated steel-and-glass pedestrian bridges or walkways. **CH-M**

Fuji-Sankei Communications Group Headquarters Building

Architects: Kenzo Tange Associates

Completed: 1996

Location: Odaiba, Tokyo, Japan

Style/Period: Metabolist

Armed with powerful new computer software, modern architects are producing ever more curvaceous buildings, whose biomorphic curves make undisguised connections with the natural world. The FCG Headquarters Building, as it is also known, offers an altogether more abstract approach to "organic" architecture, with its seemingly mechanistic grid hiding a secret debt to microbiological processes. Kenzo Tange, the senior figure in Japan's metabolist group, had a design approach that emphasized a building's ability to meet future needs through dynamic expansion instead of remaining fixed in its initial form. The name "metabolist" was derived from the group's use of natural metaphors, such as the cycle of accumulation and reduction displayed by cells found within living tissue.

Rising 25 stories out of the artificial island of Odaiba, the grid of the FCG Headquarters Building leaves many gaping voids between its walkways, suggesting that this mega structure has the capacity for further, inward, regeneration. After the first four floors, the building splits into two separate towers, linked by an immensely strong web of hollow box girder walkways that help brace them against the shock of Japan's frequent earthquakes. Caught in this net of aluminum-clad conduits hangs a gigantic titanium sphere, 105 feet (32 m) in diameter and divided into three to house a domed observation platform, restaurant and machine room. With its distinctive "Death Star" silhouette, the FCG Headquarters Building has become entirely synonymous with its media occupants and now forms a natural extension of their corporate iconography. **PC**

Museu De Arte Contemporânea

Architect: Oscar Niemeyer

Completed: 1996

Location: Niterói, Rio de Janeiro, Brazil

Style/Period: Late Modernism

Perched upon its rocky peninsula overlooking Guanabara Bay, the Museu De Arte Contemporânea (MAC) hovers like an architectural throwback to the science fiction comics of the 1950s. Despite the gallery's science-fiction aesthetics, its architect, Oscar Niemeyer, provides a surprisingly organic interpretation of its aerodynamic white form. In his eyes it is a budding flower, rising on its single stem from the nourishing pool of water at its base. The elegant form does indeed bear a marked resemblance to another florally inspired object, the iconic fiberglass Tulip chair by Eero Saarinen (1956), albeit on a much grander scale.

Rising on a "stem" some 30 feet (9 m) thick to a height of 52 feet (16 m), Niemeyer's reinforced-concrete flower holds a three-level gallery that displays João Sattamini's personal collection of Brazilian contemporary art. The gallery owes its existence entirely to Sattamini, whose long-term art loan to the city of Rio was conditional upon their commissioning Niemeyer to build a suitable means of display. Visitors enter in theatrical style by ascending a spiraling red boarding ramp that loops around to touch first one story then the next. The small footprint of the single column form allowed the architect to wheel his 164 feet (50 m) wide UFO to the very edge of the narrow site, improving the spectacular views from its 360-degree black-tinted windows. With this vantage point it performs the dual function of educational art-house and sensational observation platform. **PC**

Museum of Fruit

Architect: Itsuko Hasegawa
Completed: 1996 (begun 1993)
Location: Yamanashi, Japan
Style/Period: High Tech/Biomorphic

The three futuristic elements of Hasegawa's Museum of Fruit rest like gigantic dormant seeds half buried in the fertile soil. Perishable foodstuffs may seem a bizarre choice for a permanent exhibition, but in the context of the Kofu Basin's primary industry its subject is not so surprising. The area yields the biggest crops of deciduous fruits found anywhere in Japan, its slopes filled with swelling peaches, plums and grapes. The museum's forms echo this natural harvest but offer up a host of other metaphors, from fruit baskets and seed pods to palm houses and tree canopies.

The central structure is the Green House, its arched roof's ribs radiating out from either end like a globe's lines of latitude converging upon the poles. Reaching 66 feet (20 m) at its highest point, the Green House's humid climate supports a seemingly "lost world" of primeval fronds laden with tropical fruits. To the left lies the low glass dome of the Events Space, its theatrical auditorium linked to the Green House by a tunnel that doubles as a subterranean gallery. The Workshop Building, whose simple four-story education block is caged within a white steel pergola that will, in time, become a living mass of creeping plants, completes the trio. All this was engineered using the latest GSA dynamic stress modeling software to ensure that these man-made seeds can resist the seismic activity of the natural world. **PC**

BAPS Swaminarayan Mandir

Architect: Pramukh Swami Maharaj

Completed: 1997

Location: Neasden, London, England

Style/Period: Hindu

This *mandir* (temple) was the first purpose-built Hindu place of worship to be constructed in Europe, and it is one of the largest anywhere in the world still in use. It is also a monument to the importance of good organization in such community-based projects. Vast quantities of Bulgarian limestone and Italian Carrara marble were first shipped to India, where they were intricately carved by more than 1,500 local craftsmen, and then returned to the building site, where some 1,000 volunteers put them together piece by piece like a jigsaw puzzle in around three years.

The temple was inspired by His Divine Holiness Pramukh Swami Maharaj, the head of the Bochasamwasi Shri Akshar Swaminarayan Sanstha (BAPS) sect of the Hindu faith, and it was built along traditional lines as laid out in sacred Hindu texts. It consists of the *mandir* itself, a cultural center

and several other rooms. The temple is in reality a focal point for the local Hindu community and has several other non-religious functions — meeting place, sports and medical facility. It also houses an exhibition that seeks to explain the Hindu faith to the many non-Hindu visitors it receives each year. **IW**

National Center for Science & Technology

Architect: Renzo Piano Building Workshop

Completed: 1997

Location: Amsterdam, Netherlands

Style/Period: Contextual Modernism

Permanently moored at the end of Prins Hendrikkade Wharf, Piano's museum of science and technology is a consummate exercise in contextual architecture. Part of a larger program of urban renewal, its inter-active exhibits bring new life to the city's declining dockyards, encouraging tourists to repopulate this once bustling port.

With its sharply inclined bows jutting out over the water, the National Center for

Science & Technology's (NEMO) maritime form makes obvious connections with the area's past, but this naval analogy also extends to its material character. An architectural interpretation of plank-on-frame construction, it uses an underlying skeleton of steel girders to define the hull-like form. To this are affixed two-story-high panels of laminated wood, which are cloaked in turn by a distinctive outer layer of preoxidized copper cladding. This references the local shipbuilding heritage since, in the age of sails, the hulls of Dutch merchant ships were similarly sheathed in copper to protect their timbers during their long voyages to the East Indies. The museum's wedgelike form provides Amsterdammers with the bonus of a sloping roof terrace, whose elevated expanse of seating offers a rare vantage point from which to admire this famously flat city. In a final nod to the nautical context, a long inclined boarding ramp rises up from the quayside to reach the rear of the roof deck, allowing eager sunbathers to quickly embark upon this land-locked liner for a few hours' imaginary cruise. **PC**

The British Library

Architect: Sir Colin St. John Wilson

Completed: 1997 (begun 1984)

Location: 96 Euston Road, St. Pancras, London, England

Style/Period: Postmodern

That the British Library, Britain's national library, today houses around 150 million items and can accommodate 1,200 readers demonstrates what a huge building it is. And it was the need for more space and modern facilities, as well as the desire to bring together the British Library's disparate and dispersed collections, that drove the move from its previous home, the Reading Room at the British Museum, to a new purpose-built structure in the nearby St. Pancras district of central London.

In appearance, the 14-story British Library is of its time, being an asymmetrical, multilayered building constructed from such 20th-century materials as reinforced concrete. But it also complements its older neighbors: the red bricks cladding its exterior echo those used for the nearby St. Pancras Station, for instance. Most of the British Library's holdings are stored in four underground levels, with individual items being called up as and when they are required. Researchers consult such reading material in either the Humanities Reading Room (in the center of the building) or the Science Reading Room (in the east wing), both of which comprise three levels. Both also enjoy the benefit of natural light, which is admitted through skylights in the Humanities Reading Room and through windows in the Science Reading Room. **CH-M**

Petronas Towers

Architects: Cesar Pelli & Associates

Completed: 1997 (begun 1992)

Location: Kuala Lumpur, Malaysia

Style/Period: Regional High Tech

Soaring up into the blue Malaysian night, the illuminated rings of the Petronas Towers lend them the appearance of pulsing energy pylons plucked from the skyline of a 1930s Flash Gordon comic. A product of the fierce commercial rivalry between emerging "Asian Tiger" economies, their twin spires rise a triumphant 1,483 feet (452 m) above the Golden Triangle of Kuala Lumpur. From here they reigned for seven years as the world's tallest buildings, until they were usurped by Taiwan's exotic Taipei 101.

Rejecting Western skyscraper models, the towers' American architects sought out local precedents for their unique forms. The applied art of Malaysia's dominant Muslim religion provided the building's plan, each tower being extruded from a pair of interlocking squares with one rotated at 45 degrees to form the eight-point star found throughout Islamic crafts. Small circular in-fills between the stars' points adds further visual interest, the whole facade being executed in alternating bands of glittering stainless steel and green-tinted glass. These materials form a polished skin for the towers' massive concrete skeletons, whose structural columns measure 8 feet (2.4 m) thick at their base, and rest upon a concrete raft foundation supported by 104 barbette piles driven as far as 344 feet (105 m) into the ground. The final flourish is the "sky bridge" — a two-story structure that spans the gap between the towers at the 41st and 42nd floors, permitting workers to conduct an aerial commute across the void. **PC**

The Getty Center

Architect: Richard Meier
Completed: 1997
Location: 1200 Getty Center Drive, Brentwood, Los
Angeles, California, United States
Style/Period: Modernism

The J. Paul Getty Trust commissioned the Getty Center's design from architect Richard Meier in order to accommodate itself and the Getty Museum, as well as the Getty Conservation Institute, the Getty Research Institute and the other Getty institutes and programs funded by U.S. oil billionaire J. Paul Getty's vast wealth.

Most of the visitors to the Getty Center's elevated site in the Santa Monica Mountains, on the outskirts of Los Angeles, come here to view its renowned collection of antiquities, pre-20th-century art and photographs.

Parking space is provided in a seven-story underground area at the bottom of the hillside, visitors then being transported by tram up to the complex. The modernist buildings here were erected from reinforced concrete and steel and then clad in beige Italian cleft-cut travertine and light-admitting glass. Artifacts are displayed in five two-story galleries, or pavilions, whose top levels are linked by means of terraces and glazed walkways, as well as by underground passages. The pavilions are arranged along one axis, while office buildings follow the line of another, at a slight angle to the first, which reflects the natural topography. Along with numerous fountains and courtyards, the Getty Center's grounds include the meticulously planned (by Robert Irwin) Central Garden, the entire complex demonstrating a harmonious fusion of nature and culture. **CH-M**

Guggenheim Bilbao

Architect: Frank Gehry

Completed: 1997 (begun 1991)

Location: Bilbao, Spain

Style/Period: Deconstructionism

Much has been written about the Guggenheim Bilbao and its almost miraculous powers of economic regeneration, but the process of its pioneering construction is frequently neglected. Intended as the European outpost for the Guggenheim Foundation's vast art collection, the museum's architect, Frank Gehry, began by making a series of energetic on-site sketches. He translated these sketches into hundreds, if not thousands, of models compiled from masses of folded and crumpled card arranged in seemingly random forms. Having achieved his ideal composition, Gehry's physical models were then laser-scanned into the virtual world. The resulting digital data was exported into a computer program called CAITA, which was originally developed by the aviation industry to design planes such as the Mirage jet fighter. Given this pedigree, the program had little difficulty adapting to Gehry's immense steel-framed fuselage skinned in gleaming lock-seamed titanium plates.

The individual components were accurately fabricated off site using computer-controlled cutters guided by the model's data before being bolted together. A projecting layer of curved steel tubes then smoothed out the superstructure's hard edges, creating the familiar graceful contours that support the shimmering skin. With the architects, engineers and contractors all simultaneously sharing the same data the project was delivered on time and on budget (£44 million sterling or $72 million) without sacrificing any of the original model's sculptural panache. It was as though Gehry had been able to mold the building with his own hands, which, in effect, he had. **PC**

No.1 Poultry

Architects: Stirling Wilford Associates
Completed: 1998
Location: City of London, London, England
Style/Period: Postmodernism

This defiantly postmodern building stands amid an impressive array of earlier imposing structures, including the Bank of England, the Mansion House and the Royal Exchange. The older buildings are solid and serious as befits their financial and administrative functions, while No. 1 Poultry is quirky but with a hint of solidity in its facade. The brief for the building required the team led by James Stirling to create what was essentially a place of business, office and retail, but one that also had some public functions. Stirling proposed putting a public walkway through it at ground level and another point of access to an underground station.

The banded, colored stone of the curved exterior is restrained compared to the interior. The interior consists of a triangular space that is partly given over to brightly glazed tiles that are punctured by a regular pattern of windows, each of which is framed in a regular pattern of equally bright colors, including blue, pink and yellow. Stirling also included other non-business spaces within the building. There is a rooftop restaurant with its own separate entrance and an observation area. No.1 Poultry is a bold, some might say unsubtle, piece of postmodernist architecture, and one that still divides opinions. **IW**

The Millennium Dome

Architects: Richard Rogers Partnership
Completed: 1998 (begun 1996)
Location: Greenwich, London, England
Style/Period: High Tech

A structure ill-served by its contents, the Millennium Dome was deserving of far better press than the muddled "Millennium Experience" it sheltered within, since its graceful white canopy was alone in being delivered on time and on budget. The largest fabric structure in the world, the Dome's impressive circular footprint measures 1,050 feet (320 m) in diameter and rises to a height of 164 feet (50 m) at its center to envelope an exhibition area of around 861,000 square feet (80,000 sq. m).

Its familiar title is actually an engineering misnomer; this "colossus of domes" isn't a dome at all. Instead of behaving like a ridged architectural element, resting on the ground like an upturned saucer, Richard Rogers' tour de force consists of a complex web of cables under tension, all hung off yet more cables under tension. Over these steel threads stretches in excess of 1 million square feet (100,000 sq. m) of tensioned PTFE-coated glass-fiber fabric capable of supporting the weight of a jumbo jet despite being just $1/26$ inch (1 mm) thick. Installed in 144 separate panels, the canopy is held to the cables by 25,000 specially designed two-piece aluminum extrusion clamps fitted by hand by a dedicated team of abseiling contractors.

Happily, the Dome has been given a new lease on life as the O2 Arena. Its decidedly generous dimensions have translated into a concert venue with a capacity of 20,000. **PC**

Jean-Marie Tjibaou Cultural Center

Architects: Renzo Piano Building Workshop

Completed: 1998 (begun 1991)

Location: Nouméa, New Caledonia

Style/Period: Regional High Tech

Exactly 20 years after his competition-winning Centre Georges Pompidou (see page 385), the revered architect Renzo Piano found himself designing a building to immortalize a prominent adversary of French rule, as opposed to its elected head. Piano had won the contest to create a cultural center in memory of Jean Marie Tjibaou, a leading figure in the campaign for the recognition of the Kanak culture in the South Pacific French territory of New Caledonia.

Emblematic of this Polynesian way of life that had been almost extinguished by French colonial policies, the indigenous forms of Kanak's "Great Houses" provided Piano with his inspiration. He proceed to fashion a series of open-sided towers whose clusters of crisply cut fingers emulated the half-way stage in the old Kanak technique for creating the conical roofs onto their palm-sapling huts. However, instead of binding their ends together to form the usual peak, Piano left them pointing to the sky, symbolizing the continued growth of a civilization brought back from the edge of oblivion. The beautifully detailed towers, with their laminated iroko ribs and stainless-steel ties, help to ventilate the adjoining low-lying structures. The prevailing breeze passes over their hidden slanting roofs to create currents that draw fresh air through the interiors. The towers' open staves and crossed-braced elements also allow the center to resist the 143 mph (230 km/h) cyclone winds that occasionally blow across this tropical paradise. A sculptural blend of tradition and modernity, Piano's solution is a worthy monument to Tjibaou's enduring legacy. **PC**

Estação do Oriente

Architect: Santiago Calatrava

Location: Parque das Nacoes, Lisbon, Portugal

Completed: 1998

Style/Period: High Tech

The authorities of the Portuguese capital commissioned this multifunctional building from Spanish-born Santiago Calatrava in 1993 after a closed international competition. The brief was to create a new transport hub to the northeast of the city, close to its international airport, which would also be the gateway to a world's fair to be held some five years later. The overall long-term aim was to use architecture to push forward the regeneration of a down-and-out area around the National Park.

Calatrava's winning entry includes a subway station, as well as various train and bus services that are close to other buildings, including a shopping mall, concert facilities and exhibition spaces. Estação do Oriente ("Orient Station") is a classic piece of Calatrava's expressionist architecture in that it has bold structural forms that take their inspiration from nature. It is imposing yet delicate. The roof has the look of a vast marine skeleton, while the stunning roof canopy is clearly inspired by palm leaves. The station has three levels — the upper is home to the rail station, the middle level has its own shops but also gives access to the mall, and the lower level houses the metro and bus stations. **IW**

Jin Mao Building

Architects: Skidmore, Owings & Merrill

Completed: 1998

Location: 88 Century Boulevard, Pudong, Shanghai, China

Style/Period: Chinese High Tech

On its completion in 1998, the Jin Mao Building that the U.S. architectural firm of Skidmore, Owings & Merrill (SOM) designed to tower above the Chinese city of Shanghai's Pudong district was the tallest building in China, at 1,380 feet (421 m) high. That it has 88 stories is significant, since eight symbolizes prosperity in traditional Chinese belief. This belief also explains the Jin Mao Building's octagonal shape, which was created by surrounding an octagonal concrete shell with 16 steel-and-concrete columns. Its eye-catching form — reminiscent of a traditional Chinese pagoda — was achieved by dividing its floors horizontally into 16 sections, each being one-eighth smaller than the section below. The structure is clad in glass, supported by stainless steel, aluminum and granite and protected by aluminum latticework.

As well as offices, the Jin Mao Building accommodates the Shanghai Grand Hyatt Hotel, which occupies floors 53 to 87, and whose spectacular barrel-vaulted atrium is especially noteworthy. With a diameter of 89 feet (27 m), it extends from the 53rd floor all the way up to the 87th, resulting in a height of around 377 feet (115 m). It is ringed with corridors and staircases, which are arranged in such a manner that a sinuous, spiral effect can be admired when looking up or down. **CH-M**

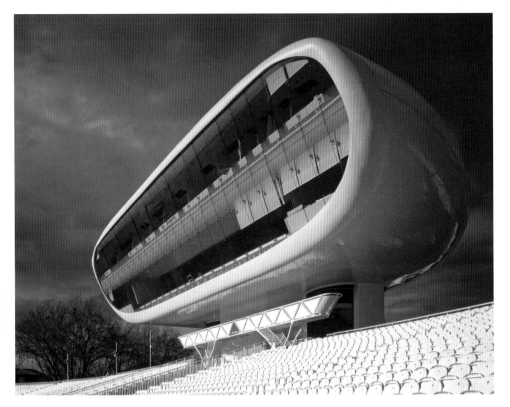

NatWest Media Centre

Architects: Future Systems

Completed: 1998

Location: Lord's Cricket Ground, London, England

Style/Period: High Tech/Futuristic/Blobitecture

The Marylebone Cricket Club may seem an unlikely patron for avant-garde architecture, but it was their hallowed corner of England that became the site of Future Systems' first major commission. Hovering between the Compton and Edrich grandstands, the NatWest Media Centre is the flying saucer of the sporting world — its Cyclops eye focused firmly on the batsman's crease. The center's banked tiers of seats regularly play host to up to 200 journalists and commentators who gaze through a long laminated-glass screen, which is tilted at 25 degrees to prevent the sun's reflection from blinding the players below.

The world's first all-aluminum building, measuring some 131 feet (40 m) long and 66 feet (20 m) deep, the center's smooth, aerodynamic skin is supported by a wealth of hidden welded struts and beams in a fabrication technique borrowed from the hulls of high-speed boats and racing yachts. The whole structure was actually prefabricated in a Dutch boat yard before being shipped across to England in 10-foot (3 m) wide sections to be welded into position. These exclusive connotations of hand-built motorboats must have sat comfortably with the spectators and players, and it might well explain why such a futuristic building was seen as perfectly palatable by a normally conservative institution. **PC**

Parc de la Villette

Architect: Bernard Tschumi

Completed: 1998 (begun 1982)

Location: Porte de la Villette, Avenue Jean-Jaurès, Paris, France

Style/Period: Deconstructionism

The Swiss-born French architect Bernard Tschumi's competition-winning design for the Parc de la Villette in Paris envisaged a park that looked quite unlike any other, in

France or elsewhere; although its red, skeletal elements did recall the work of such Russian constructionist architects of the 1920s as Vladimir Tatlin. In fact, Tschumi's park has been hailed as an important example of deconstructionist, anti-modernist landscape architecture, his stated aim being to create "the largest discontinuous building in the world" and thus to put form before function.

Tschumi worked toward achieving his aim by erecting 35 red-painted steel pavilions, or "follies," at various points in the park's grounds. The appearance of the follies, all deconstructed cubes, was abstract and varied, and their purpose was often unclear. In addition, although he planned the incorporation of a music center, a science museum, playgrounds, themed gardens and sports areas, functions were not obvious from forms. Few of this defiantly urban park's components looked particularly harmonious. Yet there was plenty to stimulate people's interest and imagination at the Parc de la Villette, and Tschumi had followed a few guiding principles in his design, which he based on the follies' points, the paths' lines and the sporting areas' planes, or curves. CH-M

Burj Al-Arab Hotel

Architects: Tom Wright and Khuan Chew

Completed: 1999

Location: Off Jumeirah Beach, Dubai, United Arab Emirates

Style/Period: Regional Modernism

The commission for this hotel — "Tower of the Arabs" in English — was given to British architect Tom Wright, who was asked to produce an iconic building that would become synonymous with Dubai. He produced a structure that looked like the sail and masts of a dhow, a traditional local sailing boat. Work commenced in 1993, and the structural work was largely completed in six years. The hotel stands on an artificial island that took three years to complete. It involved driving 230 concrete piles into the bedrock and then linking the new island to the mainland by a curved private bridge.

The overall shape is reminiscent of a sail

held between two wings, each a steel exoskeleton wrapped around a reinforced tower and split into a V-shape that echoes the shape of a dhow's masts. The space between the two wings, which is enclosed with Teflon-coated fiberglass panels, is actually a vast atrium and is the tallest in the world. The

five-star hotel, which has 202 rooms and even its own helipad, was once the tallest hotel in the world, at 1,053 feet (321 m). It has an overall floor space of 1.2 million square feet (111,500 sq. m). Anglo-Chinese designer Khuan Chew was responsible for the opulent interior. **IW**

Samsung Jong-Ro Tower

Architects: Rafael Viñoly Architects

Completed: 1999 (begun 1994)

Location: Seoul, South Korea

Style/Period: High Tech

It is easy to understand why the Samsung Jong-Ro Tower in Seoul, South Korea, is nicknamed "The Bottle-Opener," since the tall steel-framed structure's most distinctive feature — the gap at the top that comprises around a third of its total height — does indeed give it a passing resemblance to this low-tech kitchen utensil. With its exposed-steel and aluminum elements and glass curtain wall, the tower is most emphatically high-tech, however, as befits a building commissioned by a global electronics company.

The tower had already been partly constructed when, in 1994, Samsung launched a competition for a design that would accommodate other commercial ventures, literally over and above the originally envisaged 20-story shopping mall.

The prize was won by the U.S. firm Raphael Viñoly Architects, whose ingenious concept incorporated the existing triangular structure. Thus, the supportive steel frame and three stair-and-elevator cores were extended, with two stories being added beneath the cantilevered steel cornice that marked the next stage of the design. It comprised office space and was further differentiated from the section below by its flat, rather than curved, facade. Only the three cores rise above the cornice to the roof (which is illuminated at night), giving a total height of 436 feet (133 m). **CH-M**

Canary Wharf Station

Architects: Foster & Partners

Completed: 1999 (begun 1991)

Location: Canary Wharf, London, England

Style/Period: Modernism/High-Tech

Improved public-transport links with the rest of London were a prerequisite of the redevelopment of the Docklands area, which saw the erection of such towering new landmarks as One Canada Square, also called the Canary Wharf Tower (see page 421). And when it came to London Underground, London's subway system, it was decided that the Jubilee Line should be extended.

Opened in 1999, the most highly acclaimed Jubilee Line Extension station is Foster & Partners' Canary Wharf, which is so huge — 1,027 feet (313 m) long, 115 feet (35 m) wide and 89 feet (27 m) deep — and so dramatically lit that it has been compared to a cathedral. The light is largely natural and is filtered through, and directed inward, by the curved steel-framed and glass-clad canopies that shelter the ground-level entrances. Above ground, the space between these entrances has been turfed and planted with shrubs to act as a public park and welcome area of greenery within an increasingly built environment. From the vast ticket hall, 20 banks of escalators lead passengers into the bowels of the station, which was constructed within the old (drained) West India Dock, where there are two platforms. Gray reinforced concrete was used for the walls and supportive columns, whose bases are clad in stainless steel. **CH-M**

The National Centre for Popular Music

Architects: Branson Coates

Completed: 1999 (begun 1996)

Location: Sheffield, Yorkshire, England

Style/Period: High-Tech

The Millennium Dome is by no means an isolated case of an excellent structure being let down by its contents. The National Centre for Popular Music opened in March 1999 with the help of an £11-million ($5 million) grant, only to close just seven months later with debts of over £1 million ($460,000). Intended as a music-orientated exhibition space, the center's poorly conceived program of "interactive music experiences," marooned in provincial isolation, failed to entice the media-savvy public. Only the architecture proved to be worthy of an encore.

Occupying a square plot, the four faceted-drums each measure 65 feet (20 m) across and are collectively clad in 2,016 panels of Sheffield's ubiquitous stainless steel. Separating them is a two-story cruciform circulation space that allows each drum to act as an independent volume — ideal for hosting temporary exhibitions or separate functions with different opening hours. The rooftop's curious curving nozzles form part of the natural ventilation system and can rotate in unison, like synchronized gun turrets being aimed at the prevailing breeze. The fact that their abstract forms were derived from the shape of a record player's pick-up arm holds a certain irony, as the drums now reverberate to the spinning vinyl of DJs entertaining the population of Sheffield Hallam University, whose student union the building has since become. **PC**

Bluewater

Architects: Eric R. Kuhne Associates

Completed: 1999

Location: Dartford, Kent, England

Style/Period: Postmodernism

The out-of-town shopping mall has special pariah status in the British media, cast as the assassin of the main street despite the latter's

self-inflicted wounds of congestion and bland uniformity. In this context Bluewater is actually creating something new: an accessible and coherent retail environment and wide-ranging amenities without traffic or bad weather. Critics may turn up their noses, but the public vote with their feet, and the throngs of shoppers that flood Bluewater every weekend validate its approach. Designed as a destination for everyone from teenagers to the elderly, its three themed malls each cater to the tastes of a different audience. Linking them together are the "anchor stores," whose product lines have broader appeal.

Architecturally, the studied use of vernacular forms, such as the ventilation cowls based on Kentish oasthouses (conical kilns used to dry hops), sets this scheme far above its peers. Each mall has a distinct visual identity, complete with artworks and paving, that follows themes linked to their county host. Of the three ceilings, the Rose Gallery's is most spectacular. Based on the shallow domes of Sir John Soane's original Bank of England, the glazed cutaway arches flood the mall with natural light to create the impression of an indoor street. All commercial architects should invest in such attention to detail. **PC**

The Reichstag

Architects: Foster & Partners

Completed: 1999 (begun 1995)

Location: Platz der Republik 1, Berlin, Germany

Style/Period: High Tech/Neoclassical conversion

Most of the Reichstag, or parliament building, that stands in the government district of Berlin, Germany's capital city, comprises a neoclassical building dating from the late 19th century. It was devastated by fire in 1933, shortly after Hitler became chancellor, heralding a 66-year hiatus in its role as the headquarters of one of the most important instruments of democratic government in Germany. Since 1999, the Reichstag has again served as the home of the German parliament, which is today called the Bundestag (Federal Parliament), rather than the Reichstag (Imperial Parliament).

This, then, is a building with a momentous history. In reconstructing its central core after Germany's reunification in 1990, the Reichstag's past, as well as its future, had to be taken into account by the British architectural firm of Foster & Partners. The dome that rises above the Reichstag's roof is an impressive centerpiece. It refers to the original cupola, as well as being a symbol of modernity and trans-

parency — literally so, as two spiral walkways leading to an observation deck offer the public a bird's-eye view of the parliament proceedings taking place below. The steel-framed glazed dome — 75 feet (23 m) high and measuring 131 feet (40 m) across — incorporates a mirrored cone suspended from the center that reflects natural light into the debating chamber. **CH-M**

Tate Modern

Architects: Herzog & de Meuron and Sir Giles Gilbert Scott

Completed: 2000

Location: Bankside, London, England

Style/Period: Moderne with Minimalist Conversion

In 2004, a panel of 500 British art-world professionals voted Marcel Duchamp's *Fountain* the most influential work in 20th century art. Duchamp's controversial "ready-made" sculpture consisted simply of a ceramic urinal signed with the comic pseudonym "R. Mutt." Unsurprisingly, the merit of transforming industrial objects into works of art through such minimal interventions continues to divide public opinion. By contrast, the transformation of Bankside Power Station into the luminous Tate Modern has been an unprecedented popular success, providing one of Britain's great art institutions with a much-needed second London home.

The young Swiss practice of Herzog & de Meuron won the competition to convert Scott's cathedral of industry, thanks to their design's sensitive retention of the original structure. They effectively created a building within a building, inserting a seven-floor steel frame inside the boiler house to provide both galleries and administration space. Peeping above the previous roofline is a double-story glass penthouse named the "Lightbeam," which holds a panoramic restaurant and private members' rooms. But the real showstopper is the turbine hall, which once echoed with the whir of a thousand fan blades but now hums with quiet conversation as visitors stand to admire its installations. These installations can be truly monumental in scale, thanks to the five-story high volume and 36,600 square feet (3,400 sq. m) of floor space. Though its galleries do indeed contain an artist-authorized replica of Duchamp's *Fountain*, it is Bankside itself that has proved to be the Tate's ultimate "ready-made." **PC**

The Lowry

Architects: Michael Wilford & Partners

Completed: 2000

Location: Salford Quays, Manchester, Lancashire, England

Style/Period: Postmodernism

Built to stimulate the regeneration of the disused Salford Quays, the £105-million ($200 million) Lowry stands at the terminal of the Manchester Ship Canal. Containing both auditoriums and art galleries, it bears the name of artist L.S. Lowry, who immortalized the city through his evocative paintings of smoking mills and factories, all populated by his trademark stickmen and stickwomen.

The Lowry's neutral stainless-steel cladding reflects both the dramatic northern skies and the still waters of the docks, imbuing it with an industrial character that acknowledges the heritage of the site. Given the numerous roles that the building was required to perform, architect Michael Wilford conceived the plan as a series of distinct volumes, each housing a separate function, that congregate within the site's triangular boundary. Largest of these steel-sided forms is the Lyric Theatre, a versatile 1,730-seat auditorium that backs onto the smaller 466-seat Quay Theatre, deftly allowing them to utilize the same backstage machinery. The funnel-like tower forms the peak of the composition, and its light diamond-patterned lattice structure pokes up out of its spiraling steel cladding. The tower wraps around a white concrete drum housing the world's largest collection of Lowry's paintings and drawings, some 430 in all, a selection of which are displayed in rotation in the galleries below. Undeniably successful, this cultural beacon for the arts succeeded in attracting over 250,000 more visitors than originally anticipated in its first year alone. **PC**

Frederick Phineas and Sandra Rose Center for Earth and Space

Architects: Polshek Partnership Architects

Completed: 2000 (begun 1992)

Location: New York, New York, United States

Style/Period: High Tech

A stunning clear-glass cube containing a huge blue-tinged sphere, the Rose Center was designed for the American Museum of Natural History as the successor to the old Hayden Planetarium (demolished in 1995), in which to accommodate and display the most sophisticated technology and latest scientific information about the universe. Built on the edge of Central Park West at 81st Street, this $210-million project was entrusted to James Stewart Polshek and Todd H. Schliemann of local New York firm Polshek Partnership Architects.

The 120-foot clear glass cube dramatically reflects its surroundings, taking on the colors of the day. The glass has been purified of the iron that gives other glass a tint. Inside, the floor is paved with black terrazzo that sparkles with crystal chips. On the ground floor is the Cullman Hall of the Universe, which houses model planets and a full-sized replica of the Mars Rover. Alongside is the Gottesmann Hall of Planet Earth, the highlight of which is the 15½-ton (14 metric tonnes) Willamette meteorite that fell in the Pacific Northwest 10,000 years ago. Major NASA events are broadcast live and breaking astronomical news is displayed on a 13½-foot (4 m) long screen. The sphere itself is supported by a muscular steel tripod and six struts. Three glass elevators take visitors up to a sixth floor bridge and provide access to the new 420-seat Hayden Planetarium. Visitors leave through a spiraling exit ramp that charts 13 billion years of stellar evolution. **SW**

Queen Elizabeth II Great Court

Architects: Foster & Partners

Completed: 2000 (begun 1999)

Location: British Museum, Great Russell Street, London, England

Style/Period: High Tech

The Queen Elizabeth II Great Court — the Great Court for short — was opened by Britain's Queen Elizabeth II herself in 2000, and since then it has functioned as an area where visitors to the British Museum can access galleries and education facilities, meet up, buy refreshments or simply rest for a while.

Designed by the British architectural firm Foster & Partners, the Great Court comprises the courtyard area — measuring 302 x 240 feet (92 x 73 m) — at the center of Sir Robert Smirke's original quadrangular building (see page 188), which was previously inaccessible to the public. At the heart of this stands Sydney Smirke's Rotunda, also called the old Reading Room (see page 208). The Great Court's most impressive feature is its vast undulating glass roof, which comprises 1,656 pieces of glass and 4,878 steel components, and which makes it Europe's largest covered public square. Small green ceramic circles dot the glass roof to minimize solar glare, so that the play of sunlight on glass creates wonderful effects but does not dazzle. The Great Court's masonry elements, including the Rotunda's cladding (which conceals 20 reinforced-concrete columns supporting the center of the roof) were mainly constructed from Portland stone, a traditional London building material. **CH-M**

Al Faisaliyah Tower

Architects: Foster & Partners and Buro Happold

Location: Al Faisaliyah Complex, Riyadh, Saudi Arabia

Completed: 2000

Style/Period: High Tech

With the Middle East awash with oil wealth, the richest producers have embarked on a major building spree and no country more so than Saudi Arabia. This tower is a perfect metaphor for the region's new status, and when it was built it was the first skyscraper in the Middle East, at some 875 feet (267 m) high. It is now the centerpiece of a complex that also includes a hotel and two other buildings. The mixed-use tower contains offices, apartments and retail outlets, all topped by a spherical three-tiered restaurant, the Globe, made of golden glass.

The architects came up with something a little different from the skyscraper norm by designing a tapering building with a sphere that was supposedly inspired by a ballpoint pen. The frame consists of reinforced-concrete spars, one at each corner, that arch elegantly to the uppermost point — the nib.

The tower was also designed with the local climate very much in mind. Various high-tech methods are employed to keep the interior cool and shade the tower from the region's fierce temperatures. **IW**

Eden Project

Architects: Nicholas Grimshaw & Partners

Completed: 2001

Location: St. Austell, Cornwall, England

Style/Period: High Tech

The Eden Project was developed in part to help rejuvenate one of the less prosperous regions in England and in part to build state-of-the-art greenhouses to conserve endangered exotic plant collections from around the world. The site chosen was a 57-acre (23 ha) disused china-chalk quarry, something of a blot on the local countryside. The architect, Sir Nicholas Grimshaw (1939–), produced a design based on a series of biomes, or geodesic domes, that each provides the right set of climatic conditions for the plants housed within it. The largest, the biggest greenhouse in the world, is the Humid Tropics Biome, and it covers 51,148 square feet (15,590 sq. m) and rises to 180 feet (55 m).

The domes consist of a number of mostly hexagonal sheets that range in size up to 29 feet (9 m) across and are made from a triple layer of ETFE (ethylene tetrafluoroethylene) thermoplastic laminate, which is held in place on a tubular steel framework. The foil was a key part of the design, as it allows ultraviolet light to pass through into the biomes and is self-cleaning. It lasts for around 30 years and is recyclable, thereby fitting in with the project's overall environmentally aware ethos. The project has become Cornwall's most-visited tourist attraction. **IW**

below, a narrow courtyard that is open to the skies, which divides the building in two. Tokyo being vulnerable to seismic activity, the structure's concrete-and-steel skeleton was protected with built-in flexibility, thanks to its rear "stepping columns," viscoelastic dampers and cantilevered floors.

The most fascinating aspect of the 13-story building, however, is its glass facade. Piano had a traditional Japanese lantern in mind when planning it, and the result is curtain walls on all four facades that incorporate 13,000 glass blocks, which are mainly opaque and mainly measure 18 x 18 inches (45 x 45 cm). A few clear-glass blocks at eye level allow passers-by to admire the Hermès products on display, and they are also used at the entrance and corners. By day the building is filled with diffused light, and by night it glows like the lantern that inspired Piano. CH-M

Museu Oscar Niemeyer

Architect: Oscar Niemeyer
Completed: 2001 (begun 1967)
Location: Curitiba, Paraná, Brazil
Style/Period: International Modernism

Although the Oscar Niemeyer Museum has existed only since 2003, some of its components have stood in the Brazilian city of Curitiba for far longer than that. The long, low and largest building of this two-structure museum was completed by the architect himself in 1967, when its intended function was to serve as an educational institute. When it was later decided to turn it into a museum dedicated to architecture, design and the visual arts, it was Niemeyer — despite his advanced age (he was born in 1907) — who remodeled it, whereupon it was opened as the New Museum (Novo Museu) in 2002. With the completion of his idiosyncratic eye-shaped annex in 2003, the complex was formally renamed the Museu Oscar Niemeyer (Oscar Niemeyer Museum), although it is popularly known as the Museu do Olho (Museum of the Eye).

Constructed from reinforced concrete, the "eye" rises on a rectangular, mosaic-adorned plinth above a pool of water and is accessed by means of the spiral walkway that

Maison Hermès

Architect: Renzo Piano
Completed: 2001 (begun 1998)
Location: 5-4-19 Ginza, Chuo-ku, Tokyo, Japan
Style/Period: High Tech

The turn-of-the-millennium building that the French luxury-goods company Hermès

commissioned Italian architect Renzo Piano to design for its flagship store and corporate headquarters in Japan combines Western and Eastern influences to elegant effect. When it was completed in 2001, the new Maison Hermès, which is situated in Tokyo's commercial Ginza district, stood tall, at 148 feet (45 m) high, and thin, at 36 feet (11 m) wide. There is a rooftop garden and, far

connects the annex with its parent building. Glass-and-steel curtain walls based on a diamond-shaped grid mask the "eye's" two flat facades, providing natural illumination for the two stories within, which accommodate an exhibition space and refreshment areas. **CH-M**

Teatro Armani

Architect: Tadao Ando

Completed: 2001 (begun 2000)

Location: Via Borgognone 59, Porta Genova, Milan, Italy

Style/Period: Modernism/Minimalism

Giorgio Armani created not only one of the world's best-known haute-couture fashion houses, but he also won a reputation for expensive, understated elegance and pared-down glamour in the process. And so, it was vital that his new global headquarters in Milan, Italy's fashion capital, reflect and project this brand image, as well as serve various business-friendly functions. Japanese architect Tadao Ando — admired for his restrained, but exquisite, light-manipulating designs and his simple use of top-quality materials like concrete, sandstone and glass — was a perfect match.

The Teatro Armani (Armani Theater), which was completed in 2001, is situated on the site of a former chocolate factory in the Porta Genova area of Milan, previously an industrial district that is now being regenerated. The low brick building is entered through a sliding panel of glass. Visitors then walk along a 328-foot (100 m) long concrete-lined and subtly lit corridor, which is bisected by a line of concrete columns as it slopes upward to the foyer at the back. The complex includes an inside courtyard, complete with decorative pool, a large dining room, administrative offices and showrooms. The pièce de résistance, however, is the theater, which was created primarily as a venue for fashion shows and accommodates 682 armchairs, which are mounted on moveable wooden bleachers on either side of a metal runway. **CH-M**

these hoards of guests is the station's most distinctive element: a 131-foot (40 m) wide disc that hovers, saucerlike, on four stilt legs clad with a gleaming skin of satin-finished stainless steel. It is the disc that announces the station's presence across the flat Expo plain, acting as an easy reference point for disorientated businesspeople. The curved steel rings a central skylight of diffusing glass, which allows light to shine directly down thorough a tube containing the steel-and-glass-walled elevator, linking ticket hall to platform concourse. Illuminated at night, this conduit takes on the appearance of a teleporter, transporting passengers at warp speed to the awaiting trains that have been guided in by its alien beacon. **PC**

Swan Bell Tower

Architect: Hames Sharley
Completed: 2001
Location: Barrack Square, Perth, Western Australia, Australia
Style/Period: Postmodernism

On June 12, 1771, the bells of St.-Martin-in-the-Fields rang out in celebration at Captain Cook's return from his antipodean voyage of exploration. Few who heard their peels that day could have ever imagined that these same bells would leave London for the land Cook had claimed for England. Removed from the venerable St. Martin's due to their damaging vibrations, the 12 bronze bells became a gift from the cities of London and Westminster to the state of Western Australia, marking the 1988 bicentenary of Australia's founding. Together with six new bells, the rechristened "Swan Bells" form the center-piece of the regenerated Barrack Square and are housed within a futuristic campanile on the banks of Perth's Swan River.

Soaring 271 feet (83 m) into the sky, the bells' new home contains faint echoes of the church from which they came: the vertical glazing bars and horizontal ringed supports recall the geometry of James Gibbs' 18th-century spire. Hung within a specially constructed six-story chamber, the bells are suspended 77 feet (24 m) above the ground to replicate their original position. Wrapping around this bell chamber are four sweeping

Expo Station

Architects: Foster & Partners
Completed: 2001
Location: Singapore
Style/Period: High Tech

The theatrical grandeur of railway stations around the world reflects their symbolic role as a point of arrival, and the place where travelers' all-important first impressions are formed. Sitting astride the twin tracks of the Changi Airport Line into Singapore, the Expo Station dutifully forms a dramatic gateway to the country at large, while acting as the principal entrance to the 62-acre (25 ha) Expo complex.

The tracks it serves run in raised cast-concrete viaducts that keep the electrified lines free from possible inundation by the region's torrential rains. The station can also cope with deluges of passengers, its efficient landing stage being capable of handling up to 17,000 people per hour. Waiting to greet

copper "sails" that hint at both Perth's maritime connections and the snugly folded wings of the river's eponymous black swans. Described by its architects as the "world's biggest musical instrument," the tower includes a system of adjustable sound-proof doors and louvers that either muffle the bells' peels during practice or direct it out toward the river or city as required. **PC**

Bodegas Ysios Winery

Architect: Santiago Calatrava
Completed: 2001
Location: Laguardia, Álava, Spain
Style/Period: High Tech/Biomorphic

The desire to expand its wine-production facilities, and to make a splash as it launched a new wine (Ysios), led the Bodegas and Bebidas group to commission Spanish architect Santiago Calatrava to design a building that would both function efficiently as a winery and be a talking point. Calatrava fulfilled both briefs with his Bodegas Ysios Winery, which opened in 2001.

The 86,114-square-foot (8,000 sq. m) winery lies amid a vineyard growing tempranillo grapes at the foot of the Cantabrian Mountains, north of the town of Laguardia. At heart it is a rectangular concrete structure — the two longer (northern and southern) walls measure 643 feet (196 m) in length and the two shorter (eastern and western) ones 85 feet (26 m). Two shallow pools, divided by a granite bridge, shimmer at the foot of the southern wall. The southern facade — the main elevation, which faces the highway — is faced with cedar slats, which are reminiscent of wine barrels, while the sidewalls are clad in aluminum, as is the roof. And the undulating roof, whose laminated wooden beams describe sine curves that echo the mountain peaks beyond, is the winery's most extraordinary feature. At the center the roof extends over a first-floor glazed balcony, the visitor's center, with wine being produced on the story below. **CH-M**

Jewish Museum

Architect: Daniel Libeskind

Completed: 2001

Location: Berlin, Germany

Style/Period: Deconstructionist

This remarkable Deconstructionist building by Daniel Libeskind was commissioned to tell the story of Germany's Jewish community from its earliest times to the present day, with particular emphasis on their mass murder and persecution during the Nazi period. The museum's very architecture, as much as its collections and exhibits, is meant to inform. The museum, of zinc-clad reinforced concrete, is meant to express and explore three central features: the community's role in Germany's historical development, the Holocaust itself and the need to remember the Europe-wide tragedy.

It was a personal project for Libeskind, who lost many family members in the Holocaust. He incorporated specific references and symbols into his design. These touches produced disorientating and unconventional spaces that have been given names such as the Stair of Continuity and the Garden of Exile and Emigration. Some exhibition space has been deliberately left empty to symbolize the loss of the Jewish community's contribution to Germany under the Nazis, while the entrance is by way of a staircase and tunnel in a concrete tower that rises through the floor of an adjacent museum dedicated to German history. The museum opened in 2001. **IW**

Modern Art Museum of Fort Worth

Architect: Tadao Ando

Location: Fort Worth, Texas, United States

Completed: 2002

Style/Period: Modernism

Some architects can be overwhelmed by large spaces, yet the prolific Osaka-born Tadao Ando came up with a monumental design that perfectly suited the 473,600-square-foot (44,000 sq. m) site and was not lost within it. He responded by creating a large modernist museum, and he added gardens and a sizeable artificial reflective lake that not only made excellent use of the space, but also gave the whole complex a light and welcoming feel. The museum, with its vast acreages of glass, shimmers above the lake and is reflected in it.

The museum actually has five rectangular blocks that are closely interrelated, and each has a double fabric. The outer structure of each consists of 40-foot (12 m) high glass panels held in place by steel frames, within which Ando constructed an altogether more substantial concrete block. The exterior structure has a flat roof that is supported on Y-shaped reinforced-concrete columns. The glass walls also allow the visitor to admire the view of the other buildings in what has been dubbed Fort Worth's cultural district, as well as the downtown area a few miles away. **IW**

Downland Gridshell

Architect: Edward Cullinan

Completed: 2002

Location: West Sussex, England

Style/Period: Eco High Tech

Set within 50 acres (20 ha) of rolling West Sussex countryside, the Weald & Downland Open Air Museum offers a window onto five centuries of wooden architecture. The majority of its 50 historic buildings arrived in component form, to be conserved then carefully pieced back together. Much of this painstaking restoration work was carried out in rudimentary facilities, but with funding the museum was able to commission a purpose-built workshop and storage facility that has become a tourist attraction in its own right.

Resting like some immense peanut shell among the trees, the Downland Gridshell's undulating cedar cladding largely obscures the root of its name. Its novel lightweight frame was constructed from 120-foot (36 m) long green-oak laths, which were fabricated using traditional wood joints combined with special modern glues. These laths were laid on top of a scaffold raised 8 feet (2.5 m) above the final floor level to create a flat sandwiched-lattice pattern four laths thick, which is held together by loose-fitting metal clamps. Previous gridshells had achieved their desired forms by brute force, employing hydraulic pistons to jack up their centers. Here a gentler approach was used: the raised scaffolding was gradually removed around the lattice's edges to permit gravity to act as sculptor. This method resulted in far fewer joint failures. Breaking new ground at almost every stage of its construction, the Downland Gridshell has successfully added a new chapter to the material history the museum has done so much to preserve. **PC**

Serpentine Pavilion

Architect: Toyo Ito

Completed: 2002

Location: Kensington Gardens, London, England

Style/Period: High Tech

Every summer, the Serpentine Gallery — an art gallery situated in London's Kensington Gardens, adjacent to Hyde Park — commissions a pavilion from a world-renowned architect. In 2002 its choice was the Japanese metarationalist Toyo Ito. Ito's pavilion — which took six months to erect and stood for three — caused a sensation during its brief existence in the gallery's grounds, where it served as an auditorium and café.

Working with British structural engineer Cecil Balmond, Ito designed a structure whose intersecting lines and geometrical shapes were both reminiscent of the elegant simplicity of his native country's art of origami and breathtakingly complex. Its computer-generated forms were created by overlaying repeating algorithmic patterns onto a square, which was then manipulated into a cube shape, so that the pavilion seemed to have been formed from triangles and trapezoids. The sections that made up the pavilion were constructed off site and then assembled like a jigsaw puzzle. Because it was made of glass and white-painted aluminum, a magical effect was created by the apparent lack of a supportive frame, as well as by the mixture of transparency and translucency. Once inside, the overall impression was rather like finding oneself at the heart of a giant light-filled square snowflake. **CH-M**

Federation Square

Architects: Dan Bates and Peter Davidson (Lab Architecture Studio)

Completed: 2002

Location: Melbourne, Victoria, Australia

Style/Period: Eclectic modernism

One of the most important architectural developments in Melbourne, the unconventional Federation Square, with its U-shaped complex and elevated plaza, has quickly become a major attraction for visitors. Designed by Don Bates and Peter Davidson of Lab Architecture Studio, Federation Square, or Fed Square as it is affectionately known, is home to a range of museums, galleries, cinemas, stores and restaurants. These facilities are built around two public spaces: the covered Atrium and the outdoor St. Paul's Court, which flows into the main square. The enclosed Atrium is five stories high with glazed walls and roof, although an elaborate underground system ensures the space is kept cool in summer and warm in winter. The paving in the Atrium and St. Paul's Court is predominantly bluestone, while the main square's ocher stone blocks follow the Outback-inspired design known as Nearamnew, created by artist and historian Paul Carter.

Stalked by controversy from the start, the original design underwent several changes. With costs soaring over budget, the Square, originally intended to be ready to mark Australia's centenary in 2001, finally opened in 2002. The square can hold up to 10,000 people and has defied its critics to become a popular site for cultural and musical events. **EW**

Cathedral of Our Lady of the Angels

Architect: José Rafael Moneo

Completed: 2002 (begun 1999)

Location: Los Angeles, California, United States

Style/Period: Modernism

Part of Spanish architect José Rafael Moneo's brief, when he was commissioned to design Los Angeles's new Roman Catholic Cathedral of Our Lady of the Angels, was to reflect the diversity of the people who live in the Californian "City of Angels." This 21st-century cathedral is situated alongside the 101 (Hollywood) Freeway, with Hollywood's larger-than-life image and industry being echoed by the cathedral's size (it is the world's third largest cathedral).

Constructed from partly textured, angular concrete elements, the cathedral's adobe-colored hue links it with the region's Spanish-mission-style architecture. Above the altar, framed by an alabaster lantern (or window), is a 50-foot (15 m) tall concrete cross that is also prominent from the outside. A bell tower measuring 156 feet (48 m) in height stands alongside the building, as does a "carillon wall." To gain access, worshipers climb steps (symbolizing ascension to the spiritual plane) that lead through a number of plazas before passing through a pair of bronze doors and then along the ambulatory, which encircles the nave. The 300-foot (91 m) long nave — all 58,000 square feet (5,388 sq. m) of it — can accommodate a congregation of 3,000. The ceiling, which is clad in cedarwood, is set at a height of 85 feet (26 m), and the floor is paved with Jana limestone. **CH-M**

Integrated Transportation Center

Architects: Terry Farrell & Partners

Completed: 2002 (begun 1996)

Location: Incheon International Airport, Seoul, South Korea

Style/Period: High Tech

The sprawling Integrated Transportation Center that the British architectural firm Terry Farrell & Partners designed for Seoul's Incheon International Airport came into its own in 2002, the year of its completion, when South Korea hosted soccer's World Cup tournament and fans flooded in from all over the globe.

The 3-million-square-foot (278,700 sq. m) site on which the complex was constructed was reclaimed land, originally having been two islands situated off Seoul's coast. Its approximately 30-mile (48 km) distance from South Korea's capital necessitated an integrated transportation center to accommodate subway and regular and high-speed train stations, as well as a bus station, parking areas, taxi stands and car-rental and other drop-off and pickup points. A huge underground level caters for the rail services and parking, while the ground-level Great Hall connects these areas with the two airport terminals located to the north and south. The extensive glazing of this steel-framed hall provides daylight, as well as views of aircraft and the landscaped gardens that have been planted with indigenous Korean plants. An airfoil consisting of glass and white stainless-steel panels stands on three legs atop the structure, above a 50-foot (15 m) wide oculus that extracts warm air when necessary. Appropriately, when viewed from the air, the overall impression is of a bird in flight. **CH-M**

Falkirk Wheel

Architects: RMJM Architects, Ove Arup and
Butterley Eng
Completed: 2002
Location: Tamfourhill, Falkirk, Scotland
Style/Period: Futuristic/High Tech

Having helped kick-start the Industrial
Revolution, Britain's canal system fell victim
to the forces it had set in motion. The
increasing movement of materials and ideas
brought about its nemesis, the railways,
whose speed and ease of maintenance put
the stately canal barges at a permanent
disadvantage. Abandoned to the elements,
or actively filled in, these former industrial
arteries have been gradually resurrected
since the 1970s as a popular form of
recreation.

An icon of this renaissance is the Falkirk
Wheel, a 21st-century solution to spanning
the 115-foot (35 m) difference between the
Forth & Clyde Canal and the Union Canal.
Emerging from the hillside along a
reinforced-concrete aqueduct, pleasure craft
enter one of two watertight gondolas, which
are held in the ringed hands of the wheel's
outstretched arms. Once the doors are
closed, 10 hydraulic motors rotate the arms
around the central axle, the gondolas being
kept horizontal by a simple system of gears.
The wheel uses Archimedes' principle to its
advantage: the boats automatically displace
their weight in the water to keep the wheel's
arms in near perfect equilibrium. Despite its
futuristic spurs, the wheel has an air of
Victorian solidity, thanks to its 15,000
specially made bolts that resist the shifting
stresses of rotation, which would have
defeated modern welded seams. With its
loaded gondolas arcing gracefully through
the air, the Falkirk Wheel is a reminder that
speed is not the only virtue of travel. **PC**

Yokohama International Passenger Terminal

Architects: Foreign Office Architects
Completed: 2002
Location: Yokohama, Japan
Style/Period: Eco High Tech

This terminal had a difficult gestation. In
1994 the city launched an international
competition to find a suitable design, but the
development was halted when the country
was hit by an economic recession. It was
finally given the go-ahead after Japan and
South Korea were picked to host the 2002
World Cup, and Yokohama was chosen to
host the final of soccer's most prestigious
tournament. The intention of the architects
was to create a welcoming point of access to
the city for ordinary travelers, although the
terminal is now largely used by large luxury
cruise ships.

The pier was considerably different from
previous designs, in that the Britain-based
architects strove to allow visitors to enter the
building by one route and depart by another.
Various different materials were used to
emphasize the different paths. The building's

main level contains arrival and departure facilities, customs and immigration, food and drink outlets, and stores, while part of the roof is given over to a public viewing platform. Yokohama was the first Japanese port to be opened to the Western world, and the terminal is an architectural expression of the links between East and West. **IW**

Beddington ZED

Architects: Bill Dunster Architects

Completed: 2002

Location: Wallington, Surrey, England

Style/Period: Eco Tech

Commissioning architect Bill Dunster to design a new community of 82 sustainable homes, the Peabody Trust created a benchmark for carbon-neutral living. Dunster's holistic approach began with the energy used to produce and transport materials. Largely sourced from within a 35-mile (56 km) radius and utilizing over 98 tons (100 metric tonnes) of reclaimed steel from Brighton Station, BedZED, as the community is known, began saving carbon before a single brick was laid.

A "Zero Energy Development," the scheme has several strategies for minimizing fuel consumption. The intelligent north-south orientation of the terraces allows homes and live-work spaces to reap the benefits of passive solar gain and strong natural light, respectively. Banks of photovoltaic cells are built into triple-glazed facades, while the roofs are populated by colorful coxcomb ventilators — part of a heat-exchange system that uses outgoing stale air to warm the fresh air they draw in. Consequently, the community's energy consumption is 10% of an equivalent standard development. Lauded and awarded by politicians and professional bodies alike, the brilliantly conceived BedZED regrettably remains a hopeful prototype. **PC**

The Deep

Architects: Terry Farrell & Partners

Completed: 2002

Location: Kingston-upon-Hull, Yorkshire, England

Style/Period: Postmodernism

Like a constant sentinel watching the confluence of the rivers Hull and Humber, Hull's aquarium, the craggy Deep, sits hunched upon its triangular peninsula. With its wedgelike form ending in a blunt, glazed nose, it mirrors the bows of the supertankers that sail by its predatory gaze. If the building looks heavy and muscular, it is because it had to be. The concrete substructure, with its piles extending 98 feet (30 m) into the peninsula, cradles the deepest single aquarium tank in Europe, going down 33 feet (10 m) in places. The volumes involved are gigantic: the combined tanks contain some 627,000 gallons (2,850,000 L) of carefully filtered water.

Raised around these tanks is a substantial frame of almost 882 tons (800 metric tonnes) of structural steel, which is clad in 13-by-6½-foot (4 x 2 m) panels of machine-cut marine-grade aluminum. The carefully stratified layers of color and pattern punctuated with fissurelike windows clearly convey the architect's concept of exposed geological strata, as if this aquarium had just been forced to the surface by tectonic activity. This seismic metaphor is continued through the sequenced exhibits that take visitors back through the history of our oceans in an abstracted slice of the earth's crust. Having descended down from the bright top floor to the dark, mysterious depths, the Deep's guests are ushered into a glass-walled elevator that whisks them back up through the shark-infested tank to emerge into daylight once more. **PC**

Bibliotheca Alexandrina

Architect: Snøhetta

Completed: 2002

Location: Alexandria, Egypt

Style/Period: Postmodernism

Destroyed in the 4th century CE, the legendary Library of Alexandria remained a fabled memory until Professor Mahdouh Lofti Diwa persuaded the Egyptian government to resurrect its legacy of learning. Intended as the catalyst for an education-led economic revival within the Middle East, the library became the subject of an international architectural competition, which was won by the unknown Norwegian firm of Snøhetta in 1989.

Twelve years and U.S.$220 million later the library was ready, with 500,000 books on its shelves and a further 8 million volumes in closed stacks. Students and scholars sit down to study them in an awe-inspiring round reading room, 525 feet (160 m) in diameter, whose 14 terraced platforms are capable of accommodating 2,200 users. Oblique references to Ancient Egypt abound, the sloping ceiling being supported by a forest of concrete columns with flared capitals that recall the temples of Karnak and Luxor. The library's exterior is simultaneously ancient yet modern, with a south facade of riven Aswan granite blocks into which the languages of the world have been incised like huge hieroglyphs. The library's simple cylindrical form tilts at 16 degrees so that

one edge sinks beneath the earth while the other rises into the air, its pitched circular roof sinking below the horizon like the disc of the sun god, Ra. Most ingenious of all is this roof's aluminum structure, in which alternating triangular sections are folded inward in order to bounce reflected light off the library's ceiling and down to the readers below. **PC**

Parliament Library

Architect: Raj Rewal

Completed: 2002 (begun 1991)

Location: New Delhi, India

Style/Period: Regional Modernism

Whereas most of New Delhi's parliament complex was designed by Raj-era British architects, the Parliament Library that was opened in 2002 was, by contrast, the creation of an Indian. In combining his country's ancient Mogul and Hindu architectural traditions with modern construction methods in an innovative design, Raj Rewal furthermore expressed India's complicated, yet dynamic, 21st-century character.

The low-profile Parliament Library comprises four stories (two of which are below ground and house book stacks). Its ground plan is based on a square enclosed by another square, with circular structures anchoring the corners (the outer, north-western corner apart). The walls of the 592,000-square-foot (55,000 sq. m) library are clad in red and yellow sandstone, with the multi-domed glass, steel and concrete roofs that rise above the main areas being the most spectacular feature. The central glazed dome contains reflective glass that illuminates but also prevents sunlight from dazzling or overheating those inside. The Parliament Library is entered by one of four lobbies, one on each side of the outer square. Inside, the area beneath the central dome acts as the hub and provides access to the reading room, auditorium, cafeteria, libraries and meeting rooms. The outer structure incorporates a cloisterlike corridor, while open courtyards fill the unused spaces between the inner and outer squares. **CH-M**

Poundbury Village (Phase 1)

Architect: Leon Krier

Completed: 2002 (begun 1988)

Location: Poundbury, near Dorchester, Dorset, England

Style/Period: Neoclassical/Neovernacular

Britain's Prince Charles, the Prince of Wales and also the Duke of Cornwall, is well known for his preference for traditional, vernacular architecture and dislike of modernism. He therefore chose an architect whose views accorded with his own to plan his experimental Poundbury development on Duchy of Cornwall land in 1988. That architect was the Luxembourg-born Leon Krier, and although other architects have since been responsible for designing specific buildings on the 400-acre (162 ha) site to the west of Dorchester in the English county of Dorset, they were working within guidelines set down by Krier.

Construction work began in 1993, and it is envisaged that Poundbury Village will eventually boast 2,500 residences and accommodate a population of about 6,000 people. The aim is to use high-quality local materials and to conform to a variety of low-rise period English building styles, so that the village looks both unmistakably English and as though its components have sprung up at random, over the course of centuries. This is also why stores and other communal buildings are situated in different spots rather than in a particular zone. And reflecting its pre–World War II inspiration and prioritizing of human beings, cars are banished to parking spaces at the backs of the houses, while streets are relatively narrow and winding. **CH-M**

Esplanade – Theaters on the Bay

Architects: Michael Wilford and Partners and DP Architects

Completed: 2002

Location: Singapore

Style/Period: Postmodernism

Designed by the UK-based Michael Wilford and Partners and DP Architects of Singapore, the Esplanade – Theaters on the

Bay is on six hectares of Singapore's waterfront overlooking Marina Bay, not far from the famous Singapore Lion.

The complex encompasses several performance areas. The 2,000-seat theater rises over four levels, but no seat is more than 130 feet (40 m) away from the stage, which is itself the largest performing stage in the country. The 1,600-seat concert hall boasts world-renowned acoustics designed by Russell Johnson, and it includes a reverberation chamber and adjustable acoustic canopy. An outdoor theater caters for open-air performances, while Singapore's first arts library is situated on the third floor. The structure also holds two smaller studios, capable of seating between 220 and 250 people, as well as a 2,314-square-foot (215 sq. m) exhibition space offering panoramic views over the bay. The twin domes, clad in glass and aluminum sunshades, are affectionately known as the "durians" because of their resemblance to the native prickly and pungent Singaporean durian fruit. Others liken them to the eyes of an insect. Since their opening in October 2002, the Theaters on the Bay have become regarded as one of Singapore's most unique and instantly recognizable structures. **EW**

Cincinnati Contemporary Arts Center

Architect: Zaha Hadid

Completed: 2003 (begun 2001)

Location: 44 East 6th Street, Cincinnati, Ohio, United States

Style/Period: Deconstructionist

Cincinnati's privately funded Lois & Richard Rosenthal Center for Contemporary Art, or simply, Contemporary Arts Center (CAC), was intended to act as a catalyst in encouraging as many people as possible to engage with contemporary art. To this purpose, the 80,000 square feet (24,384 sq. m) of space within hosts an ever-changing, interest-stimulating selection of exhibitions. The building is situated in a busy urban location at the intersection of Walnut and 6th Street, and, thanks to the vision of London-based architect Zaha Hadid, it entices passers-by to enter it.

One of the ways in which Hadid's wide but narrow rectangular six-story creation draws in visitors is by means of an "urban carpet," which is an expanse of concrete that leads from the sidewalk through the columned portico, into the lobby and on to the mezzanine level, ending in a curve behind the staircase. This, in turn, takes visitors on a narrow, zigzagging route upward to the galleries, which are of different shapes and

sizes and interconnect in a way that Hadid likened to the pieces of a three-dimensional jigsaw puzzle. When viewed from the outside, these spaces protrude according to their interior design, and it is this uneven, geometrical effect, along with the mixture of reinforced concrete, steel, aluminum and glass, that makes the facade's appearance both eye-catching and unique. **CH-M**

Kunsthaus Graz

Architects: Peter Cook and Colin Fournier (Spacelab)

Completed: 2003

Location: Graz, Austria

Style/Period: Blobitecture

Nicknamed "the friendly alien," the 197-foot (60 m) wide and 75-foot (23 m) high Kunsthaus Graz (Graz Art Museum), begun in 2001, was built to celebrate the city of Graz's position as Cultural Capital of Europe in 2003. Built of reinforced concrete over a steel frame, its huge external shell is covered in blue Plexiglas with nozzles erupting from its surface, which were designed to admit daylight. It is impossible to overlook or ignore. Within the outer casing on the east side of the structure lies a matrix of 930 fluorescent tubes, and the brightness of each can be changed individually. Through this BIX facade (BIX is short for "big" and "pixels"), the building itself becomes a giant screen overlooking the city center and capable of displaying messages or films relevant to the exhibitions held within. It is a work of art built to display other works of art.

The Kunsthaus' role is to exhibit modern and contemporary art from the 1960s onward. The glass-enclosed lower level holds a store and café, and visitors reach the upper exhibition spaces via vast moving walkways. Designed by Peter Cook and Colin Fournier, working together as Spacelab, the Kunsthaus was shortlisted in 2004 for the Royal Institute of British Architects' Stirling Prize for excellence in architecture. **EW**

from the shimmering chain-mail dresses of designer Paco Rabanne, combining chic fashion statement with shock-value structure to inject the Selfridges brand with some much-needed adrenalin. The monolithic blue bulk of the exterior is coated in Monolastex, a durable liquid plastic normally used for painting lighthouses, which should give many more years of wear than the average impulse purchase.

Inside, a vast tapering central atrium with progressively wider openings creates a core of natural light that floods into every floor. The void is crisscrossed by sleek futuristic escalators whose white fiberglass and reinforced-plaster-clad curves appear to morph seamlessly into the walls. With every organic element seemingly molded from a single block of plasticine, Selfridges is the epitome of "blobitecture." PC

Spaarne Hospital Bus Station

Architects: NIO Architecten

Completed: 2003

Location: Hoofddorp, Netherlands

Style/Period: Biomorphic/Blobitecture

Polystyrene might seem an unpromising material for architecture, but the avant-garde NIO Architecten have successfully employed the ubiquitous white foam to create the largest building in the world made entirely from synthetic materials. Wrapping around itself like a snoozing boa constrictor, the Spaarne Hospital Bus Station looks as though it might contemplate swallowing the green and blue buses that nervously circle its concrete plinth. Its architects dubbed it the "Amazing Whale Jaw," imagining the bonelike forms to be the beached remains of a vast ocean-going mammal.

An impressive 164 feet (50 m) in length, the whole building was made off site using computer-controlled cutting machines, before being delivered in five sections to be glued together and sprayed with a final unifying coat of polyester. The lightweight sections were easy for workmen to maneuver into position, but they wasted no time in bolting the snake to the ground, as it would have slithered away in a strong breeze. All the necessary functions have been

Selfridges

Architects: Future Systems

Completed: 2003

Location: Bull Ring, Birmingham, England

Style/Period: Blobitecture/Biomorphic

Poised, as if preparing to devour the schools of shoppers that flow across its curving footbridge, the new Selfridges department store looms over Birmingham like a creature from the black lagoon. Its retro reptilian skin is a glittering array of over 15,000 anodized-aluminum discs, like polished pinheads, bolted to the undulating facade of sprayed-concrete render that hugs the contoured layers of expanded steel mesh. Future Systems' inspiration is said to have come

accommodated within the form, including trash cans, bench seats, recesses for lighting and even a staff room for the bus drivers to sit in, quietly drinking tea in heavily insulated comfort. Originally an off-white hue, the station soon began turning a mottled green, adding still further to its serpentine aesthetic. PC

Walt Disney Concert Hall

Architect: Frank Gehry

Completed: 2003

Location: Los Angeles, California, United States

Style/Period: Deconstructionist

With its sequences of shivering lines and undulating waves, Walt Disney's daring *Fantasia* offers an abstract vision of classical music. A very personal project absorbing many thousands of dollars, Disney's 1940 masterpiece took 28 years to turn a profit, but it is now regarded as a modern classic. Wishing to create a permanent legacy of her husband's love of music, Lillian Disney gifted $50 million in 1987 toward the creation of a home for the Los Angeles Philharmonic. The competition to realize this vision was won by Frank Gehry with a scheme that addressed orchestra, audience and the city at large.

Designing from the inside out, he focused on the acoustic quality of the 2,265-seat auditorium, using a steeply banked "vineyard" arrangement to bring patrons closer to the musicians. His generous Douglas-firclad lobby opens directly out onto the street, welcoming pedestrians into a "living room for the city." Begun in 1992, work stalled in 1994 when a series of natural and economic disasters befell LA, causing funds to dry up. Work thankfully resumed in 1999, aided by Gehry substituting steel for stone to save $10 million. This economy allowed him to explore increasingly fluid geometries that were more evocative of sound. The new billowing-sail forms were made from Japanese stainless steel, with wire-brushed surfaces to prevent excessive glare. Opened in 2003 to rapturous reviews in the music press, the energetic abstract lines of the Walt Disney Concert Hall add an appropriately animated presence to a regenerated downtown LA. **PC**

Tod's Omotesando Building

Architect: Toyo Ito

Completed: 2004

Location: Tokyo, Japan

Style/Period: Modernism

Completed in 2004 and standing seven stories high, the Tod's Omotesando Building is a striking example of modern architecture reflecting and interacting with the natural world around it. Set within Tokyo's tree-lined Omotesando Avenue, the intricate branch displays of the trees resonate in the building's external lattice design, particularly in winter months when the trees are bare. With 270 windows, the overall impression is one of light and space, and glass and concrete blend together seamlessly with impressive results. In common with many other structures in Japan, Tod's Omotesando Building is set on a shock-absorbing foundation.

The building, designed by Toyo Ito for the Italian footwear retailer, covers over 86,000 square feet (8,000 sq. m); it is a focal point within this busy up-market shopping area, and it is ideally designed to reflect the luxury of the goods available within. Inside, the external design is again reflected by the stairways, by the size and shape of individual sections and by the overall sense of light, both natural and artificial. Alongside the store itself, the Tod's Building holds offices and, on the top floor, the Tod's headquarters boardroom that opens out onto a roof garden. **EW**

30 St. Mary Axe

Architects: Foster & Partners

Completed: 2004

Location: City of London, England

Style/Period: Eco High Tech

Modern office towers are synonymous with conspicuous consumption, their electricity meters whirring around the clock as they power elevators, pump water and circulate air over many floors. No strangers to tall commercial buildings, Foster & Partners began a quest for greater office efficiency with the help of an enlightened client, the insurers Swiss Re. The return on Swiss Re's architectural investment was 30 St. Mary Axe (also known as the Swiss RE Tower and quickly dubbed "the Gherkin" by an irreverent press), whose entire design is geared to minimal energy consumption.

Looking ready to blast off from London's Square Mile, its sleek ballistic exterior is a rigid exoskeleton that acts as both facade and structure, creating a column-free interior that can be fully penetrated by natural light. It stands 590 feet (180 m) tall with 41 floors, and each of its circular levels is divided into six radiating fingers, leaving six triangular shaped voids in between. This standard plan is then rotated on each successive floor, linking the voids together to form the tower's distinctive black lines, which twist around like the rifled grooves on an immense artillery projectile. These voids are the building's lungs, which draw fresh air up the tower through natural convection, contributing to an overall energy saving estimated at up to 50 percent. The spirals end beneath a tinted glass "nose-cone" containing an occupant-only restaurant, whose dramatic views must have proved a crucial sweetener for many a business lunch invitation. Ever ingenious, Foster & Partners have delivered that rarest of things: an office tower with green credentials. **PC**

Scottish Parliament

Architects: Enric Miralles, Benedetta Tagliabue
and RMJM
Completed: 2004
Location: Holyrood, Edinburgh, Scotland
Style/Period: Regional Modernism

Yoked by the Act of Union, generations of Scotland's elect sat grudgingly in their neighbors' capital to participate in the democratic process. Alongside their English colleagues, they debated within London's Palace of Westminster until a 1997 referendum devolved many powers back across the border. Mindful of the centuries of forced separation, Scotland's First Minister Donald Dewar sought to break with past conventions and forge a physical union between the legislature and the land it governs. The result of his persuasive campaign, the new Scottish Parliament remains a controversial structure, both economically and aesthetically, and a stark contrast to the almost authoritarian formality of Westminster.

The competition-winning design was by Spaniard Enric Mirralles, and its plan is said to represent the concept of the ancient Greek "agora," an open place of public assembly where people gathered to support the democratic ideal. Instead of a completed scheme, Mirralles presented the jury with a seductive design proposal — a handful of bent stalks and folded leaves, which he proceeded to arrange upon the table, creating an organic diagram for a complex that seemingly flowed out of the landscape. Those leaves and stalks are everywhere, woven into the fabric of the building from sinuous steel microphone stands to the lobby's 12 sweeping skylights, jostling like a school of fish. An ode to natural materials and contemporary craftsmanship Mirralles' visual vocabulary successfully conveys Dewar's concept of the parliament embodying the land itself. **PC**

Taipei 101

Architects: C.Y. Lee & Partners

Completed: 2004

Location: Taipei, Taiwan

Style/Period: Regional High Tech/Megastructure

Rising a decisive 184 feet (56 m) further than Malaysia's Petronas Towers, the record-breaking Taipei 101 was officially declared the world's tallest building on December 31, 2004. Topping out at 1,667 feet (508 m), its 101 floors are serviced by the world's fastest elevators, whose double-decked cars can make the ascent from ground to 89th floor in a mere 39 seconds. Eight identical stacked modules, whose sides lean out at 7 degrees to reduce solar glare and improve the panoramic views for its occupants, create the tower's distinctive stepped profile. The building's weight is borne by an underlying structure of eight "megacolumns" devized by American engineers Thornton-Tomasetti. Reaching up to the 62nd floor, these immense elements have a cross section of 10 x 8 feet (3 x 2.4 m), and their steel walls are up to 3 inches (8 cm) thick, being packed with concrete pumped in at 10,000 pounds per square inch (703 kg/sq. cm).

Though the architects cite the native bamboo shoot and flower as their initial inspiration, the tower's estimated 771,619-ton (700,000 metric tonne) weight places an entirely unnatural amount of stress upon the earth's crust. In a region where earthquakes are common, this strain has become a controversial issue, but still the competition to be the tallest building continues unabated, and it may not be long before Taipei 101 finds itself usurped by an even loftier contender. **PC**

Seattle Public Library

Architects: Rem Koolhaas/OMA

Completed: 2004

Location: Seattle, Washington, United States

Style/Period: Eclectic Modernism

Opened in May 2004, Seattle Public Library's unorthodox and striking diamond-shaped steel, glass and aluminum 11-story structure rises majestically through eight horizontal layers. Chosen from among 29 bidders to design the building, Dutch architect Rem Koolhaas, named the Pritzker Architect Prize Laureate in 2000, worked with Joshua Prince-Ramus to create a fascinating modern library on a steep site with a 29-foot (9 m) height differential.

The five internal platforms are designed to appear to be floating, increasing the sense of space and light, while bright yellow escalators add strong blocks of color. The several distinct areas include a vast "living room" that lies under a 49-foot (15 m) high sloping glass wall, the "book spiral" that runs over four stories and displays the entire non-fiction collection in a continuous series of shelving, and a 275-seat auditorium on the ground floor. In total, this 362,987-square-foot (34,000 sq. m) library has the capacity to hold some 1.4 million books and other reading materials. The library also contains 400 public computer terminals and parking for 143 vehicles. In 2005 the Seattle Public Library won an American Institute of Architecture (AIA) Honor Award, and in 2007 it was listed 108th in an AIA public poll on America's favorite architecture. **EW**

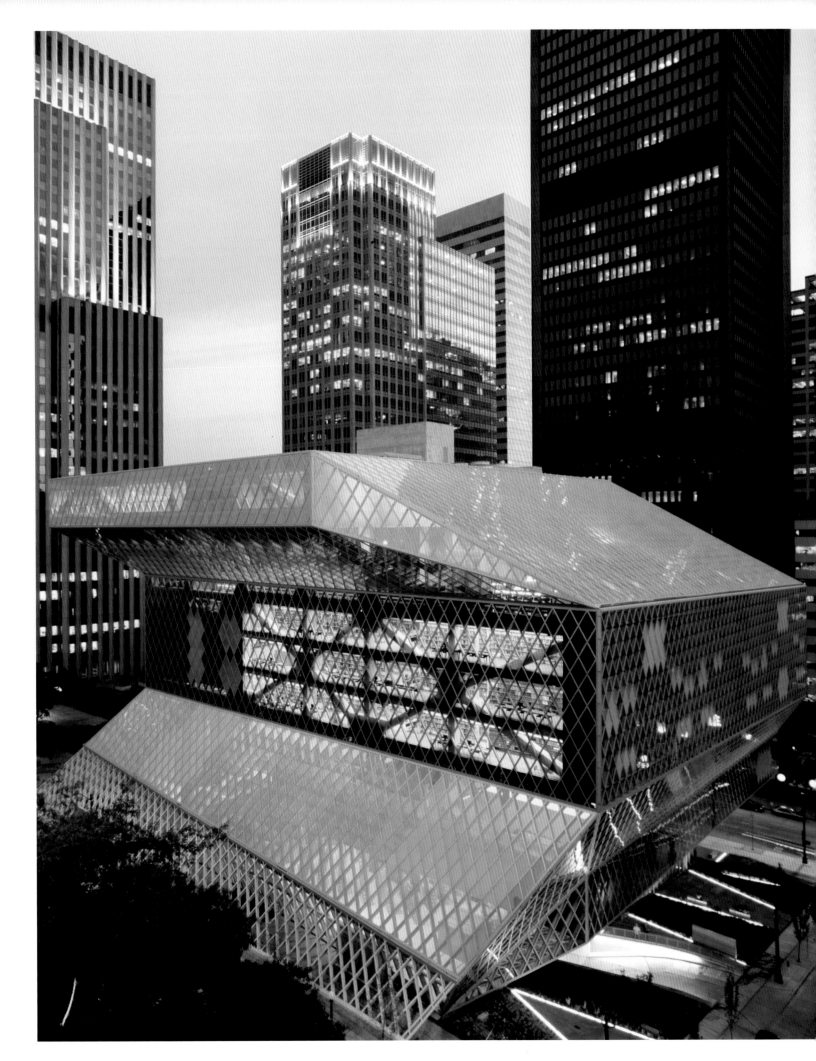

Millau Viaduct

Architect: Foster & Partners and Michel Virlogeux

Completed: 2004

Location: River Tarn Valley, Millau, France

Style/Period: High Tech

Come the months of July and August, a French exodus occurs as the urbanites of Paris take to their cars and head off to holiday on the Mediterranean coast. Many choose to take the Route A75, a modern toll-free highway that runs 211 miles (340 km) from central Clermont-Ferrand to coastal Béziers. Having driven at speed for much of their journey, vacationers used to find themselves ensnared by the notorious traffic black spot of Millau, a small town lying in the trough of the Tarn Valley. With its modest river bridge causing polluting tailbacks that could be measured in miles, a solution to this annual problem was urgently needed.

The result was the world's tallest vehicular bridge, whose cable-stayed road deck allows motorists to fly across the void at an average of 886 feet (270 m) above the valley floor. Seven slender pylons, whose graceful concrete profiles help reduce the deflection caused by prevailing strong winds, support the 1½-mile (2.46 km) long bridge. The tallest pylon rises to a staggering 1,125 feet (342 m) — higher, in fact, than the Eiffel Tower. Taking just over three years to construct, this ambitious project cost 394 million euros (around U.S.$600 million). Far from sending the now bypassed Millau into decline, the viaduct has stimulated unprecedented growth, with hotels, restaurants and business parks springing up in its wake. It seems the viaduct designed to help vacationers along their way has become a regenerative tourist attraction in its own right. **PC**

Phaeno Science Center

Architects: Zaha Hadid and Mayer Bährle

Completed: 2005

Location: Wolfsburg, Germany

Style/Period: Deconstructionist

The home of automotive giant Volkswagen since 1938, Wolfsburg boasts a long history of advanced engineering. Looking to re-brand the town as a center of science and technology, the local council held a competition for an interactive museum to kick-start their education-based economy.

Cruising at low altitude, like an angular star destroyer, the concrete prow of Zaha Hadid's winning Phaeno Science Center marks the launch of this campaign. Its unworldly appearance is enhanced by the undulating ramps and curves of the surrounding lunar landscape that visitors must negotiate before boarding the craft. The center floats 23 feet (7 m) above the plaza on 10 inverted concrete cones that erupt from this park of dunes and craters. By elevating the building, Hadid created a second public realm beneath the vessel's hull, which is eerily illuminated by dozens of fluorescent tubes hidden in square cast recesses. Carved into one of the cones, the blue glow of the coffee bar shines out like a teleporter waiting to whisk visitors to the wonders of the galleries above. Once inside the museum, visitors are confronted with a similar rolling landscape of seamless poured resin, which is sucked down in places by the concrete vortexes of the supporting feet. This unrestrained fluidity was only made possible through the largest single use of self-compacting concrete ever attempted in Europe. A special super-plasticizing additive permitted the concrete to flow freely into its futuristic mold without trapping pockets of air, neatly placing new technology at the heart of Wolfsburg's education initiative. **PC**

Casa da Música

Architects: Rem Koolhaas/OMA

Completed: 2005

Location: Porto, Portugal

Style/Period: Deconstructionist

Officially opened in April 2005, four years behind schedule, the Casa da Música has received international critical acclaim. Designed by Dutch architect Rem Koolhaas, it was originally intended to celebrate the city of Porto's position as Cultural Capital of Europe for 2001. The building's unusual white faceted-concrete exterior houses two auditoriums, rehearsal rooms, a restaurant, a roof terrace and parking for 600 vehicles. A continuous route of stairs, platforms and escalators allows access to all the spaces around the main auditorium.

The main auditorium seats just over 1,200, and its stage is large enough for 110 musicians and 143 choral singers. The smaller auditorium provides a flexible space capable of holding 300 people sitting or 650 standing. Corrugated glass across two walls in the main auditoriums was designed both for optimal acoustic effect and its striking good looks; it also allows diffused daylight into the concert space. The innovative design, however, retains the conventional shoe-box shape for the auditoriums, which is considered to provide the best possible acoustics. Folded glass "curtains" elsewhere in the building provide slightly distorted views of the city. In 2007 the Casa da Música won the prestigious Royal Institute of British Architects' European Award, with the jurors describing it as "intriguing, disquieting and dynamic." **EW**

National Assembly for Wales

Architects: Richard Rogers Partnership

Completed: 2005

Location: Cardiff Bay, Cardiff, Wales

Style/Period: Eco High Tech

"Transparency" has become something of a byword in politics, and while the politicians may not always live up to their rhetoric, the same cannot be said for the architecture of Richard Rogers' National Assembly for

Wales. Perched upon its stepped plinth of dark Welsh slate, the seat of the newly inaugurated assembly translates the transparency of Mies van der Rohe's Farnsworth House (see page 328) into the public realm, wrapping its many functions in a curtain of crystal-clear low-iron glass.

To create a suitably stately presence, the architects designed a startling signature roof whose undulating surfaces suggest the motion of the waves in Cardiff Bay beyond. Its underside clad in western red cedar, the roof's steel structure allows it to extend far beyond the glass box's walls like a broad hat brim. It shelters the wide flights of steps that welcome the electorate up into the lobby, from where they may take their seats in the public viewing gallery that rings the circular debating chamber. Set deep within the plinth, the chamber is capped with a conical ceiling whose skylight incorporates a mirrored cone to bring natural light flooding down onto the assembled members below. Externally clad in cedar, this ceiling can be seen erupting out of the plinth like a wooden volcano to morph into the roof's underside. A model of modern democratic architecture, the Welsh assembly has a clarity that few institutions can equal. **PC**

De Young Museum

Architects: Herzog & de Meuron and Fong and Chan Architects

Completed: 2005

Location: San Francisco, California, United States

Style/Period: Modernism

Following an earthquake in 1989, the original De Young Museum, set in San Francisco's Golden Gate Park, was deemed vulnerable to further tremors, a conclusion that quickly impacted on its ability to attract exhibitions. The decision was made to build a new structure capable of withstanding further quakes, and the new state-of-the-art facility opened to the public in October 2005.

Designed by the Swiss firm Herzog & de Meuron and Fong and Chan Architects in San Francisco, the building addresses the problem of its location near the San Andreas Fault by incorporating a series of sliding plates that allow it to move up to 3 feet (1 m). Equally important was integrating the building into the park. As a result, over 163,120 square feet (15,000 sq. m) of copper — which will change to a greenish hue as it oxidizes over the years — cover the entire structure, while other natural materials, including stone, glass and wood, have been used. Over 300 new trees, including redwood and eucalyptus, have also been planted inside and outside the

building, and pathways weave in and out, providing a seamless continuity between museum and park. A distinctive feature is the 144-foot (44 m) nine-story spiral tower topped by an observation deck giving panoramic views over San Francisco's famous bay. **EW**

Torre Agbar

Architect: Jean Nouvel

Completed: 2005

Location: Barcelona, Spain

Style/Period: Modernism/High Tech

Rising 474 feet (144 m) into the sky, the, sometimes controversial, bullet-shaped Agbar Tower — named after the first syllables of its owners, Aguas de Barcelona — has four basements, 35 floors and 4,400 windows with sensor-regulated louvers that automatically tilt to eliminate direct sunlight. Designed by French architect Jean Nouvel, it opened in June 2005 and was inaugurated by the King of Spain in September of that year.

Nouvel described it as "not a skyscraper in the American sense [...but] a unique growth in the middle of this rather calm city." Bearing in mind that the owners were a water company, he also described it as like "a geyser under permanent calculated pressure." The third highest building in Barcelona, the Agbar Tower stands straight as far as the 14th floor, where it curves inward, and is topped by a glass and steel dome. Across the facade are set 4,500 yellow, blue, pink and red LED lights, allowing spectacular illuminations at night. The reinforced-concrete structure also contains aluminum panels in earthy tones of blue, green and gray. The service and emergency stairwells are in the central core, allowing the individual floors to be free of columns and the workspaces to be open. **EW**

Seoul National University Museum of Art

Architects: Rem Koolhaas/OMA

Completed: 2005

Location: Seoul, South Korea

Style/Period: Deconstructionist/Modernism

Working on awkward sites has become something of a specialty for Dutch architect Rem Koolhaas, (see Seattle Public Library page 492) co-founder of the OMA (Office for Metropolitan Architecture) collective. OMA is an award-winning partnership, rightly acclaimed for their imaginative and complex buildings around the world. The

Samsung Corporation were the main sponsors behind the Seoul National University Museum of Art, and they reportedly allowed Koolhaas a free hand in the museum's design. Construction began in 2003 and the building, on the university's main Gwanak Campus, was completed in 2005.

Built on a sloping site, the angular and irregularly shaped building resembles a long horizontal box that is wider at one end and balanced on a concrete core. It runs parallel to the incline of the earth with an overhang at the top of the slope. The steel-and-glass shell appears to hover above the landscape, and the interior utilizes glass where possible to exploit natural light. With three stories below ground and three above, the 48,000-square-foot (4,450 sq. m) museum is centered around a bright stairwell atrium and incorporates six galleries, an auditorium, office and a media lounge, which are all linked by Koolhaas's trademark zigzag walkways. Surprisingly, there are plenty of

conventional fittings inside, such as hardwood floors, but imaginative use of plywood paneling and thin walls of translucent plastic and fluorescent lights lend a thoroughly modern air to the building. **JM**

Allianz Arena

Architects: Herzog & de Meuron

Completed: 2005

Location: Munich, Germany

Style/Period: Modernism

During a referendum on building a new stadium in Munich held in October 2001, the overwhelming majority of local citizens voted in favor. Taking just three years to build and opened in 2005, the bubblelike Allianz Arena, designed by Swiss architects Jacques Herzog and Pierrre de Meuron, has been the home ground of both the Bayern

München and TSV 1860 soccer teams.

Capable of seating nearly 70,000 fans across three terraces, the stadium bowl is made up of concrete and steel frames. The 409,000-square-foot (38,000 sq. m) roof is formed from 2,800 membrane air-filled pillows that have earned the building the nickname *Schlauchboot* ("the inflatable boat"). From a distance, the pillows look white, but each one can be lit as required to become red or blue, allowing the correct color to be displayed depending on which of the home teams is playing. Measuring 846 feet (258 m) long, 745 feet (227 m) wide and 164 feet (50 m) high, the Allianz Arena also houses team, coach and referee locker rooms, stores, warm-up areas, 550 toilets and 9,800 parking spaces in four four-story car parks. The playing field itself measures 344 x 223 feet (105 x 68 m) and was one of the venues for the 2006 World Cup. **EW**

City of Arts and Sciences

Architect: Santiago Calatrava

Completed: 2006

Location: Valencia, Spain

Style/Period: Biomorphic

Built in the dry riverbed of the River Turia between Valencia and Nazaret, Santiago Calatrava's huge 86-acre (350,000 sq. m) City of Arts and Sciences is a "city within a city." It celebrates, as its name suggests, artistic and scientific heritage, and it houses the Principe Felipe Science Museum, the Reina Sofia Arts Palace, the Oceanogràphic underwater city — designed by Felix Candela — and the Hemesferic planetarium. Built as a millennium project to mark the advent of the 21st century, Calatrava described it as "a city to be discovered by promenading."

The rotund glass and aluminum planetarium, the Hemisferic — reminiscent of a human eye — was the first landmark to open in April 1998, followed by the interactive science museum with its whale skeleton-type structure in 2000. The 861,000-square-foot (80,000 sq. m) Oceanogràphic houses 45,000 examples of 500 different marine species and 80 plant species from around the world in 10 distinct areas, while the spectacular 1,800-seat, 230 foot (70 m) high arts palace, El Palau de les Arts Reina Sofía, is an ideal showcase for performing arts. Water plays a prominent part in the city. As Calatrava himself explained, "As the site is close to the sea and Valencia is so dry, I decided to make water a major element for the whole site, using it as a mirror for the architecture." **EW**

The Palace of Peace and Reconciliation

Architects: Foster & Partners and Tabanlioglu
Architecture & Consulting

Completed: 2006 (begun 2004)

Location: Astana, Kazakhstan

Style/Period: High Tech

Once a constituent republic of the USSR and since 1991 an independent nation, Kazakhstan, in central Asia, put itself on the architectural map with the completion, in 2006, of "The Pyramid," as the Palace of Peace and Reconciliation is popularly called. And it is not difficult to appreciate how this 253-foot (77 m) tall building in Astana, Kazakhstan's new capital city— which was designed by the British–Turkish architectural collaboration of Foster & Partners and Tabanlioglu Architecture & Consulting — acquired its nickname.

The pyramidal structure has a footprint of 203 x 203 feet (62 x 62 m) and is 203 feet (62 m) tall and set on a 50-foot (15 m) high podium whose additional dimensions are 315 x 315 feet (96 x 96 m). The Pyramid's triangular appearance is echoed by the stainless-steel triangular-patterned lattice that describe five levels on each side, the lower levels being clad in gray granite, and the upper levels showcasing a stained-glass design incorporating doves. Its primary purpose being to accommodate the triennial meeting of the Congress of Leaders of World and Traditional Religions, an important part of the Pyramid is the circular assembly chamber at the top. This surrounds a central atrium that extends as far as the oculus roof of the 1,500-seat opera house that is situated within the podium. **CH-M**

National Grand Theater of China

Architect: Paul Andreu

Completed: 2007

Location: Beijing, China

Style/Period: Eclectic Modern

China's rise to economic superpower status has been matched by some monumental building projects, especially in its capital.

This work has not been without controversy, largely because areas of traditionally styled and often domestic buildings have been swept away en masse and replaced by vast public edifices that shout about the country's new position in the world. This theater complex by Paul Andreu is just one example of the trend. The architect was asked to create a building that could hold three different venues — an opera house, a concert hall, and a theater — alongside exhibition areas, shops, and food outlets.

Andreu opted to build in concrete, titanium, and glass, and produced a huge, domed structure that stretches some 696 feet (212 m) along one axis and 471 feet (144 m) along the other. It rises to a height of 152 feet (46 m), dwarfing many of the traditional residential areas around it, and is surrounded by a large lake that covers an area of 382,000 square feet (35,500 sq. m). Entrance to the building is by way of underground walkways, while the whole edifice is internally lit at night to reveal the facilities inside. **IW**

National Stadium

Architects: Herzog & de Meuron
Completed: 2008
Location: Olympic Green, Beijing, China
Style/Period: Eclectic Modernism

This stadium, which was created by Swiss architects Jacques Herzog and Pierre de Meuron, was built as the centerpiece of the 2008 Olympics held in the Chinese capital and is a remarkable structure by any measure. It has been nicknamed the "Bird's Nest" by local people, largely because of its remarkable open facade, which consists of massive steel columns (running some 22 miles/36 km in total) and struts that rise out of the plinth on which the stadium is set and then curve over, becoming interlinked to form the roof. The effect, previously unknown in a public building, gives it a light, almost delicate, feel despite its obvious monumentality.

The stadium's sculptural qualities somewhat belie the fact that it is a functional building. Inside, there is seating room for around 91,000 spectators, and there are also underground areas that give access to the venue and provide space for various other activities, including media centers and retail outlets. Color is used sparingly throughout — the steelwork is silver, the seating is bright red and parts of the interior a flat black. The stadium reflects the epic qualities of public architecture in communist China, but it also articulates the progressive qualities of this newly emerging economic powerhouse. **IW**

Bahrain World Trade Center

Architects: Atkins Architects

Completed: 2008

Location: Central Business District, Manama, Bahrain

Style/Period: High-Tech

The small, oil-rich state of Bahrain has grown exceptionally wealthy by exploiting its underground resources. However, its wells will run dry at some point in the future, and so the recent aim has been to reposition the Gulf state as a leading commercial center and international tourist destination. This 787-foot (240 m) skyscraper is not only part of the on-going efforts to make Bahrain into a trading center, it also includes features that reflect the eventual decline in oil production and the search for new power sources.

The building consists of two sweeping and tapering tower blocks that are aerodynamically shaped like a pair of dhow sails. They act as airfoils and suck in winds that blow in off the Persian Gulf. The towers are connected by a number of walkways that carry three 164-foot (50 m) wind turbines that should be able to generate between 10 and 15 percent of the towers' energy needs when they come on line. The architects have created a superb high-tech building that is not only redolent of a nation in economic transition, but one that also symbolizes the country's post-oil aspirations. **IW**

Sagrada Familia

Architect: Antoni Gaudí

Completed: Not completed

Location: Barcelona, Spain

Style/Period: Art Nouveau/Neogothic

Appearances can be deceptive. Beneath the elaborate, almost organic facades of Gaudí's church, Sagrada Familia, lies a building so advanced for its day that some critics have declared it a work of "proto-modernism." At the age of just 31 Gaudí took over the church's construction and was presented with a crypt completed by the initial architect, Francisco del Villar, who had resigned in 1883. Laying Villar's master plan aside, Gaudí spent the next 37 years exploring his own unique ideas about structure and color, using them to articulate his deeply held religious beliefs and sense of Catalan national identity.

At first glance his forest of tapering pinnacles, emblazoned with Catholic texts and embellished with mosaic finials, seem a purely sculptural variation on European cathedral Gothic. Yet these same elongated spires are essentially a work of modern engineering: a group of mutually supportive columns that reach heady heights from a narrow footprint. Faith was not Gaudí's only guiding force, as gravity helped sculpt his forms. His scale models used loops of cord suspended from his studio ceiling to form perfect catenary arches, which he then weighted with lead shot to simulate the stone they would need to bear. If the viewer mentally inverts the finished spires and imagines them as stalactites, dangling in some dripping grotto, then the method becomes clear. Still incomplete upon Gaudí's death in 1926, the Sagrada Familia continues to rise in fits and starts as funding allows, like a venerable tree of life, slowly growing for eternity. **PC**

Bibliography

Able, Chris, *Sky High – Vertical Architecture*,
Royal Academy Publications/Thames and Hudson, London, 2003

Byars, Mel, *The Design Encyclopedia*,
Laurence King Publishing, London, 1994

Campbell, James W. P., and Pryce, Will, *Brick: A World History*,
Thames and Hudson, London, 2003

Co, Francesco Dal and Forster, Kurt W., *Frank O. Gehry – The Complete Works*, The Monacelli Press, New York, 1998

Conti, Flavio (translated by Patrick Creagh), *The Grand Tour: Individual Creations*, HBJ Press, New York, 1978

Cunliffe, Sarah, and Loussier, Jean (Eds.), *Architecture Styles: Spotter's Guide*, Saraband (Scotland) Limited, Glasgow, 2006

Curtis, William J. R., *Modern Architecture Since 1900* (Third Edition), Phaidon, London, 1996

Erlande-Brandenburg, Alain, *The Cathedral Builders of the Middle Ages*, Thames and Hudson, London, 1995

Fairley, Alastair, *De La Warr Pavilion: The Modernist Masterpiece*, Merrell, London, 2006

Fleming, John, Honour, Hugh, and Pevsner, Nikolaus, *The Penguin Dictionary of Architecture*, Penguin Books Ltd., Harmondsworth, 1991

Frampton, Kenneth, *Modern Architecture: A Critical History*, Thames and Hudson, London, 1992

Frampton, Kenneth, *The Renzo Piano Logbook*, Thames and Hudson, London, 1997

Gale, Iain, (with photography by Richard Bryant), *Living Museums*, Mitchell Beazley, London, 1993

Glancey, Jonathan, *C20th Architecture – The Structures That Shaped The Century*, Carlton Books, London, 1998

Gibson, John, *Anatomy of the Castle*, Saraband (Scotland) Limited, Glasgow, 2001

Gill, John, *Essential Gaudi*, Parragon, Bath, 2001

Hollingsworth, Mary, *Architecture of the 20th Century*, Grange Books, London, 1988

Hausen, Marika, et al, *Eleil Saarinen: Projects 1896–1923*, Ginko Press Verlag GmbH, Hamburg, 1990

Lyall, Sutherland, *Masters of Structure – Engineering Today's Innovative Buildings*, Laurence King, London, 2002

McCarter, Robert, *Frank Lloyd Wright*, Phaidon, London, 1997

Melvin, Jeremy, *. . . isms: Understanding Architecture*, Herbert Press, London, 2005

Morgan, Conway Lloyd, *Jean Nouvel: The Elements of Architecture*, Thames and Hudson, London, 1998

Nicoletta, Julie (with photography by Bret Morgan), *The Architecture of the Shakers*, Norfleet Press, New York, 1995

Nuttgens, Patrick, *The Mitchell Beazley Pocket Guide to Architecture*, Mitchell Beazley Publishers Limited, London, 1980

The Phaidon Atlas of Contemporary World Architecture, Comprehensive Edition Phaidon, London, 2004

Slavid, Ruth, *Wood Architecture*, Laurence King Publishing, London, 2005

Slessor, Catherine, *Eco-Tech – Sustainable Architecture and High Technology*, Thames and Hudson, London, 1997

Sudjic, Deyan, *Norman Foster, Richard Rogers, James Stirling: New Directions in British Architecture*, Thames and Hudson, 1986

Thiel-Siling, Sabine (Ed.), *Icons of Architecture: The 20th Century*, Prestel Verlag, Munich, 1998

Index

Brunoni, Ugo 430–1
Brutalism 353, 356, 368–9, 395
Buddhist style 37, 64–5, 74, 98
Bullfinch, Charles 212
Burbage, Cuthbert 127
Burckhardt, Johann 49
Burgee, John 392–3, 400
Burgess, William 222–3
Burj Al-Arab Hotel, Dubai 455
Burlington, Lord 154
Burnham, Daniel 229, 238–9, 276–7
Burton, Decimus 200–1
Butterfield, William 224–5
Byzantine architecture 52, 105

C

Ca'd'Oro Palazzo, Venice, Italy 94–5
Caernarfon Castle, Wales 82–3
Calatrava, Santiago 428–9, 452, 469, 502–3
Cambodia: Royal Palace 266–7; Siem Reap City 70–1
Cambodian architecture 266–7
Camerson, Charles 169
Canada 364–5, 367, 410–11
Canadian Museum of Civilization, Gatineau, Quebec 410–11
Canary Wharf Station, London 456–7
Capability Brown 91
The Capitol, Washington D.C. 212
Capra, Villa Capra or La Rotonda, Vicenza, Italy 118–19
Cardiff Castle, Wales 222–3
Cardinal, Douglas 410–11
Carl Larsson's House, Sweden 263
Carrol, Charles, junior 178–9
Carson, Pirie, Scott and Company Department Store, Chicago 12, 14, 235
Casa Batlló, Barcelona, Spain 246–7
Casa da Música, Porto, Portugal 498
Casa de Pilates, Seville, Spain 112
Casa Hernández, Mexico City 418–19
Casa Malaparte, Capri, Italy 319
Casa Milà, Barcelona, Spain 256–7
Case Study House No. 8 (Eames House), California 322
Case Study House No. 21 (Bailey House), Los Angeles 342–3
Cassels, Richard 158
Castle Drogo, Devon, England 286–7
Catedral Metropolitana Nossa Senhora Aparecida, Brasilia 372–3
Cathedral Church of the Holy Cross, Turkey 58–9
Cathedral of Our Lady of the Angels, Los Angeles 475
Catherine de Medici 107
Cavalier Hotel, Miami, Florida 309
Central Station, Amsterdam, Netherlands 228–9
Centre Georges Pompidou, Paris, France 385
Cesar Pelli & Associates 444–5
Chalgrin, Jean Francois Therese 195

Chamberlain, Powell & Bon 395
Chambers, Sir William 162–3, 166, 168–9
Chand, Ustad Lal 174–5
Changdokkung Palace, Korea 91
Chapel of the Holy Shroud, Turin, Italy 144–5
Chareau, Pierre 300
Chechulin, Dmitry 394
Cheng, Jia Huan 434
Chenonceau Château, France 122
Chermayeff, Serge 305
Chew, Khuan 455
Chiat/Day Headquarters, Santa Monica, California 420–1
Chicago Early Modern style 238–9
Chicago School 235
China: Beijing 92–3, 504–5; Great Wall 120–1; Shanghai 434, 452–3; Xian 122–3; Zhejiang 108–9
Chinese style 62, 108–9, 120–1, 122–3
    High Tech 452–3
    Ming Dynasty 92–3, 122–3
Chinoiserie 162–3
Chiswick House, London 154–5
Choga Zambil, Dur Untash, Iran 28–9
Christian Classicism 52–3
Christian IV of Denmark 132
Chrysler Building, New York 284–5
Church of the Light, Ibaraki, Japan 415
Church of the Sacred Heart of Our Lord, Prague, Czech Republic 296–7
Church of St. George, Ethiopia 73
Cincinnati Contemporary Arts Center 483
City of Arts and Sciences, Valencia, Spain 502–3
Classical Architecture 140–1
Classical Revival 216
Coates, Wells 302–3
Cockerill, Samuel 177
Colonial Georgian style 168
Colosseum, Rome, Italy 40–1
Commercial Romanesque style 230–1
Constantine, Roman Emperor 51, 52
Contextual Modernism 442–3
Cook, Peter 484–5
Corbett, Harrison & MacMurray 316–17
Coventry Cathedral, England 352–3
Creek Vean, Cornwall, England 362–3
Crete, Knossos 26
Critical Regionalism 406–7, 415
Cromford Mill, Derbyshire, England 166
Crystal Palace, London 202
Cubist style 249
Cubitt, Lewis 204–5
Cullinan, Edward 473
Cumberland Terrace, London 187
Cuypers, Petrus 228–9
C.Y.Lee & Partners 492
Czech Republic: Brno 286; Prague 246, 296–7, 434

D

Daily Express Building, London 298–9
Damascus, Syria 56
Dancing House, Prague, Czech Republic 434
Danish Renaissance 132
Darb-I Iman, Iran 98–9
Davanzati Palazzo, Florence, Italy 87
Davidson, Peter 474–5
de Klerk see Klerk
De La Warre Pavilion, Bexhill-on-Sea, England 305
de Meuron, Pierre see Herzog & de Meuron
De Young Museum, San Francisco 499
Deane, Thomas 210–11
Deconstructionism 389, 398–9, 412, 420–1, 426–7, 434, 446–7, 454, 470, 483, 487, 496–7, 498, 500–1
The Deep, Kingston-upon-Hull, England 480
Deming, Elder William 212–13
Denmark,
    Copenhagen 317
    Sjaelland 132
Derngate, No.78, Northampton, England 262–3
Diane de Poitiers 107
Die Wies Pilgrimage Church, Bavaria, Germany 160–1
Doge's Palace, Venice, Italy 96–7
Dollmann, Georg 226–7
Dôme des Invalides, Paris, France 144
Dome of the Rock, Jerusalem 54–5
Don Fadrique de Ribera 112
Don Per Afán 112
Doric style 31, 32
Downland Gridshell, West Sussex, England 17, 473
DP Architects 482–3
Dryák, Alois 246
Dubai 455
Duca, Jacopo del 122
Dudok, William Marinus 290–1
Dulwich Picture Gallery, London 180–1
Durham Cathedral, England 70
Dushkin, Aleksei Nikolayevich 312
Dutch Colonial style 172–3
Dutch Renaissance 132

E

Eames Charles 322
Eames, Ray 322
Early Bronze Age 20–1
Early Christian 57
Early High Tech 367
Early Modernism 244, 255, 274–5, 294–5
Early Neoclassical 178–9
Early Perpendicular 108
Eclectic Modernism 334–5, 341, 474–5, 492–3, 504–5
Eclecticism 166–7, 288, 387
Eco High Tech 473, 479, 488–9, 498–9
Eden Project, Cornwall, England 464–5
Edward I of England 82

Edward IV of England 109
Église Sainte-Trinité, Geneva, Switzerland 430–1
Egypt 24, 25, 26–7, 35, 480–1
Egyptian House, Penzance, England 94–5
Eiffel, Gustav 228
Eiffel Tower, Paris, France 228
Einstein Tower, Potsdam, Germany 270–1
Elizabethan style 125, 126–7
Ely, Reginald 108
Empire State Building, New York 296
Engineering Faculty Building, Leicester University, England 356
England: Bath, Somerset 38–9, 165; Berkshire 109, 257; Birmingham 486; Brighton 184–5; Cambridge 108; Cheshire 100–1; Cornwall 194–5, 362–3, 464–5; Coventry 352–3; Derbyshire 125, 164–5; Devon 286–7; Dorset 482; Durham 68–9; East Sussex 96–7, 305, 308–9; Greenwich, London 9–11, 133, 146–7; Kent 210, 458–9; Kew Gardens 162, 200–1; Leicester 356; Liverpool 198, 366–7, 388–9; Manchester 461; Northampton 262–3; Norwich 368–9, 384–5; Nottingham 301; Oxford 138–9, 158–9; Oxfordshire 151, 414; Portsmouth 219; Salisbury Plain 22–3; Staffordshire 198–9; Suffolk 180–1, 382–3; Surrey 110–11, 145, 479; Warwick 90–1; West Sussex 241, 473; Wolverhampton 231; Yorkshire 458, 480; see also London
English Baroque 138–9, 151
English Colonial 137, 142
English Palladian 158–9
English Renaissance 145
Erechtheion, Temple, Athens, Greece 35
Eric R. Kuhne Associates 458–9
Erskine, Ralph 422–3
Espinasse, Francois 254–5
Esplanade – Theaters on the Bay, Singapore 482–3
Estação do Oriente, Lisbon, Portugal 452
Ethiopia 73
Evans, Arthur 26
Évry Cathedral, France 432
Exoticism 184–5
Expo Station, Singapore 468
Expressionism 246–7, 270–1, 317, 346–7, 348–9, 350–1, 354–5, 404–5, 428–9

F

Falkirk Wheel, Scotland 478
Fallingwater, Bear Run, Pennsylvania 308
Farnese family 118, 124–5
Farnsworth House, Plano, Illinois 328–9
Farrell see Terry Farrell &

Company
Fawley House, Oxfordshire, England 414
Federalist style 178–9, 208–9
Federation Square, Melbourne, Australia 474–5
Fiat Factory, Turin, Italy 274
Finland: Helsinki 264–5, 370–1; Luoma 236–7; Paimio 302; Savonlinna 116–17; Säynätsalo 332–3
Finnish National Romantic style 236–7
Flemish Gothic Revival 228–9
Florence Cathedral, Italy 95
Folly Farm, Berkshire, England 257
Fong and Chan Architects 499
Fontainebleau, the Chateau of, France 114
Fontana, Carlo 150, 154
The Forbidden City, China 92–3
Ford, Captain W.H. 180–1
Fort Carré, France 142–3
Fort McHenry, Locust Point, Baltimore 176
Foster & Partners 456–7, 459, 462–3, 463, 468, 488–9, 494–5, 504
Foster Associates 382–3, 384–5, 402
Foster, Norman 13, 362–3, 382, 384–5
Foulston, John 194–5
Fournier, Colin 484–5
Fowke, Captain Francis 216, 221
France: Albi 102; Antibes 142–3; Bourges 80; Chartres 77–8; Évry 432; Fontainebleau 114; Lyon 428–9; Maginot Line 314–15; Marseilles 332, 427; Millau 494–5; Nimes 37; Normandy 66–7; Raincy 276, 277; Remoulins 40–1; Versailles 141; see also Paris, France
France, Roy F. 309
François I of France 114
Frederick C. Robie House, Chicago 252–3
Frederick Phineas and Sandra Rose Center for Earth and Space, New York 462
Frederiksborg Slot, Denmark 132
Frigimelica, Girolamo 162
Fuente de los Amantes , Mexico City 362
Fuji-Sankei Communications Group Headquarters Building, Tokyo 436–7
Fuller Building(The Flatiron), New York City 238–9
Fuller, Richard Buckmaster 367
Fumihiko Maki Associates 400
Functionalist 332–3, 356, 386–7
Future Systems (architects) 454, 486
Futuristic 370, 396–7, 454, 478

G

Galleria Vittorio Emanuele, Milan, Italy 218–19
Gallus/Gallarus Oratory, Ireland 57
Gamble House, Pasadena, California 250–1

Garden Grove Community Church, California 392–3
Gardner-Pingree House,Salem, Mass. 176–7
Garnier, Charles 217
Gate of Nations, Persepolis, Iran 31
Gatwick Airport Terminal Building, England 308–9
Gaudi, Antoni 246–7, 256–7, 506–7
Gehry, Frank 389, 412, 420–1, 434, 446–7, 487
Gehry House, Santa Monica, California 389
Georgian House, Edinburgh, Scotland 173
Georgian style 165
    Georgian Colonial 152–3
    Georgian Industrial 164–5
    Georgian Neoclassical 170–1, 173
German Pavilion, Barcelona, Spain 280–1
Germany: Bavaria 160, 166, 196–7, 226, 377; Berlin 190, 192–3, 252, 459, 470–1; Darmstadt 237; Dessau 278–9; Dresden 152; Munich 501; Potsdam 270–1; Stuttgart 397; Weil-am-Rhein 412, 426–7; Wolfsburg 496–7
Geselius, Herman 236–7
The Getty Center, Los Angeles 445
Ghengis Khan 66
Gibberd, Sir Frederick 366–7
Gibbs, James 150–1, 154, 158–9
Gilbert, Cass 260–1
Gilles le Breton 114
Giotto di Bodone 96
Glasgow School of Art, Scotland 250
Glass House, New Canaan, Connecticut 322–3
The Globe Theatre, London 126–7
Goldberg, Bertrand 356–7
Goldfinger, Elmö 313
Gothic Pastiche 338–9
Gothic Revival 10–11, 198–9, 206, 210–11, 214–15, 216, 220–1, 222–3, 224–5, 232–3
Gothic style 66–7, 68, 74–5, 77–8, 94–5, 99, 102–3, 108, 166–7
    Early 80
    English 78–9, 90
    Flemish 80–1
    High 80, 103
    Italian 85, 94
    Late 108
    Southern 102
    Victorian 225
Gowan, James 356
Graham, Bruce 371
Grand Central Station, New York 258–9
Grand Hotel Europa, Prague, Czech Republic 244
Grand Opera, Paris, France 216–7
Great Ball Court, Chichén Itzá, Mexico 64
The Great Kremlin Palace, Moscow 202–3
Great Mosque of Djenné, Mali 251
Great Mosque Hassan II, Morocco